Relational Agency and Environmental Ethics

Relational Agency and Environmental Ethics

A Journey beyond Humanism as We Know It

Suvielise Nurmi

LEXINGTON BOOKS
Lanham • Boulder • New York • London

Published by Lexington Books
An imprint of The Rowman & Littlefield Publishing Group, Inc.
4501 Forbes Boulevard, Suite 200, Lanham, Maryland 20706
www.rowman.com

86-90 Paul Street, London EC2A 4NE

British Library Cataloguing in Publication Information Available

Library of Congress Cataloging-in-Publication Data Available

ISBN 9781666904543 (cloth)
ISBN 9781666904550 (ebook)

*For Arto,
Pietari, and Marisofia*

Contents

Acknowledgments

No doubt, I could not have written this book without being a part of countless webs of interaction, and this outcome is just one expression of the processes that have been going on in all its various participants and their sensemaking interactive relationships. As a deeply relational agent I want to share the honor to have this book published with all those collaborative processes, individuals taking part in them, and the various environments in which they have taken place, though the list necessarily remains sadly inadequate. I want to express my gratitude for the funding that made it possible to write this book. I give thanks to the Alfred Kordelin Foundation, Finnish Cultural Foundation, Finnish Concordia Fund, Research Institute of the Lutheran Church of Finland, and the Association of Finnish Nonfiction Writers. At the early stage of this project, I also had a great opportunity to work within a wonderful community at the University of Helsinki, teaching ethics for theologians and building up multidisciplinary networks of sustainability scientists while doing research surrounded by brilliant colleagues in philosophy, theology, and interdisciplinary environmental science. I am grateful for my alma mater for its innovative atmosphere, inspiring, interactive environment for creative work, and active advancement of interdisciplinary work through the Helsinki Institute of Sustainability Science.

While trying to identify the blind point of environmental ethics to explain its weak efficiency at that time, I had numerous nurturing conversations and discussions, for instance, on the strategies of environmental ethics and their philosophical challenges especially with Jaana Hallamaa, Reijo Työrinoja, Mikko Yrjönsuuri, Heikki Kirjavainen, Timo Koistinen, Tage Kurtén, but also many other colleagues. I also want to thank Frans de Waal and Michael Ruse for their critical and constructive comments on my thoughts at the Venice Summer School conference on Human Uniqueness. At the second stage of the process, I concentrated on the idea of relationality, and an account of moral agency. I am especially grateful to Simo Knuuttila (in memoriam) for support, encouragement, and inspiring discussions that challenged me to think ever further, though in the beginning he was suspicious of using term "relational" in the first place. Another person with whom I had some great discussions on relationality and moral realism is Sami Pihlström. I want to thank him for trust and support, things which I greatly value. I want to give special thanks to Virpi Mäkinen, dear colleague, encourager, and friend, and Lisa Sideris for their constructive comments and discussions in the final stages of the book. I also want to thank the International Society for Environmental Ethics for the opportunities to meet and discuss with brilliant colleagues around the world and for the possibilities to present my most recent ideas at the ISEE Annual and ISEE session at the American Philosophical Association 2021, and ISEE president Marion Hourdequin for supportive comments regarding the idea of relationality. Special thanks to Lana García for the great help with correct English, for comments, and copyediting, and to Benjamin Hale for recommending her.

I am grateful for having the honor of sharing my life with a brilliant ecologist, Arto Nurmi, who is ready to help with scientific questions whenever needed. I am also thankful for the numerous times he has pushed me to hike Lapland fjelds, wander in the forests, or sit hunched in a blind in the middle of a bog to watch black grouse and other animal relations. I want to give special thanks to my adult children, cognitive neuroscience researcher Pietari Nurmi and geographist Marisofia Nurmi, who have been eager to commit themselves to long, inspiring discussions on cognitive science, scientific methodology, and various ethical and environmental issues besides a whole range of issues concerning human condition. Although not connected to the book, all this has been influential. I cannot go without mention of my closest nonhuman companions: our dear dogs and all the surroundings of my home office by a little Finnish lake. In daily interactivity with the forest rich with species, including European otters, lynx, owls, flying squirrels, dippers, frogs, deer, and, of course, various plants, berries, and mushrooms, each lifeform has collaborated with me.

October 2022
Suvielise Nurmi

Introduction

Who are we as moral agents? What does the answer have to do with current and future situations on Earth that appear perilous for most life-forms of the biosphere? This book is a journey toward the self-understanding of ethics inspired by considering how ethics is shaped by the kind of picture we conjure when we look in the mirror. Environmental ethics works as the vehicle of this journey. It is a field of philosophy that openly challenges our present understanding and pushes the big picture of ethics toward an inner sustainability transformation by asking critical questions of ethical theories. What issues of the nonhuman and material world concern ethics? What matters for ethics in the first place? What means does ethics have to discuss systemic environmental problems? At the core of the self-understanding of ethics is the picture of the moral agent. The journey of this book defends the claim that the concept of moral agency of human beings determines the means and ability of ethics to deal with the critical problems of our time and, hence, whether ethics can efficiently play its role in humanity's most challenging issues.

The function of ethics is to offer tools for solving practical problems. If the tools do not match with the problems we face, as it seems, theoretical and conceptual revisions are necessary. Ethical discourse has often gotten sidetracked from the complex issues concerning institutionally and culturally maintained processes and conducts that are fatal for the biosphere. Actions, decisions, and practices behind such processes are still widely considered morally trivial, amoral, or even morally praiseworthy as they advance some of the interests of human society. The powerlessness of ethics in environmental issues is a tragedy of philosophy. It originates, at least partly, from the conceptual structure of the common moral theories that adopt a modernist account of humanity and human moral agency. Interdisciplinary sustainability scientists actively criticize the modern philosophical framework of political, institutional, and cultural discussions for distorting human-nature relationships, and they call for more systemic understanding of the human condition. Since ethical theories are not equipped to meet complex environmental issues, they

1

are easily left for the scientists to solve. Environmental philosophers who are suspicious of the practical relevance of conceptual philosophical work often prefer identifying themselves as environmental scientists rather than philosophers. Environmental philosophy has also had difficulties with philosophically valid methods, which has not lifted its profile as a part of mainstream theoretical philosophy. Some of the difficulties have to do with how the idea of relationality can be used in environmental philosophy.

Therefore, the journey to the self-understanding of ethics in this book focuses on the basic presuppositions of modern humanist ethics concerning moral agency as a unique capacity of an individual human intracranial mind. Many philosophers are, however, cautious about criticizing the modern humanist account of uniqueness of human moral agency, although it has been deemed scientifically incorrect. Partly they are cautious for good reasons, since reducing ethics to scientific explanations could conceptually threaten the possibility of taking the critical viewpoint, without which ethics seems impossible. But philosophy that stops when facing a dilemma is lazy philosophy. I shall argue that basic conceptual philosophical work can substantially enhance the cultural conditions of sustainability transformation. Philosophers should feel encouraged to exercise their specific contribution to sustainability not only in applied or political philosophy but also in theoretical and conceptual work.

The conceptual dualisms, dichotomies, and binarities characteristic of the modern framework of ethics that divide humans from nature have been a permanent subject of criticism in discussions about the ability of modern ethics to plausibly deal with environmental issues, even from inside the modern framework. For example, John Rawls acknowledges the problem and argues that we should recall "the limits of a theory of justice. Not only are many aspects of morality left aside, but no account can be given of right conduct in regard to animals and the rest of nature" (Rawls 2003, 448). But commonly offered alternatives have also been questioned. It has been common to think that overcoming dualisms implicates holism that easily slides either to speculative metaphysics or lacks normativity (the is-ought fallacy): awareness of the fact that the world is a unified whole does not automatically obligate promoting its harmony. Normativity in holism can, of course, be argued through considering the whole as a subject with its own interest of survival, like the Gaia hypothesis claims. But as it easily subordinates the individual parts to the good of the whole, philosophers are cautious to defend it. The focus of debates seems, however, misplaced. The fundamental dichotomies that need specific reconsideration are the ones that split the human agent internally into two: human nature and human moral agency. This has been surprisingly little discussed, and the dichotomized nature of the human agent is considerably more accepted in environmental ethics than dualism dividing between human and nonhuman nature. The aim of this book is to fill this gap.

Through the journey I shall introduce and defend the *relational shift* concerning the concept of moral agency and examine its philosophical and normative implications. The general idea of relationality, as such, has been among the leading themes in environmental thinking since the dawn of ecology that emphasizes the systemic interactivity between organisms, and it is among the central concepts of social ecology. But unlike the most common understanding, relationality is approached here from the *agential* perspective: it concerns cognitive and moral agency. Recent studies especially on cognition, philosophy of mind, and anthropology have significantly enlightened the relational nature of mind and agency. With the help of both philosophical and interdisciplinary discussions I shall sketch an account of agential relationality that refers to agency as embodied and embedded and to the systemic ecological processes combining the various factors of agency. But locating relationality in the very operations of agency, namely reasoning, autonomy, and action, makes it not only play an explanatory role in ethics, but also have wider philosophical and ethical implications. If relationality questions assigning agency to an isolated individual mind, profound discussion is required concerning the ideas of autonomy and responsibility, as well as the role of various environments in moral agency.

Philosophers are masters of criticism. But when discussion turns to the question of moral agency, critical tones against the dichotomized concept are fewer. The question is especially tricky for environmental ethicists. For the purposes of this study, I define environmental ethics as a part of environmental philosophy that has a general purpose to sustain philosophically valid and environmentally efficient normative ethics. Environmental ethics is then a group of strategies that formulate theories to point out principles concerning the environment and justify their normativity. Such strategies need to protect the conditions of responsibility, and the possibility to take a critical viewpoint and act otherwise, and to think that the moral reasons to act sustainably are universally authoritative. But at the same time, they need to protect the practical relevance of moral actions: moral commitment to environmental ethics must have positive impact on material and nonhuman reality. For an environmental ethical theory to be practically relevant, its postulates must be scientifically valid, including its account of moral agency. The modern notion of human agency seems, however, empirically suspect, and it hinders moral theories from being successful. Environmental ethics thus has a dilemma. Environmental ethics tends to defend, at the same time, both the critical point of view of ethics, which refers to the autonomy of ethics from the factual state of affairs, and its practical relevance and efficiency, which refers to the scientifically valid explanations of presuppositions, which also concern moral agency. In terms of metaethics, many environmental ethicists thus strive to combine contextual and embodied explanations of human morality with moral realism and universal moral rationality. Although these aspirations seem contradictory, it is worth asking how much their confrontation originates from the modern conception of human agency.

Moral agency represents the ideal of human existence. Conceptions of moral agency thus constitute a normative view of humanness. They also set a criterion for granting membership in the moral community. In modern humanist ethics moral agency marks exceptionality: It is a feature specific to human beings and is not expected to perform elsewhere. In modern humanist ethics, since the definite elements of moral agency are autonomy in the strong sense of freedom, rationality, and impartiality, they mark the members of a moral community. Moral relevance of others is trivialized. Taking seriously our shared fate with the nonhuman sphere, the modernist notion of moral agency requires revision—for the sake of ethics.

Modern ethics has been a captive of its humanist concept of agency. As binding obligations, such as duty, right, and justice hold true only in the context a of moral community, the function of moral conduct is to evaluate actions between free and rational agents. The primary strategy of environmental ethics to overcome this has been to point out reasons to extend the community of morally relevant beings to cover more-than-human entities. However, since it remains humanistic and individualistic by logic, it can be called extended humanism. The secondary strategy has been to focus on alternative ontologies. But relationality of agency shifts not only the presumptions of humanist ethics but also of its critics. The modern idea of agency is most clearly criticized by environmental ethicists drawing on two mutually opposing philosophical traditions: evolutionary naturalism and ecofeminist constructivism. Many ethicists also take an agential approach to relationality and face the hard question of the autonomy of an (individual) agent. Ecofeminism and evolutionary ethics can thus offer options to escape humanism without speculative assumptions, but in both approaches there also lurk hazards from the viewpoint of the aspirations of environmental ethics: antirealism lurks in posthumanist ecofeminism and reductionist determinism, and the is-ought fallacy lurks in evolutionary naturalism.

The journey will start with a walk through these different strategies of environmental ethics. The parallel aspirations of the ecofeminist and evolutionary naturalist frameworks regarding human agency as constituted by (social or natural) relational processes will then be taken as the point of departure to construct a relationally revised concept of agency. The perspective of the study will extend to include external multi- and interdisciplinary research on the relational nature of being, knowing, and acting in order to clarify and develop the parallel aspirations of critical environmentalists. What will come out opens a novel track beyond the unnecessary fetters of modern ethics. The journey is not without dangers. Criticism may threaten the idea of responsibility, and hence, the normative force of ethics. But when the stakes are high it is worth taking a risk and nearing the edge of the cliff. A walk with the conception of moral agency in environmental ethics can take us beyond humanism with implications that extend to concern ethics in general. But can a relational shift then solve the dilemma? Is natural relationality of agency possible without violating autonomy and normative authority of ethics? And can a turn of focus to relationality help an ethical theory to meet complex environmental problems?

An agential approach to relationality seems to have potential to tackle the basic dilemma that bothers environmental ethics. Though it rejects extreme freedom as the condition of responsibility and even risks the critical perspective of ethical assessment, it still seems to allow for a narrow channel that does not deny the autonomy of ethics nor its normative authority. I shall argue that relational ethics can be realist, however modest. Relational agency will, however, revise some of the metaethical categories and blur some common borderlines. Implications that seem to follow for environmental ethics are both theoretical and normative. In case of the idea of environmental responsibilities, the shift will be notable as everyday life actions seem to become morally praiseworthy or blameworthy as actions influencing relational moral agency.

The book travels through four landscapes. The first task is to explore the concept of moral agency in different strategies for environmental ethics. After the brief analysis of the modern humanist concept, the focus turns to the two critical strands, evolutionary ethics and ecofeminism, and their parallel aspirations. The second landscape consists of interdisciplinary discussions on systemic and relational understandings of human agency. It will introduce examples of discussions concerning the relational conditions of being, knowing, and acting as a moral agent. Empirical natural sciences, such as cognitive science and evolutionary anthropology, will be brought together with humanities, such as psychology, philosophical anthropology, social philosophy, philosophy of mind, and discussions on collective agency. In this part the task is to sketch the relational conception of moral agency. The emphasis will be on issues crucial for moral agency, autonomy, and rationality. The third part takes us to the landscape of the philosophical implications for ethical theories. It returns to the two frameworks for taking critical stances against modern ethics, namely naturalism and constructivism, to see how they change due to the relational shift of the account of agency. The last part aspires beyond the framework known as humanist ethics by taking us to the relational conceptual landscape and initially sketching the outline of an agential type of relational ethics. The focus will be on the questions crucial for the dilemma of environmental ethics: compatibility with moral realism and the source of normativity, and the ethical relevance of complex environmental issues. Among the conclusive arguments I shall defend the view that environmental responsibilities can be considered as responsibilities for relational moral agency, from which their normativity can be derived. The journey will conclude with some normative implications for environmental ethics. A relational shift seems to bring an ethical theory closer to virtue ethics, though of a nontypical form, perhaps. But the justification of normativity in a relational theory also may resemble a Kantian one: one must act in accordance with environmental imperatives because it is the way to maintain one's own autonomy and rationality.

PART I

Moral Agency in Environmental Ethics

The first three stops of the journey take us to the philosophical discussion of environmental ethics during the past four decades. The first stop briefly explores the foundations of modern ethics regarding the moral role of the relationships between moral agents and the rest of the world, and especially how they influence environmental ethics. The two following stops stand in opposing sides of the road and scarcely acknowledge, not to mention appreciate, each other's starting points. One is rooted in the natural sciences, while the other leans on mainly phenomenological feminist philosophy. But environmentalists on these stops have a common enemy that makes their projects interestingly parallel: both attack against the concept of human moral agency embedded in the core of modern moral philosophy. In this book, these starting points will be discussed as parallel approaches in terms of their parallel aspirations to reconsider moral agency from a relational point of view. A third stop that shares this aspiration—which gathers environmentalists from clearly alternative metaphysical and religious starting points—will here be passed by only a light touch because the focus is in sketching the widest possible route for so-called mainstream discussion.

The three stops of this part represent three strategies for environmental ethics. Their main purpose is to find a justified way to integrate the relationships between human agents and other elements of the natural world in the moral discourse in a plausible and normatively noninstrumental way. As the journey of this part continues, it will follow the shared aspiration of the strategies openly critical against the modernist and humanist presuppositions. It will also dive into the interdisciplinary context of discussion about relational account of agency.

Chapter 1

Exceptional Humanism and Its Extensional Counterparts in Environmental Ethics

HUMAN UNIQUENESS IN THE
LOGIC OF MODERN ETHICS

Origins of politically mainstream moral theories are in the Enlightenment humanist tradition, and they include the idea of human uniqueness entailing exceptional moral agency. The focus is on the relationships between moral persons: the terms of binding and serious obligations—such as duty, right, law, and justice—hold only within the community of free and rational individual agents. Environmental ethics thus faces the exceptional features of humanity, rationality, and free will as the borders of moral standing and community. Applying this kind of a theory to cover obligations concerning nonhuman beings is possible either by deriving these obligations from obligations to other humans or by extending the definition of moral community to include certain nonhumans. However, the borderline between those who deserve moral attention and those who do not is derived from the definition of the genuine members of the moral community, namely human beings.

According to Immanuel Kant's famous anthropocentric argument, indirect duties toward nonhuman animals are based on the analogy between animals and human beings. Even though we cannot have direct duties toward nonrational beings, we can have indirect duties toward (nonrational) animals for rational moral reasons. As Kant puts it in his *Metaphysics of Morals*, "the duties to animals are duties only insofar as they have reference to ourselves. Hence, we shall reduce all duties to those towards other people" (Kant 1996, 443). Normativity emerges from the analogy with moral agents. The duty not to mistreat persons, directly or indirectly, is clear for rational moral agents, and by argument from analogy, indirect duties toward animals are justified: Maltreatment of such animals would lead, before long, to maltreatment of other humans. Hence, we should respect nonhuman others insofar as they include manifestations of human nature. According to Kant, domestic animals should, perhaps particularly for this reason, be treated "just *as if* they were members of the household" (ibid.).

The strengths of Enlightenment ethics are in universalizing moral discourse based on common reason, and in detaching it from metaphysical and essentialist links. But the claim for justified moral conduct to be universalized requires a shared rationality among the members of the moral community, or a shared nature as the ground of morally counting interests. Reciprocity can be universal and all-encompassing only in the community of relevantly similar members. Conversely, the sphere of ethics can extend to include nonhumans via conceptual similarity. The method of modernizing moral discourse is then based on the existence of relevant features that make the moral status of individual entities equal. Human-nonhuman relationships thus become trivialized when confronted with social relationships or individual well-being, and at the same time, nonindividual things as well as other parties are excluded. The ability of Enlightenment-derived normative theories to deal with the complex ecological and systemic changes, or with the relationships between human individuals and their nonhuman environment, is limited. Consequently, these theories appear unable to provide efficient guidance in the most acute issues of environmental ethics, which are complex and systemic by nature. Environmental ethics is thus not just an issue of applying ethics to new areas of questions, but also something that forces ethics to self-reflect. Historical development that made environmental manipulation and human supremacy possible has thus posed a drastic challenge to the typical modern logic of universalizing ethics: ethics seems to fail to protect both life and social coherence. It is inefficient in critical aim setting, value rationality, and conceptualization of the good and the right in the changing conditions on earth.

The idea of indirect duties to nonhumans derives from the premodern outlook, but the reasons animal mistreatment is linked to moral corruption depend on the adopted views of human beings and the source of moral reasons. The ethical outcomes depend on these presuppositions. Distinctive for modern ways of interpreting indirectness of duties to nonhumans is to consider humans as the source of moral reasons combined with the individualist conception of the human agent.[1] In spite of partly appealing to its classical and medieval predecessors, the Kantian idea of indirect duties to nonrational beings is an individualist approach that has even more limited possibilities for dealing with ecological issues. To compare, the medieval Thomistic view repudiates mistreatment of animals for reasons derived from the *telos* of the human agent: mistreating animals, irrespective of how similar they are with human beings, makes the human agent less virtuous as a person and restricts achievement of her *telos*. A virtuous human has compassion for all creatures. Since virtuousness is a condition of correct reasoning, bad treatment of nonhumans corrupts human intellect and weakens further reasoning (Stump 2003, 103–6, 278–80).

Contrary to this, Kant repudiates mistreatment of animals only because of its impact on members of the moral community: it is wrong because it leads to mistreatment of our fellow humans. Indirect duties to animals remind us of other humans. The justification thus lies in the moral community and (indirect) duties derived from the analogical features of animals that remind us of other humans. Such a justification can, however, be weakened by, for instance, narratives that alienate humans and nonhumans and definitions of morally significant human features that are considered as distinctively human. The problem of modern ethics in environmental issues seems at first glance to lie in valid justification of moral conduct. But justifications of moral conduct in modern ethics strongly rely on a fixed idea of human moral agents. The features that make humans moral agents and members of the moral community form the normative measure for all entities. This is the key reason why the conceptions of human agency should be focused on in different strategies of environmental ethics. All the strategies that clearly focus on agency seem to share interestingly common points in their criticisms against the modern framework. It is, however, worth noticing the difference between anthropocentrism as a notion of justification and as a metaethical position. Modern humanist moral theories are usually anthropocentric in a justificatory sense: they refer to certain types of humans as the source of moral reasons and value and, thus, to the content of moral conduct derived from the will of that kind of human agent. For metaethical anthropocentrism, the focus is on the conceptual limits of morality due to the nature of moral agency: moral deliberation and each incident of actual conduct are bound to the agent's perspective. Although this usually refers to human prescriptions, the agency may include more than humans too. Distinction between justificatory and metaethical anthropocentrism elucidates the difference between humanism and an agency-based ethics.

How did we then become modern (if we ever did)? A brief genealogy of modern humanism is worth consideration. The commonly shared view in Western moral philosophy is that humans are unique natural beings: they have an exceptional moral agency that provides them with the ability to act for moral reasons. Humans are on a continuum with other animals on account of their nature, but are exceptional on account of their moral agency, which signifies the fundamental dichotomy of the modern idea of humankind. This dichotomy is at the core of the logic of modern ethics, and as an implication, the conceptual gap between a moral agent and the rest of the (contingent) world is among its fundamental preconditions: agents must consider themselves detached, isolated, and above the various natural and social webs to practice their autonomy and act morally. Contingent issues derived from material and social contextuality are stripped away from a human being when considered as a moral agent. Defined as noncontingent, moral agency depicts the ideal for humans to transcend their nature as "superhumans." This is the case, for instance, in Kant's ethics: moral agency considered as detached from environmental contexts implies an ideal that does not encourage improved relations with ecological others. For an environmentalist who is concerned about the correct understanding of nature both within and outside a being, the modern notion of a human agent may be inconvenient. Such a view seems scientifically implausible if we take a moral agent to be a natural human being, a member of a certain mammal species, rather than a nonnatural entity. Although essentialism of human nature is rejected in modern ethics, the concept of a moral agent may still be essentialist due to the dichotomized notion of the agent. Since moral agency is not expected to appear in other forms of life, humans have a special status and a unique worth: they form a moral community of exceptional beings with mutual responsibilities. The logic of moral reasons and even the source of normativity in modern theories is internal to the moral community.

The historical baggage of humanism in modern ethics descends from the conceptual divergence between the philosophy of nature and philosophy of mind (concerning the activity of human autonomous operations) on the one hand, and between the mental operations of will and intellect on the other. The first foundations for modern ethics were laid in the late medieval theological conflict between *via antiqua* (Thomas Aquinas) and *via moderna* (Duns Scotus, followed by William Ockham) in the thirteenth century. Two significant new lines of thought were united in *via moderna*: (a) suspicion about universals and eternal essences, and (b) belief in the strict causal determination of physical nature. Together they influenced the self-understanding of ethics in many ways. Among other things, the tension between the human mind and physical matter was highlighted: unlike matter, the mind was conceived of as being beyond the mechanisms of causal determination. An important historical step in the philosophy of mind was William Ockham's voluntarism, according to which the source of good reasons for action are in God's legislative will. Although legislative will came to refer to human will, particularly by Kant, for Ockham it remained the divine will. The crucial thing is that he clearly set will free by distinguishing it from any natural necessities: free will represents an exception in the world on account of its ability to reach beyond the causalities of nature (Hoffmann 2017). From an environmental point of view, important philosophical implications of the victory of *via moderna* concerned philosophical anthropology: First, agents (as well as objects) were described as individuals. Second, the processes of valuing and deliberation were defined as free actions of will. Third, mind and matter were ontologically and functionally divided. The concept of a moral agent absorbed the three isms: individualism, voluntarism, and dualism. Consequently, morality was detached not just from nonhuman nature but also from the natural sides of human agents. In a way the activity and subjectivity of "an agent" were asserted by sentencing "objects" to passivity.

Environmentalists sometimes discuss the influence of Christian theology in environmentally destructive courses of thought. Among the possible influences this medieval debate seems especially relevant. Although both before and after the debate it was clear that a Christian should respect the created world and is not allowed to manipulate it, the reasons for respecting it changed. Distinction made between God's intelligence and God's will, and the focus on God's dictating will as the only source of obligations in *via moderna* gave rise in ethics to the Divine Command theory. This relocated the reason to respect the nonhuman world from virtuousness to the religious order: God did not create this particular world, because it *is* the best possible world, as Thomas Aquinas claimed, but on the contrary, this world is the best because God *chose* it (Työrinoja 1995). Therefore, respect for the creation is justified by the Divine legislator through respect for God's will. The consequences actualized only within the progression of time. First, this schism resulted between medieval and modern detached philosophy and the natural sciences, and the latter became privileged. And second, along with secularization in ethics that undermined theological justifications, it became the task of the best possible (non-divine) legislator to choose and design the best possible world. More influential than the turn to the mortal human was the fact that the decisive element of moral legislator was identified as an exceptional and separated part in the individual human mind: the core of ethics and the source of obligation became a mysterious free part of mind that can be isolated from both body and external environments. Together these changes paved the way for the new type of natural sciences and enabled entirely new technological liberty to manipulate the environmental conditions of life. The view that the actual world is contingent rather than necessary, and that something being good does not result from (God's) wisdom of recognizing its goodness but from (God's) free choice encouraged humans to conceive of their freedom as creative (Työrinojan 1995). Individual free will thus became appreciated as the source of obligations, and hence the core of being human, while reason directs the means. Respect for nature may remain, but it results from the human act of valuing only, or possibly from nonhuman acts of valuing. In this sense, a medieval debate set the standard for the oddity of non-anthropocentric environmental ethics.

The culmination point of solidifying the view that human will is free to determine moral obligation irrespective of the limits of the earth came later through the influence of Renaissance humanism that divided the human agent internally by separating free will and instrumental rationality. The idea that humans can and may use their own freedom to cultivate and construct the world in accordance with their own mind took its full formulation in Renaissance humanism. The writings of Italian Renaissance humanist Giovanni Pico della Mirandola (1463–1494) express how classical humanism ended up holding the mental capacities of human agents to be nearly omnipotent.[2] According to Pico, freedom of will releases a human from the laws of nature. Although Pico's ideas—the immensity of the mind, the insatiability of curiosity, the infallibility of the memory, and confidence in one's intellectual capacities to fashion oneself—did not as such survive for long, the basic line of thought, especially concerning the will, remained. In consequence, the conceptual structure of moral philosophy asserted an active role for human voluntary actions, while the other partners in the action became objectified into passivity.

The most drastic influence of humanism concerned the concept of human agency, which became internally heavily divided into two realms: free will as an exceptional part of human mind and instrumental rationality. These realms depict the hierarchical structure of the world both inside an individual agent and more widely. During the following centuries, several other ideas were developed that strengthened the dichotomized picture of a moral agent. For example, René Descartes's internalism and epistemological skepticism, David Hume's moral philosophy, especially motivational externalism, and Immanuel Kant's conception of radical autonomy. In the field of philosophy of nature, separation gained one of its culmination points in Francis Bacon's mechanistic natural philosophy. Together these ideas generated the basic presuppositions of the modern ethics of a split man.

In contrast to premodern theological ethics, the authority of principles and moral codes in modern ethics are based on the sovereignty of those who exercise free will. Typical examples of this kind of position are, of course, Kantian formalism and contractarianism, exemplified, for instance, in Rawls's wide reflective equilibrium. The claim of modern ethics that the source of moral reason is grounded in human legislative will, which follows the basic logic of the Divine Command theory. This, as such, does not have to threaten serious environmental commitment or the ability of ethics to give efficient guidance. It does adopt a view of the moral agent as an individual entity divided into two mutually isolated realms, one of which represents the contingent, empirically perceived, and causally determined natural agency, and the other, free, moral agency. And that the latter, conceived as the ideal and genuine unique humanity, is free in the sense that it isolates one from her bodily, environmental, and other relationships. Environmentalists have commonly blamed modern humanist ethics for human-nature dualism, but the main problem lies, in my view, in creating an internal schism within the individual. An agent is seen internally split.

A dichotomized concept of a human agent and the following conceptions of autonomy and reason dominate modern moral rationality and rules the logic of modern ethics in a way that is harmful for its capacity to deal with complex environmental issues. Therefore, extensionalist environmental ethical strategies, which are built on the modern framework that do not question the modern presuppositions concerning the agency remain inefficient.

According to the modern moral rationale, social and material determinants are strictly placed within instrumental premises, which should not be confused with moral reasoning. Moral reasoning must be universalized and impartial. As moral agents, human beings are thus free from both sociocultural and biological-emotional bonds. This implies that they should be able to isolate their moral agency from other aspects of being human. This provides equal, inherent moral agency to all humans, while natural agency that is bound to the context is manifested in both human and some nonhuman living agents, for instance, in their mating, caring for offspring, and predation. The natural and exceptional sides of humankind consist of conceptually distinct realms: natural agency expresses contingent reality, while moral agency can provide normativity. Implications of such a split seem significant in ethics. Internal dichotomy reflects the structure and logic of modern ethics: the universality of moral reasons (reasons of true moral conducts) has its foundation in universal moral reasoning—an individual's ability and norm to cross cultural, social, and material bonds—but this requires that agents consider themselves isolated from contextual contingences to practice moral agency. Exceptionality that splits the human agent into conceptually separated parts of natural and moral agencies also implies that reason and will are mutually separated.

The dominant view after Hume has been to locate moral and factual reasoning, as well as cognitive and intentional actions, in conceptually different categories. This forms the background for the modern type of transcendentalism in ethics: the free element of mind represents the core of morality and ensures moral agency, while skepticism about the possibilities of reason to directly reach moral truths is justified. Intentionality refers to the autonomous ability to set ends and it is seen as a subjective activity. Modern solutions to the problem of combining particular moral activity with objective and non-contingent moral truth lean on human autonomy, as does Kant's ethics. The possibility of moral realism in modern ethics is thus connected with autonomy as an ability to overcome what is natural: the moral agent finds transcendence in himself. But autonomy considered as freedom of an individual will does not just represent a person's moral agency, but also marks human uniqueness and superiority: the logic of modern ethics is based on exceptionalism (see Kagan 1989, 399–400; Peterson 2001, 38, 44).

The conceptual framework for human agency plays a crucial role for the normative outcomes. In the modern context, whatever definition of moral agency is *de facto* adopted dictates in practice what is considered worth striving for in order to deserve the membership of the moral community. Therefore, identification and critical evaluation of the concept of moral agency used in environmental ethics helps in analyzing its challenges as well as possibilities to efficiently guide action toward nonhumans. Environmentalists widely recognize the modern notion of humanity as environmentally problematic. Many of the critics consider the problems to be so profound that they call for help from alternative ontological or religious views, as well as indigenous worldviews and wisdom.[3] Although such alternatives offer, of course, important stimuli, critical self-reflection of the background presuppositions of the prevailing ethical discourse should not be dismissed, since we need widely acceptable alternatives to practically provide for cultural sustainability transformation. While bringing in ontological alternatives may provide speculative discourse, my purpose is to sketch a conceptual revision on the grounds of empirically plausible and philosophically sound understanding of moral reasoning and action.

The question is whether a human agent *can* be separated from human nature, or whether this is an idealized view that misguides rational deliberation. Since ethical approaches based on the supposition of separate aspects of human agency—one relative to other animals, another relative to nonnatural divine legislator—has far-reaching ramifications, such a supposition should be empirically supported. The question of scientific plausibility of the presuppositions of modernist humanism has been raised in many fields, including environmental ethics. Recent representatives of the critical discussion often make use of the recent trends of cognitive science and psychology, as well as the philosophy of mind and cognition, about the interrelatedness between the operations of the will, the intellect, and action. According to these critics, if epistemic and voluntary activities were considered not as isolated but as more interwoven, the role of the complex connections between values and facts could be better uncovered for practical normative theories.

Conceptions of the ideal manifestation of agency have changed several times in the history of Western moral philosophy, and the history of philosophy will no doubt continue to change. Therefore, critical reflection of the concept of agency may also have significant ethical implications. Environmental ethics as a part of the self-reflective discussions of modern ethics plays a role of critical evaluator. If environmentalists adopt the logic of the modern exceptionalist framework and accept that impartiality achieved by isolating oneself from the contingent conditions of life is the precondition of morality, they sustain mental structures that made ethics environmentally toothless in the first place. Therefore, conceptual revisions are required for moral theories to be more capable of dealing with the systemic issues of the sustainability crisis. I suppose that these revisions should not require deep metaphysical conversion, but even revisions in the concept of agency can make a radical difference in modern ethics and bring environmental concern from the margin to the core of ethics.

EXTENDING UNIQUENESS

A common line of thought in theoretically oriented environmental ethics endeavors to construct ways out of the limited human-centered perspective and dichotomy between human and nonhuman entities by justifying inclusion of various others into moral discourse through extending the domain of morally counting entities or moral community. The strategy for environmental ethics is thus considered as a strategy to widen the narrow anthropocentric view by justifying that the category of inherently morally counting entities can be extended, first, to individual animals, and then to other living beings and systems, and perhaps further to ecosystems, species, and/or other wholes including possibly also nonliving entities. According to this kind of extensionalism, the task of environmental ethics is to justify the extended application scope of the used moral theory by arguing as a universal claim that at least some nonhuman entities deserve moral status. Consequently, it has been a common way to categorize environmental ethical arguments in accordance with the extent to which they widen the domain of morally relevant entities, resulting in a continuum from narrow anthropocentrism to individualist animal ethics, to biocentric arguments, and further to ecocentric and holistic arguments, some of which adopt an alternative ontological approach. An extensional strategy for environmental ethics is grounded on the internal logic of the selected moral theory, which is shown to be applicable to wider issues than it has been used. The criterion of being morally considerable, or having moral status, then is the key for an environmental argument. The question is whether some nonhuman others deserve moral status and whether they can thus address moral claims or responsibilities to the agent in a way that the other humans do.

Obligations can be extended either by analogy or by ontology, but arguments that wish to avoid metaphysical suppositions usually represent extension by analogy. The objective criteria to judge which relationships should be considered from a moral point of view are then derived from notions of similitude or analogy: morally relevant features, due to which humans deserve moral standing, must provide equal moral standing to whatever entity is under consideration. For a justified moral claim to be impartial, obligations should be extended to all relevantly similar entities, for example, those capable of having interests (Singer 1993, 56), capable of being subjects of their own life (Regan 1983, 199–200), or capable of pursuing life (Goodpaster 1978, 308–25). The most common moral theories used in extending the scope of ethics are utilitarianism, articulated most famously by Peter Singer in his animal ethics (Singer 1976, 1991; see also McShane 2011), and deontological ethics, used by rights-based animal ethics and some other monistic approaches to environmental ethics, such as Tom Regan's (1983), Paul Taylor's (1989), Robin Attfield's (1987), Andrew Brennan's (1988), and J. Baird Callicott's (1980), and sometimes also contractarian ethics (e.g., Rowlands 2002). Although common forms of extensionalism are individualistic approaches, extension by analogy is used even in the case of systemic wholes, including nonliving things. James Lovelock (1979), for instance, argues for responsibilities to Gaia by describing the earth as an intentional entity. An extensional argument for responsibilities to a systemic whole, such as Gaia, requires, however, that the whole is considered as an integral entity comparable to an individual.

I argue that the extensional line of thought has a misplaced focus. By focusing on the nonhuman partner of the relationship, extensional environmental ethics sticks to the conceptual presuppositions of the modern exclusive humanist ethics it tried to oppose in the first place. In my view, the focus should be moved from the question of what kind of entities inherently deserve moral status to the questions of what kind of entity a human moral agent is, and what we can say about the moral aspects of the relationships between the agent and other entities based on those grounds. Turning the focus to the ways in which human moral agency is understood in an environmental ethical argument also alters the classification of the arguments for extensiontal ethics. When the focus is on the *objects* of moral consideration, the strategy that places different arguments on a linear continuum from anthropocentrism through biocentrism to ecocentrism calls us to take further steps in this line when we try to deepen the perspective of ethics in environmental issues. But if the focus is on the concept of *agency*, the shape of this continuum becomes twisted from a line segment into a horseshoe model. In both ends, the "humanist" one as well as the "naturalist" one, the arguments are more open to critically question the modern concept of human agency and the idea of deriving measures of moral status from a human individual and more likely to focus on the entire relationship instead. In either ends, hence, there is more hope for a deeper inclusion of environmental relationships in ethics than there is in the middle, where the extensional arguments are located, if only the idea of moral agent is reconsidered.

The extensional strategy is grounded on the internal logic of the normative theory it aspires to apply to the extended contexts. The idea of universalized justification of moral conduct is especially important for a successful extension: the utilitarian argument, for example, is extended to other sentient entities by pleading to its internal impartiality and universality. Following Jeremy Bentham's *Introduction to the Principles of Morals and Legislation* (1789, chapter 18, sec. 1), since any partial reason to limit moral concern is invalid, moral status can only depend on morally counting significant features such as the ability to suffer (Singer 1976, 152–53; 1993, 56–57; Goodpaster 1978). It is thus central for an analogical justification of extension that the criterion for moral status is independent from morally trivial categories and factual differences. But by claiming such an impartiality the argument insists that the criterion of having moral status is isolatable from other features of the object. For instance, sentience as the natural condition for having interests in Singer's theory does not count morally as such, because only the consequences of actual interests count. The criterion is in fact derived from what is understood to be *exceptional* in the moral realm compared to the contingent world—which refers to the exceptional moral agency of a human being— and this exceptionality is then extended toward more-than-humans, too. The criterion is thus derived from the established conceptions of human moral agency. This emphasizes the irrelevance of material, social, ecological, and evolutionary contingences in ethics, which are seen as insignificant for moral rationality and the way morality is conceptualized.

Extensional strategy thus has a problem: By making use of the modern type of universalism to avoid humanist exclusivism, it in fact adopts the exclusive humanist logic of the modernist framework. A theory using extensional strategy is grounded on the internal logic of the normative theory it aspires to extend. Therefore, it also sticks to the problematic notions of humanity of that theory. By widening the sphere of moral standing, the strategy out of the human-centered outlook in fact strengthens the idea of humans in the center of the widening circles and as the measure for the criteria of having moral status. If morality is an issue of a human, individual deliberator, whatever criterion we use for extension, it reflects some human features: those that make a human exceptional as a moral agent. This seems to diminish both the scientific plausibility and the practical efficiency of environmental ethics. Obligations, rights, and principles that regulate the relations among humans are thought to be extended to the relationships with nonhuman beings, if we only can find a way to make them morally considerable as separate entities by pointing out that they match with the universal conditions of the moral status. An extensional strategy just expands the scope of humanist ethics. The criterion of being morally considerable is derived from the unquestioned members of the moral community, that is, human individuals. A notable feature of the modernist tradition in ethics is that in order to reach the moral perspective a moral agent needs to isolate himself from the contingencies of his own life and from those to which he is related. Such an internal transcendence is required to ensure autonomy and impartiality of the agent. The idea of an exceptional, isolated core of human (moral) agency remains the center of moral worth in extensionalism. While focusing on the moral standing of the others, it does not critically examine or challenge the adopted concept of the human agent that functions as the center for extended arguments, nor the humanist preconditions of extended theory.

Extensionalism has been criticized both as being limited regarding the natural entities it can cover, and as inefficient in so-called wicked systemic problems. Despite the practical power of extensional projects in animal ethics, in cases of complex environmental issues, such as biodiversity or climate change, they seem to make little difference, if any. The basic dilemma for extensionalism is that while seeking for universal justification to take environmental relations seriously, it sticks to the ethical framework, the mistakes of which it wishes to overcome. Most notably, extensional theories adopt the modern humanist concept of human moral agency that explicitly denies the moral relevance of environmental relations. They in fact seem to strengthen the idea of human exceptionality and supremacy and fasten a human individual to the center of the widened circles of moral consideration as the source of the criteria for moral status. The main problem is that extending the domain of morally relevant others implies a fixed center that offers the criterion for extension. Whatever criterion we use for extension, it reflects human features, which are taken for granted: those that make a human exceptional as a moral agent. Extensional strategy thus remains as a counterpart to exceptional humanism: the idea of a moral being refers, first and foremost, to features of humanity that remain conceptually untouched. As a point of departure, this kind of approach to ethics denies that bodily or environmental relationality could have any moral relevance; relations belong to contingences. The traditional idea of the human individual agent remains as the genuine core of ethics however extended it may be.

As the notion of humanity remains central in environmental ethics, it is significant to consider what is meant by humanity. The definition of humanity determines what we think about the nature of morality and the focus of ethics. Theoretical approaches to justify moral relevance of the relationships between moral agents and nonhuman entities are also tied with the adopted conception of agency. If we wish to develop the ability of moral discourse to contribute to the condition and future of the biosphere, and to enhance the plausibility and efficiency of environmental ethics, the essential task is to focus on the concepts of the human agent and moral agency, and to critically evaluate the adopted concepts in ethics. An agential approach is an opposite strategy for environmental ethics compared to the extensional one.

Conceptual criticism against the modern framework caused wide interest in alternative philosophical frameworks and vivid ontological discussion among environmental ethicists especially from the 1970s to the 1990s. This is especially true of deep ecologists, moral holists, and those influenced by the ecosystem ecology, such as Holmes Rolston III, J. Baird Callicott, and Arne Næss, respectively, who each called for some kind of a paradigm shift. Their influence in the field has also been enormous. However, despite the fact that an ontological shift can offer an attractive sensitivity with respect to ecological interactivities, a metaphysical paradigm shift does not automatically have positive implications. For example, metaphysically demanding arguments are weak from the viewpoint of practical efficiency: a clearly ontological or religious project excludes those who do not accept the premises of the discussion, and ontological revisions are not easily accepted. Despite being fascinating, such a project may fail in producing solutions to the sustainability crisis of ethics. Therefore, due to the urgency of the crisis, frameworks that are widely accepted in political discussion have been favored by mainstream environmental ethics. Among them, however, the increasing criticism against the Enlightenment ethics has made, for instance, pragmatist framework popular (see Light 1996; Norton 1987, 2005; Weston 2004, 2009).

Holistic and deep ecological arguments do not form an ethically coherent strategy. Some of these arguments represent a modified type of extensional strategy, while some others offer a clearly alternative approach based on some critical account of humanity and/or the rest of the nature. It is also worth distinguishing between ecological and moral holism. Gaia theory (Lovelock 1979), and Arne Næss's ecosophy (Næss 1973) are examples of ecological holism holding some wholes as ontologically new entities. Næss (1988), for instance, argues for the moral self that extends to cover all the ecological relationships to a whole. This means, roughly put, that all others become parts of the exceptional self. According to critics, this kind of strategy is reminiscent of ethical egoism (Plumwood 1994, 156–57). Moral holism, on the other hand, is an ethical view that opposes individualism and prioritizes the good of, say, a species or an ecosystem, as does, for example, Aldo Leopold (1949) and J. Baird Callicott (1999). Still another way to integrate ecosystem ecology into ethics is the sociobiological approach most famously represented by E. O. Wilson (1975). As an openly naturalistic approach it straightforwardly argues against the concept of the human agent in modern ethics. Besides various holistic and socioecological approaches, however, early ecohumanists and especially ecofeminists aimed beyond traditional humanism by criticizing modern ethics about the narrow conceptions of both nature and the human agent (e.g., Warren and Cheney 1991). According to the ecohumanist Andrew Brennan, for example, freedom, autonomy, and rationality in the sense required by modern moral theories are practically never manifested (Brennan 1988, 27, 65, 135–36, 143–44, 199–200, 211, 221).

The radical arguments in both humanist and naturalist ends of the continuum of environmental ethical arguments focus on the conceptual problems concerning the agent, instead of justifying the extension of the objects. A specific target of criticism on both ends is the idea of isolated and exceptional human agency behind the moral theories used in extensionalism. I am quite convinced that a novel and practically influential environmental ethics cannot avoid conceptual revisions concerning the concept of agency in ethics, which makes me somewhat skeptical of the possibilities of the traditional holistic approaches. However, the agent-focused strategies pose their criticism against the modern concept from mutually different frameworks and starting points. At the after-modern or posthumanist end, for instance, ecofeminism scrutinizes problems of the rationalist tradition and focuses on the processes of reasoning and epistemology, while at the naturalist end, the strategy drawing from the Darwinian science or ecosystem ecology focuses on the empirically plausible concept of will and intention. Despite their mutually opposing backgrounds, their criticisms as well as the alternatives they offer share surprisingly much. This makes it important to examine their critical voices against the humanist presuppositions in environmental ethics side by side. As the aspirations to reconceptualize the problematic presuppositions of humanism and extensionalism thus attack them from mutually opposing directions, it seems that a comprehensive critical approach, the one that takes criticisms of both ends into account, could offer a promising starting point for a novel strategy to approach complex environmental issues. Therefore, it is both interesting and inspiring that the critical alternatives of the opposing ends and mutually opposing philosophical frameworks are parallel in their criticisms against the traditional modern idea, and in a way, in fact, approach each other. Especially of note, this concerns aspirations to reconsider *human agency as a relational issue*. In parallel, they seem to take promising steps beyond the conventional battle lines and toward a new approach to environmental ethics while distancing themselves from the extensional strategies that rely on the modern logic of ethical theory based on the similarity argument.

Ethics should be among the leading cultural means of sustainability transformation. However, this seems not to be the case. The contribution of ethics to sustainability transition has been weak, which is partly the fault of extensionalism representing the most popular approach of the past decades. To summarize, six critical points, at least, can be made about extensionalism as an environmental ethical strategy. First, the morally significant relationships are defined by referring only to the facts about the object, regardless of the agent-derived facts; second, the criterion of moral relevance is derived from the idea of similarity with the subject, which derives moral relevance of other beings from that of humans who are unquestioned members of the moral community; third, they imply the centric structure of ethics, which makes it conceptually exclusive and imperialist; fourth, the justification is based on the idea of a morally demanding analogy between the agent and the object, which provides for universal arguments but fails to deal with strangeness and partiality; fifth, they include implausible presuppositions concerning the agent's moral and epistemic abilities; and sixth, they give an instrumental role to factual reasoning and knowledge, which implies a trust in the neutrality of science and epistemic optimism. Let us take a little closer look through the four first points.

First, evaluation of whether a relationship counts morally or not is made by focusing the evaluation only on the *quality of the object*. Both the object and the relationship as such are isolated from the agent and the agent-derived facts: the considering agent is and should stay impartial. Extension is based on the idea of impartiality of moral conducts and moral consideration: the legacy of a moral theory can be extended to various objects by appealing to impartiality. Since impartiality is considered to express reasonably justified ethics (Singer 1976, 100–1 and 1995, Goodpaster 1978, 308–9),[4] it makes extensionalism normatively motivating. However, obligations, rights or principles regulating social relationships in a human community can be extended only due to some universal condition that makes different entities worthy of moral consideration, only *if* they meet that condition. The basis of the argument lies in Kant's view of the moral community (Callanan 2013). The focus of the extensional strategy is, thus, on the other, the object. Kenneth Goodpaster (1978) defines the general structure of a moral relationship by the formula: "For all A, X deserves moral consideration from A." Both A (rational moral agent) and "consideration" (defined by the extended theory) are fixed, while the only open term is X. This turns the focus to the criterion. The main question for environmental ethics is then reducible to the question about the kinds of beings to which the category of X impartially refers: all beings verified to meet the criterion—if only the objective criterion is found—have moral standing and mandate practical respect from humans. Despite differences, arguments representing an extensional strategy in general rest on the originally Kantian idea of moral status as something inherent in the object, independent from its relationship with the agent or context. The criterion for moral consideration should be objectively and impartially applied to each object that deserves it. Intrinsic features that qualify the object are conceptually connected to selected theory and simplified to make different entities commensurable. A being either meets or does not meet with the criteria, and if the being does match the criteria, it deserves moral status universally and independently from the agent. Definition of the borders of the moral domain is absolute. Somewhat similar critical questions that arise in the case of modernist anthropocentrism about an essentialist assumption of a universal qualification for morally countable beings, also arise in the case of extensional arguments. Environmental ethics is understood as a project of seeking for the qualified members of "our club" to save their rights against nonmembers. This offers ethics a very narrow pathway to contribute to environmental issues or relationships with nonhuman entities.

Second, the criteria of moral relevance are derived from the *idea of similarity* with the moral agent, which reduces moral relevance to the unquestioned members of the moral community. Extension can be justified only if different cases are identified as relatively similar or analogical, and hence comparable with those who unquestionably meet the criteria. This makes extensionalism fixed to human-centeredness. Similarity, rather than difference or otherness, awards membership to the club. For Kant this similarity is first and foremost rationality. However, Kant leaves the door open for some nonhuman primates to enter in, if they only qualify for the intrinsic value-conferring property, which is morally significant similarity. Kantian extensional strategies redefine this criterion that makes humans and some nonhuman entities equal as moral patients, although they cannot be considered moral agents (for criticism see Callicott 2002). In this logic it seems necessary that features providing moral status should be seen as isolated from any specific features or relationships. This implies not only that the inherent features that count morally are independent from any agent-derived features, but also vice versa, that the core element of the agency stands untouched by contingent relationships. Morally relevant similarity thus refers to exceptional agency and practicing of moral rationality is isolated from particularities and contingent relationships.

Third, the implied (anthropo)centric structure of ethics makes an extensional strategy for environmental ethics conceptually exclusive and open for criticism about *moral imperialism*, and the structure of justification based on the idea of a morally demanding analogy between the agent and the object fails to deal with strangeness and partiality. As it is central for extensionalism that the core of what counts morally is both impartial from trivial categories and differences between the entities, and that it is not reducible to any factual features of the object, a morally relevant similarity is a kind of abstraction, something isolatable from the other features of an entity. In a consequentialist interpretation, for example, the underlying principle on which extension relies is that of equal consideration of interests. Having interest does not rely on, for instance, sex, race, age, or species. But having interests is not the same as being sentient, although sentience is the decisive analogy. Peter Singer's strategy is to extend the utilitarian moral argument to everyone whose interests could be hurt, i.e., all sentient beings capable of suffering (Singer 1976, 152–53; 1993, 19–21, 56–57). Despite being a necessary condition for having interests, sentience as a factual feature is not, however, a sufficient condition for moral status rather than interests. Interests are not reducible to any experience of pleasure or pain, but are independent from their necessary bases, the ability to suffer and enjoy (Singer 1993, 57, 77; 1999, 328). What then matters for an agent is the consequence of her action from the point of view of the actual interests of sentient patients. So, an interest deserves moral consideration when it exists, not when there is potentiality to have interests. What follows is that the more interests one has, the more moral attention it deserves.

Three problems arise: First, the moral domain is quite limited: only enti-ties that are "free" enough can have strong interests, because physical reac-tions are weaker interests than free desires (Singer 1976, 159; 1993, 14). What is regarded as an interest also heavily relies on the agent's perspective. Second, among sentient beings those who have more interests deserve more attention, since each interest deserves equal respect (see Singer 1976, 149; 1993, 21–23). This trivializes the relevance of nonhuman beings compared to complex cultural agents: due to the agent's perspective, other-than-human entities seem to have fewer interests, and those who have more interests, count more. Third, as the feature that guarantees moral status does not depict factual similarity, the possibility of a human agent to gain information about the good he or she should promote, namely interests of those who deserve moral consideration, is very limited.

Kenneth Goodpaster (1978) criticizes sentience as the manifestation of the interest criterion, since it is biologically reducible to just some means for survival. He prefers "being alive" as a more valid gatekeeper instead. Being alive could also hold for a wider sphere of objects, covering nonsentient animals and plants: the need for light and water are the interests of plants, although they do not feel pain when not given them. Goodpaster's version of extended utilitarianism thus criticizes Singer's classical argument for con-necting moral status to irrelevant descriptive features. Instead of arguing that sentience is ontologically or morally justificatory ground, however, Singer appeals to the analogical similarity between the sentience of an agent and that of other creatures as decisive for the obligations this relationship addresses to the agent. By analogy, according to him, the agent can identify with the feel-ings of an animal: he can, although weakly, understand its suffering (Singer 1993, 68–70, 277). This refers again to another difficulty that is linked with the adopted view of the agent: the theory implies trust in the agent's reasoning: the agent must achieve information not only about the other's expressed experience, but also their interests, which are not reducible to these experiences. A somewhat similar problem is included in the argument for rights-based extension on the side of deontological theories defended by Tom Regan. He argues that the right to be respected and treated well is justified for all that have inherent value. Having inherent value depends on whether the entity can be seen as a "subject-of-a-life," which is Regan's criterion for any morally considerable being. But a practical problem concerns the possibility and authority to define from the point of view of an entity and decide whether it is a subject-of-a-life or not (Regan 1983).

Analogy as an abstract similarity entails two types of difficulties for the arguments: they subscribe to a modernist neglect of the body and the physical structures as morally insignificant, and they admit the problem of strangeness: a human moral agent can never fully understand what counts as the good for the nonhuman other. Goods for and duties to are then derived by analogy from the goods for and duties to those whose moral status is unchallenged—rational, healthy (Western) adult humans. The obligation to recognize a particular relationship as morally relevant depends on what the agent recognizes as inherent in the object. The argument defended by Paul Taylor, for example, claims that having a good of its own provides a being both necessary and sufficient reason to be appointed inherent worth and to be respected accordingly. However, there is no way for "having a good of its own" to straightforwardly obligate agents, but rather the obligation arises when the agent *sees* another living organism as a teleological center of life and, hence, an analogical bearer of inherent worth. When an agent recognizes this analogy, it obligates him to follow the ultimate moral attitude of respect in relationships with these entities. According to Taylor, we recognize this analogy only if we give up narrowly human belief-systems and adopt a biocentric outlook that depicts all living organisms as teleological centers of life, and thus, as entities having goods of their own (Taylor, P. 1989, 42, 72, 76–80, 101, 119, 168). This kind of analogy cannot be verified or unverified by science; it is a question of outlook.

Individualist extensional arguments, especially, highlight the ability of an agent to rationally evaluate the moral relevance of nonhuman others and take the correct attitude toward them. But since interests, rights, or values of the entities are not quite reducible to empirical facts about their condition features, the decisive issue is that the agents have empathy with the interests of the sentient others, adopt the correct outlook, or have the right attitude of extending respect to the inherent value in all subjects-of-life. All this is possible because of the analogy. Singer, for instance, makes an epistemically optimistic supposition that an agent can and does recognize what is in the interests of the animals that are sentient, like the agent himself.[5] However, there is asymmetry in the empathy and rational recognition of animals by agents that provides a problem of foreign extraction, even an "imperialistic" relationship. The perspective of a human agent, considered as impartial, dominates what can be seen as good or bad for various nonhuman partners. And as the analogy refers to the modernist idea of a "plain" moral agency (which remains untouched in an extensional argument), the moral relevance of the other partner also is seen as something isolatable from material, social, and ecological contingencies.

Fourth, suppositions about the agent's *impartiality, empathy, and rational abilities* to understand the nonhuman entities are implausibly high in these kind of theories. In addition to the scientifically questionable presuppositions of exceptional agency that an extensional theory adopts from the modern moral theory, such as absolute freedom and impartiality, arguments for analogical extension assume trust in the agent's benevolence and epistemic capacity to understand nonhuman others. The role of factual reasoning and knowledge also remains instrumental in extensionalism. This implies a trust in the neutrality of science and epistemic optimism, and in fact subordinates the practical outcomes of moral reasoning to science. What then can be said about the role and influence of the nonhuman world on the moral agent? First, as an agent's environmental relationships are contingent, they are insignificant for moral reasoning. This is a philosophically clear claim but as a description of a human being, a member of the mammal species, it sounds scientifically implausible. Second, moral reasoning conceptually separates voluntary action as the source of values from instrumental reason that points out the means. The view of moral agency is thus internally split into mutually isolated will and reason. Will isolated from the contingencies of the world is not totally natural, while cognitive abilities may be seen as particular capabilities dependent on, say, genes and education. This split implies that the spheres are conceptually monolithic in the sense that reason, at least, does not have a significant influence on the ability of the will, which is thus free.

A DILEMMA THAT REMAINS

Extensional arguments for environmental ethics remain conceptually exclusive and centric models: extensions are based on some relevant similarity with a certain center, to which all moral relevance is reducible. Despite that the emphasis is on inclusive equality, the requirement for similarity or analogy between relevant moral parties implies that differences betoken exclusion. The criterion for moral standing depends on the concept of the center—of the human moral agency. Human exceptionalism, as a part of an extensional strategy, as well as traditional humanism, can be criticized for (human-derived) exclusivism, and extensional arguments problematically implicitly strengthen the view that moral agents who best can meet the criteria stand at the center. The concept of human agent is thus central for the success of this kind of a moral theory—both in social ethics as well as in animal and environmental ethics. This is well understood in the criticism by feminists, minorities, and indigenous people, for instance, who push back against the ideal of an adult white wealthy man as the one who unquestionably qualifies the measure.

Whether a modern ethical theory has practical efficiency in environmental issues partly relies on the reliability of the adopted view of human moral agency. According to the prevailing conception, isolation, freedom, autonomy, impartiality, and rationality are perquisites of autonomy of a moral agent. If they are conceptual preconditions for morality, they should be unchangeable and as eternal as morality itself. Is it too dangerous a question to ask whether the modern view of the moral agent is reliable? Would it undermine ethics if human agency was not conceptually exceptional? Does the autonomy and authority of ethics rely on the traditional humanist presuppositions of modern ethics? The basic dilemma behind the debates in environmental ethics concerns, on my view, the conceptual division between moral and factual concepts, or normative ethics and descriptive explanation, embodied in the concept of human agency: It splits the agent internally into two conceptually incompatible parts, natural and moral agency. Environmentalists would be pleased to combine them. But reliable explanations of human agency that question this internal dualism are conceived of as threats for ethics.

As said earlier, definitions of the sphere of morality, as well as its limits, depend on the adopted notion of moral agency. Even if the problems of extensional arguments would otherwise be solved, an applied concept of agency still maintains the environmentally harmful structures of moral theories (Cuomo 1998, 95–97; Plumwood 1993, 22). The concepts of freedom and knowledge that dominate the modern view of human agency depict human supremacy and the authority to decide about the future of the earth. The problem for environmental ethics is not anthropocentrism as such, but the modernist presuppositions about the human to which it is connected. We do not even need ethics to see the drastic mutuality and interdependence between humans and nonhumans in the biosphere.

The international scientific community has reached quite a wide consensus that the current geological era should be known the Anthropocene, the human epoch, due to the influence of human activities that have profoundly altered the conditions and processes on our planet in an ultimate and irreversible way (International Commission on Stratigraphy 2019). Geologically they include significant changes in erosion and sediment transport (caused by colonization, agriculture, climate change, and urbanization); chemical composition of the atmosphere, soils, and oceans; perturbation in the cycles of carbon, nitrogen, phosphorus and metals—and derived changes in environmental conditions (including global warming, ocean acidification, and other changes in the oceans)—as well as changes in the biosphere on both land and sea (due to habitat loss, predation, species invasions, and human-caused physical and chemical changes), including an irreversible species mass extinction.

However, many philosophers who criticize the modernist notion of the human, such as Donna Haraway and Rosi Braidotti, are concerned about the cultural emphasis given on the power of human expressed by the name of epoch including "Anthropos" (e.g., Braidotti 2018; Haraway 2016). But the point of the term is, for me at least, that nature to which we are intimately tied responds with our own weapons. The Anthropocene indicates the start of degeneration of human species. It calls for reconsidering humanity and the place of humans in the world—to diagnose the megalomania of a species that cannot escape the threat it creates to itself and to act accordingly. The Anthropocene highlights how profoundly humans and nonhuman nature are intertwined. Natural contingencies are not trivial but rather determine the conditions in which the "free and rational" human mind exists. Likewise, human influences are integral to nature. These influences do not remain "out there," but degeneratively change our own conditions and destructively shape the natural world in and through which human agents identify themselves, socialize, feel, reason, deliberate about good and right, decide, become motivated, and act. We now constrain our own freedom and shape future humanity as well as nonhuman actions. We are parts of the same eco-cultural systems as nonhumans. The Anthropocene highlights the complexity of the mutual interconnectedness between different elements and agencies on earth, and by demonstrating the destructive influence of humans, it also demonstrates "the decline of the primacy of universalist 'Man' and of supremacist *Anthropos*" (Braidotti 2018, 243; see also Braidotti 2019; Haraway 2016, 57).

As Braidotti remarks, the discussion on the Anthropocene intersects with the ones on posthumanism and post-anthropocentrism. Posthumanism focuses, according to Braidotti's definition, "on the critique of the humanist ideal of 'Man' as the universal measure of all things," while post-anthropocentrism "criticizes species hierarchy and human exceptionalism," and "their convergence is producing a trans-disciplinary field of posthuman scholarship." The focus of recent environmental humanities is strongly influenced by these three discussions. As Braidotti points out, recent environmental humanities differ from traditional humanities with two regards: they do "not assume a concept of the 'human' identical to the humanist 'Man,' nor [are they] compatible with anthropocentrism." Instead, they foreground "the relational, self-organizing, technologically mediated, material systems of expression of forces that—before the Anthropocene—we used to call 'nature'" (Braidotti 2018, 242–43).

One thing that we could learn from the Anthropocene is that the conceptual division between moral and nonmoral actions is much more unstable than commonly thought. Moral actions are often said to be those by which we may harm or benefit someone, but if the consequences of my everyday nonmoral actions stay at the biospheric and geological levels for millions of years to harm or benefit beings to become, it is almost impossible to separate between moral and nonmoral actions. I can never know for sure whether the action I am performing counts as a moral action or not. In fact, I should think that I can be morally blamed or praised about each of my steps. It seems that in practice it is impossible or at least not easy for me to be rational with my actions or conscious of my motives. This invites us to reconsider the category of moral actions, as well as the idea of moral rationality. An interesting question is whether *indirect actions* should be recognized as morally blameworthy or praiseworthy in virtue of their influence in the material, ecological, social, or cultural conditions that provide the environment in which one's own agency and others' agencies are constituted. If this is the case, we should also think of these actions as partly responsible for *moral rationality*, which should then be seen as *relational* and partly contingent and.

Empirical research on humanity, such as anthropology, has been a somewhat guarded topic in modern ethics, because the empirical explanations of moral agency most often question the modern notion of an autonomous individual agent, which is seen to undermine responsibility and to imply ethical reductionism. But the environmental dilemma forces moral discourse to scrutinize the implications of modern humanist suppositions for moral reasoning, and also the self-understanding of ethics in general. According to the modernist presumption, it is the human exceptionality of moral agency manifested in independence and impartiality that entails a moral perspective. But subscribing to this as an environmental strategy strengthens conceptual anthropocentrism, in which the ability to detach oneself from nature and from social others is at the core of being moral and is hence a norm. At the same time, environmentalists widely acknowledge that the idea of human uniqueness has become suspicious in the light of scientific evidence. Therefore, sticking moral agency to such features represents implicit essentialism. Those who criticize human exceptionality often focus on naturally or socially reductive anthropology, but sometimes it also implies the reduction of moral concepts to natural or cultural phenomena, especially in non-environmental contexts. This is not, however, the only direction for valid criticism. On the contrary, it seems that more sophisticated criticisms can be put forward if the target is correctly specified. Rejecting isolated autonomy and absolute freedom as preconditions does not necessarily imply determinism about human agency, let alone reductionism concerning moral reasons. A relational view that connects the mechanisms of an agent to the social and ecological contexts does not deny the unique complexity of agency itself (see Cheney 1998,

265; Preston 2000, 240; Plumwood 2002, 49, 54–56, 206, 215–16, 227–29; Raz and Wallace 2003; Ingold 2022).

Among environmental philosophers, critical voices have actively attacked humanist and individualist overtones and their ethical implications in the extensional strategy, such as moral monism indicated by both individualistic and holistic extensionalism. For instance, Anthony Weston, a pragmatist philosopher and critic of a monocentric view of ethics, argues that the strategy fails because it simply replaces anthropocentrism with a wider centrism and calls for critical conceptual analysis. According to Weston, ethics should be de-centered to take the multiplicity and complexity of the natural world seriously (Weston 2004; see also Narayan and Harding 2000). He makes use of the dialogical approach formulated originally by Martin Buber as one of the first prominent formulations about the truly respectful relationship between different kinds of beings in modern Western philosophy. It Is worth noting that Buber's dialogic principle essentially transforms the concept of a human agency by focusing on intersubjectivity. According to Buber's central claim, no isolated "I" exists; individuated elements always realize themselves only in dialogue between "I," "Thou," and "It." Dialogical relation to another (*I-Thou*) makes each figure a mysterious center of value.[6] Buber's dialogic principle works as the basis for Weston, as well as for many other critics of moral monism, who call for a paradigm shift in environmental ethics to consider moral worth with diverse centers (Weston 2004, 26). In the current environmental discussion, it is common to stress the plural centers of value and talk about a multispecies moral community, thanks much to the popularity of Donna Haraway's writings (Haraway 2016; Haraway and Clarke 2018, Haraway 2019), but monistic extensional strategies are still powerful in academic ethics due to the established theories on which they rely. Multicentrism, as Weston calls it, starts with de-centering humanness and disentangling worth from any one qualification. In ethics this implies that we should not talk about abstract respect rather than a "willingness and ability to make the space, not just conceptually, but in one's own person and in the design and structure of personal and human spaces, for the emergence of more-than-human others into relationship" (Weston 2004, 31). A challenge emerging from this kind of thinking is that it does not fit into traditional metaethical categories. The ethical realm is not real enough to be reached by reason, nor is it unsubstantial enough to lack foundations in the real world.

Much of the criticism against the conceptual dichotomy of modern theories targets comparing qualifications of morally relevant others to features derived from the quality of humans as moral persons. However, the role of these others, as well as the nature of a human person, in the drama of life often remains invisible. This notably restricts the ability of a theory to take all the perspectives of complex environmental problems into account. I shall go a little further and argue that the most decisive features of a human agent, whose scrutiny could help here, are *freedom of will* and *cognitive reasoning*. As I shall show, the common conceptions are currently under wide critical scientific discussion. Despite the categorical difference between ethical and empirical discourses, the properties of agency should be open to debate in the light of the most recent scientific understandings of the human mind, rationality, and the nature of intentionality. This is especially important because of the status given to the moral agency as the core of noble humanity: as such it represents the normative ideal. If the evidence that will be given in the following chapters concerning natural humanity is correct, the features praised as marks of the core of moral standing should be revised. By leaving exceptional human agency unquestioned, an environmentalist strategy consolidates ethical structures that waters down the relevance of ethics in the battle against sustainability crises.

Specific attention should be paid to the conditions and mechanisms of moral action, especially the processes of voluntary actions and knowledge formation. Instead of just repeating the modern story of the Kantian philosophy that "free choice entails a form of metaphysical 'subject' or 'agent' by way of the 'Will,'" which is a distinctive "faculty" of the mind (Solomon 2003, 204), the focus should be on the conditions and mechanisms that produce intentional action. If acting for moral reasons is thought to require genuine impartiality from the agent, the agent needs to identify himself in isolation from his social and environmental surroundings to apply moral principles in the correct way. Moral autonomy is usually considered to require radical freedom, while autonomy as a parent, lover, or economic agent may admittedly be more partial and contextual, but is such a strict division justified? Freedom of will is emphasized especially in nonnaturalist ethics: an agent as an autonomous subject guarantees the nonnatural character of moral values. This is thought to imply separation between two realms of the human subject. Naturalists, for their part, struggle between empiricism and essentialism. According to a widely shared modern view, moral agency should be somehow released from natural causalities to be capable of taking an impartial "third person's point of view," while natural agency remains under natural causalities.[7]

To clarify the dilemma, it is helpful with regard to this question to remind ourselves of the crossroads at which modern ethics originated. The debate that culminated between Thomas Aquinas and Duns Scotus in the thirteenth century concerned the mutual influences between intellect and will, and the role of each in moral reasoning. Thomas argued that virtuousness of will enhances intellect to better reach the moral facts, the best understanding of which is accepted by the will. Intellect can be either cultivated or corrupted by (the vices and virtues of) will. If the outcomes of intellectual operations fail, they may misguide the will. According to Scotus, the will is free from the guidance of intellect, and intellect can correctly serve bad will without being corrupted. This implies that reason is instrumental, which is, again, a distinctive feature of the modern view: Outcomes of intellectual operations are neutral regarding voluntary actions. Intellectual operations as separated from attitudes and voluntary orientation emphasize the objectivity and neutrality of the information they give; the autonomy of science becomes highlighted. Questions about how the objects and facts of the world are conceptualized or constructed, or how cognitive relationships, like the recognition of objects, modifies our intentions and will, for example, are beyond moral discourse and evaluation.

In the history of moral philosophy, a move toward voluntarism was important for the autonomy of ethics: moral actions were clearly not any more bound to a better or worse understanding of facts, but on the contrary, moral crimes could be committed by the well informed. However, there are significant side effects to this line of thought. According to critics, both the freedom of voluntary actions and the neutrality of intellectual capacities play a bigger role in modern ethics than seems plausible. I agree and argue that in the context of environmental ethics, at least, the implications include normative inefficiency regarding complex issues about the conditions of life. Philosophical and cultural traits of thought together with scientific development, increasing technical skills, political situations and economic conditions made the modern conceptual changes acceptable and dominant, allowing the notion that a human can represent ideal moral agency without caring for the factual ecological state of affairs. It slowly emerged in the common understanding in Western societies that human agents can manipulate their own future without moral restraint. Developing science promoted the notion of humans constructing a better world for themselves, leading to the expansion and differentiation of civilizations. However, even Bacon worried that the power of science could be misused and, in fact, argued that science should not be separated from moral evaluation (Klein 2016). An important thing in the cultural change, a change that recent environmentalists have called a conceptual mistake that encouraged *hubris* concerning the contingent natural and social conditions of our moral agency, was that the new science considered the human mind as an exceptional knot of causalities and finalities. Over the centuries, a common understanding came to hold that humans as moral agents represent a unique point in the universe and that the causalities of the world could be enslaved by an autonomous individual.

The modern concept of freedom has recently been criticized by philosophical anthropologists. According to Robert Solomon, for example, free action can be seen as connected with "the rest of a person's character, circumstances, and culture, including his or her reflections on these." Freedom and responsibility should then be evaluated in relation to the narrative of one's life: an act that "fits and makes sense in one's life story" is free enough to be called freely chosen. According to Solomon, this is the view that David Hume also suggested (Solomon 2003, 204–5). From the viewpoint of this book the question concerns what the implications are of such a modest or narrative approach to the concept of agency—and to a self-understanding of ethics, through that. If the concept of agency is not restricted to the limited realm of the will, it is possible to think that choosing one's values, for instance, is deeply tied with nonconscious and quasi-intentional aspects in the agent's processes, but can, nevertheless, be called freely chosen if it is narratively justified (Solomon 2003, 206, 232). On the practical level, at least, Solomon's modest view of freedom represents a huge step from the Enlightenment tradition: the absolute autonomy of free will is not among the prerequisites of moral responsibility. The narrative relationships between will and the other aspects of agency are complex.

I agree with these critics. Supposing that the agent's relationships with her home landscapes, pets, or surrounding climate do not matter concerning the way she conceptualizes the moral significance of extraction, torturing of pets, or caring for plants, simplifies the idea of moral perspective (e.g., Preston 2001; Rowlands 2003). In modern ethics, a strong belief seems to prevail that the agent's nonmoral actions do not influence the conditions of moral agency. Such belief hinders ethics from being practically reliable and should, therefore, be questioned in order to reconsider the role of environmental issues in ethics. Appealing to a theory without conceptual criticism about its view of humanity does not seem to be a way to solve the basic dilemma of environmental ethics. The moral arguments grounded on the analogy between moral agents and moral patients carry on the idea of an isolated exceptional agent and the otherness of those who are different.

To sum up, I argue that the extensional strategy for environmental ethics includes problems that weaken its efficiency and motivation, since it misplaces the core focus of environmental ethics: the focus of the criterion for something to have moral status simply strengthens the idea that ethics is restricted to a concern about the relationships between exceptional individuals who are isolated from a cruel nature. Despite its practical usefulness in some issues of animal ethics, the extensional strategy maintains the modernist presuppositions of justificatory anthropocentrism. This makes it weak in facing the general problem of moral theories to solve complex environmental issues. The focus should be turned to the quest for an alternative idea of moral agency.

The dilemma between moral autonomy and the contextual human mind will not be solved in this book. Perhaps it never will be, or at best it will take a long time for our most astute philosophers to solve it. But meanwhile, I argue that explanations of operations of the human mind—will, reason, perception, and motivation—and the meaning of these explanations for the theory of ethics—the idea of moral reasons, and the autonomy and authority of ethics—should be critically examined in the light of the contextual, embodied, and embedded relationality of a human animal. At least for environmental reasons. Among environmental ethicists, evolutionary ethicists (by appealing to natural sciences) and ecofeminists (by appealing to social sciences and philosophy) pose perhaps the strictest criticism against isolated agency. They insist on taking the contextuality of the agent better into account, and upon a nuanced definition of freedom. Recent vivid discussion of the gap between freedom and nature has highlighted the idea of a less-than-absolute dichotomy.

NOTES

1. Reasons given in premodern ethics for neglecting animals as moral partners were metaphysical instead: Different modes of life have different purposes, and therefore, humans and animals cannot be fellows. Thomas Aquinas, *Summa Theologiae*, 2a2ae, 25, 64, a. 1.

2. An illustrative passage from Pico della Mirandola's *De Hominis Dignitate (Oration on the Dignity of Man,* 1486), translated by Richard Hooker (1996), describes God's words to Adam after creation: "whatever seat, whatever form, whatever talent you may judge desirable, these same may you have and possess according to your desire and judgement. Once defined, the nature of all other beings is constrained within the laws We have prescribed for them. But you, constrained by no limits, may determine your nature for yourself, according to your own free will, in whose hands We have placed you. We have set you at the centre of the world so that from there you may more easily gaze upon whatever it contains. We have made you neither of heaven nor of earth, neither mortal nor immortal, so that you may, as the free and extraordinary shaper of yourself, fashion yourself in whatever form you prefer. It will be in your power to degenerate into the lower forms of life, which are brutish. Alternatively, you shall have the power, in accordance with the judgement of your soul, to be reborn into the higher orders, those that are divine."

3. Among the popular inspiring sources besides the indigenous cultures are process metaphysics by Alfred North Whitehead as well as Confucian and Buddhist ontologies, from which also deep ecologists, such as Arne Næss, draw inspiration.

4. A commonly used argument here is R. M. Hare's impartiality thesis in his *Freedom and Reason* (Oxford University Press 1965) and *Moral Thinking* (Oxford University Press 1981).

5. Singer's optimism concerning the agent's ability to interpret the interests of a sentient being is based partly on the similarities between animal and human nervous systems. Singer 1991, 11–16; Singer 1993, 69–70. Impartial perspective also requires rationality on the part of the agent. Singer 1995. For Singer's empiricism, see Crisp 1999, 94–95.

6. For Buber, the dialogical *I-Thou* relationships that refer to the interactive nature of reality are possible also with different animate beings, such as animals, trees, or with the Divine Thou. See Buber 1970.

7. Kant, for example, thinks that the division between what "is" and what "ought to be" refers to the dichotomy between determinism and freedom. See Kant 1990 (*Foundations of the Metaphysics of Morals*), 13–14, and Kant 1987 (*Critique of Judgment*), 35.

Chapter 2

Moral Agency in Evolutionary Environmental Ethics

A Naturalist Alternative to Dichotomized Agency

NATURAL SCIENCES, HUMAN NATURE, AND ENVIRONMENTAL ETHICS

Environmental ethics has its historical roots in the natural sciences and environmental activism (in addition to traditional moral and philosophical discussions) and the attempt to find a scientifically sound model of ethics has remained central. However, the use of the natural sciences varies and may even be selective (Sideris 2003, 11–44; Sideris 2015, 137). The difficult outcomes of scientific inquiry are sometimes subsumed under notions that are found to be more helpful, such as the ecological model of nature.[1] Therefore, it is not only that environmental ethicists' use of scientific arguments may imply deriving "ought" from "is," but more notably, "the *ought* they are deriving" may represent "only a part of nature's *is*, as science understands it" (Sideris 2003, 26–27).

Due to Darwinian influence, shared animal nature, the evolutionary continuum between human and nonhuman nature, and ecological interrelatedness are widely defended by environmental ethicists. These issues also reveal a dilemma for environmental philosophy: such notions may call autonomous moral agency into question. The challenging implications for ethics are not often properly worked out and, perhaps, metaphysical revisions are called for to resolve the dilemma instead. A continuity thesis, for example, is often simply taken as a support for extending the membership of a moral community on the grounds of sameness, or analogy. Interrelatedness, on the other hand, has been used to justify holist notions of the moral self as grounds for ontological extensions of agency—sometimes, for example by Næss (1988), even to the extent that applies to ethical egoism (for criticism, see Brennan 1988, 143–44; Plumwood 1993, 180; Warren and Cheney 1991). It seems that some basic philosophical difficulties in facing the facts of human and nonhuman nature have mainly been disregarded in environmental ethics, reducing the use of natural sciences either to pointing out "morally relevant" (a term used unquestioningly as such) similarities between human and animal nature, or to justifying metaphysical holism.

But interdisciplinary work in environmental philosophy should be interested in taking the challenges of science seriously, though not blindly. A tendency to closely tie a theory of ethics to its scientific explanations is common, for instance, among sociobiologists and evolutionary psychologists. E. O. Wilson (1998) calls it the "consilience" of science. Sometimes, science is seen as a worldview with a myth of its own, offering not just explanations, but also reasons, meanings, and values.[2] Among these challenges, those posed to the concept of moral agency and the meaning of human animality are crucial: evolutionary mechanisms and the systemic structures of nature can fundamentally elucidate human ways of acting and reasoning. Reliability of normative theories and their political use require scientific plausibility. There are, however, a twofold threat of science for philosophy. First, explanations that put humans on the same level with other natural beings may threaten the idea of moral autonomy—and in consequence, the responsibility of the agent. Second, empiricism that reduces moral motivation and conduct to natural explanations about cultural manners or religious outlooks may threaten the autonomy and authority of ethics, as well as the idea of normativity (Stenmark 2001). Rejection of scientific understanding is not an answer: it would threaten the plausibility and practical import of ethics in the human way of life, societies, and culture. It should also be noted that scientific theories about human nature are numerous. Approaches that critically aspire to avoid both simplified explanatory and justificatory reduction, as well as rejection of the challenging facts are, to my understanding, urgently needed in environmental ethics.

For a theory of moral *agency* that could deal with human relationships in relation to nonhuman reality, the relevance of a theory of human *nature* is in the features that deal with the mechanisms of creating meanings and values, setting aims, reasoning, evaluating, and being motivated to act. Theories of human nature are, however, combinations of views that in fact take up positions in relation to different questions. With regard to moral traits, the building blocks for explanations include views that concern human nature as compared to nonhuman agents, as either constructed (blank paper) or given (full paper),[3] as plastic or fixed, as material or mental, as determined or free, as causal or teleological, as naturally motivated or not to act morally (optimistic versus pessimistic views), as mortal or immortal, as self or non-self, and the notion of human nature as either purely descriptive or also pre-scriptively laden, allowing the use of concepts like flourishing normatively (Stenmark 2012). While it is not insignificant whether human nature is given or constructed, mental or material, these questions are not as decisive as questions of freedom, plasticity, optimism, and the normative status of human nature. For environmental ethics, however, comparison between human and nonhuman nature plays an interesting role. On the one hand the moral importance of ecological interrelatedness, the unity of life, and the continuity between human and animal nature are strongly emphasized. On the other hand, however, human animality that rules out the nonnatural, transcendental exceptionality of moral agency, may potentially threaten the entire idea of demanding moral duties, at least in the objective sense. Therefore, an interesting question is whether the non-reductionist naturalist arguments can help in avoiding problematic aspects of exceptionalism as necessary prerequisites of moral agency.

Despite possible confusion and misinterpretations, the attempt to take ecological and evolutional realities into account in a scientifically sound concept of moral agency makes environmental ethics of great value for wider discussion on ethics and its self-understanding. If moral philosophy cannot face the challenges it has in dealing with human-caused planetary changes, the authority of ethics will degenerate. Theoretical research on ethics should not close our eyes from constantly increasing our scientific understanding of human, as well as nonhuman, nature, action, intentionality, motivation, and social life, if morality is regarded as worth being preserved as something that plays a role in people's practical life. Without tools capable of guiding actions in the world of environmental destruction, morality may appear useless. Sciences also have instrumental value: they offer information to evaluate environmental consequences, assess political objectives, analyze discussions on values, and contribute politically.

NATURALIZING MORAL AGENCY: DARWIN AND HIS FOLLOWERS

Freedom of choice, moral reasoning, and the motivation to act for moral reasons are morally decisive features that are considered to emerge from the exceptionality of human moral agency. With these respects, humans and nonhumans are usually considered as different "in kind," rather than just "in degree." These features of agency amount to autonomy, which is—in one form or another—a prerequisite of any idea of moral responsibility. While in ethics humans are generally seen as unique rational and free moral agents, human uniqueness and exceptionality of the features that enable humans to act for moral reasons have been called into question by evolutionary explanations of morality.

The idea of human uniqueness has been an incessant target of suspicion among evolutionary scientists ever since Charles Darwin's *The Descent of Man* (first published in 1871). Evolutionary biologists, anthropologists, sociologists, and psychologists have offered empirical explanations for human capacities and dispositions associated with moral behavior, such as altruism and cooperation. Darwin emphasizes humanity as part of the unbroken chain of life. According to Darwin, moral senses make the most definite difference between humans and other animals, but, even that, "great as it is, is certainly one of degree and not of kind." Moral senses are naturally evolved by social instincts, and lead to morality "with the aid of active intellectual powers and the effects of habit" (Darwin 2001, 101, 130–31). The fact that people universally in all cultures pass on values and behave according to certain standards supports, for Darwin, the notion that it is part of human nature to have moral senses. Despite depicting a specific nature of human species, the origin of moral dispositions is in natural evolution. There is nothing nonnatural in the idea that human beings are moral agents and have a sense of right and wrong (Darwin 2001, 103). Hence, Darwinian understanding justifies nondualism between humans and nature.

Evolutionary theories are currently widely taken seriously in moral philosophy. Environmental ethicists value the idea of the biological origins of morality and the continuum between human and nonhuman actors especially for two reasons. First, they highlight the value of material, ecological, and animal realities as central to the evolutionary history of human agents, which again maintains the aims of environmental ethics and deepens the theoretical discussion. It also opens philosophers' eyes to the study of animal behavior, including elements from which we can learn about ourselves. Second, recognition of the natural origins and naturalness of the highest expression of human uniqueness or exceptionality—our moral agency—forces us to humbly focus on the fact that the best future for earth is not necessarily the one that we have created based on our best understanding. We are bound to our limited perspective—at least as individuals and groups containing communities of somewhat similar other individuals. Approaching the meaning of truth, good, and right would require other species' perspectives and an embracing the mechanisms by which various things in nature are interrelated, too.

So-called evolutionary ethics goes further. In the Darwinian spirit, all evolutionary ethicists argue that moral senses, dispositions, and traits are evolved through natural selection by adaptation. Usually, they also argue that such dispositions are evolutionarily profitable. Profitability may refer to genetical adaptations (genetic reductionism), or to a wider notion that also takes psychological and social adaptations into account. Explanations of moral senses and traits vary, however, due to the adopted theory of natural selection. Moral senses can be seen to result from survival-oriented selection as profitable adaptations at the level of individuals (e.g., following Herbert Spencer's theory of social Darwinism), species or populations (which may be closest to Darwin's own view), relatives (following William Hamilton's kin selection theory), groups (e.g. sociobiologists and evolutionary psychologists loosely following V. C. Wynne-Edwards and Konrad Lorenz, or John Maynard Smith, for example), or genes (a view made commonly known especially by Richard Dawkins). In addition to different biological interpretations of natural selection, moral tendencies and dispositions may be reduced to a synthesis of several scientific fields, including most notably psychology and anthropology. Besides reductive approaches, an empirical approach may also take a non-reductive form to seek reasons for certain manifestations of morality to occur. Although moral dispositions are evolved as capacities, their use and cultivation may still be unprofitable for genetic fitness and express some culturally developed aims instead. Different explanations have different philosophical implications, and this should be kept in mind.

Altruism, sacrificial love, and cooperative sacrifice as traits that exist did not fit into the original Darwinian theory, and explanation of moral behavior compelled evolutionary scientists to develop further theories to explain moral behavior (Schloss 2004, 10). Social Darwinism, developed by Darwin's fellow scientist Herbert Spencer, argued that there is progress in the natural evolution of species, and this biological progress is depicted in the development of society, art, and other fields of human activity—including morality, as evolution goes hand in hand with social development (Farber 1994, 118–19, 122).[4] After the world wars social Darwinism declined in popularity and was treated as ethically suspect, though some followers developed the idea by appealing to Freudian psychology. Julian Huxley, an architect of neo-Darwinian theory, was among them. He argued that evolution is a progressive process with three distinct stages: cosmic, biological, and sociopsychological. Huxley's view is based on the theory originally defended by his grandfather, Darwin's contemporary Thomas Henry Huxley, who argued that morality is exclusively a cultural innovation that sets the human psyche at war with its own nature (Huxley, T. 2009, xxv–xxxiv, 35–36, 75–76). Unlike Darwin, but like his grandfather, Julian Huxley thus argued for discontinuity between man and other species by differentiating between biological and sociopsychological progress: humans are thus unique in kind. Cultural progress is not based on biological trends. Because of the psychosocial stage of evolutionary progress, cultural and moral development is exceptional. Huxley also argued that the only "path of unlimited progress" is the one that is included in human mental abilities (Huxley, J. 1941, 115; Farber 1994, 130–36; see also Michel Ruse's

"Introduction" in Huxley, T., 2009). He also believed that the only—or at least best—progress takes place in the self-control and independence of the human mind. As a progressivist he thought that cultural progress through moral development necessarily creates ever better civilizations.[5]

The problem of neo-Darwinian theory lies in the supposed discontinuity between humankind and the rest of nature, which is against the basic Darwinian notion of evolution, and belief in the inevitable progress of development. Together they implicate the superiority of the human moral agent over the "lower" species, and hence, perhaps even justify subordination of nature as well as cultural hierarchy. From the point of view of the idea of moral agency, the fact that neo-Darwinian theory denies, following Huxley, the Darwinian idea of qualitative continuity between different forms of life resulting from gradual evolution is significant: Discontinuity maintains the idea that complex mental and moral abilities are *separated* from the nature of agents. Moral abilities emerge from cultural development distinct from the material environment influencing adaptation. Such a view has been criticized by, for instance, primatologist Frans de Waal (2005, 2006), who argues that Huxley's theory is scientifically implausible in the way it contrasts moral abilities with natural humanness and abilities of other species. According to de Waal, Huxley's morality is a "thin veneer" over human nature determined by constitutive selfishness (de Waal 2006, 7–12). In addition to breaking the continuum between humans and the rest of the nature, Huxley's position thus splits humanness into natural and nonnatural elements (for discussion, see Kitcher 2006; Singer 2006). However, the neo-Darwinian appeal to the progress of cultural evolution, on the one hand, and the synthesis of natural, psychological, and social sciences, on the other hand, attracts some environmentalists, especially those who prefer a mythic story as a background for moral conducts. Scientific optimism and the harmonious story of nature unveiled by unified science represents for certain environmentalists a source of wonder comparable to the religious one; science as the crown of human culture emphasizes the exceptionality and mythic power of humans (for criticism, see Midgley 2004; Sideris 2017, 32–35; Sideris 2015, 139, 144–46; Deane-Drummond 2015, 172).

Most evolutionary psychologists and ethicists after Huxley adapted a psychoanalytical explanation of moral obligation, whereas before explanations were derived from biology. Philosophers commonly regard both evolutionary explanations of morality with suspicion: the link between empirical facts and their moral implications is not clear. Although the validity of moral sentiments could be derived from the psychological nature of human species, the relevance of these sentiments for ethics cannot, as Henry Sidgwick, for instance, argued (Farber 1994, 134). In twentieth-century moral philosophy, biological foundations were put aside, and the study of the origins of ethics focused on the history of philosophy and social sciences. Especially influential was G. E. Moore's criticism of moral naturalism, which turned the focus to philosophical issues, especially moral language. This had an influence in divorcing questions about (human) nature from moral philosophy, especially in the case of rationalist and cognitivist theories.

Moore's legacy dominated the framework for normative ethics in the late twentieth century when environmental ethicists tried systematically to justify responsibilities for nonhuman nature. Therefore, there were natural reasons for some environmentalists to take up a renewed interest in the evolutionary approach along with sociobiology, launched by Edward O. Wilson in his *Sociobiology: The New Synthesis* (1975). Sociobiology emerged as a biological explanation of human culture and behavior on Darwinian and neo-Darwinian grounds, and critical questions about moral agency became a vivid part of environmental discussion especially through Wilson's influence. Many of the notable lines of environmental ethics owe a debt to sociobiology, among others, Peter Singer's utilitarian subjective naturalism (1991) and holistic naturalism defended, for example, by Holmes Rolston III (1999), in addition to philosophers who more clearly focus on the implications of sociobiology in ethics, such as Mary Midgley (1994) and Michael Ruse (1999), although they strongly oppose each other.[6]

According to Wilson's sociobiology, natural selection has a strong explanatory force for the ongoing processes of both biological and cultural evolution: nurturing, cultural manners, moral senses, and behavior can be explained by the interaction between genes and the environment (Wilson 1978, 17). Besides moral senses, morality as a phenomenon, moral rationality, and perhaps even the content of moral conducts are also explainable by biology and the evolved sociality of our species. Wilson adopts William Hamilton's kin selection theory to explain altruistic social behavior: through altruistic behavior organisms best improve their inclusive fitness. Morality can thus be justified by the study of genetics. It is our natural inclination to be moral for the sake of our genetic progress: altruism ensures a greater number of similar genes to be passed on than non-altruistic behavior (Wilson 1978, 153–54; Ruse and Wilson 1989; Ruse 1999, 174). Morality as a phenomenon is "the morality of the gene," and the study of moral agency is, in theory, reducible to the study of genetics. Moral conduct is based on moral senses, which are explained by the function of emotional control centers in the brain, especially in the limbic systems that evolved through adaptation in evolutionary time. Evolutionary ethicists after Wilson's *Sociobiology* mainly deny, however, that either individual or group-selfishness, by which morality can genetically be explained, would as such be profitable for evolution. Explanation of complex moral systems requires a wider empirical perspective on motivation since culture also influences survival. Wilson himself later noted the problems in explaining morality by reference to profitability and admitted that morality and religion form the most interesting and humbling challenges for science. Wilson's theory is, however, reductionist in the end, although he softened it in his later works (cf. Wilson 1975, 3; 1978, 41, 68; 1998, 183, 276–78, 296).

Environmental ethicist and sociobiologist Michael Ruse argues that there is no reason to think that psychological capacities could not be motivated by the biological self. Instead of selfishness, it is morality—one based on altruist claims—that brings about "the best" environment for the genes of an individual human to survive in. Morality is thus an adaptation like hands and genitals (Ruse 2004, 44–45; 1999, 174; 2010, 297, 303). Ruse's conception of moral agency delineates three levels of desire. Basic desires at the lowest level motivate both human agents and nonhuman choice-makers to action. Humans alone, however, have second-order desires through reflective self-evaluation: at this level free will is used to choose between competing first-order desires. Moral choices are made at the level of third-order desires, by which we can prioritize our already reflected on volitions that are mutually competing. Third-order desires form like an advanced chess-playing machine that uses more general principles instead of calculating all the options. Moral sentiments of altruism are thus naturally evolved, but they must be distinguished from biologically profitable "altruism" and altruism in the literal sense, referring to the feeling of the need to act kindly "simply because this is the right thing to do" (Ruse 2001, 212–15). Ruse's metanarrative about ethics is, however, that of efficient evolution: morality (altruism in the literal sense) is the best pragmatic strategy to attain biologically profitable quasi-altruism ("altruism"). This means that to serve our "selfish genes" most efficiently, we should not be selfish (Ruse 2001, 191–92, 195). The failure of social Darwinism, according to Ruse, was that it tried to justify moral codes by making an appeal to the progressiveness of evolution by claiming that ethics promotes this progress. Ruse denies belief in progress and argues that ethics has no other reason to exist than biological adaptation: it just is as it is as an adaptation of social humans to live a social life. But because this view of ethics does not commit anyone to sacrifices, Ruse claims that we have created systems to justify "that it is more than it is." Thus, he argues that "ethics is an illusion put in place by our genes to make us good social co-operators" (Ruse 2010, 297, 303, 307–9, 311–12).

The sociobiological view of human nature and agency is criticized for its essentialism and genetic reductionism. According to critics, among which there are many feminist philosophers, by explaining all kinds of human behavior—sexuality, aggression, dominance, the caste system, labor division, parental care, and religion—in terms of genetics, sociobiology strengthens essentialism. Characteristics profitable for evolutionary fitness are seen as essentially better than others. Through genetic reductionism, this kind of sociobiology reduces not only emotions and motives, but also ethical systems to genetics (cf. Ruse 1998, 123–26). On the side of feminist constructionists, this criticism is then part of their fight against an essentialism that legitimizes unequal socioeconomic structures. Critics also notice that Wilson's view of humankind endorses the biases of his social and cultural class (white, middle-class, heterosexual males from the US South). He describes social and behavioral differences, such as homosexuality, as differences requiring a biological explanation: differences among men are abnormalities, eventually evolved for somehow strengthening the normal traits of behavior (Wilson 1978, 143–46). Yet another criticized feature is Wilson's belief in progress: all social behavior, including intentional activities and ethics, work toward evolutionary progress. Wilson acknowledges, however, that "the evolutionary epic" is a "myth" and that this "myth" is the core of scientific materialism. But he thinks it is the best explanation for the whole universe that we see and experience today (Wilson 1998, 295–96; 1978, 201; cf. Ruse 1999, 185, 188, 190–91).[7]

Contrary to both Wilson and Ruse, an evolutionary ethicist, philosopher of biology, and feminist Mary Midgley seeks for a more complex, and explicitly *non-reductionist* approach to evolution, which she calls a "middle way" (Midgley 1994, 159). For both reductionist and non-reductionist accounts of moral agency, each agent is individually affected by the whole evolutionary history of the human body, and the limbic system releases hormones that drive us to certain actions. But according to non-reductionists, such as Midgley, responses to evolved bodily messages are not hardwired. Rather, the way the brains are trained by the environment, especially by the social community, is a definitive factor in how people respond (Clayton 2004, 319, 325).

Evolutionary psychology, currently the dominant evolutionary explanation of morality, has softened the role of determinism by combining humanitarian perspectives with the originally sociobiological position. In Jerome Barkow, Leda Cosmides and John Tooby's *The Adapted Mind* (1992) three theses are defended. First, universal human nature "exists primarily at the level of evolved psychological mechanisms, not of expressed cultural behaviors." Second, these mechanisms "are adaptations, constructed by natural selection over evolutionary time." Third, "the human mind is adapted to the way of life of Pleistocene hunter-gatherers," which means that the modern circumstances may be radically different compared to those our mind is adapted to. In sum, the human mind and its functional design features should be seen as responses to those demands that were faced by our hunter-gatherer ancestors, and the adaptions of the mind, such as morality, ensured quick and efficient responses to environmental challenges (Barkow, Cosmides, and Tooby 1992, 4–5). Slightly varying explanations have been developed on this ground by psychologists, anthropologists, and neuroscientists.

In contrast to sociobiology, evolutionary psychologists consider that besides genetic fitness, social experiences and learning determine human behavior. They argue that evolved moral psychological manners and changes in them often reflect cultural rather than genetic adaptations: people adopt them because of some wider interests of a larger group of beings, bound together by a common fate and common prospects. In the environmental discussion Elliot Sober and David Sloan Wilson, for instance, defend this kind of idea and criticize individually and genetically oriented interpretations (Sober and Wilson 1998, 335–36. Cf. Ruse 2004). Evolutionary psychology thus extends the sphere of explanation by adding social and cultural determinants to the biological ones (Lewontin 1991, 123; cf. Wilson 1975, 548). Therefore, in moral philosophy, evolutionary psychology is more sensitive to cultural variety than its predecessors. However, the design features of organisms, the human mind included, are seen as causally related to adaptive problems. The mental design generated through adaptation is then panhuman and universal for all members of our species (Barkow, Cosmides, and Tooby 1992, 5, 8). This means, among other things, that standard evolutionary psychology implies the acceptance of a functionalist notion of ethics. But in contrast to suppositions of selfishness as the guiding principle for adaptation, evolutionary psychology emphasizes the complex mechanisms that make cooperation profitable: social life and cognitive adaptations for altruistic, cooperative traits are its explanatory focus (see Barkow, Cosmides, and Tooby 1992, 161–62).

Extension of the scientific ground for empirical explanation does not negate reductionism as such. Despite distancing from simplistic genetic determination and adopting more complex explanations of moral reasoning and codes, evolutionary psychology still seeks universal *explanations* for particular cultural expressions through the idea of "the adapted mind" (Barkow, Cosmides, and Tooby 1992, 45). As an empiricist approach to morality, evolutionary psychology reduces *reasons for* action to scientific *explanations* of the adapted mind. Hence, it maintains a monistic view and ignores the possibility of interactivity between actions and adaptive mechanisms in, for instance, moral development. From the philosophical point of view, the question about the reductionism of moral agency remains quite alike in both sociobiology and evolutionary psychology.

The perspective of evolutionary psychology has, however, some benefits from the point of view of environmental ethics. First, it offers the connection between environmentally functional behavior and moral inclinations. Second, it advises not to straightforwardly listen to these inclinations, since they are adaptations to a very different environment than we currently deal with. Third, it calls for a more social understanding of not just emotive but also cognitive mental operations. The second point could be applied to the argument for cultural obligations to be aware of these inclinations and to formulate codes that function best in meeting environmental challenges. The third point refers to the meaning of cooperative adaptations. It could be used in justifying the need for environmental non-selfishness and collective duties. More broadly, evolutionary psychological arguments can benefit the moral philosophical discussion especially at three points: they question the common understanding of individual and extremely free moral agent, they cast light on the embodied nature of mind, and they concentrate on scientific evidence that denies dualist human nature (Barkow, Cosmides, and Tooby 1992, 49–50). In this sense, evolutionary psychology follows the original Darwinian view of qualitative continuity between species.

Serious aspiration to combine the empiric biological, psychological, and neurological evidence with the philosophy of mind has notably developed the understanding of the human mind and mental operations as what I will call *relational*: fundamentally interactive, embodied, and environmentally extended. Hence, these are steps toward non-reductionism that Midgley called for in the naturalist approach to ethics. However, evolutionary psychology seems to stick to scientific biological imperialism in its ideal of explaining the universal "panhuman" design of the mind by the unified scientific method. In this sense, much of the criticisms made against its sibling sociobiology also hold for evolutionary psychology. But the steps it has taken to guide an evolutionary approach toward a more complex understanding of human agency and mental operations open a road to a more relational view of natural agents.

AUTONOMY AND MORAL
RESPONSIBILITY THREATENED?

Scientific demystification of humanity promotes our nonhuman kin and removes humans from a conceptually exceptional status. Evolutionary naturalism also challenges human exclusivity with respect to autonomy and morality: as adaptations, moral capacities may also be adapted by other species. But the Darwinian nondualism that provides such demystification also challenges the common understanding of the conditions of autonomy, and could, therefore, also be seen to diminish moral responsibility. There are three common responses to this threat. According to the first, the idea of genuine morality and autonomy includes mystical elements, and it is abandoned. For the second, some vital element of a miracle-type self-determining power is thought to remain. For the third, Darwinian naturalism is seen as compatible with the capacities of autonomy, responsibility, and free action to at least the extent that it does not threaten normative ethics. In addition, a fourth response has entered the discussion. It calls for the reconceptualization of the notions of autonomy, free will, and morality: despite being vitally important and distinctive for human animals, these features are neither miraculous nor nonnatural.

The Darwinian defense of the qualitative evolutionary continuum between human culture and the rest of nature is conceptually important for reconsidering the uniqueness of human moral agency and the nature of animal agency. According to Darwin, natural agency and moral agency are not disconnected. "Nature" as such can develop agency for genuinely unprofitable behavior. Darwin's conception of human nature is, thus, optimistic. In contrast, Thomas Henry Huxley, Julian Huxley, and more currently, for example, Richard Dawkins, argue that there is a gap between evolved, selfish nature—in which actions are determined—and morally potential, culturally developed agency—which is capable of restricting selfish genetic determination (Dawkins 2016, 247–59).[8] At the end of *The Selfish Gene* (1976), Dawkins expresses optimism about human unselfishness and cultural progress: "We are built as gene machines and cultured as meme machines, but we have the power to turn against our creators. We, alone on earth, can rebel against the tyranny of the selfish replicators" (Dawkins 2016, 260). More than anything, this represents pessimism about the innate human nature, together with which it calls for the culturally developed capacities—to which the idea of freedom is restricted—to resist this natural selfishness. Dawkins's pessimism derives most importantly from genetic reductivism. Through game theoretical analysis about successful strategies, Dawkins argues that in contrast to genetic evolution, human memetic culture should prefer cooperation and niceness—especially a tit-for-tat type of strategy (Dawkins 2016, 271–84, 292–93). Frans de Waal's criticism defines this idea about moral agency defended both by Huxley and Dawkins as a "veneer" laid over the cruel (human) nature and isolated from it (De Waal 2005, 19–23). Wilson agrees with Darwin's basic idea of continuum between humans and the rest of nature but believes that culture is primarily a human species-specific property, although some traits of culture can also be found in animal communities. As an exceptionally human phenomenon, culture goes beyond purely biological evolution. Human nature was adaptive "at the time of its genetic origin," but due to gene-culture coevolution, this turns into what he calls a paradox: "At the same time that culture arises from human action, human action arises from culture" (Wilson 1998, 183). Ruse follows in many respects Wilson but defends evolutionary naturalism and skepticism in a stricter sense (see Ruse 1995, 241–42; Ruse 2010, 312).

An acute question for an evolutionary approach toward human agency concerns the prerequisites for responsibility, among which freedom of will is the most discussed. Cartesian dualism that dichotomizes the body with machinelike causal activities, and mind with free intentional agency, represented for Darwin an attempt to preserve an essentialist idea of the human subject as an ontologically exceptional entity. What Darwin's theory in general, first and foremost, attacks against, is the essentialist view of any biological being. For Darwin, morality is thus a natural issue, while Huxley's dualism in a way "pits morality against nature and humanity against other animals" (Desmond 1994, 599; see also de Waal 2006, 8). The continuity thesis is a challenging idea for the traditional understanding of autonomy and responsibility. But the discontinuity thesis seems scientifically poorly explained and philosophically problematic due to its detached optimism and passing over the natural conditions of agency as positive limits for the design of the future. As critics of Huxley and Dawkins argue, defense of the discontinuity thesis may just have emerged from a supposition that radical freedom is a prerequisite for moral agency—as if adding the idea of exceptional freedom to humans would make a radical evolutionary theory about human nature more acceptable to philosophers.

As will become clear, the argument of this study disagrees with such a supposition. And it seems that environmental ethics has suffered from the fact that attempts to formulate more modest conceptions of freedom and autonomy, scientifically plausible but still uncertain, have not been properly acknowledged in moral philosophy. This is, perhaps, due to the inclination of some notable evolutionary scientists to adopt a philosophical supposition that for moral actions to be unprofitable would require properties that are disconnected from evolutionary forces. Disconnection between natural and ethical properties, and the absolute, Kantian way of understanding freedom are central presuppositions of so-called evolutionary debunking arguments that reduce ethics to natural science (Kirkman 2009, 218; FitzPatrick 2017, 6–7; Sideris 2007, 76–78). The hardwired evolutionary debunking arguments on the one hand, and arguments for the superiority of human (cultural/moral) species to exceed its own (selfish) nature on the other, have dominated the discussion on the ethical implications of evolutionary science. In contrast to them, most environmental ethicists want to take seriously the complexity of evolutionary mechanisms, and they seem widely ready to defend Darwin's continuity thesis about moral agency. Different questions should, however, be distinguished: it should be recognized, for example, that the Darwinian idea of continuity in capabilities cannot be equated with the genetic reduction of morality. The latter would rule out much of the traditional meaning of responsibility, while the former does not imply determinism. Despite this, the continuity thesis forces moral philosophers to closely scrutinize whether common suppositions about deliberative operations included in ethical theories hold in scientific examinations. Such a humble conceptual scrutiny of the function of human moral capacities is what normative ethics urgently needs—not only for environmental ethics, but for various contemporary ethical discussions, for example, those concerning artificial intelligence and biotechnology.

Evolutionary approaches to ethics can, roughly put, defend either reductionism or non-reductionism concerning moral deliberation and action. While reductionist explanations hold moral traits to result from survival-oriented natural selection, hardline non-reductionist explanations are often connected with the defense of the nonnaturalness of genuine moral traits. But more modest interpretations are possible. In particular, interdisciplinary discussions on philosophical anthropology and philosophy of mind and cognition, closely connected with the recent scientific findings, encourage one to question the idea that the non-reductionist concept of moral agency would require a non-natural notion of moral capacity.

Sociobiology argues that the human species has evolved into a species consisting of beings that cooperate through morality. Morality is a unique system that may internally motivate altruist action as it connects people emotionally with each other. But as this system of morality takes place, according to sociobiology, for the sake of genetic survival of the species, moral motivations emerge from, perhaps unconscious, egoist inclinations: to be moral for the sake of my genetic progress (Ruse and Wilson 1989, 316). All social behavior—ethics included—ultimately works for evolutionary progress because humanity is generated to improve genetic survival (Wilson 1978, 201; 1998, 284–85). Morality thus has an instrumental role in the evolutionary epic, being as such a "lucky fake" that makes us do what is profitable for our genes (Ruse 1999, 176). Whether sociobiology then commits a fallacy that violates Hume's "no is from ought," is a debated issue even among evolutionary ethicists. The strict separation between emotion-motivated "quasi-moral behavior" (observed also in some primates) and exceptionally human reason-based, "genuine moral behavior" is widely questioned. Hence, Wilson's idea of progress as inevitably good, at least, is criticized as representing the naturalistic fallacy (see Ruse 1998, 214; 1999, 185–88, 190–91; Sideris 2015, 2017). Considering the conditions of the fallacy statement might be helpful here. For a modernist view, natural "is" represents objective, causally determined facts, while "ought" represents norms set by the free legislative will. To understand this correctly, it is necessary to understand the ethos of modern science and the instrumental role of knowledge included in that. Historically speaking, objectivity of factual truths was adopted into modern ethics, most notably from Descartes. According to Kant, for instance, moral reasoning is free from all determination that qualifies nature (Kant 1987, 35; 1990, 3–4). This easily amounts to the interpretation that moral reasoning must not be anything naturally explainable: moral autonomy as the freedom of a legislator belongs to the nonnatural sphere. But autonomy as radical freedom is only possible in comparison with the world of objective, determined facts. In case the view of the natural world is not mechanistic in the Cartesian sense, the modern idea of practicing autonomy becomes more complicated.

Choosing between the continuity thesis with an optimistic view of human nature and the discontinuity thesis with a pessimistic view of human nature also influences what is considered to motivate people to act morally or care about being moral. For the continuity thesis, moral capacities can be naturally motivated. People may construct cultural structures as they are inclined to enjoy cultivating their moral capabilities and increase their flourishing through moral action. According to Ruse, an ethical social contract theory, such as John Rawls's, for instance, coincides with a Darwinian view (Ruse 1995, 244–45). But even if human nature is considered as determined by selfish genes, following the discontinuity thesis, cultural development may still motivate people through their selfish emotions. As Thomas Hobbes's classical externalist theory of ethics supposes, people are totally selfish, and they want to satisfy their desires to the maximum extent, but as they are rational, natural desires motivate them to seek peace, security, and freedom, which can only be realized by a commodious life. For personal commitment to morality, however, this type of motivation offers weak justification. Whether an evolutionary approach to motivation is internalist or externalist depends on its attitude to natural selfishness (see Brink 1989, 46–47, 49).

ETHICS EXPLAINED NATURALLY

Evolutionary theorists disagree whether genuine moral behavior—namely actions that cannot be reduced to evolutionary profitability—originates in nature. While Darwinians argue for the continuity between natural and moral behavior, those who highlight that natural behavior is always genetically profitable argue that unprofitable actions must be grounded on nonnatural aspects in human culture and free will. The Darwinian naturalist thesis that even genuine morality has its origin in nature is currently the dominant one among evolutionary scientists: Human agents are moral animals that differ from other animals only in degree, not in kind (Darwin 2001, 130). Human morality is thus a product of natural social evolution, "a direct outgrowth of the social instincts that we share with other animals" (De Waal 2006, 6), or "a form of inquiry in which innovators recognize and respond to external constraints" (Kitcher 2011, 204). Emergence of genuine moral reasons has to do with adaptation, and animal social tendencies function as the building blocks for morality. Evolutionary theorizing that focuses on human agency can thus explain moral motivation, perhaps even morality, as a natural phenomenon. In any case, natural continuity between animal altruism and human morality is acknowledged (Ruse 1998, 2004, Kitcher 2007, 2011).[9]

For those who hold morality as a distinctly cultural innovation, the discontinuity between evolutionary and cultural reasons should be kept clear, and morality, as an issue of reasoning, must be separated from evolved, and therefore selfish, emotions. *If* there are reasons for genuinely altruistic actions, they do not originate in nature; instead, we have culturally adapted to social life and developed social codes to survive. Morality may even be a device for selfish beings to promote their fitness. According to Dawkins and Ruse, for example, we are lucky to have morality due to our ancestors, who became moral by the power of their nonnatural choice (Dawkins 2016, 180–81, 260; Ruse 2001, 212–13; see also Dennett 1984, 72). The dichotomy between nature and culture is thus striking. The metaethical implications of Huxley's, Dawkins's, and Ruse's views are that evolutionary theorizing either disproves all foundations of ethics—and thus leads to an evolutionary debunking argument—or ethics must have nonnatural foundations in culture or religious beliefs that have emancipated humans from genetic selfishness. The evolutionary explanations are seen to reveal the groundlessness of ethics: moral reasons are, in fact, fakes. But some argue that objective moral codes exist due to an evolved rationality shared by moral beings. Objectivity then arises from the need of social animals to justify their actions to others. If ethical realism is defended, it is conceived nonnaturally. According to critics, this interpretation of evolutionary explanation implies a narrow conception of evolution and discontinuity between physiological evolution and the human mind: mechanisms of biological and social adaptation are falsely mutually isolated (FitzPatrick 2017, 6–7; 2018, 551). The idea of human nature is pessimistic and of human agency dualistic: if there is morality for naturally selfish humans, it is "presented as a thin crust underneath of which boil antisocial, amoral, and egoistic passions." Culturally evolved moral agency is needed to make humans capable of getting beyond natural selfishness (de Waal 2006, 6–12).

According to the Darwinian optimistic view of human nature, since human beings are first and foremost social animals, their moral capacity has evolved to guide them in social conflicts. But while some Darwinians argue that actions in accordance with evolved moral emotions as such could be called moral (Westermark 1917, 738–39; Barkow, Cosmides, and Tooby 1992; Cosmides and Tooby 2013), some others think that they convey objective moral imperatives by functioning like moral intuitions in Kantian ethics (Haidt 2001; Wright 1994; de Waal 2006). But again, some others conceptually separate moral conduct and natural good, and only stress the earthly nature of ethics through the human perspective: since humans are mutually dependent, evolved predispositions and the moral system protect our species-specific natural goods (Foot 2001; Kitcher 2011, 2013). "Biology holds us 'on a leash' and will let us stray only so far from who we are. We can design our life any way we want, but whether we will thrive depends on how well the life fits human predispositions" (De Waal 2005, 54). Different adaptational explanations lead to different metaethical positions among the Darwinians, and both naturalism and nonnaturalism about moral facts can be defended. Most usually morality is related to natural fellow feelings: emotionally grounded action can be, due to our psychological structures, genuinely altruistic.

Answers to the question "Why should I be moral?" are thus connected with the question of whether the idea of *moral agency* is separated from the idea of *human nature*. Moral naturalism drawing from an evolutionary approach calls for not separating moral reasoning from the normative forces that motivate action. This means that if humans are individual egoists by nature, morality can internally motivate action only when it underpins one's rational interests. Usually, people are considered selfish, but not necessarily: natural rational interests rely on one's self-understanding and identity *as an agent*. There can also be external reasons for altruism, but they are less confident, as they are generated by fear of external punishment. Many philosophers argue that natural egoist reasons are not the reasons of a moral agent however rational they would be: autonomous moral agency requires acting for reasons of its own type (Nielsen 1972, 541–43). Moral reason entailing a moral act should then be nonnatural.

However, social, and relational self-understandings of the agent challenge the egoism of moral naturalism from another angle. Understanding humans as altruists by their social nature, inclined to seek for a nonindividual common good, makes the motivation more confident, but the metaethical questions remain: are reasons to act morally (altruistically) then *moral reasons*? Is altruism *morally motivated* if agents are naturally social and their innate instincts make them inclined to be altruistic? According to the common answer, natural sociality may *explain* morality as a phenomenon but cannot *justify* norms. The usual conclusion is that contingent nature is irrelevant for norms, which can only be followed by choice of will, which is necessary for moral motivation: the source of normativity cannot be equated with the source of natural inclinations.

However, a wide range of recent philosophical discussions calls into question the idea of a strictly separated will indicating moral autonomy, an idea that presumes a modernist, individualist, and dualistically split view of the agent, to which there are plausible alternatives. Debate over the primary role of motivation and reason maintains the split of the capacities of agency into natural and non-natural—into the mutually isolated willing agency and reasoning agency. Can will, in fact, be free from reasoning? Or should the possible freedom of intention be seen in the complex process in which reasoning and will are both involved? The evolutionary approach to social codes, supported by empirical social sciences, denies a strict separation between reason and will. For instance, sociologist Émile Durkheim criticizes Kant for separating the logical structure and the normative force of ethics, which makes normative force extrinsic to the very idea of morality. For this reason, according to Durkheim, Kant's philosophical anthropology is an anthropology of a "double man" (Bernstein 1995, 94–95). Whatever we think about Durkheim's argument, it is worth acknowledging that the separation of logical structure and normative force may cause an anthropological side effect where cognitive moral processes, such as reasoning, are separated from the emotional processes carrying motivational power.

Reduction of moral capacities to innate social instincts should not be equated with the reductive notion of moral reasons for action. Even though evolutionary explanations are often taken to support ethical reductionism, it does not have to be the case. According to non-reductionist naturalist explanations of morality, the simple survival mechanisms of natural selection are not enough for moral reasons or even a full explanation: morality refers to fundamental sacrifice, giving without hope of reward (see Midgley 1979; Waller 2003, 541). Darwinism thus does not deny an obligation to try to be autonomous and altruistic. But morality as a phenomenon cannot be reduced to genetic selection. According to Mary Midgley, even freedom can be defended without denying that all major human motives are innate in the sense that they are not separable from natural reasons (Midgley 1984, 74). Midgley aspires for a scientifically sound Darwinian type of evolutionary approach to ethics and argues that Darwin was in fact not a reductionist, and therefore, an evolutionary approach to ethics should reject the strict Humean dichotomy between prescriptive and descriptive. Midgley attacks the idea of "an antiskeptically isolated human essence, a purely spiritual or intellectual pilot arbitrarily set in a physical vehicle which plays no part in his or her motivation," but she also claims that "we surely must reject the crude, mechanistic, reductive accounts of motive . . . and the fatalism that goes with them" (Midgley 1994, 145, 159).

According to Michael Ruse, although autonomy and altruism are important for morality, the causes of human behavior in fact always remain determined: a degree of autonomy exists as a self-corrective mechanism in the second-order level of altruism, but such an altruism can be seen as an evolutionary demand (Ruse 1998, 214, 258; Ruse 2001, 212–13). The interesting feature in Ruse's view is—despite its metaethical reductionism—that it emphasizes that moral agency plays a role in evolution. Human cultural practices and actual moral conducts are not meaningless for the course of biological evolution: medical science, for instance, has altered natural selection (Ruse 1985, 210). The capacity of being a moral agent combines natural causalities, moral inclinations and, through imagination, orientations based on the hope of something not yet realized. Together they influence the future adaptations of moral agents, and thus determine the innate motives of future humans. This refers to moral agency as an evolving issue that can be actively enhanced or degenerated.

Naturalist explanations of morality are alternatives on offer for environmental ethicists to prevent an exceptional human agency that presumes nonnatural autonomy governed by absolute freedom, but reductionist explanations are rarely defended in environmental ethics. Instead, they often seek a more relational approach to explain moral behavior. There are then at least two options to soften explanations of the moral autonomy of actions: by considering actions as relatively free, due to the complexity of operations by which they are generated (see Midgley 1984), or by considering responsibility as not requiring absolute freedom (see Waller 2003). It seems to bother many environmentalists that the juxtaposition between evolutive nature and free action underestimates the complexity of human mental operations and the interactive nature of the agency. A notable number of philosophers criticize the absoluteness of the gap between freedom and nature, and the derived operations of will and reasoning, which has dominated moral philosophy, largely due to Kant's influence, and has been defended by both empiricist and rationalist humanists—and even by evolutionary ethicists. Their criticism gets support from empirical science: the presuppositions unquestioned in the Enlightenment tradition concerning the operations of human agency are widely implausible from the empirical point of view. This is, I argue, an important reason for environmental ethicists to raise a critical question about the self-understanding of ethics. From the environmental point of view, it is especially problematic if philosophical argumentation maintains factual presuppositions that are suspicious in light of the empirical sciences. Environmental ethics cannot sustain science skepticism without being self-contradictory.

The evolutionary origins of traits and dispositions associated with altruism and cooperation can be investigated as empirical phenomena, and they can also explain much of moral capacities. The problem, however, arises when moving from explaining phenomena to explaining the exercise of moral capacities: it requires clarifying the relationship between causal adaptations and reason-giving explanations. Complications in moving from one type of explanation to another elucidate the problems included in attempts of evolutionary debunking arguments to reduce ethics to evolutionary biology or psychology (FitzPatrick 2017, 2–8). Some questions are worth asking in order to clarify the conceptual map when talking about evolutionary explanations of the mechanisms of moral reasoning. One set of questions concern the explanation of moral reason: Does evolutionary theorizing explain a) moral reasoning, b) reasons for acting morally, or c) moral reasons? Another set of questions concerns the conceptual reducibility of morality: does a positive answer to the explanatory questions imply a) that the moral reasons are reducible to the explanations, which would mean that ethics is not autonomous, b) that the truth-aptness of moral concepts is reducible to the explanatory facts, which would rule out the authority of ethics, or c) that the normativity of moral reasons is reducible to the explanatory, say, psychological facts, which would rule out the idea of normativity. The philosophical implications vary in accordance with the answers. For example, arguments that derive the truth value of moral concepts from natural facts represent naturalism, but arguments for reducing the normative authority of moral reasons to evolutionary factual explanations "debunk" ethics. Debunking arguments renounce the autonomy of ethics: it is reduced to empirical science.

Quite a few evolutionary psychologists argue that not only moral senses, but also moral conduct and manifestations of current morality, are adaptively explainable. Some even claim that the reliability of moral codes can be justified on evolutionary grounds. Elliot Sober and David Sloan Wilson argue that evolution provided altruism, which is thus coded in the agent's psychological capacities besides egoist and hedonist motivations (Sober and Wilson 1998, 324–27). Metaethically, evolutionary psychology is usually used in arguments against moral realism. The justificatory status of moral beliefs is argued to become undermined by an appeal to the empiric explanations. Although evolutionary explanations are usually conceived to undermine moral realism—at least in its robust sense—use of the evolutionary genealogy of moral dispositions and reasoning does not imply debunking arguments nor even modest forms of moral realism. One of the decisive questions for whether naturalist explanations undermine types of moral realism concerns the nature of moral agency and its role in the theory of ethics. The prevailing notions of autonomy and freedom should be open to scientific and philosophical criticism. Evolutionary genealogy may in fact offer valuable tools to revise modernist presuppositions about the moral agent and processes of moral reasoning common to modern ethics, and to reconsider the idea and role of the material environment in moral realism. Linking moral reasons or the truth value of moral concepts to the nature of the moral agent is nothing new. Together with other versions of naturalism, such as Aristotelian or neo-Aristotelian agent-based virtue ethics, evolutionary approaches to realist ethics face the question: What makes natural reasons normative for the agent? While traditional Aristotelian naturalism dissolves the problem by essential humanness, evolutionary naturalism, as well as neo-Aristotelianism, allows for contingences of nature as constitutive for the actualized types of humanness and the reliable manifestations of virtue (e.g. Cela-Conde and Ayala 2007, 353).

In this chapter, a distinguishing feature among evolutionary ethicists appeared to be their attitude to the genuine naturalness of morality. Positions differed regarding the Darwinian idea of a continuum between animal and human agencies. According to the Darwinian view, although the processes for moral reasoning are complex, they do not require nonnatural agency, while authors following Huxley's view argue that moral ability, if it exists, is a nonnatural addition by culture. Naturalist Darwinians also seem more inclined to scrutinize the nature of the processes that decisively constitute moral reasoning and actions, and to defend non-reductionist naturalist explanations of freedom and autonomy. The view of isolated moral agency that has been eagerly defended in modern ethics seems both unnecessary and implausible, but this does not necessarily imply the reduction of agency into causal determinism. Instead, the processes of nature themselves are far more complex than generally thought in modern philosophy. I argue that this fact has not been recognized in ethics as widely as it should be.

NOTES

1. Ecosystem ecology has deeply influenced environmental ethics and thoughts about its philosophical implications, though in various ways. Sometimes environmental philosophers also refer to a romanticized notion of a natural community as a self-regulating superorganism, though such a view is only loosely based on ecosystem ecology.

2. For example, in *The Universe Story* (1992) Brian Swimme and Thomas Berry displace the grand narratives of religions with the epic of evolution and its universal "sacralized science" that has also a mythical or spiritual role. According to critics such as Lisa Sideris, Richard Dawkins (2011) also implicitly makes such a move. See Sideris 2017, 31–35. For criticism of the overemphasized role of science in environmental philosophy, see also Midgley 1985, 2000, 2004.

3. For the criticism against both "full paper" and "blank paper" theories of human nature, see Midgley 1978.

4. According to Spencer, progress was a move from the undifferentiated to the differentiated: as complexity increases individuals become more developed in the prescriptive sense. Spencer held progress of moral culture as inevitable, although culture is not a function of natural selection but a sphere of human spiritual and psychological activity. Spencer 1851, 323–24. See also Ruse 2004, 29–30.

5. Huxley's view represents a kind of "religious humanism" or "religion without revelation" which he hoped could overcome the dichotomy between human intentional purposes and the natural causalities. For a closer analysis about Huxley's view, see Farber 1994, 127–31, 148–49, and for its current modes in religious environmentalism, see Sideris 2017, 157–60.

6. While Ruse asserts that ethics is what it is for biological reasons, Midgley thinks that biological and cultural elements are interwoven in natural processes, both concerning moral capacity and norms.

7. Ruse argues that Wilson tries here to reformulate his deep religious faith into the scientific model.

8. For Dawkins, the cultural, exceptional content of replication are "memes," which are replicated by the mechanism of "imitation."

9. Philosophers avoided this view for a long time because it was politically used to justify racism and eugenics. which in the current discussion is usually considered as a misinterpretation. See Richard Weikart, *From Darwin to Hitler: Evolutionary Ethics, Eugenics, and Racism in Germany* (New York: Macmillan 2004).

Chapter 3

Moral Agency in Feminist Environmental Ethics

A Constrained Constructivist Approach

ECOFEMINISM AS ENVIRONMENTAL
PHILOSOPHY AND FEMINIST ETHICS

Perhaps the most prominent critics of adopting the Enlightenment-based framework for environmental ethics are ecofeminists. Feminist constructivism also offers a clear alternative to approach human moral agency. Philosophically speaking, evolutionary naturalism and feminist constructivism are contradictory positions regarding the concept of human nature as well as ethics. Naturalist approaches seek objective nature-based truths about being human, whereas feminist philosophy denies absolute meanings and universally shared concepts. In ethics, to put it roughly, naturalist understanding of human nature usually implies an understanding of moral conducts either as conventions based on (empirically verified) natural psychological needs and structures of human agents (the Humean approach) or on some essentialist theory of human nature (the Aristotelian approach). In contrast to this, socially constructed human nature implies a rejection of any universally shared foundation for normative conducts, and instead rests either on cultural practices of care and love, or on the methods of discourse and political life (e.g., approaches by Rawls, Jürgen, and Habermas). In a way, ecofeminism locates itself in between the two philosophical opposites from the beginning. Although ecofeminism is a part of feminist philosophy, ecofeminist conceptions of human agency refer to a conceptually more modest constructionism that I call *constrained constructivism,* in accordance with Katherine Hayles (Hayles 1991, 76–85). Constrained constructivism implies that the concepts of nature, human nature, and moral agency, as well as the nature of moral reasons, should be approached humbly, expecting neither true representations nor pure narratives.

Ecofeminism stands at the crossroads of feminist philosophy and environmental ethics. As a type of environmental ethics ecofeminism is typically classified as a variant of radical ecophilosophy because it questions the modernist conceptual role of the relationships between human and nonhuman entities. According to ecofeminism, falsehood is implicitly interwoven into the concepts of modern ethical framework, which is incapable of holding nonhuman objects as morally demanding and providing sound arguments for sustainable relationships. Ecofeminism[1] differs from nonfeminist contextual environmental ethics most pointedly through the idea of twin domination that makes a conceptual connection between the subordination of nature and the subordination of women. Carolyn Merchant's twin domination argument in *The Death of Nature* (1980) stresses that the metaphors that connect women to nature are parallel to those by which nature is subordinated in culture (Merchant 1993, 2–4, 270–73).[2] The interpretations of the interconnection between women and nature, as well as ways to overcome the twin oppressions, are, however, various. Supremacy over nature and inequality between sexes, races, and social classes is widely seen to have common roots in dominant Western structures of thought that follow "the logic of domination." This generates subordination by means of conceptual dualisms, for instance, between reason and emotion, culture and nature, and mind and body (Warren 2000, 47–56; Plumwood 1993, 55–59; Mellor 1997, 115; Hekman 1999, 110–13).

As feminists and environmental ethicists are allies in their struggle against this logic of domination, ecofeminist projects use feminist methodologies and widely engage in the discussions of non-environmental feminists. However, the social constructionist idea of the human self as a moral agent is among the debated topics because of the different roles ecofeminists and other feminists give to both the body and nonhuman, material, and ecological others in the construction of moral identities. The basis for feminist critique of the mainstream concept of the self is in descriptions of woman as the Other, nonsubject, nonperson, non-agent, or body (Beauvoir 2011), which indicates not only subordination of women's selfhood, but also nonhuman entities and people of various minorities. In contrast to the modern understanding of the moral self as a free, autonomous, and rational person isolated from particularities, relationships, and a wider social arena, feminists promote a wider perspective of moral selves and their agency. Moral selves are embodied and embedded, not totally free, nor autonomous: freedom is better to be defined as an aim rather than a prerequisite (Meyers 2000, 12, 16).

One of the main ideas of mainstream feminist ethics is that by giving voice to the experiences of women and other oppressed groups as moral selves and agents they will be *emancipated*. Ecofeminism builds upon feminist philosophies. But, in contrast to one of the standard strategies for overcoming dominant patriarchal culture that *liberates* women from being linked with nature—which has been the standard interpretation of emancipation—ecofeminists argue that the solution is not, conceptually thinking, to spread the power of the oppressing ones to the oppressed ones. It would only shift the problem but maintain the conceptual dualism. Instead, ecofeminism admits and foregrounds the material, bodily, and social constraints of *all* agents; no one is liberated from natural determinants. Ecofeminism propounds an anthropology that recognizes the necessities of cooperation, interconnectedness, and mutual love and care as essential for maintaining life in both nature and human communities (see Mies and Shiva 1993, 5–19). Subjects are vulnerable and profoundly mutually interdependent, and their subjectivity can flourish only if these dependences are acknowledged. Western cultures that internalize dualisms create harmful isolation from material surroundings and nonhuman others. Patriarchal structures cannot thus be removed by "liberating" women from their metaphorical or concrete likeness with nature and by giving them domination over nature. Instead, the relational interconnectedness with, and recognition and appreciation of, otherness—whether it is experienced as other human beings, nonhuman living beings, the body, or the physical world—ought to be strengthened. Oppressed ones should not be drawn further from nature, but rather, those in power should be drawn closer to it. Ecofeminist reconceptualization thus does not focus on the subjectivity of those considered as "others," but rather on those considered as the noble "ones," unquestioned subjects, rational, free, and impartial moral agents (see e.g., Cuomo 1998, 97–98). Ecofeminism is an agential approach to environmental ethics that refuses to merely focus on the objects of patriarchal discourse. New insights for reconsidering *genuine* moral agency emerge from the perspectives of the disvalued.

Besides its explanatory task, ecofeminist philosophy has had, from the beginning, a cultural and political agenda that aims to disrupt oppressive and alienating moral culture by criticizing its foundationally exclusive structure. Ecofeminists describe the traditional approach to ethics as "the arrogant perception," in contrast to "the loving perception." The structural failure of the arrogant perception is that it "presupposes and maintains *sameness* in such a way that it expands the moral community only to those beings who are thought to resemble (be like, similar to, or the same as) 'us' in some morally significant way." Therefore, it "builds a moral hierarchy of beings and assumes some common denomination of moral considerability by virtue of which like beings deserve similar treatment or moral consideration and unlike beings do not" (Frye 1983, 75–76; see also Warren 2000, 104–5). A basic problem lies in exclusiveness: qualifications for morally significant others are based on some similarity that is needed in order to mark out the individuals that belong to the moral others. The emphasis on moral standing focuses on the demarcation of insiders from outsiders, members of a "club" from nonmembers. Human agents with the ability to make such definitions have power over the status of others, which makes the whole question of morally considerable others "imperialistic" and ethically problematic. This widely shared criticism positions ecofeminism against the extensional strategies.

The oppression of women and exploitative subordination of nonhuman nature abide by the same damaging logic in which the relationship between the "agent" and the "other" is that of the conqueror and the conquered. The dominators not only have power, but they also believe that their power is justified. Practicing this logic implies its own justification and, therefore, alternative logics cannot emerge within such practices. The way out of the logic of domination requires reconceptualization of the powerful self, the agent, as well as the sources of his "justified" power. Without dismantling the patriarchal view of the human agent, it is impossible to formulate sustainable relationships between human and nonhuman nature (Cuomo 1998, 61). In this sense, the political and the philosophical projects cannot be separated (Mies and Shiva 1993; Warren 2000, 207, 211).

Despite the shared aims of ecological and feminist ethics in their parallel cultural criticisms against the logic of domination, the most rigid criticism against ecofeminism comes from those feminist philosophers who argue that the emphasis on the material and biological features and interrelatedness of the self problematically refers to either essentialism or biological determinism (e.g. Davion 1994). A typical anti-essentialist argument insists that admitting the conceptual link between women and nature implies essential female nature, and hence, replicates the damaging logic (Cuomo 1998, 112, 114, 117). Ecofeminists mainly deny this criticism, although the question is also divisive. The question concerns whether women's experiences are worth privileging in epistemic or moral knowledge construction for sustainable ecological culture and politics: positions close to conceptual naturalism stress the privileged position of the experiences of the oppressed in the discourse (e. g. Salleh 1997, 39, 323), whereas a more humanist approach highlights that women and nature just form a conceptual community of fate under oppressive structures. Both highlight that exclusion of material or biological issues originates in the oppressive logic against which feminism has always fought. Conversely, any environmental ethics that does not take the twin domination seriously cannot prosper (Warren 2000, 62; Warren 1996, 19). However, most ecofeminists consider identification between women and nature as a constructed idea expressing dualism and, hence, useless in ethics (Plumwood 1994, 33).

A question for ecofeminism thus is, politically speaking, whether either the damaging identification between women and nature, or the converse idea of women's deeper ecological wisdom can be used positively in order to overcome oppressive structures, or whether the strategy should be to liberate women and nature by rejecting the image of that linkage as a sexist biological reduction.[3] A problem is that both strategies implicitly presuppose culture-nature dualism. Therefore, philosophically oriented ecofeminists have not been interested in debating whether women are "closer to nature" than men, but rather in uncovering the conceptual framework that makes this question relevant and in constructing a new methodology and ethical framework that reaches beyond humanism. The framework in which features representing the natural are excluded from or devalued in whoever's politically or morally recognized agency, and in which ideal human agency is isolated from and opposed to the biological and material (human) nature should be replaced by a view that appreciates the material and collaborative nature of agency (see e.g., Warren 2000). Donna Haraway calls such agency a sympoietic becoming within the compost society of companion species (Haraway 2016). Humans are as embodied as other animals, and their bodies are as biological, sexual, and ecologically contextual as others—perhaps in addition to being something else, too (Mellor 1997, 178).

At least three strategies are used by feminist environmentalists to overcome the oppressive conceptual frameworks. The first strategy embraces biological, bodily, and ecological conditions as essential factors for the epistemic and moral agent. Advocates of this strategy are most opposed to extreme deconstructivism of some traditional forms of social feminism. According to these ecofeminists, sustainable gender equality cannot be achieved by focusing on elevating the oppressed or boosting their status by focusing on their equal powers. On the contrary, the focus should be in conceptual "diminishing" of the idealized, abstract idea of moral agency or free self, which has been elevated above the determinants of nature and other people as a property of the selected ones. This strategy often calls for giving epistemic priority to the experiences of those who are "closer to nature" in the construction of sustainable moral principles; for this reason, it is often criticized for adopting some type of essentialism. The second strategy goes together with postmodern anti-essentialist critiques against the oppressive framework, although most ecofeminists criticize postmodern feminism for its simplistic interpretation of the criticized view. According to ecofeminist advocates of this strategy, privilege for women or indigenous people is not justified without metaphysical assumptions about nature and the human self. An ecofeminist project is thus discursive and political by nature (see Cuomo 1998, 112–40).

The third strategy does not hold material determinants and socially constructed concepts as opposites but as partners in the construction of the self

(Cuomo 1998, 124–25; Mellor 1997, 178). Advocates of this strategy can be called conceptual ecofeminists, and sometimes their view is called "strategic essentialism." Karen Warren, Val Plumwood and Chris Cuomo, for example, highlight that since the link between the domination of nature and the subordination of women is a conceptual one, so must the solution be. They argue, first and foremost, for an ecological conception of humanity. Instead of claiming similarity as a precondition for equality, they stress the role of diversity for both beings and values (Plumwood 1994, 147,153; Cuomo 1998, 132, 134). Recognition of the real diversity of qualities and things is important for an accurate construction of the self, which is always constructed in a web of these things and qualities. Each individual agent exists as a part of her web, comes into existence by it, and constitutively influences it. Disvaluing the other determinants participating in the web (whether they represent her body, habitat, culture, or her social or ecological surrounding) might imply degeneration.

Regarding the dominant conception of a moral agent, ecofeminist criticisms offer three particularly interesting and promising points of focus. They concern (1) the diversity of moral identities, (2) refusal of the internal split of human agency, which excludes ecological relationships from the constitutive ingredients of the construction of the moral self, and (3) the view of the moral self as a self-in-relationship. In what follows, I shall explore the ecofeminist approach to moral agency more closely from these three perspectives.

DIVERSITY, MATERIALITY, AND RELATIONALITY

According to a classical formulation of social constructionism (expressed by Glifford Geertz, Thomas Kuhn, and Peter Berger and Thomas Luckmann), which is an important framework for feminist ethics, culturally formed interactions between individuals and their social environments are constitutive of what it is to be human. This formulation denies any view of essential human nature. According to Berger and Luckmann, "in the dialectic between nature and the socially constructed world the human organism itself is transformed. In this same dialectic man produces reality and therefore produces himself" (Berger and Luckmann 1966, 183). Another formulation by Clifford Geertz insists that a human entity requires cultural impact to become fully human: being human is constituted by the culturally formed interactions between individuals and their social environments. Environments, cultures, symbols, and symbolic structures particular to each time and place shape the idea of humanness. Diversity is impossible to destroy, because humanity as a concept refers to diverse expressions of being human rather than to any universally shared idea (Geertz 1973, 35, 53; Peterson 2001, 53). Each approach to humanness is shaped by a particular culture, by symbols, and by historically situated semantic structures. All constructed concepts, such as "man," "woman," or "Arab," for instance, may thus carry power-related meanings. Conceptual differences depicting humanity generate oppression in social life if, but only if, we believe that some pure, true human nature exists. Compared to any idea of an ideal human (whether it is understood as essential or constructed), some manifestations of humanity can be claimed to be better than some others (Peterson 2001, 54; Hekmann 1999, 85; Cuomo 1998, 114; Mellor 1997, 161, 178).

Appreciation of genuine diversity stands at the core of various types of feminist ethics. Humanity only exists in modes of being human in the contingent world. Being human is thus constructed via interactions with different others; it is in essence being and acting in relation to different others and can never be found in isolation (Warren 1990, 143). From an ecofeminist point of view, moral agency emerges from ecologically structured processes of interaction with material, biological, and social others; in relation to nature a human being is in relation to the constitutive elements of her own being. The idea of humanity, or a moral agent, need not, however, be rejected. Yet a possible consensus about the idea cannot be based on imposed similarities between all people. Humanity as a concept consists of diverse ways of being human and is constructed in relationships that should be respected as influential origins for emerging ways of being human. Ignoring fundamental diversity among beings of equal value would bring about polarization, value-dualism, and oppression. If socially formulated conceptions are held to be universal, they entail the "logic of domination": marginal perspectives on human life become oppressed by structures of domination (Warren 2000, 105; Plumwood 1993, 55–59; Mellor 1997, 115; Hekman 1999, 110–13). From the political perspective, the fact of the constructed diversity of agents implies that if there are normative notions about the way that human nature, or the nature of the morally considerable other in general, should be performed, these norms only express particular power structures. Feminist ethics highlights emancipation of the marginalized experiences of being human as the way to improve the moral culture. Since all expressions of humanity are culturally constructed, no one should be elevated over some other: everyone should take up their right to be an equal expression of humanity (Peterson 2001, 52–53).

Constructivism is a heavily humanist approach, while ecofeminism strongly opposes the humanist presuppositions of modernist ethics. This tension makes ecofeminism especially interesting from the viewpoint of the possible futures of humanist ethics. Whether ecofeminism overcomes its humanist backgrounds or offers new insight for the post-Enlightenment humanist ethics by revising the included concept of human and hence reforming its conceptual framework divides its current advocates. It seems that there are two stark options for traditional humanist ethics to contribute to the discussions on the most urgent challenges of the current world, according to ecofeminist philosophy: either to conceptually regenerate itself, or to step aside. As the main target of ecofeminist criticism is anthropological presup-positions—which are guilty of many problems in humanist ethics—it has potential to fruitfully advance modern discourse even without abandoning all its basics. Ecofeminist philosophy has also inspired other philosophers to revise the traditional presuppositions of modern ethics. The key issues of ecofeminist approaches to moral agent include diversity, nondivided human agency, and relationality.

First, in a moral relationship, authentic diversity holds for both moral agents and moral objects, and claims for "similarity" seem inconsistent. The idea of fundamental diversity among moral agents taken seriously challenges the traditional idea of a moral community: a moral community cannot be conceived as a group of beings capable of reciprocity on the ground of shared identities. But withdrawing similarity from the conditions of moral relation-ship means that moral judgments cannot be grounded on shared convictions, a common idea of good life, or a shared idea of truth (see e.g., Hekman 1999; Barad 2007). This brings about another metaethical threat for non-extensional environmental ethics besides the reductionism involved in the strong forms of evolutionary naturalism.

The threat of relativism especially worries environmentally oriented femi-nist ethicists. Since contextual social relations are not seen as external but as constitutive to a moral agent, personal viewpoints cannot be externalized in the construction of moral principles. From the viewpoint of environmental ethics, this sounds problematic because the material limits of the Earth—especially benign conditions for human species—are not just socially con-structed, but rather a tragic physical reality to which our moral rationality is bound more than we would wish. Despite this dissonance, feminist environ-mentalists do not, with some exceptions, defend a monistic idea of human good. On the contrary, they have broadened the sphere of beings with which we shape a community of meaningful relationships: it should be seen to include nonhuman members. Diversity refers not only to that among human individuals, but also to various types of entities, in dialogue with which moral selves are constructed. Hence, the moral community should be seen as a multispecies community (e.g., Haraway 2007, 2016). The picture of the Anthropocene, the world in which we face the influence of our own actions, seems to challenge the standard feminist view of constructionism as restricted to social contexts. It calls for acknowledging that social construction never occurs in isolation, but rather, social, cultural, ecological, and physiological interactivities are interwoven, and all involved in the processes of conceptual construction, too. Recognition of diversity requires recognition for the multifaceted and multispecies context of social and cultural processes. This is what ecofeminists have emphasized, and currently philosophers are widely taking seriously the intimate relationships between material elements and the identity of the agent. Diverse relationships can be seen as mutually influential and even constitutive for the very idea of agency.

The second point of focus in the ecofeminist conception of a moral agent is the emphasis on the role of the material aspects of humanity in moral agency. Whereas environmental ethics usually locates the criticized dualism between human/cultural/social reality on the one hand, and natural/material/ecological reality on the other, ecofeminism often locates the most problematic dualism inside a human being, that is, within the moral agent (Plumwood 1994, 146–47). I see this as helpful for ethics. The problem lies in the conceptual separation between the "natural" and "moral," that is, the material or determined side, and the free one in human agency. As Mary Mellor argues, humanity escapes its own material conditions and oppresses its own materiality if the interconnections between the biological and social are ignored. According to Mellor, in order for moral theories to be adapted for the use of environmental ethics, they must renew their understanding about the relationships between the genuine aspects of humanity and the material world, in addition to unsustainable social relations. Problems caused by dualisms can only be overcome by opening eyes to the role of the material relationships for human moral agency (Mellor 1997, 180, 182–83; 2000, 108, 114; see also Alaimo and Hekman 2008).

Analysis of the ecofeminist criticism against the modern frameworks of ethics shows that the most problematic conceptual dualism concerns the inner nature of the human agent. Therefore Mellor, for instance, calls for rediscovering the fundamental immanence of humanity, and acknowledging that the supposed transcendence of the human agency in modern thought is just a social construction itself, contrary to the natural world, which is "not dead or dumb or a product of human mind" (Mellor 2000, 115). Ecofeminists who employ various strategies all fight to overcome the internally split concept of human agency by valuing the material, bodily, and biological features disvalued in the dominant masculine culture. Because the characteristics connected to men have been considered to represent noble humanity, and as superior to those connected to women or nature, culturally formed identities and the ideals of human agency have systematically encouraged the domination of both women and nature (Plumwood 1994, 144). From the point of view of ethics, it seems more important, therefore, to question conceptions concerning the dominant (conceptualized as "male," "human," "moral self," or "the agent") rather than the oppressed ("female," "natural," "moral object," "the other"), or even the dualism between the two. A sustainable relationship with the rest of nature requires critical rethinking of the cultural identities of human agents with the help of women's perspectives.

Ecofeminists criticize standard (non-environmental) feminist ethics for adopting a type of social constructionism that commits them to world alienation. Ecofeminist or material feminist philosophers thus defend types of earthly feminism (see Midgley 1994; Mellor 2000; Mann 2005; Grosz 2008; Hekman 2008). According to Mary Midgley, the problem of constructionism lies in the supposition that what is essential for humanness is reduced to social and conceptual influence, and therefore, there is nothing conceptually important "out there," just an empty landscape out of which human identity is constructed by conceptualization. She calls this a "blank paper" theory of human nature and argues that neither that nor the "full paper" theory referring to biological or genetic reduction are true or acceptable (Midgley 1978, 18). "Blank paper" theory reduces constitutive agency to the human mind, excluding material determinants. In fact, then, constructionist aspiration for anti-essentialism may be as reductive as essentialism itself. Reduction into conceptualization separates humans and other animals in a way that makes this kind of constructionism exceptionalist; this is the view that critical environmental ethics wanted to attack, in the first place, by adopting feminist constructionism (Midgley 2004, 137, 141). Presuming that humans only "possess an essential quality, the capacity to construct meaning, which all other species lack" also gives humans a privileged position (Peterson 2001, 73).

The idea of emancipation defined through "free" discourse, in contrast to the "necessities" of the determination of the material and social world, resembles the Kantian sublime transcendence, and hence, maintains the domination of nature, according to materially oriented ecofeminism. But while postmodern constructionism may undermine human relationships with the world as real, it can still help us in reaching a new understanding of that relationship: nature that is not conceived of as external and fixed would not just exemplify environmental or material "necessities" rather than productivity. In the postmodern register, the agent itself is produced by the "chains of signification" in discourse. Sublime transcendence can be seen in that "the discourse subjects the subject in the double sense; it both oppresses and makes. Somehow, almost magically, the productive function of discourse disappears the realm of 'necessity' in the old sense and sets the subject 'free' in the process" (Mann 2005, 57). This kind of postmodern view adopts, however, the Kantian Euro-masculine idea about what we must be free from: freedom is domination over the necessities. The postmodern tendency to overcome necessities then simply continues the failures that justified male/human supremacy by referring to freedom (connected to human culture) and oppressed women as representatives of the realm of necessity (connected to nature). The problem lies in understanding emancipation as freedom from material relationships, which are seen as "necessities." The postmodern notion of emancipation is thus like the early modern humanist fantasy to overcome the limits of human agency. Bonnie Mann argues that more than protesting against the association of women with the realm of (either biological or social) necessities, feminism should protest against the "dissociation of human beings in general from this realm": freedom from the Earth is "suicidal" (Mann 2005, 52–54, 58, 60). I agree and add that conceiving the material world as the realm of necessities is also a fantasy that needs correction.

The third focus of ecofeminism concerning the idea of agency is relationality. Feminist care ethicist Eva Kittay argues that recognition of dependence and relationality as universal human conditions can form a basis for the ethics of care. Experience of dependence is the place from which we can know what is essential for justice and good social policy (Kittay 1999, 49–50, 75, 79–82). Relationships with nature, too, only can be known and articulated from the "place" of our dependence on the Earth. This way of thinking represents a relational account of the moral subject, and ecofeminists also use the logic of care ethics but add the importance of including material dependencies in the picture. Earthly dependencies form a productive place that enables and empowers moral deliberation and action: "The earth is not our prison, but a productive place we inhabit, that constitutes and enlivens us moment by moment" (Mann 2005, 59–60; see also Peterson 2006). This refers to the discursive interaction to which material partners and nonhuman others are joined already prior to the social discourse. Mellor places the inter-relationships, discourse, and narrative into the historical processes that tie us to nature. Human activity is neither natural nor unnatural in the sense that we could claim that nature would be better or worse off without humanity. The relationship between human agents and their nonhuman partners is essentially a moral question about the quality of continuous mutual interaction (Mellor 1997, 13, 188).

Ecofeminism argues for conceptually non-divided and dynamically relational agency. Conceptual rethinking should lead to repositing and revaluing the excluded and despised features of existence and agency. Dependencies and features that represent the conquered or oppressed (dependency, contextuality, or emotionality) in the modern view should be appreciated as authentic and ideal features of humanity and definitive features of a moral agent—instead of or at least besides rationality, individuality, and self-constitution. When the features of the conquered, devalued, and strange are recognized as constitutive of the moral agent, they bridge between moral agents and those agents conquer. Such a bridge restores the continuity between humans, animals, and the material world without assimilation or losing the value of "difference" (Plumwood 1994, 154).

Relational features, such as gender, place, race, religion, social class, friends, and opportunities are features that shape our way of being a self, as well as our modes of knowing and capacities to act. Ecofeminists usually also describe being human as a *moral* self in terms of dynamic relationality: A moral self is fundamentally a self-in-relationship. That means that even autonomy is thought to require relationality, as many feminist ethicists, such as Diana Meyers (1989), Catrione Mackenzie (2000), and Marilyn Friedman (2000) argue. For ecofeminists, however, relationality is central for human agency in sense of both embodiment referring to materiality, and embeddedness widely referring to the relationships in which this embodiment takes place. A human being retains the essential character of being a self-in-relationship also when acting as a moral agent. Ecological embeddedness includes an idea of relative activity among all different things in the world: hence, various material/biological as well as social/cultural dynamics are essential for what it is to practice human capacities, and the essential features of agency cannot be isolated from their contingent dependencies, nor unique in a sense that essentially differs from the agency of other animals in kind. In this sense, at least, ecofeminist and Darwinian views are allies: material and social conditions are constitutive for moral agency (Warren 2000, 90; see also Grosz 2008).

According to my interpretation, the ecofeminist project recognizes that it is more important to reconceptualize the idea of moral agency than the idea of the self. They seem convinced that considering the ecological conditions of human life to be quintessential for moral rationality, rather than external to it, represents a remarkable difference in the ability of moral theories to face environmental questions. The tendency of modern ethics to devalue necessities that influence moral deliberation overemphasizes the importance of impartiality. Despite the fact that total determinism would undermine agency, devaluation of dependencies may lead to denying or ignoring them, which also harms moral culture. Like care ethicists (Noddings 1984), ecofeminists argue that relational features that bind us bodily, emotionally, biologically, and socio-ecologically, should not be detached from moral deliberation, and a sound theory of ethics needs to take this into account. In environmental ethics this means that human attention to "nature" cannot be impartial in the modern sense. Val Plumwood and Lori Gruen, for instance, talk about "engaged empathy" when they talk about the commitment to those we are related to as important for both moral knowledge and motivation (Gruen 2009; Plumwood 1999; see also Little 2007b).

Appreciation of diversity, materiality, and relationality of agency influences values and ought to inform them: ideal humanity is not isolated from biological or ecological realities but intimately related to them. As Karen Warren argues, "relationships are not something extrinsic to who we are, not an 'add on' feature of human nature; they play an essential role in shaping what it is to be human." Relationships through which a human life comes into its existence and through which concepts are constructed, are constitutive rather than external by nature. Therefore, moral relationships are always relationships between materially and socially contextual and mutually interdependent parties. Being human essentially is being and acting in relation to different others: there is no "being human" in isolation—it is always being human "in the world" (Warren 1990, 143). Relationality also involves dynamicity and instability. Construction of one's moral identity is heavily embedded in the changing contexts and the relationships in which it takes place. Becoming an agent is a continuous process that requires commitment to the dialogues that influence one's knowledge, norms, and meanings. As an agent, a human being both constructs her very nature through conceptual, cultural, and social structures, and is constructed. As is clear, the perspective of an agent always remains particular. But the fact that universality is impossible does not mean that the relational perspectives are arbitrary—they are just relational. The contingent epithets of humanity or the historical, cultural, social, and material settings, or the narrative of the agent's own life make agency possible, though situated.

Jim Cheney, Donna Haraway, and Val Plumwood, for instance, defend an interactive argument about both knowledge and moral meanings. According to them, epistemic as well as moral knowledge is constructed, in Plumwood's words, "in conversation with nature" (Plumwood 2002; Cheney 1989, 126, 129; 2005, 110; Haraway 1988, 589–90; see also Preston 2000, 230). The role the agent's relationships and partiality play in ecofeminist ethics parallels the role they play in feminist epistemology, especially in feminist standpoint theory: interactivity in particular relationships is essential for knowledge construction, as well as for the construction of moral norms (Code 2006a; Harding 1998; Longino 2002; Plumwood 2002; Hekman 1999; Hartsock 1998; Haraway 1988).[4] Epistemic validity requires valid activity from the part of the epistemic agent: the criteria of knowledge are derived from the criteria of valid constructive activity. Therefore, epistemic virtues can be seen to rely on moral virtues. If knowledge construction is conceived of as a dialogical process, it requires offering space and respectful listening to a partner who is the object of knowledge. Valuing and disvaluing are central methods for offering and denying space. Following Cheney and Weston, epistemology is thus "ethics-based" (Cheney and Weston 1999).

Ecofeminists reject the modernist claim of the idea of shared absolute freedom as the core of moral agency, or as a mark of equal partners of moral community. Impartiality as an idea emerges from a narrow and implausible view of humanity that externalizes the necessary relationships of an agent from her genuine moral agency. Ecofeminists and often also other feminists argue that such an externalization works for the logic of domination. The core of a humanity connected to the noble feature of being a moral agent should better be seen as a unique type of relatedness, a capacity to be a human "in the world." A definition of human "uniqueness" in terms of relationality offers a theoretically fertile alternative to the individualist, stable idea of agency in ethics. At the same time, it brings animals and humans to share the same community as mutually dependent and respecting agents. The idea of stable and untouched agency is mistaken, harmful, and needless.

If the ecofeminist notion of relationality is correct, it seems impossible for any moral theory that does not take the relational nature of the agent into account to succeed in promoting the good life. According to Plumwood, denial of the importance of particularity and situatedness for moral life exemplifies itself in an attempt to control these human properties by glorifying superior, "interest-free" and "masculine" reason. Environmental ethics seeking to guide us to live in harmony with the environment within the framework that alienates us from our own ecological structures would be, however, incoherent (Plumwood 1994, 142–43).

RELATIONAL AUTONOMY IN FEMINIST ETHICS

The three aspects highlighted by ecofeminists as conditions of moral agency—diversity, inner nondualism, and relationality—pose challenges to the dominant understanding of the moral agent as an autonomous and rational agent. Hence, implications for the structure of moral theory are also to be expected. Constructionist anthropology implies that social particularities are constitutive for one's moral deliberation and acting. Both the identities of agents and the knowledge agents can achieve are bound to the relationships by which they are constructed. Relational features thus shape human ways of reasoning and being autonomous. Both practical deliberation and all modes of knowing possible for human agents are relational. This calls for reconceptualization of the dominant concept of autonomy.

A claim for conceptual revision of autonomy is not an easy one for ecofeminists, as it brings with it questions about the limits of responsibility and moral truth. The concept of autonomy is important for feminism, especially for discussions about giving voice to the subordinated, while at the same time, embodiment and embeddedness of each human agent are inalienable features of feminist ethics. Perhaps for this reason, feminist ethicists, especially feminist bioethicists and ecofeminists, have carefully scrutinized autonomy and developed notions of contextual and relational autonomy (see Mackenzie and Stoljar 2000). Positions are, however, various, and due to the tension between the feminist aspiration for emancipation and the environmentalist aspiration for recognition of the genuine agency of ecologically relational beings, positions that ecological feminists defend may somewhat contradict each other.

According to one line of thought about autonomy in mainstream feminist ethics, famously defended by Simone de Beauvoir (2011, ch. 14), autonomy is important for the full realization of one's agency. Autonomy is also possible but requires releasing people from oppressive relationships and empowering them through supportive relationships to use their own freedom. So, supportive relationships, solidarity, love, and care are necessary conditions for a person's ability to use her own voice and perform autonomy. The use of noble agency requires liberation, but actualization of autonomy requires conditions in which it is possible. Autonomy of relational beings thus sets moral obligations to recognize the selfhood and agency of the oppressed, and to free them to use their full autonomy. Autonomy is here defined in terms of freedom, and the claim for giving full moral agency to the oppressed arises from the assumption that moral agency is compromised by oppression. Many ecofeminists criticize Beauvoir's view about devaluing the agency of the "Other," which may be different from that of the "One." According to them, claiming transcendent freedom implies a supposition of freedom as emancipation from relationality and determinacy, which implies that oppression diminishes moral agency, and thus, those who are oppressed are not so much moral agents as those who are not oppressed (Cuomo 1998, 58–59, 76; Mann 2005, 52–54; Hoagland 1999, 92–93). Relationality and particularity that may tie an agent to the constraints of autonomy may also function as the means for liberation and full autonomy. However, since the notion of "noble agency" represents the idea charged with the imbalance of nature, many ecofeminists find this interpretation suspicious and call for a conceptual revision.

Another line of feminist thought reconceptualizes autonomy in a way that admits the causal and cultural limitations of freedom as not compromising moral autonomy. Instead, they can be seen as positive forces on which each and every human needs to build his or her autonomy. The types of autonomy may be diverse: the autonomy of oppressed partners also represents the idea of noble agency, even though it would differ from the autonomy of those in power. Unconstrained or isolated autonomy is, however, an illusion. Admitting relationality does not mean subjection to the powerful. According to this view, relationalities may play a positive role in moral deliberation without a transcendent target of liberation. Unwillingness to admit that humans are fundamentally embedded in the social and natural environments only reflects the modernist supposition that relationality would devalue human worth. This is why ecofeminists tend to defend the contextual and relational view of autonomy rather than the liberational view. Ecofeminists usually argue that the only autonomy one can achieve is relative to the environments one is embedded in: autonomy is only possible with the help of the contextual and relational nature of human agency (e.g., Plumwood 1993, 22–24; 1994). The idea of a moral agent as a self-in-relationship entails that an agent's moral capability is constructed in relationships with various others (Kittay 2011). Value concepts, such as interests and well-being, should be seen to refer to inter-relative elements. Ecofeminists also emphasize the environmental harmfulness of an individual, isolated notion of autonomy.

Feminist philosophy, in general, criticizes the modern concept of autonomy regarding the implied conception of the un-contextualized, incorporeal, individual agent. Particularly in the field of feminist bioethics it is widely accepted that autonomy cannot be entirely separated from the social and biological determinants of an agent. The ideal of absolute individual autonomy makes sense only together with "assumptions about selfhood and agency that are metaphysically, epistemologically and ethically problematic," and thus diminishes the practical relevance of ethics (Mackenzie and Stoljar 2000, 3). Lorraine Code calls such an idea a "perversion" (Code 2000, 184). The concept of autonomy should then be revised in a way that takes seriously the realities and conditions of human life and agency. Revisions made by feminist bioethicists and ecofeminists are in many respects congruent. Relational autonomy is suggested to replace the conception of autonomy as an absolute and definite feature.

There are two clearly different ways to consider autonomy as relational in this discussion: *procedural* and *interactive* approaches differ from each other on the question of whether the relationships practiced are considered as a means to develop one's individual autonomy, or as constitutive for the very concept of autonomy. The procedural concept of autonomy makes use of the psychoanalytic conception of self, according to which we need to be connected, cared for, and guided in order to learn how to make our own choices. In concordance with the procedural view, Marilyn Friedman (2000) argues that social relationships form the only proper means for humans to become autonomous as an individual. Therefore, influences of our close relationships, transference of cultural values and parental consulting, should not be seen as limits to autonomy. On the contrary, social upbringing and ongoing personal interactions are necessary conditions of autonomy because they impart resources for critical reflection and self-concept: an agent carries the normative and authoritative influence of her (early and close) relationships as conditions for her (later) autonomy. Freedom is included in "reflective self-understanding or internal coherence" and "an absence of . . . manipulation by others" (Friedman 2000, 40–41, 46). This kind of procedurally relational concept of autonomy focuses on the constituents of autonomy as the socially constructed abilities of an individual to develop and express autonomy in her decisions. Autonomy requires the ability to act effectively on one's values with the help of social impact. Procedural relational autonomy thus partly resembles the idea of emancipation, but compared to Beauvoir's approach, the interactivity takes place in a deeper level of the identity formation.

The interactive view calls for a conceptual shift and considers autonomy as such as a relational issue. According to the interactive notion of relational autonomy, defended for example by Diana Meyers (1989), Catriona Mackenzie (2000), and Anna Peterson (2001), it is not possible to separate autonomy from the conditions of action if the social and material embeddedness of a human agent is taken seriously. In contrast to the idea of radical freedom as the core of autonomy, autonomous choices should be understood as choices between constraint alternatives. Autonomy can be practiced without absolute individual freedom. Relational autonomy is possible in conditions of constraint freedom, too, and in fact, this is the normal case. Individuals are not absolutely free, but autonomy should not be seen as an individual issue. By humbly holding oneself to the notion that the conditions of one's actions in social and ecological relationships are relevant, one can make a difference in the course of the development of these conditions. The agency actualizing in the interactive relationships can make changes, although the actor is not an absolutely free individual. Meyers argues for an idea of autonomy as competence, which includes self-reading and self-actualizing skills. Instead of uninfluenced choices, the autonomous agent practices skills of actualizing oneself in relation with those influencing in her identity. The difference between being autonomous and failing to be autonomous is that an autonomous person is not passive but reflectively engages with the social determinants that partly shape her life (Meyers 1989, 53, 59, 82–84). This emphasizes that autonomy need not be thought of as a property—as if the term was separated from the agent that owns it—but as an element of action.

While the procedural notion considers relationships as conduits for becoming autonomous in a sense of freedom, the interactive notion considers relationships to be constitutive for autonomy: relationships are needed as constituents of rationality, by which the agent develops her virtuous identity to better morally engage with others. Both relational notions of autonomy, but especially the interactive one, represent a virtue perspective on being an agent. Restrained rather than radical autonomy develops virtuousness: "The emphasis upon constraint and its ethical correlate restraint, points to a balance between recognizing our real power to construct and change the world, on the one hand, and the equally real limitations of that power, on the other" (Peterson 2001, 211). It is worth noticing that relational autonomy is not reductive: autonomous actions can*not* be *reduced* either to social or physiological determinants. Rather, considering agency and included autonomy as relational concepts refers to a nonindividualist conception of self: particular relationships constitutive for the self imply that autonomy and self-governance are fundamentally relational, too (Oshana 2013; Mackenzie and Stoljar, 2000b, 21–26).

CARE FOR OTHERS AS CARE FOR
ONE'S OWN MORAL ABILITY

A relational concept of autonomy does not, at least not necessarily, entail relativism. But it means that the target of the struggle for becoming more ethical beings and doing the "right" thing should be located differently. Given that historical, cultural, social, and ecological structures are constitutive for the agent, it is impossible to purify one's "noble agency" from their influence. Assuming that some act or standpoint is neutral or free only authorizes its domination and maintains oppressive moral structures. Regarding epistemic and moral truths and objectivity, relational autonomy refers to an attitude that resembles the feminist standpoint theory in feminist epistemology (Haraway 1988; Harding 1991, 2004; Hartsock 1998; Hekman 2004). Privileged perspectives cannot express complete truth, but neither can any perspective alone. However, truth can be approached—although not perhaps reached in the objective sense—through being connected with other perspectives. The relational notion of autonomy stresses the crucial role of interactivity between the representatives of the various perspectives. But if one's moral ability relies on the quality of his or her relationships, the struggle for better (knowledge, social structures, or moral agents) should be retargeted. Approaching the good or the truth is possible only through approaching the *best possible relationships* (cf. Harding 1991, 2004).

Relationally assisted autonomy requires the kind of attitude toward others that constructs the best possible ability to make decisions. But the good result does not just benefit the individual, it also benefits the wider collective around her. Hence, the relational interpretation of autonomy does not take agency merely as a description, but also as a prescription. Because of the shared idea that relationally functioning autonomy emphasizes the quality of relationships, care ethics (see Gilligan 1982; Noddings 1984; Ruddick 1989) is seen as a strong ally of ecofeminist ethics. According to Karen Warren, a coherent ecofeminist ethics "involves a shift *from* a conception of ethics as primarily a matter of rights, rules, or principles," and instead, turns towards ethics that emphasizes the role of the "values of care, love, friendship, trust, and appropriate reciprocity—values that presuppose that our relationships to others are central to our understanding of who we are" (Warren 1990, 138, 141, 144). Warren argues that nonfeminist environmental ethics cannot offer an alternative to the notion of human supremacy over nature, since they approve of assumptions that promote and maintain notions such as ethical absolutism, ethical monism, objective moral knowledge, and conceptual essentialism (Warren 2000, 90–91, 106–9). A relational, care-sensitive ethics denies these assumptions and, therefore, it can adopt the relational view about moral decision-making. Relational autonomy also seems capable of clearly preventing a dualism between reason and emotion. Additionally, it is applicable to various types of relationships that hold between a diversity of entities. Situated moral principles can more fruitfully be used in the kind of agency that takes place in dialogical types of reasoning.

According to Warren and Plumwood, for instance, relational agency emphasizes the agent's ability to care and love as central for ethics, instead of equal treatment, which refers to the idea of comparison and thus requires measures of similarity. Warren defends a modification of care ethics that she calls care-sensitive ethics as an appropriate way to formulate the morally justified relationships between humans and nonhuman nature. The care approach appreciates diversity in the moral community and thus suits multi-species communities. Conditions for a care-sensitive ethics are the ability to care about oneself and others, consideration of ethics as being situated universality, and consideration of the appropriateness of principles and practices by care practices (see Warren 2000, 106–9; Plumwood 1994, 145–46). The care tradition is particularly relevant for environmental ethics, according to Warren, because of its emphasis on the relational nature of the diverse moral community. A caring perception maintains difference in a moral relationship—even with a rock: "A loving (or caring) perception presupposes and maintains difference—a distinction between the self and other. . . . A moral community based on loving perception of oneself in relationship with a rock is one that acknowledges and respects difference, in addition to whatever sameness or commonality also exists" (Warren 2000, 105). Since the partiality of the relational agent is inescapable, moral principles or rules are also situated rather than absolute, although they can carry on elements that make actions morally comparable. Contrary to the usual conclusion that situationism implies relativism, the relational concept of agency reaches beyond the division between absolutism and relativism in ethics.

Understanding the agent as a self-in-relation involves not just a revised understanding of autonomy, but also a revised understanding of rationality. Plumwood criticizes rationalistic culture for distorting many important spheres of human life. According to her, the ecological crises we must face due to human ("rational") activity shows that what has been held as a reason-centered culture "has become a liability to survival." Rationalism, as we are used to conceive it, fails to give the whole picture of rationality in its full complexity, because it has shut out important aspects of both human and nonhuman reasoning and agency. According to Plumwood, rationalism lacks an awareness of "ecological embeddedness, nature's agency and limits, and human dependency on the non-human sphere" (Plumwood 2002, 45). According to rationalism, knowledge is the product of pure reason, and excludes "the senses or the body." An alternative, ecologically sound rationality should be essentially dialogical, which includes care for those with whom we communicate. The core failure in the dominant conception of rationality is the separated narratives of the knowing subject and the known natural object. The transformation needed in science is thus not just political, but also epistemic. Plumwood talks about "care models of knowledge" that break down the radical subject/object division and allow agency for the known in the dialogical relationship. The quality of the dialogical relationships is decisive for the epistemic outcome: "caring rationality" considers ethics and responsibility as crucial even for science (Plumwood 2002, 44–47, 53–55).

Search for appropriate moral rationality for relational agents draws the discussions on moral reasoning and epistemology closer to each other. Most usually it is thought that there is a one-way influence between epistemology and ethics, though recently this view has been vigorously impugned. But as Cheney and Weston argue, a more plausible way would be to think that "the world we inhabit arises most fundamentally out of our ethical practice." In order to know something about the world, we need to offer "space" and "invite" the hidden possibilities of the world to meet with our awareness. Ethical action is thus a requirement as well as a response (Cheney and Weston 1999, 115–18; see also Weston 2004, 32). Moral reasons are the first reasons, not just in ethics but also in epistemic activity through the need to choose a "loving perception" toward the known, to put it in Warren's words. According to her, the required moral condition is "the ability to care." It is not just the basis for choosing right for the correct reason but itself a crucial aspect of moral motivation, moral reasoning, and moral practices, which means that there need not be any external reason to "be moral" besides the bona fide moral reasons for an essentially relational moral agent to commit to caring for those with whom she shares her world (Warren 2000, 104–5, 108–12, 156).

What has been said here about the conception of the moral agent in ecofeminism shows that the adoption of an ecofeminist approach to environmental ethics calls for conceptual rethinking that also plays a role in the formulation of ethical theories. Compared to mainstream feminist constructionism, which is said to celebrate the linguistic or narrative turn in ethics, ecofeminism represents a constrained type of constructionism. The material and even determined perspectives of the agency are celebrated as the internal part of the narrative. This makes the ecofeminist conception of agency interesting also from the viewpoint of constructivism as an ethical theory. I also argue that the ecofeminist aspiration to relationally reconsider autonomy as well as epistemic and moral rationality offers a valuable insight for other environmental ethicists struggling with the question of how to combine the factual contingencies of the moral agent with a universally binding responsibility for ecological sustainability.

One of the most notable ethical implications is that the relational concept of autonomy turns the focus from the moral contents to the methods of being moral. Understanding human lives in a relational narrative implies that living one's story and shaping one's agency require a constant effort to see one's own world from the perspectives of others in order to approach what is good. This is, however, impossible without commitment to the various webs of interactivity that restrict one's individual freedom and isolated identity. There are thus moral reasons for relational care and love that should be seen practically as the first reasons for both ethics and epistemology. An appropriate act must be to choose a "loving perception" of others in order to know or understand, not just for moral reasons (Warren 2000, 104–5). Care is an appropriate method to evaluate reliable versus unreliable knowledge, as well as to evaluate moral principles. Anna Peterson argues, for her part, that we are responsible for mediating moral truths by acting according to this method in relationships with earthly others—both dialogically and by recognizing the reality with which we construct our moral agency (Peterson 2001, 211–12). In contrast to the epic of evolution, which is causal by nature, or the traditional one-way influence between epistemology and ethics, the dynamical structure of the relational agent involves complex two-way influences between various partners. Time must also be considered. Imagination of the future and beliefs concerning it, for instance, are present in the current process of identity formation, and hence of agency construction.

The relational concept of autonomy seems to have extremely interesting philosophical and metaethical implications. What makes it especially promising is that it can preserve requirements of *responsibility* without claiming individual freedom. It makes, however, the conditions of autonomy more modest. Ecofeminists usually defend moral realism, unlike many other feminists. The conceptual shift about ecological relationality that concerns the concept of agency has a restraining effect on constructivism in ethics: the shift in the concept of an autonomous agent, who is the source of obligation according to constructivism, changes the entire idea of humanism that is thought to be involved in it. At the same time with these promising issues, relational autonomy is a concept that should make us humble; it claims that our own moral ability is bound to others and to their benevolence to support us and to commit to caring dialogue with us. It thus leaves us in uncertainty regarding both autonomous action and moral knowledge. The best we can do is to care for our relationships and the quality of interactions with our various cohabitants on this planet.

To conclude my remarks about ecofeminist discussions at this stage, I would like to emphasize three features of ecofeminism that should, I think, be taken into consideration when cherishing hope for the ability of ethics to contribute to sustainability transformation. First, the plurality of perspectives resulting from the diversity of genuine agents and their modes of knowing implies that the reasons for actions are also plural. In order to seek for universal commitments to, say, environmental conducts, the formulation of such ethical conducts cannot be separated from the ways in which different perspectives and viewpoints are taken into account, or the ways different agents are interconnected with each other. No one can alone achieve a justified moral reason for action. But justified moral reasons cannot, according to an ecofeminist perspective, be achieved inside a human community alone, either. Therefore, ecofeminist approaches claim that help from, and cooperation with, nonhuman partners that share the ecological community with us is highly needed in the construction of moral principles and conducts.

Second, an agent should not be internally divided into the spheres of moral and contingent agencies, but rather seen as bodily and materially relational also when reasoning and acting as a moral self. Ecofeminist wavering between constructionist and realist views about the nature of things expresses an aspiration to combine two approaches that represent metaphysically contradictory positions about human nature into a coherent view about human agency when it is observed from a spatially and temporally wider perspective. Social construction does not only concern concepts (about nature or the direction of emancipation), but in some sense, also the "real world." This is because the constructed concepts adopted by a particular agent are considered to influence the interventions he or she makes in the material world, and these interventions are seen to cause such environmental changes that, again, have an impact on the abilities of agents and societies to make further constructions about concepts.[5]

Third, ecofeminism conceives autonomy as relational autonomy, derived from the fundamental conception of a moral self as self-in-relationships. Moral agency as committed to partiality and fundamental relationality signals the need to reconceptualize autonomy as relational, both in the social and the material ecological sense. This is a modest notion of autonomy but, I argue, enough not to undermine the idea of responsibility, although that should be understood a relational concept, too. One possible interpretation about the specific ecofeminist way of understanding relational autonomy highlights the "loving perception" as a condition of autonomy. The agent's particular way of being related to the issue she is describing influences her ability to make moral deliberations concerning that issue. Her autonomy depends on the quality of her relationships with the partners who are the objects of her actions or deliberations.

The supposition in ecofeminism seems to be that conceptual rethinking concerning these issues can also make moral theories more capable of efficiently dealing with environmental issues. However, insisting on change in the way that human or nonhuman nature is conceptualized does not necessarily seem to refer to changes in an understanding of how things are, but rather to one's moral attitude and practical relationships towards epistemic objects. Choosing one's descriptive notions (that is, constructing the world) is an ethical task with real effects (on the world and on the agent). The next questions are: What are the moral reasons for making these choices? What makes some relationships better than others? and How can we know what they are? From the ecofeminist perspective, answers to the metaethical question of justification seem to be closely connected with answers to the questions about the agent: Who are we going to be? Or who do we want to be? But these are not in any sense private questions. Our wishes and beliefs are dialogically bound to those of other people and to our material and multispecies living surroundings. Wishes and beliefs concerning the future of humanity also direct our actions. By describing the world, we transform humanity; and by interventions in material processes, we construct our own nature, reasoning, and agency, as well as of various others'.

NOTES

1. Following Karen Warren, I use ecological feminism and ecofeminism as synonyms. Warren 2000, 53. It is also worth noting that ecological refers also to social and cultural ecologies.

2. According to Merchant, nature has been identified with either of two feminine metaphors: a nurturing mother and a wild, uncontrollable, dangerous female, originating from, respectively, medieval philosophy and Francis Bacon's early modern philosophy. According to Plumwood, the origins of the metaphors maintaining twin domination are already in the rationalist tradition of classical Greek philosophy. Value dualisms between masculine/feminine, reason/emotion or spirit/body connect masculinity with ideal humanity. Plumwood 1996.

3. Women's ecological wisdom may be seen to emerge either from the real differences of consciousness, or from the historical fact that women have been treated more like animals, which has influenced their understanding of nature.

4. Code, Harding, Longino, Plumwood, and Hekman represent relational feminist epistemology, while Hartsock's and Haraway's referred works represent social feminist epistemology.

5. This implication of ecofeminist notion of relational agency parallels interestingly with the basic enactivist claims in the recent cognitive science and their ethical implications. See more in chapters 5 and 7.

Chapter 4

Relational Agendas

PARALLEL AGENDAS TOWARD RELATIONAL AGENCY

Naturalists and constructivists criticize the predominant notion of moral agency from philosophically opposite directions, and ecofeminist and evolutionary ethical approaches are commonly located on opposing extremes in environmental ethics. From the point of view of the aspirations of environmental ethics concerning a non-relativist, universally acceptable, and practically efficient ethical theory, the hardwired forms of both social constructivism and evolutionary ethics are, however, problematic: Both scientific reductionism and social explanations of agency threaten the notion of moral autonomy required for responsibility, and perhaps also the idea of normative conduct. According to Mary Midgley, they suffer from the scientific ideal of simplicity. Midgley herself could be categorized both as an evolutionary ethicist and a feminist, but she criticizes the non-environmentalist forms of both (Midgley 2004, 29–32; 1994, 58–59).[1] In so doing, she points out the common aspiration of environmentalists drawing from each framework: they tend to approach each other and by so doing they soften the threatening ramifications connected to hardwired evolutionary psychology and postmodern feminism. Midgley criticizes their explanations of human nature because of their reductionism. A "full paper theory" of human nature reduces human agency to causalities, especially genetic and neurophysiological activity, while a "blank paper theory" reduces them to the social determinants considering the material body just as a platform for cultural constructions to take place. Adopting a biologically reductionist full paper explanation implies determinist reduction in ethics, while adopting a blank paper explanation implies moral relativism. According to Midgley, neither theory can alone explain the agency of a human animal; processes providing actions should be seen from a broader perspective of the interactivity between biological

83

and social determinants (Midgley 1978, 3–24, 54–57, 162–63, 285–88). She argued as early as the 1970s that all communities are "mixed" in the sense that they are "multi-species ones" (Midgley 1998, 111; cf. Haraway 2007, 2016). Individuals and species are mutually and complexly tangled, and therefore, the study of moral reasoning should also take it seriously that human animality and ecological relationality are present in the moral agency both through one's innate animal instincts and the multispecies community in which one grows and lives.

Common for current environmentalists drawing either from evolutionary naturalism or feminist constructivism is that they call for careful investigation of the physical, ecological, and social conditions of moral reasoning. Both thus aspire beyond dichotomizing material-biological and mental-cultural influences in human agency—in contrast to their original background frameworks. This makes their argumentations cross into each other's territory. They tend to make use of each other's perspectives—ecofeminists of the role of physiological, material, and ecological relationships in human and animal agency, and evolutionary naturalists of the social interactivity and phenomenological perspective—especially when they try to resist reductionism. In both camps they also often call for recognition of the wide-ranging dynamic and systemic interactivity in which agency develops and performs. This can be seen as their shared positive call to make a shift toward a more *relational understanding of agency* and, consequently, to reconsider the conceptual prerequisites of modern ethics, such as autonomy (Nurmi 2011, 2020).[2]

As parallel agendas, evolutionary and ecofeminist approaches to agency share similar types of challenges, but they also point in parallel to the same direction for overcoming them. Both acknowledge that the hard interpretations of their own frameworks imply a reductive explanation of agency, which may threaten moral autonomy and, hence, responsibility, but possibly also morality. They are similar in, at least, in five respects: First, both claim that human nature is neither essential nor fixed. Hence, human agency can be scrutinized as an empirical and changing phenomenon in terms of evolutionary, ecological, and social factors and cultural definitions. Second, both groups try to soften reductionist explanations, on the one hand, and steer clear of a dualist understanding of the nature of the human agent on the other. They attack the idea of dividing agency into being either naturally or socially determined or free and moral. Autonomy should be seen as a complex issue: A plausible condition of moral agency overlaps social and biological determinants without reduction. This means that there is an implicit link between discussions of the compatibility problem and environmental ethics, though these discussions seldom meet. An articulated relational approach will fill this gap, I believe.

Third, both admit that human conditions are not insignificant for the concept of moral agency: If an earthly being can be a moral agent, her morality is limited. But they argue that human contingencies do not undermine responsibility or the critical point of view of ethics, but rather, they compromise the modern idea of absolute freedom as a necessary condition for moral responsibility. Fourth, among the main problems of the current ethical discourse they critique the dismissal of fundamental interactivity of all earthly beings and processes, human noble agency included. Ethics that focuses on the quality of interactive structures instead of individual features also find questions about, for instance, individual freedom more trivial. Fifth, they claim that underrating contextualities in a moral theory and having a detached view of moral reasoning also cause harm for ethics and its practical applicability. Therefore, conceptual revisions are necessary, in addition to the scientific credibility that modern exceptionalism has lost. A glorious concept of moral agency dazzles moral theories into not recognizing the logic of domination nor the meanings of evolutive mechanisms in their reasoning.

A question remains, however: what kind of role do causalities play in *moral reasoning*, and can the concept of a *moral reason* for action be defined without reduction? Moreover, is the difference between causal explanations and moral reasons a conceptual one, do they belong to separate realities, or is there some third interpretation in between? Regarding the role of explanations, both strategies prefer arguments for a third view between reduction of moral reason to factual explanations, on the one hand, and acceptance of conceptual dualism on the other. The most significant point of convergence between the parallel lines of thought is the nonindividualist and interactive understanding of agency. This does not, however, simply refer to metaphysical or moral holism, but to the use of the scientific and anthropological notions of the complex mechanisms of eco-social interactivity. A shared claim is that the role of this interactivity in the processes of deliberation and action should be taken into consideration in the theory of ethics and its anthropological presuppositions. The focus should be turned to the relationships (either ecological or social) that make us moral agents. They also agree in that the interactions in various relationships should be included in the sphere of moral actions: As they influence the constitution of our own agency, they are—even in a more strict and concrete sense than Kant thought—*duties to ourselves*. The role we play in our ecological place, as well as our sociocultural role, influences not only the "world out there," but also our manifestation of moral agency.

Environmental ethicists on both the naturalist and constructivist ends thus target their criticism on the modern myth about moral agency and aspire to resist the reductionist explanations of the hard interpretations of their own traditions. But do their parallel agendas indicate a converged view? I find it a convincing idea. My proposal is that their point of convergence is an *ecologically relational notion of moral agency* entailing a relational shift in ethics. The epithet "ecological" here refers to ecologically embedded interactivity in the sense that social, cultural, and biological relationalities and their functioning structures are mutually inseparable and form a complex nexus of interactivity. From the point of view of an agent, this means that the interactivity by which her agency is constituted involves natural interactivity bound to the particular ecological reality where it takes place, as well as social and cultural interactivity bound to the constructed realm.

Naturalist and constructivist environmental ethical approaches considered as parallel lines of thought directed toward a convergent aim open new prospects to revoke traditional dichotomies. Inclined to question the extreme interpretations of their own traditions, authors on both sides seek more modest positions: *chastened or constrained constructionism*,[3] *nonreductionist*, and *soft naturalism*. The common direction to which they head takes seriously the scientific understanding of human naturalness, nonindividuality, and fundamental interactivity, but seeks to restrain reductionism. Conceptually, it is not an easy task. The initial steps taken along this path, however, show potential to elucidate the nature of moral agency in a way that reveals hidden processes as parts of moral reasoning without violating the conditions of moral realism and the authority of ethics. If my hypothesis is correct, examination of the lines of thought toward which these critical approaches aspire can unveil new possibilities for improving the theoretical basis of moral discourse concerning environmental issues. I also suppose that aspirations to consider moral agency as relational are not philosophically insignificant. On the contrary, they may appear to have interesting implications for philosophy of mind and metaethics.

In the following parts the focus will be turned from the distinctive features of environmental arguments to the aim of articulating the concept of relational moral agency and to understanding the role of earthly determinants and cultural constraints in the human mechanisms of reasoning and motivation. The complex web of interactions taking place in the agent's operations when an act is performed should be recognized and respected in order to understand what is possible or desirable for a moral agent. Naturalists tend to focus especially on the natural factors that constitute voluntary operations: motivation, purpose-giving, meaning-generating, valuing, and intending are not separable from the representational operations of perception, cognitive processes and sensory awareness, or biologically evolved and physiological inclinations. Constructivists focus on relationships constitutive for cognitive operations, such as perception and knowledge formation. Social, cultural, and moral commitments and practices influence what satisfies the conditions of knowledge; therefore, affections, emotions, and valuations, for example, are involved through representational operations. Knowledge is not only a question of whether our "computational" operations work correctly.

If the processes of agency are relational by nature, it is misleading to conceptualize agency as something demarcated under the skin of an individual (agent). Operations manifesting agency are better seen to take place in a dialogical network than in the individual mind. Although discussions heading toward relational agency somewhat overlap discussions on collective agency, relational agency emphasizes the fact that the nonhuman partners and elements of a collective must not be excluded. Multispecies collective design ecologically structured manifestations of agency. As the functioning of such complex collectives, or mixed communities, to use Midgley's terms, influence manifestations of agency, moral reasoning and motivation should also be seen as constituted in a structure that extends "beyond the skin." Experiences of place, weather, and landscape, as well as the consumption of ecosystem services (breathing, eating, etc.), for instance, are not irrelevant for moral identity, but are instead heavily involved in the ways that moral reasoning and valuing take place. Meanings and values are formulated in the agent's mind not simply by voluntary actions, nor are they just given by mental processes that contribute to their existence. They are outcomes of the interactivity between internal and external things. But meanings do influence moral activity: the things one loves have a different influence on the evaluation of one's actions than the things one hates, or things that one hardly acknowledges (see Preston 2009, 176, 180, 182). The external aspects on which agency depends, if understood relationally, highlight the role of respect (or disrespect) for others and the material environment: the normative meaning of ethics relies on the conditions in which moral agency can be manifested, and the conditions in which an agent becomes and remains responsible.

Relational shifts in the concept of agency called for by empirical natural and social sciences challenge the traditional notions of autonomy and reasoning, and perhaps of moral reason and autonomy of ethics, too. But the challenge should not be bypassed just on the grounds of the possible threat to the traditional self-understanding of ethics. Instead, I argue that identification of the point where the aspirations of ecofeminist and evolutionary environmentalists converge, and articulation of the relational shift, can clarify the ramifications of the challenge and open a new perspective beyond the problems that modern ethics has in dealing with the moral relevance of the external material world. A successful definition of nonindividualistic agency would also have implications in discussions beyond environmental ethics concerning, for instance, collective agency and agent-based virtue ethics (see Slote 2013; Pettigrove 2018). Criticism against modern exceptionality encourages us to pose questions concerning moral agents: Are human agents the only mixtures of natural causality and free finality on earth? And are the two realms of human activity as separable as thought in modern ethics? Or is it possible to think of natural (nonmoral, causally explainable) and moral (nonnatural, requiring reason-giving explanation) activities as interactively dependent on each other? A negative answer to the first calls for recognizing animal agency in a continuum with human moral agency, while a negative answer to the second calls for revising an understanding of the processes required for moral deliberation and motivation, and hence, the responsibility and autonomy of the agent. On a more theoretical level, criticism of the common interpretation of responsibility and autonomy is challenging. However modest this criticism is, it brings about discussion about stable truths and reasons for action.

The attempt to revise the idea of human moral agency manifested parallelly by environmental ethicists drawing from opposing philosophical frameworks points to a conceptual crisis in modern ethics. Human earthly beings are not the beings that have been supposed in the logic of the post-Enlightenment humanist ethics. As moral agency is central for a humanist theory of ethics, it should be based on the well-justified notions of humanity and processes of agency. The idea of an isolated individual whose reasoning and intentions are exceptionally isolated from his surroundings has been deemed invalid. But now it seems that it is not even ethically desirable.

ONTOLOGICAL APPROACHES TO
THE RELATIONAL SELF

Quest for a relational notion of the human agent—one that does not slide into reductive naturalism, postmodern relativism, or metaphysical essentialism—often turns the mind to alternative ontological approaches that define self as relational. Although relational agency is not, as such, bound to any metaphysical view, it is worth briefly discussing such approaches. The concept of a relational subject is common in an environmental philosophy that draws from, for example, process philosophy, deep ecology, or Asian philosophies that may offer illuminative frameworks for a relational definition of moral agency. But when the relational shift is based on the shifts in some specific worldview or requires adopting a particular metaphysical system or religion, the ethical discourse based on them is exclusive.[4]

As an ontological issue, relational agency exemplifies itself in positions that break down the boundary between the static world and the active subject. Metaphysical frameworks that focus on relationships as ontologically primary can overcome the bifurcation between (material/passive) objects and (mental/active) subjects in the world, as well as between physical/external and mental/internal aspects in human agency. Not surprisingly, environmental philosophers find them interesting, even though they may be philosophically marginal views.[5] A relational approach to the subject and agency is familiar in various philosophies, such as Heraclitus's thought, process philosophy, several indigenous spiritual traditions, Buddhist and Confucian philosophies, and in some Western theological, dialogical, and phenomenological philosophies. These approaches fascinate environmental philosophers precisely on account of their included potentiality to talk about environmental ethics from a wider perspective than traditional Western modern ethics. Many environmentalists find valuable, for instance, the indigenous visions that indicate that the very nature and operations of the self are tied to relationships with particular places, and with communities of material and living partners. Some focus on the Buddhist view of relational identity formation, which coincides especially with holistic environmentalism (see Næss 1998, 207–8; Callicott 2008; Fox 2003, 252; Devall 1990; Ferré 2001, 209–10), or on the environmental benefits of Confucian or Taoist insights (Tucker 2001; Tao 2004; Wong 2004; Hourdequin and Wong 2005). A wide discussion of its own draws on process philosophy (Cobb 1972; McFague 1997; Muraca 2010). Most of these approaches share an emphasis on the complexity of the physical, mental, and semantic relations and its meaning to the very being of the self, or the agent. I shall introduce two famous examples of ontologically relational approaches to the self and agency, process philosophy and Confucian virtue ethics, in order to enable comparison with the present project.

Process philosophy, originating in Alfred North Whitehead's (1861–1947) work, is one of the most used alternative ontologies in environmental philosophy. It has inspired environmentalists and theologians by its thoroughly relational, non-substantive understanding of human and natural activity (see Whitehead 1978). Whitehead offers a clear alternative to the dominant dualisms without sliding either into a vague holism or into haphazard pluralism, and instead exemplifies a genuine pluralism of interconnected parties and activities. Since process philosophy combines mental and material relationships into a fundamentally relational and process-based ontology, it can also offer a valid foundation for rejecting the juxtaposition between naturalism and constructivism—and it has both constructivist and naturalist advocators. Whitehead constructs a profoundly articulated speculative system in which the aspects of active, responsible agency and the physical world are intertwined. Being is fundamentally connected with acting: becoming constitutes being, and creativity, as a relational term, is considered the ultimate power and authoritative principle. Instead of talking about substances, process philosophy lifts up events to represent what is: "*how* an actual entity *becomes* constitutes what the actual entity *is*" (Whitehead 1978, 23), while all other things that "are in any sense of 'existence,' are derived by abstractions from actual (entities)" (Whitehead 1978, 113). By not subscribing to substantialist ontology, process philosophy entirely denies essentialism in which things have natures apart from their relations by which they are organized: "A single fact in isolation is the primary myth. . . . Connectedness is of the essence of all things of all types." Physical and mental actions are not distinguished, and relationality is the basis for anything to happen or to become—that is, to be (Whitehead 1956, 12–13, 205).

One reason for environmentalists to prefer process thought is its ability to go beyond the dichotomy between moral and factual reality without confusing their different roles. Moral reality and the laws of nature are intertwined: the laws of nature are relative to the activity of entities and to every novelty that comes into existence through process. In the process of becoming, the "many" in the world are all the time reunified to create a new "one" that joins to the "many," and all the partners of that process are active, none passive (Whitehead 1978, 21).[6] This holds for self-formation of the moral agent, too. But at the same time, this fascinating ontology may cause problems for process ethics to join in general moral discussion. For example, event-based ontology questions the temporal duration of self (especially of intentionality), which is conceived to be a prerequisite of the integrity of an agent. However, Whitehead does not dispense with personal identity, but sees it extended to the conditions of its being realized, the relationships in which the becoming of a person again and again takes place (Whitehead 1951, 690). The Whiteheadian environmentalist Frederic Ferré, for example, argues that distinction categories of subjective and objective are valorized in modern ethics due to included substance metaphysics, which is just a metaphysical system to which process ontology can offer an alternative. Subjectivism in ethics could work, according to him, if only subjects were seen as parts of "the reality of multiple subjective centers of real relationships" (Ferré 2001, 105–7). In the moral self, the dynamic of relationships, two "poles," are involved (subjective and objective, mental and physical, or cognitive and emotional), but in process and action they are never separable. Therefore, persons are "capable of initiating causal changes in the physical world by making mental judgements guided by ideal norms," but not without being embodied (physically relational), which is a requirement of agency (Ferré 2001, 59–62, 105–7, 236). Although the practical power of process metaphysics may be questioned, Ferré is correct in arguing that ontological presuppositions remain influential in all frameworks, and the value of ontological debates should not be underestimated.

According to classical Confucian writings, the self is intrinsically relational in two senses: personhood is relational by nature, and particular persons are constituted by their relationships (*Analects*, *Mencius*, and *Xunzi*). A biological organism becomes a person by entering into relationships with others: one realizes one's humanity by realizing "inborn capacities to enter into a network of responsibilities," such as feelings of compassion, shame, courtesy and a sense of right and wrong. The constitutive dispositions of identity are not traits *simpliciter*, but traits performed for particular people: among whom we choose to spend our time is not without consequences for our very identity (Wong 2004, 422–23). But besides being relational as a person, relations are necessary for becoming a moral agent (Hourdequin and Wong 2005, 20–21). David Wong highlights the fact that the sphere of constitutive relations includes both social and environmental relationships. Persons are not autonomous as individual selves, but rather they influence the constitution of collective agency (and autonomy) by cultivating certain relationships rather than others (Wong 2004, 428–29). Continuous retraining and reshaping the character in harmonious relations with nature is necessary for both the cultivation of one's identity and for getting nurture from nature (*Xunzi*, Book 9.18 and Book 17.3). In the right kind of relationships, an agent can increase her wisdom and autonomy.

Confucianism also respects differences: "the way of humans" is distinct from "the way of Nature," but both "ways" require each other and each other's activity. This is called the "relational resonance" between humans and nature (Tao 2004, 6, 8). If relations rely on one's actions, which in turn shape one's agency, then, however comprehensive one's autonomy is, the agent can never see a general rule or universal moral claim as an absolute "rightness" (associated with *yi*). Relationships with places and commitments to others are ethical necessities that force one to keep on searching for what is right (Hourdequin and Wong 2005, 21–22, 31).[7] Relationships never become indifferent. Moral agency thus calls for two virtues: the virtue of epistemic flexibility and the virtue of some firm, non-relational truth, but not a general principle. In the Confucian context such reality is called *yi*. One of the fascinating insights in the Confucian view is that the structures of the world and agency (human and other) are interconnected in a way that makes it impossible to absolutely distinguish between the conditions of action and the actions themselves. Environmental values emerge from the relational self (Hourdequin and Wong 2005, 27).

Metaphysical approaches to relational agency can form valid foundations for environmentally insightful relational approaches to ethics. In the practical level, however, adopting metaphysically loaded environmental arguments entails adoption of an entire worldview, which may be demanding and exclude people from various cultures from the ethical discussion. This, again, weakens the practical effects of such approaches. Therefore, my choice here is to seek for minimally demanding options and focus on the multidisciplinary scientific discussion on the mechanisms of agency rather than on their ontological explanations. The empirical fact that material surroundings modify and shape the ways we think, feel, believe, reason and act, for instance, involves as such deep ethical challenges for the modern culture.

However, it is worth reminding that not even science is free from metaphysical presuppositions.

SOME CONCLUDING REMARKS

The first part of the journey we have traveled through in this chapter the landscape of environmental ethics from the perspective of the several understandings of human moral agency. The three stops in humanist exceptionalism, its extensionalist version, naturalist evolutionary ethics, and ecofeminism showed that the agential perspective taken in environmental ethics uncovers problems in the modern framework of ethics that are not restricted to applications to environmental ethics. The account of moral agency in modern ethics is not scientifically convincing nor socially or ecologically sustainable. The two critical strategies appear to call in parallel for reconceiving moral agency as an essentially relational issue and for questioning the strict contradiction between the contingent, empirical explanatory reasons for action and the noncontingent reasons for action derived from free human mind, because such mind seems not to exist. The arguments of the critical approaches against the modern concept of agency and its negative impact in environmental ethics are convincing.

However, I argued that environmental ethics has a dilemma in relation to Enlightenment humanism that has given strong justifications for individual responsibilities as well as for the autonomy and authority of ethics in general. Most environmental ethicists wish to defend the autonomy and authority of ethics. It is important for environmental ethics that a critical point of view is possible, so that we can distinguish between better and worse from the point of view of the real world. This means that ethics is autonomous, not reduced to the factual state of affairs nor to social narratives. It is also important for environmental ethics to give a justified notion of normativity, which means that ethics has authority and commits the agent. In addition to these, environmental ethics cannot approve of basing a moral theory on scientifically false or socially unsustainable concepts, which will, practically speaking, undermine its scientifically relevant environmental effects. This dilemma seemed to be the reason for many environmental ethicists on both naturalist and constructivist sides to reject the hardwired modes of their own frameworks. Both include problems: the naturalistic fallacy lurks in the evolutionary approach and relativism lurks in the postmodern constructivism. I interpreted their main aspiration to be the conceptual shift to take the relationality of an agent as constitutive for her agency, in sense of both embodied and embedded agency. Both ends criticize the division between nature and nurture in agency.

Interactivity between material and mental, evolutive and social is seen as constitutive for agency and for processes providing action.

NOTES

1. For Midgley's debates with sociobiology, see Midgley 1979, 1985, 2000, 2004. For her criticism against feminists' way of trivializing genetic and intra-bodily determinants of behavior, see Midgley 1978, 1984.

2. Patrick Curry calls a position that opposes both ontologically realist and relativist types of reductionism *relational pluralism*, which finds inspiration from, for example, Barbara Herrnstein Smith, Bruno Latour, William James, and Ludwig Wittgenstein. Curry 2008.

3. Chastened constructionism is used, for instance, by Anna Peterson and constrained constructivism by Katherine Hayles.

4. In case of environmental ethics aspiring to offer practical tools for policy makers to handle the urgent crises, promoting exclusive philosophies is not enough, however coherent and inspiring they may be.

5. Among environmental philosophers there are notable persons who have renounced their credibility as "proper philosophers" to find philosophical alternatives to the common way of thought, such as Richard Routley, Fritjof Capra, and Arne Næss. Even Alfred North Whitehead was at least partly motivated by the awareness of the ecological destructiveness of the modern framework.

6. Whitehead's famous phrase, "The many become one, and are increased by one" (Whitehead 1978, 21) points to the difference between metaphysical holism and relationism.

7. According to Hourdequin and Wong, what is right in the world is always variable, but sensitivity to what each context calls for as a trait is itself not dependent on the context but on something absolute. The question of partiality and impartiality is a question of scale.

PART II

Relational Moral Agency

The interdisciplinary landscape of discussions on the relational understanding of being human or knowing and acting as a human being is diverse and covers approaches drawing from various fields of study, from biology to anthropology, psychology, cognitive science, and social philosophy. Despite their diversity, in common they indicate that individualist and non-embodied account of human agency is questionable under scientific inspection. Not even moral agency can be isolated from the bodily processes or evolutionary history, because such an agent does not exist. This part of the journey consists of several short stops, each focusing on the issue from the perspective of one or another example of selected fields of inquiry which in some cases are partly overlapping. Since moral deliberation and action represent the most unique human activities, explanations of morality are eagerly pursued. Through the interdisciplinary perspectives, hints of the proof will be gathered to dive into the relational shift of the concept of agency. It is worth acknowledging, however, that the referred fields move rapidly on, and any still picture is always limited, and several other fields are left out. But the overview is enlightening, and an interestingly wide range of separate discussions currently focus on one or another aspect of relationality in human being and agency.

Among the topics of continuous debate between scientists and philosophers are those concerning human freedom of will and the source of moral facts, as scientists are often suspicious of nonnatural explanations of morality.[1] In debates about the possibility of free choice, ethicists usually defend individual freedom without vivid critical debate on its description, because it is seen as the prerequisite of autonomy, responsibility, and any ethical demand. A common answer to scientists who explain moral codes by psychological or evolutionary reasons is that scientific facts are explanations of the contingent world, while moral facts are noncontingent, prescriptive facts, and therefore, factual and moral languages should be conceptually distinguished. But such a distinction in fact supposes a moral agent that can overcome factual contingences and isolate her free acts in a way that is scientifically challenged. Distinction is usually made between contingent human nature and free human agency located in certain mental operations considered internal to the mind and detachable from the explanations of human nature. However, according to current understanding, bodily processes as well as external material and social factors play profound roles in the core mental processes constituting human moral agency. Mind and cognition are profoundly embodied, which philosophers need to take seriously (e.g., Lakoff and Johnson 1999; Gallagher 2005; Rowlands 2010). But because of the complex and dynamic interactivity of both body and mind, neither reductionist nor dualist accounts are plausible. The question to which this part seeks preliminary answers asks what is distinctive for considering moral agency as relational.

If there are convincing explanations that the processes of mind are embodied and interactively constituted in connection with external material, social, and cultural events, such explanations not only concern contingent facts about the human agent but also the very understanding of what it is to deliberate or act as a moral agent. Explanations that change the idea of what it is to make moral decisions also influence theories of moral conduct. We cannot escape the fact that the concept of relational agency may have philosophical implications that are not easy for ethics. But I am convinced that they are far from destructive for ethics—or humanity. Although agencies emerging from interactive processes challenges the modern idea of isolated, untouched, free agents, it also prevents hard determinism and reductive ethics. A relational account of agency also calls into question the exclusion of nonhuman entities from the moral community. If ecological dynamics are constitutive for agency, even moral reasoning, autonomy, and the ability to set moral ends are engaged in ecological relationships. Ethics that is concerned about the ability of humankind to solve environmental problems should not dismiss the mechanisms of cooperation constitutive for human moral agency.

NOTES

1. It is worth noticing that although Kant importantly criticized the idea of achieving moral knowledge by pure moral reason which cannot be detached from the limits of human nature, he at the same time strengthened the idea of the unique, detached, and isolated nature of human moral agency by focusing on the moral role of the freedom of autonomous will.

Chapter 5

Being Relational

RELATIONAL INHERITANCE

In this chapter I shall introduce examples of arguments in favor of context sensitivity in human evolution, social cognition, the embodied and extended mind theses, and the idea of place-based ethics. Taken as perspectives on philosophical anthropology they elucidate the role of various interactions for biology, psychological development, cognitive operations, and moral capacities of a human agent. Common to researchers who work on these perspectives is an awareness of the complexity of natural human processes. Some also seek a synthesis between biological, eco-social, and cultural factors to explain their coevolution. Together the various arguments give an overview of the range of discussions, according to which human agency is generated and developed through relational processes. My unique question is whether they provide support for the hypothesis that to conceive of moral agency as embodied and bound to ecological and social relationships does not imply debunking ethics or moral responsibility.

Evolutionary explanations of morality used by hardwired naturalists are grounded either in reciprocal altruism (altruistic behavior leads to evolutionary gains through reciprocal responses by others) or inclusive fitness through kin selection (although I lose, some of my kin gain). These evolutionary approaches are criticized because of their genocentric view of inheritance. An alternative route to define morality emphasizes the complex development of human nature and agency. Among the classical theories representing the systemic approach to evolution are developmental systems theory (further DST; see Oyama 1985; Oyama, Griffiths, and Grey 2001a)[1] which focuses on relational ontogeny, and niche construction theory (further NCT; see Laland, Matthews, and Feldman 2016) which emphasizes ecological inheritance. In the background there is the notion of the epigenetic regulation of gene expression. According to both, genomes are activated and regulated not only by genetic determination, but by cellular processes, which also include various signals from both internal and external environments. These "nongenetic" influences are sometimes generational. Epigenetic evolution is thus not just about passing genes on to the inheritor under the selective pressure of the environment, but also about ways to read and express the genes that are transmitted. In a sense, information acquiring can also be placed on the level of ontogeny.

In contrast to overemphasized genocentrism, DST and NCT thus argue that nature and nurture are integrated in developmental systems in an interactive way: the ontogenic information required by evolution, for instance, is neither in the genes nor in the environment alone, but evolutionary changes result from constructive interactions between various elements (Oyama, Griffiths, and Grey 2001b, 4). Complex interactivities and mechanisms of ecological dynamics play a decisive role in inheritance together with genes. According to DST, the disjunction between genes and the environment, nature and nurture, or form and matter is unjustified, but instead of simply replacing disjunction by conjunction with genes and the environment, their connections should be seen as systemic and complex.[2] NCT extends this to the broader systems, such as populations and ecological structures.

Despite also being an independent theory, NCT is an umbrella concept for various types of theories that bridge the biological and cultural sciences. Broadly speaking, it argues for the dynamic coevolution of genetic and nongenetic factors, also called ecological inheritance. Organisms and their ecological niches are intimately interactive and interdependent: one-directional causation should be replaced by "reciprocal causation." By claiming that "niches are themselves part of the evolutionary process, so that an interactionist theory replaces an externalist theory" the idea of ecological inheritance is placed side by side with the genetic and cultural inheritance, possibly leading to more rapid adaptation than with evolution by selection (Deane-Drummond 2014, 220; Kendal, Tehrani, and Odling-Smee 2011, 786; also Laland, Matthews, and Feldman 2016, 192–96). A definitive feature of niche construction is that there are "organism-induced changes in selection pressures in environments" (Laland, Matthews & Feldman 2016, 195). It thus acknowledges the critical role of nongenetic inheritance: an organism or group as involved in the process of nongenetic inheritance also influence genetic inheritance (Kendal, Tehrani, and Odling-Smee 2011; Sterelny 2001, 337).[3] Social cooperation has been a vital component of the niche in early human societies, but the role of human influence has substantially increased through cultural development, industrialization, and environmental manipulation (Deane-Drummond 2014, 222). If the influence of an organism in the niche construction can modify the selection of human genes, humanity as well as the capacities of agency are mutually interconnected with ecological, social, and cultural contexts that form a "niche" for the construction and process of agency (Rowlands 2005, 7).

Although the idea of the influence of an organism is not clearly argued from the philosophical point of view, it seems to refer to the way systemic approach changes the notions of causation and freedom: neither is isolatable from the systemic processes. This, in consequence, refers to the relative freedom included in the natural evolutionary processes through the interactive webs of agency. In this sense, systemic approaches to evolution also can be seen to bring about a nontraditional perspective to the actions a moral agent should be seen as responsible for: this includes how responsibility about the future development of human as well as other forms of life is addressed in everyday life actions, "moral" and "nonmoral" alike, through which environments are influenced, even if they would not have direct consequences to any living organism. Scholars today widely agree that the interactive cooperation between genes, environments, and the organism's own activity is crucial in explanations of selection. In cases of the most complex features required for moral agency, such as reasoning, the emotional capacity for intersubjectivity, and sociality, previous cultural processes and behavioral and symbolic systems seem to play an especially influential role (Laland, Matthews, and Feldman 2016, 197; Kendal, Tehrani, and Odling-Smee 2011; Tomasello 2009, 1–47; Deane-Dummond 2014, 124–52, 196–234).

These examples of evolutionary science point to some relevant ideas for the discussion of human moral agency. First, the evolution and development of organisms (humans included) complexly depend also on the actions of other organisms (humans included) with which they share ecological niches. Interaction with other organisms may thus modify even complex human abilities, such as cognition and capacities of reasoning. Therefore, human agency, (and not just human "nature") seems to be intimately interconnected with the ecological webs even at the evolutionary level. Second, since humans indirectly modify their own inheritance—willingly or not—through niche construction by culturally learned habits and symbolic systems, these habits and symbols should be of moral interest from the perspective of future humanity. Accordingly, conceptions of morally relevant actions, as well as the criteria for the moral standing of nonhuman organisms, should be critically evaluated and revised. Third, human uniqueness, namely features that have made our species extremely powerful, has to do with the way social interactivity and cooperation have been exploited in human communities: from quite an early stage of evolution, humans had more nongenetic ways of transmitting information and engineering the environment than other species, and they formed extremely cooperative groups and communities with shared goals (Tomasello 2014, 191–92; Sterelny 2001, 338, 334–35). To be sure, this explains why humans have had the possibility of subjugating other species, though it does not justify human supremacy.

It is worth noticing that, in addition to the discussion in evolutionary science, the interest in evolutionary mechanisms has also recently been vivid among cognitive scientists and philosophers of mind. Their focus, as well, is in the role of interactivity. Relational tones have been developed in several contexts, perhaps most clearly in theories of embodied mind and enactivism. In their seminal work *The Embodied Mind: Cognitive Science and Human Experience* (1991) Francisco Varela, Eleanor Rosh, and Evan Thompson reformulated the post-Darwinian idea of "evolution by natural drift" by considering the differences in interactive relationality as a source of difference in development. According to them, the basic unit of evolution is a network "capable of a rich repertoire of self-organizing configurations," which triggers change in the viable trajectories without specifying it. The mode of change is "the interwoven (nonoptimal) result of multiple levels of subnetworks of selected self-organized repertoires." Inner and outer causal factors are "coimplicative," because "organism and medium mutually specify each other" (Varela et al. 1991, 196–97). The receptiveness of genes and the environment and their mutual interaction shows how physical "objects" play a role in the subjectivity in question (Preston 2003, 50–53, 107. Cf. Searle 2004, 108–10, 113–18). The dichotomy between what constitutes the "active" subject and what constitutes the "passive" object of an act is conceptually questioned. Rather than talking about objects, it might be more correct to talk about "partners" in order to appreciate their active role in one's subjectivity. Replacing the adaptationist outline with relational mechanisms of evolution has implications in the evolutionary explanations of cognitive and other mental operations, and consequently in the conceptions of human agency and morality which these explanations influence. I shall return to enactivism later in this chapter.

MORALITY FROM ULTRA-SOCIALITY

Sociobiologist E. O. Wilson predicted in the 1970s that a philosophical approach to morality will be replaced by evolutionary psychological explanations. He believed that it could be empirically revealed how biologically adapted emotive centers in the brain guide moral intuitions (Wilson 1975, 563). According to sociobiology, moral norms are sociocultural correlates of biologically evolved behavior and, thus, are derived from biological evolution. Even moral pluralism is thought to be explicable by evolved reactions of the brain to different situations. Although criticism of the denial of contingent factors in moral philosophy is justified, explanations of morality put forward by sociobiology contain serious problems due to the confusion between evolutionary explanations and philosophical concepts. However, despite the evident problems of sociobiology and evolutionary psychology, for instance, empirical explanations can valuably enlighten the nature of human moral agency, which as such should be distinguished from the question of evolved moral norms. According to the evolutionary biologist Francisco J. Ayala, the expression of moral behavior is natural for humans, "because their biological makeup determines the presence of three necessary conditions for ethical behavior: the ability to anticipate the consequences of one's own actions, the ability to make value judgments, and the ability to choose between alternative courses of action" (Ayala 2010, 316, 322–24). Cognitive and psychological abilities and tendencies are prerequisites of a moral culture. Therefore, in order to critically evaluate moral theories, it is important to understand how these abilities to deal with moral issues or tendencies of commitment function.

Evolutionary anthropologists, developmental and social psychologists, and cognitive scientists have recently targeted criticism against individualistic conceptions of the mind and agency. The evolutionary anthropologist and developmental psychologist Michael Tomasello, who scrutinizes the psychological backgrounds of human agency, is one of those who compellingly highlights the role of interrelatedness for moral agency. Based on the comparison between the psychology of infants and chimpanzees, he argues that the unique feature of the human species is that we are not just social but ultra-social animals. Moral agency is a sign of human sociality evolved from mutualistic cooperation, in which interactions amongst humans are beneficial to all. Interdependency causes ultra-social mutualism and explains how sociality takes form in our cognition, moral intuitions, and behavior. It changes social behavior, modifies cognitive processes, and explains much of the need to construct moral theories and find objectivity (Tomasello 2014, 192–93; see also Tomasello 2016).

Tomasello's studies show that many of the crucial features of human cognition and moral agency are explainable by capacities based on human ultra-sociality. Human agency requires capacities to understand others' intentions, share attention, and form joint intentions with others in order to make changes in the world, and to identify oneself to the collective in order to enforce norms and conform to normative standards. According to Tomasello, two ecological changes in the evolutionary history of the human species forced humans to collaborate as equals, and later to develop group-minded and collective intentionality. The first was caused by the scarcity of resources attainable for separate individuals, by which collaboration became necessary for survival. Humans learned to perceive each other as equals when taking part in joined activities. Joined intentionality evolved because humans could not manage without joint action. Psychologically the adaptively proximate mechanisms were care and sympathy, which, in turn, are crucial for the development of distributive justice—found only in human agency. The meaning of collaboration for survival also entailed that the capability to form joint goals, a commitment to these goals, and trust in others became important. According to Tomasello, even at an early age, young children conceive of themselves as partners of agency with joint goals and attention, and hence they care for each other's welfare. The second important change in evolutionary history was caused by demographic factors: competition between *ad hoc* collaborative foraging groups turned into tighter social groups and increasing population size. They, again, turned into tribal organization, meaning that small active groupings together form a cultural supergroup (Tomasello 2014; 2016, 123–37). Ultra-social humans became group-minded: they identified themselves with a certain culture, actively conformed to others, and enforced social norms on others. These features are unique to human sociality. Imitation skills developed active conformity to coordinate activities with in-group strangers, and to display one's group identity and commitment, revealing one's trustworthiness and knowledgeableness as a partner. Human beings need to be accepted by the group, which binds them to actively identify with their cultural group, to feel collective pride, shame, and guilt, and to care for the group as an independent entity (Tomasello 2014, 191–92). The relational nature of humans led, first, to the conceptualization of self-other equivalence, and later, to equal treatment of the others on the base of "deservingness" of equivalent collaborators (Tomasello 2016, 150).

The main implications of human ultra-sociality are, according to Tomasello, three: First, humans can conceptualize the situation from various social perspectives, which means that they have a sense of "objectivity." Second, humans are somehow collectively self-reflective so that they can make conclusions about others' intentional states, as well as their own. Third, humans are capable of social self-monitoring from the normative perspectives and standards of the group and of others. This can be seen as the basis for human norms of rationality. The big difference between ape and human social interaction and cognitive processes is that whereas for great apes it is a matter of instrumental rationality aiming at individual gains, for humans it is about acting on "shared intentionality" and understanding the world "together as a kind of plural subject." Humans came to commit to cooperative partnership by becoming responsive to non-instrumental normative reasons. The development of the features that depict the specific nature of human moral rationality, including self-regulation and autonomy, are thus explainable by the relational nature of humans (Tomasello 2016, 143–48). Without such skills of collective intentionality, central features of morality and self-regulation, such as "the reflective endorsement of moral decisions and a full-fledged sense of guilt," self-regulation would not have emerged (Tomasello 2016, 152).

Tomasello considers this as crucial evidence for his claim that right and wrong as moral judgments arose from the social norms and cultural practices in a "moral-structural" way. The self-regulation of a collective partly generates from strategic (instrumental) reasons, but not totally: it also has a moral dimension. The self-regulation by the plural agent becomes a part of the moral identity of its participants through them being relationally interconnected. So, the moral structure among the members must be based on "self-other equality" in order for collective self-regulation to commit and obligate (Tomasello 2014, 192; 2016, 142–47, 151). Contrary to mainstream evolutionary explanations, Tomasello argues that this relational structure of self-regulation "constitutes a new kind of cooperative rationality based not only on instrumental success but also on a sense of fairness in one's partner or compatriot to live up to our shared ideals" (Tomasello 2016, 152).[4] Equality and impartiality are thus naturally understandable through the relationally structured plural subject. One interesting point here is that the conceptualization of equality does not require (biological or mental) similarity, but rather commitment to collective collaboration, which makes the partners "equally important" (Tomasello 2016, 160–63). This notion refers to the relational nature of humanity, which is entirely natural, but provides features that depict the exceptional type of reasoning required for moral agency. If the cooperative relationality of human agency is an empirically valid notion, it can form a conceptual link between natural explanations and the authority of moral reasons for action.

Tomasello's theory is interesting not just because it explains collective and relational backgrounds of agency in terms of evolutionary psychology but particularly because it gives empirical support for the philosophical importance of interdependence, the collective mind, and joint intentionality. It especially supports the two levels of collective agency introduced by Raimo Tuomela, namely "I-mode" and "we-mode" agency, in accord with Tomasello's notions of the two steps in evolution, and the two types of "joint" and "collective" intentions. Tomasello's idea also shows that human morality "represents the internalized interactive processes—both cognitive and motivational—that structure human's ultra-cooperative ways of living" (Tomasello 2014, 193; cf. Tuomela 2013). I consider that the facts concerning human agency—such as the interdependency behind the tendency in human morality to deal with distributive justice, and the group-mindedness behind the tendency to conform to the norms as an end in itself—can also enlighten the nature of moral theories. However, norms and conventions may vary from one culture to another. Tomasello's view differs from most other evolutionary explanations of morality in that it does not overrule conceptually autonomous moral reasons for decisions (see Tomasello 2016, 141–42, 160).

It should be noted that Tomasello's studies only deal with groups of somehow equivalent individuals. This does not, however, rule out the fact that group-mindedness may well be addressed to groups of various kinds of members, including nonhumans. In fact, this seems quite empirically evident, because human social groups are always heterogeneous (including infants, aged men, and disabled people). The dead members of the group, and often also (at least domestic) animals, some plants, and rocks, as well as parts of the landscape can be counted as cultural groups. The ecosystems and land-scapes with which the history of cultural groups is tied are often respected as bearers of moral norms, too (Tomasello 2016). Norms, as well as knowledge, develop in dialogue with the nonhuman members of the ecological system in which they emerge. The fact that norms of rationality and moral standards are grounded in processes of cooperation can also hold for heterogenous cooperative groups, including members that cannot take part in self-monitoring or mutual imitation as human partners do.

The increasing volume of research on animal morality resonates with these recent empirical approaches to the social and ecological functions of moral agency. Similarities between human and animal behavior do not demote human agents, nor do they reduce their agency to determined biological facts, instead, they mark the mechanisms by which earthly modes of agency function and develop. However, studies on animal morality disprove the presumption that moral agency conceptually requires attributes that are uniquely human. Such attributes may be found beyond our species. The differences between the agency of humans and other animals are not due to any one specific character, but more to the complexity of social relations and the physico-mental operations we perform (for more about animal morality, see Rowlands 2012; Korsgaard 2012, 2018; Nussbaum 2023; de Waal 2005; de Waal 2006).

EXTENDED AND INTERACTIVE MIND

During the last centuries, philosophy and the natural sciences have mainly respected each other's autonomy, even to an unnecessary extent that has caused, for instance, counterproductive separation between fields of inquiry and the illusion of objectivity of scientific knowledge. As the fortress of human uniqueness and the apple of philosophers' eyes, moral agency is traditionally considered untouched by natural sciences, and attempts to conceptually bridge human nature and human moral agency have mainly suffered from provocatively reductionist tendencies. Therefore, new directions in the philosophy of mind and new empirical information about human cognition that turn focus to the complex meshes of relationships behind cognitive processes, consciousness, reasoning, and even intentional actions, are welcome. Human morality as a phenomenon, and motivation of people to take care of others or to act in accordance with social conduct, owes a debt to biological sociability, bodily structures, and ecological facilities, in addition to the social practices, sensitivity to impartiality (the ability, in principle, to widen the moral instinct to one's kin to everyone), and the ability to understand principles and formulate theories that also inform morality. None of these factors nor their interconnectedness should be ignored when trying to redirect trends of human behavior in relation to the environment. Therefore, it is promising that some of the most influential recent trends in cognitive science, such as theories of embodied mind, enactivism, and extended mind, argue for the relational and interactive nature of mental processes. They seem to offer steady scientific support for aspirations of environmental ethicists to revise presuppositions of humanist ethics and to understand moral agency as relational, as well as the human moral self as a self-in-relationship.

Cartesian philosophy of mind and its metaethical implications are among the specific targets of criticism for environmental philosophers who criticize the traditional modern framework of ethics. Besides the already mentioned critical strategies, environmentalists interested in philosophy of cognitive science, such as Mark Rowlands, who himself is also philosopher of cognitive science and defender of so called 4E cognition (see below), and Christopher Preston, who draws on the work of cognitive scientist Mark Johnson, form an interesting group of critics. Rowlands argues, for instance, against Cartesian interactionism, which holds that mental operations do not actually interact with the body or other external realities. He argues instead that the mind is intimately connected with the body and with external reality (Rowlands 1999, 2001, 2003). This aligns with Johnson's philosophy of embodiment, according to which the complexity of human nature can only be explained by such an account of the embodied mind that consists of multiple nonreductive levels of explanation (Johnson 1987, 2007, 2008). These lines of thought seem not only scientifically plausible but also philosophically clear in contrast to the idea of the disembodied mind.

Although few philosophers currently regard themselves as Cartesians, the Cartesian problem of the interaction of mind and body has remained a central question for the philosophy of mind since Descartes. According to Cartesian internalism, the mind is interiority, a ghost in a machine. This is widely criticized as an environmentally destructive conception. Descartes did not see how thinking could be governed by the mechanical principles that govern the physical world. Thinking was an activity of a subject directed toward the objects to be thought of. But he was skeptical concerning the possibilities of overcoming the gap between the thinking activity and the external world. Extreme skepticism led him to the idea of the mind as interiority: mental operations are thought to be located inside bodily individuals—like psychic monads in the physical world (Rowlands 2003, 12–19, 225).[5] Compared to the Cartesian view, conceiving of cognitive systems by their operational closure, as enactivism argues, implies a conceptual shift in the understanding of cognitive operations and their relation to other mechanisms in the world.

Although current theorizing about mind often denies Cartesian dualism, it usually sticks to internalism. This especially holds for the common understanding of noncognitive operations of moral agency after Kant: however misguided human reason might be (the Kantian criticism of pure reason), freedom of will remains untouched by bodily or external interferences in the Kantian concepts of the moral agent and autonomy. A Kantian moral person has a core that remains internal to the mental sphere of an individual. By peeling away features that we cannot trust while hunting for the moral truth, the remaining core of the moral person becomes strong and independent, untouched by misleading influences. Cartesian internalism in a way is crystallized in the Kantian concept of the moral agent.

Internalism consists of ontological, epistemological, and axiological components. According to ontological internalism, a mental phenomenon spatially located inside the subject (S) that experiences it or undergoes it (the location claim), and also the possession of a mental phenomenon by S, does not depend on any feature external to S (the possession claim). Epistemological internalism results from a skeptical argument: if the existence of the objects of knowledge (such as my body) is doubtful, but the existence of the thinking thing is definite, then the thinking thing and the object are distinct from each other. Thinking lacks any real connection with the objects it is directed toward. Even though the argument for certainty does not work as an argument for dualism (for there can still be a continuity of things that I am not aware of), it works as an argument for internalism: each subject knows her or his mind first and best. Axiological internalism, which is grounded on ontological and epistemological internalism, is an influential presupposition of subsequent metaethical theories, most notably David Hume's. According to axiological internalism, the source of value is either in the inner activity of a monad-like subjective mind, or in the mechanistically governed physical world. Since the mind is, for ontological reasons, an individual issue, moral concepts must also have their foundation either in individual minds or in the determinist external world, but not in their interaction. The only alternative to the subjectivist value theory for an ethical theory that adopts Cartesian internalism is, therefore, the objectivist value theory. Hume's decision was to separate factual from value properties, so that factual properties are objectively in the world, external to the subjective mind, while values are internal: Through sensory experiences one can describe the facts of the crime of murder, but the wrongness of murder can only be explained by subjective psychological states and feelings. It should be noted that the arguments dichotomizing subjectivism and objectivism imply internalism as a presupposition (for a closer analysis, see Rowlands 2003, 13, 27–31).

In order to prevent the necessity of dichotomizing between subjectivism and objectivism, Rowlands offers an externalist counterpart to internalism. He argues that knowing, as well as valuing, should be located to the relationships by which the subject's operations are constituted rather than in a private mind. Both objectivism and subjectivism are implausible from the point of view of the currently valid scientifical understanding of mental operations: "objectivism makes the gap between value and the valuing too great" but "subjectivism . . . makes the gap . . . too small" (Rowlands 2003, 210–11). However, the distinction between subjectivism and objectivism can be diminished by a third, relational option based on a scientifically evidenced notion of the mental processes providing agency. Externalism is related to extended mind thesis, which belongs to the group of theories in cognitive science that are often referred to as theories of 4E cognition theories.

Relational theories of mind have been developed in several contexts, but perhaps most clearly they are defended by theories, or theses, of 4E cognition (for an overview, see Newen, de Bruin, and Gallagher 2018; Varela, Thompson, and Rosh 1991). According to these four theses beginning with e, cognition is *embodied*, *embedded*, *enactive*, and *extended*, and perhaps also *affective*. Discussion on 4E cognition was activated by Francisco Varela, Eleanor Rosch, and Evan Thompson (1991), and it has grown into a full multidisciplinary approach in the intersection of philosophy and cognitive neuroscience. According to the basic claims of 4E cognition, cognitive processes are embodied by bodily processes, which means that they are either partly constituted by or party dependent on these processes, and correspondingly, they are embodied by extrabodily processes (Clark 1998; Gallagher 2005). In the strong form this means that cognitive processes are extended to the world (Clark and Chalmers 1998; Chalmers 2018; Clark 2007; Rowlands 2010; de Jaegher, di Paolo and Adophs 2016), while in the weak form they are considered just as embedded. Enactive cognition refers to cognition "*enacted* in the sense that it involves an active engagement in and with an agent's environment" (Newen, Bruin, and Gallagher 2018, 6; see also Noë 2004; Hutto and Myin 2013).[6] Cognition also involves affections (Colombetti 2017).

According to 4E theories in general, cognition cannot be explained without addressing the complex dynamic interactivity between the brain and the body and external physical, social, and cultural environments. Cognition takes place in the interaction *between an organism and its environment*, which means, especially according to extended mind thesis, that it is not restricted to the intracranial processes nor is it under one's skin: the mind extends to the world beyond an individual (e.g., Rowlands 2009, 57–62). Among 4E cognition theses, enactivism is the most wide-ranging, radical, and most debated. According to it, cognitive systems do not operate by representation, but instead they "enact a world as a domain of distinctions that is inseparable from the structure embodied by the cognitive system" (Varela et al. 1991, 139–40). Alva Noë exemplifies the interactive nature of enactive perception by visual sensation that works through anticipations of how the experience would change with certain types of action. He writes: "As you move with respect to the cube, you learn how its aspect changes as you move—that is, you encounter its visual potential. To encounter its visual potential is thus to encounter its actual shape. . . . To experience the figure as a cube, on the basis of how it looks, is to understand *how* its look changes as you move" (Noë 2004, 77).

From the point of view of agency, the emphasis of enactivism on the relational, interactive nature of mental processes conceived as dynamic and mutually influential is especially important: mental processes involve external operations which take the form of *action* (Rowlands 2009, 56). Cognition is not just interaction, but by mutual dynamics the interactants are also constitutive of each other: "living beings and their environments stand in relation to each other through mutual specification or codetermination" (Varela et al. 1991, 198). The processes that are crucial for consciousness are not "one-way causal-explanatory relationship between internal neural representational systems and the contents of consciousness" but a "two-way or reciprocal relationship between embodied conscious states and local neuronal activity" (Varela and Thompson 2001, 418). The dynamic two-way interactivity refers to cognitive processes as participatory sense-making (see de Jaegher and di Paolo 2007; Fuchs and de Jaegher 2009). The interactive brain hypothesis (IBH) defended in recent social neuroscience by, for instance, Hanne de Jaegher and Ezequiel di Paolo, argues that "social interaction processes play enabling and constitutive roles in the development and in the ongoing operation of brain mechanisms" (di Paolo and de Jaegher 2012, 2). This implies that an isolated human brain does not function properly: processes that occur in the brain are "not fully constitutive of social cognition" but require additional events that "involve relations between the brain and (parts of) the rest of the world" (de Jaegher, di Paolo, and Adolphs 2016, 2). The idea of enactive cognition considers human mental processes as intimate parts of the dynamic world, not detached from the external partners or the natural world that is considered as a system consisting of actively collaborating elements, together with whom we form ourselves and how the world appears to us.

Giovanna Colombetti emphasizes that enactive cognition is also an affective issue, which also highlights the ethical relevance of enactivism. An organism is "a network of interrelated processes that has to work continually in order to maintain itself, to counteract the unstable and decaying tendencies of its component processes" (Colombetti 2018, 574–75). This vulnerability or precarious nature of the living system makes it seek continual interactions with its environments. The organism cannot be, by definition, indifferent to its environment: "it touches, strikes or affects the organism as significant" (Colombetti 2015). This means that the agency of an agent is intimately something we share with our environments and with all the others we interact with and co-construct our environments. Participatory sensemaking is not only a cognitive but also an affective phenomenon. This makes enactivism ever more relevant for moral theories. According to Colombetti, affectivity is not a distinct part "that merely 'interacts' with other, non-affective parts" of the mind, for instance, in moral deliberation. Without affectivity, "we do not have a mind any more." Affectivity is a capacity to be "touched" or affected by something, which is required for things to matter. It thus entails "a sensibility, interest, and concern" (Colombetti 2018, 574).

According to enactivism, the basis of cognition is biological, and cognitive structure is basically common to all living organisms from a cell to a human being. Although this interestingly connects enactivism with the aspirations of environmental ethics, it has been almost completely ignored in environmental philosophy (Werner and Kielkowicz-Werner 2021). Even simple organisms are cognitive systems that also have a certain level of sense-making activity and adaptive autonomy in virtue of their organization. However, this adaptive autonomy refers to the "interdependence of the constituent processes of the living system," while autonomy of sense makers refers to their self-organization under precarious circumstances in which they participate in each other's sense-making (Colombetti 2018, 574; see also Varela et al. 1991, 175; Thompson 2007; de Jaegher 2018). What is especially notable here is that all cognitive systems are autonomous and, thus, importantly dynamical and self-organizing processes that are not restricted to an individual mind but extended (Colombetti 2018, 578–79). The subjects of autonomy are not defined as individual human or animal beings but as cognitive systems, which are not necessarily restricted to an individual mind or body. Knowledge construction and other mental operations should then be described as cooperative processes between an organism and its environments and other agents. According to radical interpretation, this means that when we *think together* with others, which is somewhat reminiscent of feminist epistemology. An epistemic community is part of me as I am part of it (McCraw 2020, 351, 366; cf. Code 2006a; Cheney 1989, 126, 129; Haraway 1988, 578, 592–93).

The way in which interactivity is emphasized in enactivism denies the modal distinction between cognition and action (Colombetti and Torrance 2009). Cognition is itself active and responds to the world and awakens the world by directing attention. This offers an especially interesting non-speculative perspective on the interface of freedom and nature and on the question of autonomy. An enactive notion of agency that denies the traditional isolation of freedom from nature entails conceptual revisions in intentionality and autonomy, besides cognitive processes in traditional sense (di Paolo 2009; Thompson and Stapleton 2009; Thompson 2011; see also chapter 7). Intentionality has been described as relational by, for instance, Mark Rowlands. One reason why reductionism in regard to agency has been popular is the belief that otherwise we should see something magical happen in the brain when a person intends. But Rowlands argues that it is not crucial what we find in brain because intentionality is determined by "the relations in which the inner items stand to things outside them." Intentionality is a "disclosing activity" in which processes in the head and (in part) also outside comprise operations that "make information available . . . by transforming the status of information in the structures from present to available, or by also augmenting that information" (Rowlands 2018, 350–51).

Through interaction, both partners become influenced. As said before, in participatory sensemaking the autonomy of sensemakers, whether they are simple organisms or human beings, refers to their self-organization under the precarious circumstances in which they interact. Hence, humans share with others the vulnerability of self-organization, and their autonomy is thus constantly in danger of harm. The feedback loops generated by mutual interaction between action and cognition are extremely interesting from an environmental viewpoint. Namely, they alter the moral status of many everyday life actions that direct our cognitive orientation, or even perceptional processes. Everyday life actions by which we participate in sensemaking with our cognitive objects, or should we say partners, may have feedback effects on our own cognitive structures and intentional mental processes, and hence, on our very agency.[7] The medium of feedback influencing the ways our cognitive structure is organized may be cultural or material by nature, such as eating habits, the built environment, carbon levels in the atmosphere, financial systems, landscapes, microbiomes, or modified ecosystems. When functioning as extensions of the consciousness, actions by which they are modified also modify consciousness. This kind of relationality heavily blurs the border between epistemic, or scientific, and moral agency. Ethics appears as a skill and it is a condition of knowledge, too.

The picture of human being outlined in the results of this kind of cognitive science resembles the picture that is outlined in the recent manifestations of relational environmental ethics, especially in ecofeminism. In contrast to projects that focus on the *inter*active relationships between human and nonhuman beings that as such are separate entities, enactivism and ecofeminist relationality focuses on the *intra*-activity constitutive for each participant of interaction. So, the focus is on the process of interaction rather than the interactants. An influential manifestation of this kind of view is Donna Haraway's

Staying with the Trouble: Making Kin in the Chthulucene (2016). According to Haraway, different kinds of entities live in constant mutual interaction that form constitutive networks for what each kind is, and this blurs our own nature and the borders of self. At the early stage, she used the metaphor of the cyborg, which has been replaced in recent works by *humus*. In her narratives, "human" becomes replaced by "humus," which refers to something that constantly becomes something new in the nexus of intra-action with others. Instead of posthuman(ism) she uses a metaphor of "compost" to illustrate this process of mutual co-shaping of the constituents internal to what is considered human (Haraway 2016, 11, 32, 40, 55, 97, 138; cf. 1991). In the agency of humus, external and internal activities cannot be entirely separated. Such an agency could be depicted as embodied, embedded, extensional, and enacted.

If at least some of the explanations given by theories of 4E cognition hold true for the processes that are fundamental for responsibility, such as intentionality and autonomy, the ramifications for ethics, especially environmental ethics, are notable. There are at least two challenges for the modern humanist concept of agency: First, the relational embodiment of mind and agency stipulates a reconsideration of the concepts of the body and external organisms or environments as just objects. Second, it must be taken seriously that the operations by which human agency is composed should be located in a multilevel web of interactive relationships. Mental processes are both internally and externally relational, and in fact, internality and externality are mutually inseparable. The body, for example, includes multiple active "external" partners, such as the continuously changing communities of microbes without which our body or brain would not function as they do. Reasoning and action involve nonneural activity both within and outside the agent. Third, the relational notion of agency based on enactivism rejects not only dualism but also reductionism of any kind: emergence of the mental operations—by which moral agency is possible—depend on genuine interactivity, which is not compatible with traditional monism. Due to the fundamental role of the interactivity for the very being of both body and mind, cognition and action, or life and consciousness, enactivism opposes both naturalist and constructivist reductionisms as well as standard Cartesian interactionism.

In their pioneering paper on an enactive approach to ethics, Giovanna Colombetti and Steve Torrance (2009) argue that enactivism requires a turn of focus in ethics: It encourages "focus on the ethical qualities of the interaction itself." According to their inter-(en)active ethics, "the ethical content or valuation of a given situation" emerges "as much from the interaction of the participants as from the autonomous decision-making or original authorship of the participants themselves." Interactions can also have ethical qualities regarding their ability to enable or constrain participation or autonomy. Social interaction that we participate in is, "to its very bones, an ethical communal sense-making or value-making," which they call "the negotiative dance of participatory sense-making" (Colombetti and Torrance 2009, 523). An enactive approach to ethics thus calls for concern for the fact that interactivity is not just a constitutive issue for our cognition but also an ethical issue. According to Colombetti and Torrance, an interactive turn can offer "an important new approach to ethics, that could . . . be seen as taking a place alongside the various primary ethical 'paradigms' that it is common to distinguish within ethical theory—namely, utilitarian (or consequentialist) theories, deontological (or duty-based or 'Kantian') theories, and virtue-based theories." However, instead of replacing the other "paradigms,"they suggest that it could be seen "as supplementing other accounts, as making good some deficiencies and silences in those accounts" (Colombetti and Torrance 2009, 516–17). In any case, the novel type of ethical understanding of particular and personal relationships—especially between dissimilar partners—provides a valuable theoretical backing for renewing the place of environmental relationships in ethics. It heavily supports claims for interpersonal and environmental care and caring practices as well as the personalized (non-impartial) look at the subjective life and ethical capacities of various subjects of cognition. (For a comparison between enactive and care ethics, see Urban 2014, 2015b.)

AGENCY IN PLACE AND THE CARE FOR IT

The embodiment of mind and agency stipulates a reconsideration of the concept of the body as just an object and as an entity that is restricted by the bounds of one's skin. Mark Johnson outlines five dimensions of human embodiment: the body as biological organism, the ecological body, the phenomenological body, the social body, and the cultural body, each of which constitutes its own level of explanation for bodily human agency. According to Johnson, the human body consists of relations with the full extent of the various environments: biological, ecological, experienced, social, and cultural. Each of the dimensions focus on the interaction between something called "the individual" and its "environment." Instead of being passive objects, bodies are seen as cooperative partners of the socio-ecological system through which we perceive and transform ourselves, and in the complexity of which mental operations are embodied (Johnson 2007; Johnson 2008, 164–67). According to Johnson, body and mind are not separate things, meaning that mental operations emerge from the body, but the body is not reductively physical. All human meaning, understanding, and reasoning are embodied. The capacity for reasoning and abstract conceptualization is largely linked with the imaginative structure of conceptual metaphor, which permits inferential structures of bodily experiences to be primary in making sense of also abstract things. This implies that the truth arises always in human context, relies on embodied meaning, and is relative to values and interests: "the trail of the human serpent is everywhere" (Johnson 2007, 277–80). Therefore, human freedom should be seen as a modest concept: an agent is free in the sense that she can contribute to the situation in a way that transforms it, and through that, herself.

A relational, nonindividualist, and multidimensional view of the body accords with the concept of "place" used in the environmental ethics of place defended, especially, by Mick Smith and Christopher Preston. According to Smith's definition, place is a particular product of some unique combination of social and environmental relations (Smith 2001, 215). The geographical term refers to the view that moral life does not consist of isolated cases for an impartial moral unit to apply universal moral rules, but rather a field in which the agent as a whole is embedded. Place is also an ecological concept: a place consists of certain types of relationships between various entities located in certain landscapes with certain distances, ties, and mutual interactions. Places connect through location and relationships which create meanings for the agent. Preston also argues that a physical landscape may form part of the machinery of the mind, and hence, a landscape should not be seen as entirely exterior to the mind: it participates in our identity and the way we think (Preston 2010, 6). Places are thus explanatory concepts for human agency. It is also an empirical fact that a "sense of place" plays an important role in how people engage in environmental activism: places and the connected meanings give reasons for people to resist environmentally destructive projects, such as mining or building a motorway. People do not necessarily resist such projects because of the fear of toxins, biodiversity loss, or other general harms, but because they feel that the area under threat is somehow "constitutive of who they are" (Preston 2009, 175). Place-based ethics thus supposes a clearly relational view of a human agent. A sense of place is important also from the point of view of ethics: since it binds identities to certain socially and culturally loaded ecological places, it motivates people to act to protect the capabilities of places in a wide sense, and also what constitutes them.

An ethics of place aspires to reconnect moral and physical spaces in a way that questions the modern suppositions about isolated moral agency. There are some similarities between ethics of place and feminist ethics worth comparing. While feminist ethicist Carol Gilligan, when questioning the value of separation and detachment in moral deliberation, asserts the importance of social situation and proximity in ethics (Gilligan 1982), ethics of place highlights the fact that situation and proximity hold not just for the social, cultural, or bodily conditions of the relational agency, but for material, ecological and aesthetic conditions as well. Smith describes the moral architecture of the ethics of place "in a spatiotemporal metaphorics, a discourse of relativity, proximity, dimensionality, distances, volumes, velocity, and so on," but underlines that "moral spaces" should not only be used in the metaphorical sense (Smith 2001, 151). Moral agency is a skill constituted and developed in place-based interactions and, therefore, it is bound to a particular place, where it is born and/or nurtured. Places are environments to be protected and respected for the reason that they help constitute who we are, but they also call for recognition of a plurality of agencies: we cannot occupy another's place (Smith 2001, 185).

A place-based ethics dispels the universal meaning of terms like rights and justice. Since interactions that constitute the agent are not explicitly codified, the norms cannot be either (Smith 2001, 152, 166; cf. a somewhat similar idea in Næss 1979, 238–39). With regard to this idea, environmentalists who focus on relational agency are in line with each other. They prefer virtue, care, or a dialogical approach to ethics as such approaches emphasize characters, tendencies to act, or structures of intentionality rather than separate actions or universal types of deliberation. The development of moral agency rather than the modification of universal static rules, influences most of the normative focus (Sandler 2007, 31; Deane-Drummond 2004). For example, if value construction is bound to the ecological, social, and cultural "places," foundations of valid values always remain tied to the cultural focus of attention. Valid value foundations are thus not necessarily fixed, and environmental values highlight some ecological structures and balances over others in the eco-social system in accordance with the cultural perspective. Ethics should then focus on the mechanisms to develop the conditions of value construction.

The relational view of moral agency implies that the conditions of moral reasoning should be seen as moral capabilities of an agent embedded in factual interactions. This has an interesting further implication: moral capacities being bound to environmental conditions, by which the skills enabling moral reasoning are constructed and enhanced, implies that in order to be moral, we are obligated to take care of these material and structural (ecological) conditions, as well as social and cultural circumstances as constituents of our own responsibility. The example of place-based ethics thus attests that the relational conception of agency maintains, and even justifies, a responsibility for protecting the environment. Such normative obligation emerges from the nature of human reason and moral intention. Maintaining human reasoning and moral skills requires maintaining the capacities of ecosystems and all that colonize them to provide these skills. Identity, intentions, and knowledge resulting from the complex activities in which physical environments are involved, implies that a general obligation to be moral entails particular obligations to the vitality of the physical environment (Preston 2010, 7). We can initially conclude by claiming that environments are constitutive for agency, and by shaping environments we also shape our structures of thought and ways of constructing moral beliefs. The very conditions of morality are, thus, at least partly dependent on the acts by which we as parts of various places shape, design, and manage them.

Moral capabilities thus increase or decrease due to our everyday life activities in the world: through shaping our environment through interactions we shape our sensitivity for various issues, and the very category of what is of moral relevance. The ways an agent pays attention to, cooperates with, and gives space for others to bear meanings when they interact in "participatory sense-making" also modifies how the agent considers herself, her motives, and her moral aims. By care and sensitivity an agent may let these others encourage herself to take various others ever better into consideration in an encompassing way. A claim approached here resembles the one put forward by relational environmental virtue ethics based on Confucianism: "If the environment can shape who we are, it can shape our very interests" (Hourdequin and Wong 2005, 27). I argue that profound recognition of these relational aspects of agency would be of great value for environmental ethics. The interactive nature of mental operations opens new insights into the question of what is possible for moral deliberation, and into the conditions that enable and shape it. The worry has been, however, that emphasis on the embodiment of the moral mind and the embeddedness of the agent would ruin the prerequisites of responsibility, and above all autonomy. Were this threat to be realized, the entire meaning of environmental ethics would be annihilated.

In the light of the examples brought together in this chapter it seems clear that morality as a phenomenon cannot be detached from evolution in which genetic and environmental factors are intertwined, but neither can it be reduced to either genetic/natural or environmental/cultural realities. Strong proposals are also given that cognition and other mental processes as constitutive for human agency should be conceived of as interactivity connecting an organism with its environment and various organisms with each other, which entails a revised concept of agency. Consequently, the question "who are we?" can only be answered by focusing on our webs of interactions by which our very agency is constituted. But these interactions are by no means detached from our own activity, at least if enactivism holds true. In this sense, the future is not determined, although it is not up to free choice either. I also argued that a relational understanding of human agency has ethical implications. First and foremost, it turns the moral focus to the quality of the interactions with various others. Identifying oneself as relational should thus bring about the motivation to appreciate and care for the others constitutive of "what I am." Agency emerges from being committed to various others and taking care of the environments on which one's cognitive and moral abilities are dependent. Since the mutual construction of the very existence of ecological networks is an empirical fact, it is impossible to separate what profits one partner of the network from what profits others. In this sense, identifying oneself as relational also implies care for the factual conditions of life for others as moral duties to oneself.

NOTES

1. The first modification was put forward by Richard Lewontin. See also Laland, Matthews, and Feldman 2016, 192.

2. For example, molecular biologist and feminist Evelyn Fox Keller stresses that a simple conjunction ignores the informing role of the organism's internal environment. Keller 2001, 300.

3. This distinguishes NCT from its relative concept, the extended phenotype, defended, e.g., by Richard Dawkins.

4. Tomasello makes here use of Raimo Tuomela's social ontology. See, e.g., Tomasello 2016, 27.

5. It should be acknowledged, however, that Descartes did not identify "I" or the "mind" with the true man, but only a part of the moral self. See Alanen 2003, 56.

6. Eactivism makes use of phenomenological philosophy, especially Husserl's and Merleau-Ponty's, in interpretating neuroscientific data. See Thompson, E. 2007.

7. For the grounds of the idea in cognitive science, see Fuchs and de Jaegher 2009; Froese and di Paolo 2011; Torrance and Froese 2011; Urban 2014.

Chapter 6

Knowing Relationally

KNOWING IN DIALOGUE, KNOWING IN PLACE

An interesting example of the dialogical understanding of cognitive processes and epistemic trust is the theory of social representation developed in social psychology (see Marková 2016).[1] As a constructivist theory of knowledge, it states that social representations are constantly converted through reinterpretations and re-presentations in the cognitive social activity: cognitive contents emerge and change in dialogical communication. However, studies applying social representation theory to the notion of dialogical rationality usually avoid confusion between social ways of knowing and the issue of truth. The method of exploiting human sociability, or ultra-social animality, in order to get through to some "truth" or "correct action" is an ethically laden mode of interaction, namely a "dialogical sense." Knowing requires communication based on epistemic trust, and such communication has a contractual, moral structure (Marková 2016, 4–5; Marková and Linell 2014a, 219, 231).

Theories about knowing as a mental operation of an individual usually attribute individual thinking with capacities for "objectivity" or "rationality" in an individual. Contrary to this, social representation theory argues that the capacity of an individual to make moral judgments is based on their dialogical capacity of reasoning. Ethics particularly requires dialogical rationality. Pursuing objectivity requires commitment to dialogical processes which, again, requires trust. Inquiries into child development in the field of sociology show that openness to relational communication and the capacity for dialogical reasoning precede the sense of autonomy or other senses relevant for moral deliberation and action (Marková 2016, 5, 128–29; Tomasello 2014). Conversely, actions of trust mark the agent's relationally dependent autonomy. Trust can thus be described as a combination of dependency and autonomy (Ingold, 2022, ch. 4). There are two types of epistemic trust: trust in the agents, who are regarded as autonomous in the sense that they can also cheat, and confidence in other beings and things in the world. In both types, trust implies agentive movements from the one who trusts and seeks to "know." By the acts of epistemic trust, the agents recognize each other as autonomous partners in a nexus in which knowledge is constructed (Cornejo 2014, 240). From the point of view of relational moral agency, it is interesting that, according to social representation theory, the abilities of a human to commit to dialogical relationships are fundamentally body-related experiences. Body-related experiences are behind the openness and commitment to others, which grows into morally laden relationality, and which makes humans capable of learning from, negotiating with, and accepting or rejecting the epistemic trust of others (Marková 2016, 129–30, 143–52; Cornejo 2014; Marková and Linell 2014b; Tomasello 2014, 189–90). These relational features also play a central role in the emergence of autonomy.

Another recent discussion to which social representation theory is connected is the one concerning the links between evolutionary explanations of natural cooperativity and collective rationality, both being grounds for moral conceptualization. As was introduced earlier, Michael Tomasello, for instance, argues that interdependence between individuals partly explains the evolutionary origins of human moral psychology. Unlike many others, Tomasello argues that the evolutionary meaning of interactivity for human moral agency is not just one of motivation to act altruistically but is constitutive for the cognitive structure in which morality emerges. In this sense, human interdependence does not only explain why basically selfish people are motivated to act morally, but also describes the cognitive structure in which the ideas of fairness, equity, and respect emerge. Interactivity explains the origins of cooperative and cultural rationality, which are grounds for conceptualizing moral obligations (Tomasello 2016, 143, 150–51).

Some scholars of collective agency argue that the "we-relationship" depicts the most fundamental experience in the lifeworld and is a prerequisite of epistemic trust (see Tuomela 2012, 2013). According to Carlos Cornejo, it is a dialogical experience in which we verify "the primacy of trust over mistrust or, in effect, the disposition to believe over the disposition to suspect." The we-relationship is a vivid, spatially, and temporally immediate face-to-face situation, "in which I become aware of a fellow human being as a person." An agent is oriented toward the other in a way that he understands the expressions of the other directly. He is with her and follows her actions without constructing descriptions of her beforehand. When such an orientation is reciprocal in the interaction, we-relationship becomes our primordial cognitive meaning sphere, the "common stream of consciousness" (Cornejo 2014, 249–50). Social or collective notions of cognition are of great interest for environmental ethics, as environmental problems typically arise from the gap between individual level reasoning and collective level habits cumulating from individual pieces of action that are separately seen as morally neutral (see Cripps 2011, 2013; Copp 2006, 2007a).

Christopher Preston, Mark Rowlands, and Mark Johnson are among the philosophers actively discussing the environmentalist approach to epistemology (see Preston 2003, 2009; Rowlands 2003, 2005, 2006, 2010; Johnson 2007, 2014). They develop notions of knowledge that take into account the relational nature of the epistemic agent described in recent philosophy of mind and cognitive science, most clearly in enactivism. As environmentally oriented philosophers they have thus taken part to the emerging interdisciplinary discussions including embodied, embedded, and extended mind theses and enactivism from quite an early stage (Johnson 1987; Lakoff and Johnson 1999; Rowlands 1999; Preston 2003). I argue that it is not a coincidence that these currently well acknowledged approaches of cognitive science have inspired environmentalists.

Moral epistemology that sticks to the disembodied view of the epistemic and moral subject is problematic for successful environmental ethics. Specific criticism is targeted against implied Cartesian internalism, in which will, intention and other "internal" operations are supposed to be isolated from external aspects, such as physical impacts, facts, social influence, and cultural practices. With this split in moral agency, moral subjectivism necessarily implies antirealism and relativism, because internalism alienates the knowing subject from the known object. Internal knowledge as exact and certain is separated from knowledge about the outside world as doubtful and isolated from the "thinking thing." In that view, a true belief must apply for justification in terms of internal certainty to qualify for knowledge. But moral epistemology that tries to formulate clear and certain "justificatory conditions of 'X knows that p,'" adopts "the computational metaphor of mind" (Johnson 2008, 159).

In contrast to the Cartesian starting points, environmentalist epistemology highlights the complex process of interaction that takes place in the epistemic event at both mental and material levels. External relationships, such as place, ecological position, and the structure of society, are not irrelevant to how and why "X knows that p"; they have an influence even in the epistemic content. Preston develops place-based epistemology, which aims at grounding knowledge in the earth, while Rowlands talks about environmentalist epistemology, but both argue for situated knowing: knowing that is possible for a human agent always remains physically and ecologically contextual (Preston 2003, 2005; Rowlands 2005). The capacity of knowing is not absolute or detached, and neither is the knowledge it can reach. The achievement of whatever cognitive content there may be is bound to the reality in which "place and mind are in a dialectical relationship, continually and dynamically shaping each other" (Preston 2003, 136). According to Preston and Rowlands, particular bodily existence, physical and geographical conditions, ecological structures and even the experience of landscapes, take part in the constitution of cognitive operations and influence their results. Despite the naturalistic emphasis, environmentalist epistemology does not conflict with the constructivist idea of knowledge formation. On the contrary, it can be seen to parallel feminist epistemology (cf. e.g., Preston 2003, 103–8, and Code 2005).

According to Rowlands, human cognitive architecture is both embodied and, at least partly, extended beyond the cognizing body. The actual information processing goes on in the relationships between an agent and the external world so that "acting upon external structures is a form of information processing" (Rowlands 2005, 19). Environmentalist epistemology calls into question the entire idea that cognitive operations are "in here," while the world exists "out there." As processes, cognitive operations "are themselves, at least in part, processes of the world." They include worldly constituents and cannot "be identified independently of the world" (Rowlands 2005, 25–26). Rowlands's view echoes Wittgenstein's solution to the skeptical paradox: meaning and understanding are things that we achieve in the world in practice, not inside our head, which makes Wittgenstein's heritage profoundly externalist. However, while defenders of the externalist argument mainly talk about content externalism, meaning that externalism applies to propositional states because of their semantic content, Rowlands defends vehicle externalism, which is about cognitive processes themselves. Content externalism does not "go far enough," since it leaves cognitive processes, such as perceiving, remembering, thinking, and reasoning to be explained in terms of internal structures. To highlight this viewpoint of vehicle externalism, Rowlands calls his position environmentalist epistemology (Rowlands 2003, 88, 94–96, 143–44, 155–82; 2005, 6–7; cf. content externalism by Hilary Putnam, Tyler Burge, David Kaplan, Donald Davidson, and John McDowell). Environmentalist epistemology is congruent to the 4E cognition research approaches, paralleling enactivism and the extended mind thesis.

According to Rowlands, externalism of the vehicles of cognitive processes extends to also cover the vehicles of the epistemic content. The environment contains structures that carry information relevant to accomplishing cognitive tasks, and that information can be made available only by acting upon these structures and effecting transformations in it: information processing does not only take place in the head or inside the skin, but partly in the world (Rowlands 2005, 16). Rowlands considers this to also hold for complex cognitive processes, such as remembering and reasoning. Thus, if epistemic environmentalism is accepted, it means that cognitive operations, epistemic content, as well as the measures of knowledge, are in conjunction with what we "do in (and to) the world" (Rowlands 2005, 24–26).[2] Cognition is essentially an environmentally relational process. Relationships with the nonhuman and material partners of the ecological place in which cognition takes place are not neutral. This means that epistemology should also be seen as a reason for environmentally responsible action.

Christopher Preston's place-based epistemology shares the external understanding of the cognitive processes and the important connection between ethics and epistemology. He argues for the ecologically relational nature of epistemic agency: "The material structures of the world, then, are agents in the authorship of knowledge" (Preston 2009, 185). He also focuses on the implications of environmentalist epistemology for ethics and argues that "ecological and geographical diversity should be preserved because 'landscape diversity is a valuable source of the diversity [of option] sought by epistemologists'" (Preston 2003, 132). Preston poses a historical criticism of Francis Bacon's influence in epistemology, the mistake being, according to him, that "the dialogue between mind and world" was transformed "into an arrogant monologue, or even inquisition" (Preston 2003, 73–74). Despite the similarities with Rowlands's environmentalist epistemology, place-based epistemology takes more insights from constructivist environmental philosophy, especially ecofeminism, than from naturalist views. The technical term "place" refers not only to physical realities and landscapes but also to cultural values, spiritual meanings, the formation of identity, and personal narratives included in a certain space. Like ecofeminism, a place-based epistemology widens the epistemological standpoint theory to include the physical and material aspects of epistemic processes and stresses that the influence between agents and place is bidirectional (Preston 2009, 2010; cf. Mann 2005; Keller 1992).

According to Preston, the development of naturalizing knowledge started historically with Kant and was significantly continued by Willard van Orman Quine. According to both, what can be known is tied to the agent of knowledge. Quine's response to skepticism, unlike Kant's response, connects knowledge production with the biological cognitive systems, especially the brain, of the human agent. This, Preston argues, was a historical turning point for epistemology, which was quickly thereafter developed to consider not just the operations of the brain, but of the whole body (of which the brain is part) in the epistemic process. This, again, has been developed into an understanding that not just the operations of the individual body, but the wider physical environment in which the bodily processes take place, should be taken into consideration (Preston 2003, 22–24). However, many followers of Quine can be criticized for sticking to scientifically naive naturalist epistemology and seeing humans as little more than an information-processing brain.

Preston argues that Quine's view should be revised to understand the wide meaning of interactions: humans are the unique corporeal, embodied actors they happen to be because of complex epistemic interactions that are largely determined by the operations of the entire body, understood in a wide, environmental sense (cf. Code 2005; Hayles 1995). Like Rowlands, Preston also has long acknowledged the value of the studies of embodied and extended mind as they offer empirical proof for the argument that human rationality is integrally connected to the animal nature of human agents. Cognitive science has proved that social structures, symbols of interaction (language), and cultural meanings can have their origins in the interactive animal nature, and not solely within the brain. Rationality is thus based on the animal nature of humans, in which various social and ecological aspects are interactively structured (Preston 2002, 434). Historically speaking, what has been needed in order to reconnect the alienated mind to the world is, firstly, "a therapeutic reconnection to the brain," secondly, "to the body," and thirdly, "to the physical spaces in which those bodies roam" (Preston 2003, 43). To be richly situated, a valid account of knowledge requires all these aspects.

For Preston, implications of richly situated knowledge and ecological agency are deeply ethical: material settings and physical structures that we modify by economy, art, and design, for instance, take part in moral actions as "actors" of the epistemic process. Therefore, physical structures can also shape our lives and how we think about our lives in an important way. The "material structures of the world, then, are agents in the authorship of knowledge. Objects are actors playing roles . . . in shaping the kinds of things we think and believe" (Preston 2009, 185). And this holds also for moral knowledge. Therefore, "probing the reciprocal relationship between what we believe and what we surround ourselves with seems like important work," and "uncovering how features of our material environment lead us to hold certain beliefs, values, and conceptions of the world seems like a central epistemological task as well as a central environmental one" (ibid.). Preston's view is environmentally insightful. Environmental everyday life actions, such as building, gardening, and urban planning certainly are epistemological and moral actions that can be praised or blamed.

Epistemic and moral agency are constituted in relation to the social and material environments of an actor, without opposing these contexts with one another. From the point of view of the modern humanist notion of uniquely rational and radically free human agency, this is a deathblow. This also influences environmental ethics: the Cartesian reason/nature divide is invalidated. Rationality cannot function as a criterion for any entity to deserve moral standing. The interactive life and cooperation we share with other animals is deep enough to also impact rationality: we share "an ineradicable component of our ability to understand our world" (Preston 2002, 436). By reference to empirical and philosophical studies, Preston even argues that the concept of reason needs to be revised. It "has started to look like an activity of engagement and involvement with the world rather than of detachment from it." This claim in fact restores the superiority of reason, but in a revised sense: "we are constantly engaging with the details. We do not live in the general" (Preston 2003, 44, 114).

THE NATURE OF RELATIONAL KNOWLEDGE

Environmental and place-based epistemologies do not necessarily entail subjectivism in the sense that knowledge is subjective, for instance, to those sharing a cultural context. Instead, they can be defined as relational epistemologies. Preston and Rowlands both defend a kind of "human version of objectivity" included in epistemic diversity, which they take to be a starting point. Despite partiality, contextuality, and physical engagement, epistemic processes function as procedures for approaching objectivity. Environmental epistemologies are, I would say, naturalist counterparts for procedural constructivist epistemologies, such as feminist standpoint theories of knowledge. They both highlight the limited capacity of any earthly epistemic system, and the inescapable partiality of any perspective to knowledge, but by focusing on the systemic interactivity of the perspectives, they defend modest objectivism. While standard constructivist epistemologies focus on the influence of socially constructed concepts on mental categories and language, their environmental counterparts also highlight the influence of material structures (whether they are "natural" or constructed) and the ecological conditions on the mental structures. The world as known is not passive but rather an active partner in the process of knowledge construction, which strengthens the "objectivity" of relational knowledge.

The concept of knowledge in environmental epistemologies differs from both standard correspondence and coherence theory. Knowledge does not represent reality but is influential through dialogue that affects the structures of mind as well as reality beyond. The idea of a picture reflected in the mind is an implausible idea since emergence of any such picture takes place through adapting the mind to the world. The physical structure of the mind, and the individual brain, for example, is influenced by what it "knows," and so it is that the outer world is "known by the mind." Instead of a reflected picture of reality, knowledge in this theory could well be defined as a piece of art. The material out of which a piece of art is designed cannot be separated from the performed idea: the known becomes present in a material form (or performs itself) for the mind and influences mental inhabitants of the subject, such as imagination and memory. Effected changes in the mental structures again influence how the "object" of knowledge will perform itself. The crucial factor for objectivity then is whether the dialogue functions in a way that provides reliable knowledge. Objectivity is embedded in relationships, and hence, epistemic reliability relies on ways of practicing relationality.

The active role of the material world is famously present also in ecofeminist notions of epistemology. According to Donna Haraway, for example, the material partner is "an actor and an agent, not a screen or a ground or a resource" in the epistemic process. Therefore, the purpose of knowing the world sets up a normative claim: the world should not be pictured "as slave to the master that closes off the dialectic in his unique agency and authorship of 'objective' knowledge" (Haraway 1988, 592). Knowledge construction takes place within ecological and sociocultural relationships. Feminist epistemologies aim at reconsidering rather than dismissing the concepts of rationality and objectivity. They argue against the dichotomizing sociology of knowing and objectivity. Ecofeminists especially argue that the earthly embedded epistemic process is intimately bound to the physical objects of knowledge, which themselves are active in the process.

According to feminist standpoint theories, objectivity increases with the help of socially (and ecologically) dynamic procedures of knowledge formation. Susan Harding's idea of strong objectivity, for instance, argues for approaching objectivity by giving a privileged role to marginalized standpoints (Harding 2004). Helen Longino uses collective objectivity to depict the procedure to approach objectivity by relational reconsideration of the epistemic agent. According to Longino, individuals are epistemic fictions rather than agents. Knowledge is produced in an interactive collective, and the structure of that collective is crucial for objectivity. Dialogue, common standards of criticism, and equal distribution of intellectual authority are examples of the means of objectivity. Standards of objectivity should involve the whole process of understanding—not just standards of epistemic contents, but of relationships, too (Longino 2002a, 128–29, 147; see also Code 2008, 193). The impact of the dynamic nature of human relationality on knowledge is especially clear in Evelyn Fox Keller's (1985) notion of dynamic objectivity. According to her, there are psychological backgrounds for our conceptual structures, and epistemic agency results from, and is transformed by, various relationships of the subject's life. The search for dynamic objectivity thus means seeking for a maximally authentic understanding of the world in conditions of uncertainty, which can be done by dynamic integrity and proper relationships between the subject and her environments. They thus should be the targets of evaluation in epistemic reliability.

Both Longino and Keller seem to understand well that an ecologically relational account of knowledge pools two approaches: naturalizing epistemology and feminist epistemology. There are remarkably parallel ideas between feminist epistemology and the recent philosophy of biology about epistemic agency.[3] Longino and Lorraine Code, for instance, also criticize mainstream feminist epistemology for not considering the ecological conditions of knowledge (Longino 2002a, 2002b, 2002c; Code 2006a, 2008). Code argues for an ecological notion of cognitive activity, by which the agent is engaged with the facts of the world. The relationality of cognitive activity thus combines material and mental aspects. According to Code, thinking is an epistemic practice that not only mirrors the world we are already engaged with, but generates new engagements and, thus, new "facts." Concepts of responsibility should especially be directed to this practice (see Code 2006a, 24; Code 2006b; Code 2008, 187–89).

Thinking as an ecologically structured process emphasizes that facts are engaged with agency in its entirety rather than with limited mental structures. Therefore, Code describes knowledge formulation as a collaboration rather than as a discourse or interaction. Collaboration bears the idea of community that grows by the process of being "more than a sum of its discrete parts." According to her, using ecological terms rather than relational ones offers "a way of both naturalizing and socializing epistemology." Code also writes about "ecological thinking" as a model of knowing "that is at once situated in and in relation to multiple aspects of the human and other-than-human world, interwoven with moral-social-political epistemological issues, and committed to exposing the effects of power-knowledge intersections, be they benign, malign, or 'in-between/in-among.'" In this sense, ecology does not only refer to ecological science, nor to socioecology: the focus is on how the mind aiming at knowledge is structured. The ecological notion of knowledge involves the fact that objectivity can be approached only through commitment, not by distancing oneself from objects. Objectivity increases by procedures of "ongoing self-reflexive and negotiative commitment" to various relationships and collaborative efforts to produce the best possible standards for epistemic practices (Code 2008, 188–95).

Relational agency calls for skepticism about certainty of (factual/moral) knowledge, but not necessarily about justification. Relational agency allows us to think that there are contextually justified (epistemic) beliefs on the basis of (morally) justified procedures and standards regulating (epistemic) relationships. Instead of insisting that objectivism should be the central pillar of the conceptual apparatus of an autonomous man of reason, modest relational or ecological approaches to knowledge accept uncertainty. However, in contrast to certainty, uncertainty serves epistemic and moral development: it forces one to better engage the world with the structures constitutive to epistemic agency. Contextually justified beliefs may thus not necessarily be true, but they are less false than some others, since they transform epistemic agency in a way that improves the epistemic skills of agency and draws, thus, future beliefs closer to the truth (see, e.g., Haraway 1988, 595–96; Code 2006b, 224). The idea of epistemic responsibility is important for relational epistemology.

Ecologically relational epistemology has implications for the concept of moral knowledge, too: moral beliefs can be seen to be collaboratively constructed in discourse with more than the human members of the community we live in (see Preston 2009, 179–81; Rowlands 2006, 91, 223–24). Approaching moral objectivity requires, then, that we "pay attention to the epistemic import of the physical environments we create and live in" and to nonhuman beings (Preston 2009, 175). This means that plurality must be respected: diversity offers more potential for interaction than a monoculture, and commitment to multiple collaborative relationships offers the potential for improving one's integrity of understanding. Whatever the procedure for the objectivity of moral judgments is thought to be (discourse, reflective equilibrium, feminist standpoint theory, or some other), physical and material aspects of the epistemic situation (e.g., ecology, geography, climate, and topology) must be involved in the successful procedure.

Embedded procedures for objectivity in a plurality of partial positions does not need to amount to relativism nor to "slipping into a pernicious environmental determinism"; we add something to the world that determines its value for us (Preston 2009, 177–79). Manipulation of environments/places/niches contributes to the epistemic architecture in which both moral and epistemic beliefs are constructed. Places (urban, wild, social, religious, and climatic) are "of cognitive or epistemic value for us" (Preston 2003, 117), and they govern the natural definitions of good and other moral terms. However, the cognitive meaning of place is not predetermined but produced in dynamic interaction between subjects and their places/niches. Knowledge is interwoven in active relationships without precise justification outside the practices of those relationships. We shall return to the relational approaches to moral knowledge and truth in chapters 9 and 10.

KNOWING BY PRACTICING

An aspect worth noticing here is that the fact that knowing is a place-based, socially propagated, and ecologically contextual process entails that the role of actions—intentional or not—for the epistemic outcomes is crucial. The conditions of epistemic processes are decisive for what can be known and to whom or what one trusts. The traditional description of knowledge as a true, justified belief has been challenged by theories that acknowledge the intertwined nature of knowledge and action. Four types of epistemologies may be of particular conceptual help here: virtue epistemology (e.g., Code 1987,

2006a; Little 1995, 1997; Zagzebski 2003),[4] theories arguing for a conception of knowledge as a skill (e.g., Hyman 2015), environmentalist epistemology (e.g., Rowlands 1999, 2006), and place-based epistemology (e.g., Preston 2003, 2005, 2009). Partly overlapping with each other and with feminist epistemology, these theories connect epistemology with philosophy of mind and action, as well as ethics, according to the definition of knowledge (cf. Haraway 1988; Hartsock 1998; Harding 1998).

In social epistemology, the focus is on the social conditions and construction of the epistemic trust between people. The claim is, in accordance with the recent philosophy of cognitive science, that cognitive agency is interactive and environmentally extended, on the one hand, broadens the view of the epistemic system and, on the other, highlights the quality of interactions as decisive for how it functions (see Colombetti and Torrance 2009). Involving the relevance of environmental embeddedness of the agent to epistemology usually calls for either scientifically or culturally naturalized knowledge production. However, enactivism and other currently notable explanations of cognitive operations combine elements from both evolutionary (naturalist/scientific) and cultural (constructivist) naturalization: as an interactive process cognition involves different kinds of active elements beyond the organism seen as the knowing agent.

Early approaches to cultural naturalizing in epistemology, such as Thomas Kuhn's and Paul Feyerabend's, focus on the theoretical, historical, sociological, and methodological frameworks of knowledge. The current understanding of mental processes has, however, raised visibility of the material strain of cultural naturalization. The material strain refers to constructionist views that highlight the contribution of known objects as well as material spaces for knowledge—such as the physical arrangements of labs—to knowledge construction. The laboratory itself can be seen as an agent of scientific development, and thus, lab reconfiguration that produces scientific theories should be seen as a product of both human and material agency. In the terms of cognitive scientist Andrew Pickering, there is a "dance of agency" between human and material actors in the lab. Lab techniques create an order of nature that mixes social and natural elements (Pickering 1995; Preston 2003, 35–41; Latour and Woolgar 1979). This highlights the indirect influence of arrangements in the lab, research practices, and (seemingly trivial) actions of the researcher in relation to the objects. The active role of the material world in epistemic processes in this way mixes the "world out there" and the "knowledge in here."

This kind of idea is familiar to ecofeminists, and it accords, for example, with what Donna Haraway calls the "material-semiotic" order of nature (Haraway 2007, 2016). Haraway highlights that material and narrative aspects are inseparable in knowledge creation. Instead of representations, there are "material-semiotic nodes or knots in which diverse bodies and meanings coshape one another." In labs using animals, for instance, the structure of material-semiotic relating means that people and animals are both subjects and objects in ongoing intra-action, in which "responders are themselves co-constituted in the responding" without preset properties (Haraway 2007, 4, 71). Instead of talking about certain animals (or humans) Haraway prefers to talk about material-semiotic "kinds," in which responses and responsibility take place (see Haraway 2016). The capacity of being responsible, namely, to respond, should not be seen "to take on symmetrical shapes." Epistemic and ethical practices also co-shape each partner. Knowledge, love, and responsibility form a kind of symbiotic web of actions, in which love is both an epistemic and (re)productive activity (Haraway 2007, 71, 97, 128; 2016, 60, 140). It seems thus obvious why Haraway and other ecofeminists oppose not only exclusively humanist but also extensional strategies in environmental ethics: response-ability, which has to do with the respective, listening, and responsive understanding of the other cannot be something that takes place "within relationships of self-similarity."

The idea of mixed, "environmentalist," or "ecological" epistemology is initially already present in the neo-Kantian insight, according to which knowledge synthesizes something brought by the scientist with something brought by the world. It can also be seen in the Quinean insight that knowledge is never totally pure nor is it totally alienated from the world. The number of factors acknowledged as constitutive to cognition has, however, expanded since the early days of neo-Kantianism and Quine. The conditions of epistemic objects—as they are active partners of knowledge construction—and various environmental conditions modifying the epistemic context should be seen as relevant to the epistemic process. These conditions are not, however, isolated from the ways in which the human partner interacts in her multispecies community and environmental relationships. The fact that the conditions on earth change for all due to the influence of human activity highlights the indirect influences of various actions through the environment on the constitution of agency and cognitive environments. Since even geological and climatic conditions and ecosystem services are dependent on cultural activities, the role of mutual interactivity between cultural constructions and the environmentally extended mind should be considered as important for the processes of knowing. The consequences of cultural practices have reached a level that cannot be ignored in epistemology or in moral theory. Cultural practices and intentional actions of destructive interaction with the environment have turned into strong determinants and limits for the freedom of future life and actions.

The decisive role of epistemic conditions and the agent's attitude and actions have been highlighted by a few philosophers who criticize representationalism and other "epistemological myths" based on the standard modern (but scientifically questioned) conception of human agency. According to virtue epistemology, knowledge is linked with the way the object of knowledge is recognized and listened to. Knowledge requires that objects of knowledge be involved in the epistemic process by adopting a virtuous attitude toward them: the relevant "informants" need to be paid attention to and trusted. As they become proper parts of the epistemic process, they contribute to the generated knowledge in an active way, increasing the reliability of knowledge. Therefore, according to virtue epistemology, better knowledge results from better interaction: the method for truth is bound to the agent's attitude toward all the relevant objects of knowledge that take part in the epistemic process, and in functional communication. The better "cared" for (and given space to contribute) the others are, the better the resulting knowledge represents them (e.g., Little 1995, 1997). Knowledge to which one has epistemic access is more reliable when more participants can contribute to its formation. Reliability of knowledge, thus, relies partly on the attitudes and skills of an agent, and partly on the number of participating elements in the nexus in which the process takes place. Without benevolent welcoming, important partners may be ignored.

In line with this, epistemologist and philosopher of mind and action John Hyman argues that knowledge should be conceived of as an ability or skill rather than as a form of belief: knowledge is "the ability to be guided by the facts, in other words, to take the facts into account, in what we think or feel or do." Instead of asking what should be added to a belief to get knowledge, we need to ask, "how knowledge gets exercised or expressed, since this is invariably how abilities and skills are defined" (Hyman 2015, 162). Through exercise, which is a practical activity taking place in some factual context, an agent has a way to be guided by the truth. Knowledge thus also differs from belief in relation to truth. While it is normally thought that the truth value of a belief is to be intellectually evaluated—for a belief to be counted as knowledge, we need to point out that it is true and justified—according to Hyman, the nature of knowledge should be distinguished from that of true belief, because the former is an ability or skill, while the latter is a statement (Hyman 2015, 164–65, 208–10). Hyman's differentiation is thus even stricter than those made by feminist virtue epistemologists (cf. Code 2006a).

The value of knowledge, compared to justified true belief, is that it offers a method of achieving the truth; the only way to be guided by the truth is through (epistemic) exercise, which is practical activity taking place in some factual context (Hyman 2015, 152–90). Such a formulation transforms both the idea of why knowledge is of value, and the understanding of how knowledge can be evaluated. The conception of moral knowledge does not remain untouched in such conceptual revisions. In light of relational moral agency, the truth-aptness of moral concepts refers—in addition to some other things, perhaps—to the practical care for the relations of the agent herself. Sensitivity to the conditions of epistemic processes and relational cognitive operations are thus conceptual conditions of knowing. Knowledge as an ability requires cultivating the skill of being guided by facts, not keeping a certain state of mind. To be guided by facts requires valuing and practicing the ability to be aware of, and respond to, the particular facts of a situation. This is, according to Hyman, what constitutes knowledge (Hyman 2015, 208–9). If we follow Hyman here, the task of moral epistemology is not to describe moral facts but to show how relational actions make ourselves able to be guided by good and right. If, thus, the truth is not a proposition, the ultimate truth of a statement cannot be justified or falsified by intellectual deliberation only. Truths are evaluable through the abilities they produce. By drawing from enactivism, the philosopher of cognitive science Hanne de Jaegher argues that the highest form of human cognition is engaged knowing which she compares with loving: Since knowing is, according to enactive logic, a process of participatory sensemaking, it "shares its core characteristics with the loving relationship, namely a personal involvement, concreteness, and mutual transformation." Knowing and loving both manifest "the same existential way of relating" and share the basic tension between being determined and determining. There is "the continual, ongoing balancing act between too much and too little determination between the knower (who lets be) and the known (who is being let be)," into which knowers as well as lovers must enter. Compared to knowledge resulting from an engaged process of knowing, abstract knowledge is either unfinished or over-determining. De Jaegher suggests that exceptionality of human knowledge should be seen in the ability to love. "A loving-and-knowing epistemology" is not just engaged but also engag*ing* epistemology. When an agent lovingly engages in the "relationship of knowing-and-being-known," then "those aspects of the to-be-known that we don't currently know change" (De Jaegher 2021, 861–64).

Ecofeminist philosophers among environmentalists, especially, highlight that epistemic as well as moral knowledge is something that can only be approached through wide intersubjectivity, relational recognition, and caring actions. It is common to hold ethics as the first philosophy; ethics is "a condition of knowing the world itself" (see Haraway 1988; Harding 1991, 1998; Cheney and Weston 1999; Plumwood 2002; Cheney 2005). Therefore, the relevant approach to knowledge construction is a moral one. According to such an ethics-based epistemology, what can be known partly depends on the nonrepresentational aspects of that epistemic relationship: valuing and disvaluing are thus epistemic methods (Cheney and Weston 1999). As knowledge is not reducible to its building blocks, intentional actions play a role in the epistemic process. For instance, Karen Warren (2000) considers "the loving perception" to the object to be a condition of knowledge concerning it, and Val Plumwood (2002) writes about "care models of knowledge" that break the radical subject/object division and allow agency to the known. Plumwood also calls for a revised idea of science through taking seriously that a correct attitude, care for the known, is a precondition of much knowing.

Two aspects characterize different cognitive processes as ecologically relational. First, epistemic processes are fundamentally dialogical or communicative in the sense that they exceed the community of human individuals. Cognitive processes involve objects and subjects of knowledge as collaborating partners in knowledge formation. Hence, nonhuman individuals and ecological wholes, like species and ecosystems, should be seen to be included in the process rather than be excluded as objects (for examples in environmental ethics, see Weston 2009, 5–6; Plumwood 2002, 165–66; Peterson 2001, 237; Midgley 1978). Valid reasoning requires an agent to enter various types of dialogues, to "listen" to the material and other partners, to "recognize" them, and to collaborate with them. Second, cognitive, and attitudinal elements are interrelated in reasoning in a way that makes the process of reasoning itself a moral issue. Environments carry the impact of human footprints, design, and manipulation. Whether it is Manhattan or an Arctic village, modified or left wild, the environment in which an agent is embedded has an epistemic value that plays a role in moral reasoning. An agent is morally responsible for the material and mental epistemic conditions she creates by her daily practices (see Preston 2003, 116–17; Cheney 2005, 106; Plumwood 2002; Little 1997).

The relational accounts of cognition and knowledge challenge the modernist conceptions that are still prevalent in moral philosophy. For example, the Kantian conclusion derived from transcendental idealism is that moral principles should be distanced from empirical knowledge because of the incapability of empirical knowledge to carry truth concerning moral facts. In contrast, environmental epistemologies call for engagement in risky interactions as the only way beyond contingences. Their strategy is inclusion, not exclusion. Knowledge requires empathy for those who cannot express their viewpoint and suspiciousness about those who have the power to offer "firmly founded knowledge" (Harding 1991, 2004). Rationality of action requires that the conception of knowledge be evaluated from the point of view of its ability to listen to the different voices of the world. Therefore, the epistemic attitude should be modest, or even humble, to provide for even pale representations of reality. The only possibility for an agent to acquire knowledge—factual and moral—is either despite or because of the relationships she lives by and acts in.

I argue that a relational understanding of knowledge construction—as it involves knowing not only social structures but also ecological constructions—will challenge the mainstream concept of rationality. The reason is that relational knowledge construction points to a complex mutual causality between actions on the one hand, and epistemic abilities, knowledge, and moral beliefs on the other. According to the mainstream modern conception of moral rationality, knowledge belongs to premises for moral action, but not vice versa. Relationality of agency calls this into question. The relational nature of cognitive operations demands taking the interdependency between *praxis* (material as well as social) and knowledge seriously in considering rationality (cf. Harding 1991, 57–60; 2004, 136; Haraway 1988). The role of knowledge in practical rationality is not just an instrumental one, at least not for agents that are constitutively related to their socio-ecological niches. Agents should see themselves as partly committed to the facts of those niches that function as conditions for their own epistemic abilities, rationality, and for their own value. If the relational notion of agency holds true, attempts to find procedures for (epistemic or moral) knowledge must take the mutual influence between praxis and belief into consideration. By making settings for our lives—whether they are material, social or cultural—we also limit, direct, and redirect our own epistemic and moral freedom and autonomy, as well as our beliefs. The relationship between material settings and beliefs can be described as reciprocal, as Preston does when writing about material setting as moral actors (2009). According to Preston,"when acting responsibly, societies will endeavor to create structures that embody the beliefs and values they hold," and "once in place, these physical structures start to influence the people that move through them." Therefore, we should "develop more respectful attitudes towards environments that we perceive as taking care of us, promoting our well-being, and providing us with pleasurable experiences" (Preston 2009, 179–81, 185).[5]

REASONING AS RELATIONAL

An important challenge that relational agency poses to moral philosophy is stated by Preston: "As empirical studies of mind have granted increasingly more significance to embodiment, and as epistemology has become increasingly more richly naturalized, *reason* has started to look like an activity of engagement and involvement with the world rather than of detachment from it" (Preston 2003, 114, emphasis added). Relational knowledge construction—regarded not just as socially and culturally, but also ecologically, bodily, and geographically situated—thus sets requirements for the concept of *rationality*. What is then required for an action to be rational? Considering operations for rationality as relational implies, most notably, that instrumental reasoning is not enough for moral rationality. Instead, for valid reasoning an agent needs to enter various dialogues, listen to its material partners, and collaborate with them.

A simple case is to consider practical rationality. The standard model of practical rationality combines some cognitive content with a directive intentional element. The major premise is the directive element that expresses, as a matter of course, justified motivation for action. It refers to value, moral belief, or preference, while the minor premises refer to facts. For example:

Major premise: Climate change should not be increased.
Minor premise: Charcoal burning increases climate change.
Conclusion: Charcoal burning should not be practiced.

The rationality of an action can be evaluated by evaluating either the logical relation between the premises, or the content of the cognitive (minor) premise. In modern ethics, the difference between the premises entails their different sources: cognitive premises emerge from epistemic processes independent of the value premise, while the value ingredient expresses the intention of the agent or a collective. In modernist ethics, moral rationality is conceived as instrumental: epistemic premises are means for intentions to be effectively realized. In the light of the relational nature of epistemic processes, the relationship between premises appears to be more complex than the instrumentalist view claims. Rational conclusions entailing the same major premise together with an objectively true or scientifically justified minor premise vary due to the contextual or relational nature of the truth value of the factual premise. The standard form of practical reasoning supposes that intellectual premises are objective in the sense that the attitude or previous actions cannot make any changes in them. However, even in a very simple case, rational action at one moment makes a change in the truth value of the factual premise at some future moment. Hence, the same action might not be rational at this moment two. Compare, for example, the following:

Major premise: The CO_2 level in the atmosphere is not preferable.
Minor premise: Forests control the CO_2 level of the atmosphere (true at moment one).
Conclusion: Protecting forests is preferable.

The conclusion is rational due to the truth of the minor premise. However, lack of action, that is, active control of the CO_2 level increase—which is not entirely forbidden though not preferable either—or certain actions, such as excessive logging, may change the factual ability of the forests to control the CO_2 level. The scientifically justified minor premise thus loses its validity due to the changes caused by either the lack of intentional action or previously rational intentional action. At a certain point, moment two, the CO_2 level in the atmosphere changes the rational conclusion:

Major premise: The CO_2 level in the atmosphere is not preferable.
Minor premise: Forests (in a certain area) are CO_2 emission sources that increase the CO_2 level of the atmosphere (true at moment two).
Conclusion: Protecting forests (at that area) is not preferable.

This is a simple example, while the connection between the premises is, in fact, very complex. Five points seem to be important here. First, since actions are heavily directed by the values and beliefs expressed in the major premise, the selection of the major premise seems to dominate the whole syllogism. Second, if actions change not only some separate external facts but also the ecological conditions of the agent's life, they also may change the agent's preferences concerning the major premise. As a result of changed ecological conditions, the agent's preferences and moral capability—the very meaning of "preferable"—changes. The conclusion "protecting forests is not preferable" is logically valid, but the practical consequences from acting in accordance with it would be disastrous from the point of view of the major premise (what is meant by "not preferable"). Third, attitudes heavily direct the attention of a rational agent. When relationally interacting with social and ecological others, the self-construction of an agent is directed more by those partners to which an agent has a positive attitude and gives attention. The attitude expressed in the major premise thus influences the knowledge formation for the minor premises. The agent's liability for the truth value or reliability of the factual premises covers her responsibility for the chosen major premise. Fourth, in turn, beliefs concerning the truth of the minor premises may limit (through self-construction and identity) the agent's freedom to choose the major premises (values and intentions). Fifth, the interaction between intentions and epistemic beliefs has an impact on the agent's epistemic skills. Skills advance by practicing. In the case of relational agency, the epistemic skills required in order to formulate correct cognitive premises cannot be distinguished from the skills of relational cooperation. However, relational cooperation requires a certain attitude toward those with whom/which one cooperates: an attitude of recognition, respect, and care. Intentions and epistemic contents thus seem complexly interrelated, and together they are influential for the agent's future capacities of rational reasoning.

Instrumental rationality has been especially criticized by environmental ethicists from an early stage of discussion and from very different angles. At the anthropocentric end of environmental discussion, instrumentalist rationality has been criticized, but there has also been a warning that environmentalists should not replace "anthropocentric moral rationalism" with "ecological anti-rationalism" (and turn to spirituality, religion, feeling, and intuition), since such replacements would only strengthen the post-Enlightenment rationalist dichotomies. Instead, an environmental rationality requires a critical revision of the very concepts of reason and rationality. John Dryzek (1987, 1990), for instance, argues in favor of an extended communicative reason in order to incorporate procedural standards that "are not obviously intrinsic to human discourse" but are "essential to good order in human interactions with the natural world" (Dryzek 1987, 118–20). Such an environmental rationality considers human intelligence as a "symbiotic intelligence" in which both human and natural properties play their roles. Making all epistemic interactions as equal as possible would then generate a rationality that is as objective as possible for imperfect agents.[6]

Ecofeminists Val Plumwood, Jim Cheney, and Donna Haraway, for instance, defend a different type of interactive argument. Because meanings are constructed together with the "objects" with which we share the agency, external nature has an active, participatory impact on reasoning (Cheney 1989, 126, 129; Haraway 1988, 578, 592–93). Humans have ecologically mislocated themselves: by dreaming about independence from material limits, they detached moral culture from scientific and technological interests and, consequently, distorted the very concept of human agency. Reasoning is cooperative in ways that requires a sensitive attitude toward cognitive "objects" and among cognitive subjects. According to Plumwood, the entire juxtaposition between naturalism and rationalism has its origins in the limited view of human and animal reason in the modern narrative (Plumwood 2002). Rather than selecting between trust in reason and trust in the nature, she calls for an ecologically revised understanding of reasoning. Rationalism fails to give a picture of the complexity of reason if it lacks an awareness of "ecological embeddedness, nature's agency and limits, and human dependency on the non-human sphere," or dismisses embodied and affective aspects of knowledge production (Plumwood 2002, 45–47). A parallel claim can be derived from the embodied and enactivist approaches to cognition, as has been described earlier. Francisco Varela argues in his *Ethical Know-How* (1999) that reasoning is fundamentally an ethical project. The premises of practical reasoning are intertwined, and things to-be-known change before they become known through the actual processes of engaging knowing that take place in concrete situations. Neither rationalism nor empiricism convinces alone but what Hanne de Jaegher calls "engaging epistemology" weaves a thread between the opposing views. The "existential dialectic of an encounter between beings," which is a caring and mattering relationship, continuously changes the participants in a way that fundamentally modulates the knower's intentions—even back and forth in time (de Jaegher 2021, 864).

What then does an ecologically relational definition of epistemic and other cognitive processes, or relational epistemology, imply for an understanding of the concept of rationality? At least two things. First, the concept of reason should not be considered as neutral or detached from will or emotion. The division between first-person will and objective moral reason, as it is considered in traditional moral realism, for instance, is too strict from the point of view of a relational conception of reasoning. Second, rationality should not be used as a concept referring to the method of reaching objective truths. The fact that various dialogues are responsible for what is called rationality should entail modest conceptions of knowledge, certainty, and truth. Moral action considered as a free, knowledge-based choice ties moral rationality to implausible conceptions of both cognitive and intentional agency. An instrumental, unilateral conception of rationality allows only extreme options for the self-understanding of a realist approach to ethics: reductionist naturalism or detached rationalism. I argue that a relationally revised conception of moral rationality calls for a more complex understanding of moral reasoning, which again calls for new perspectives on a mutual relationship between moral reason and the normative force of ethics, which is often considered as a problem for moral realism.[7] One of the recent arguments for crossing the strict division between instrumental rationality and intention comes surprisingly from evolutionary moral psychology. Michael Tomasello's interdependence hypothesis argues that due to natural human interdependencies the structures of rationality are fundamentally cooperative. Cooperative rationality thus cannot have an instrumental role in reasoning since it emerges from second-personal, joint intentionality; we could even talk about collective rationality based on collective intentions (Tomasello 2016, 143–46, 148–50; cf. Hourdequin 2012).

NOTES

1. Theory of social representation is originally introduced by a social psychologist Serge Moscovici, inspired by Émile Durkheim's notion of collective representations, and developed later, for example, by Ivana Marková. See Serge Moscovici, *La psychanalyse, son image et son public* (Paris: Presses Universitaires de France, 1961).

2. Rowland's idea of body language implies a strong type of vehicle externalism according to which we "cannot separate, not even logically, representation from action" in relation to the world. To avoid conceptual ambiguities, he uses the term deed, or preintentional act, instead of action in his argument on representation in action. Rowlands 2006, 83, 91, 93, 102–11.

3. For an enlightening discussion between Longino and Philip Kitcher, see *Philosophy of Science* 69 (2002).

4. Modes of virtue epistemology are, for example, virtue responsibilism by Lorraine Code, affective virtue knowledge by Margaret Olivia Little, neo-Aristotelian epistemology formulated by Linda Zagzebski, and virtue reliabilism defended e.g., by Ernst Sosa.

5. Preston exemplifies this by a story about Amish people, who maintain the type of life they conceive to be sustainable. See also David Orr, *The Nature of Design: Ecology, Culture, and Human Intention* (Oxford: Oxford University Press, 2002).

6. In ethics Dryzek does not give up the argument from analogy, and cannot, on my view, thoroughly exploit the possibilities of ecological rationality.

7. This problem seems to hold both for arguments that defend clear, even robust realism, and modestly realist constructivism. For the former, see e.g., FitzPatrick 2005; for the latter, see Korsgaard 1996, 2007b.

Chapter 7

Acting Relationally

RELATIONAL FREEDOM

The concept of freedom is central for a definition of moral agency. But definitions of freedom required for moral responsibility and reasons for action vary. Philosophers are anxious about relational descriptions of human operations mainly because of the threat they may cause to autonomy and moral responsibility. Both evolutionary explanations of human moral actions by relationally generated natural inclinations and constructivist explanations of moral codes as socially reliable constructions based on dialogical communication for functioning society may involve a threat to moral autonomy. In hardwired forms, both reduce moral agency to external reality. I shall argue, however, that a critical attitude toward individual reason on the grounds of the relational notion of agency does not rule out moral autonomy, though it challenges the standard conception of it.

The idea of radical freedom of an individual defended famously by Kant as a prerequisite of moral responsibility is compromised by a relational approach that considers social and material interactivity as constitutive for human agency. The idea of relational moral agency thus raises questions about the possibility of freedom connected with the philosophical question of compatibilism: Does psychological determinism rule out moral responsibility and the autonomy of ethics, or is it compatible with them? Or, as some philosophers put it: Is determinism conceptually distinguishable from intentional action? While defenders of compatibilism often refer to the conceptual or categorical difference between determinism and freedom, from the point of view of relational agency, this solution is not fully satisfactory. For one thing, it is not certain that causal determinism holds true for nature (Barad 2007). For another thing, it is not necessary to think that moral responsibility should rely on whether causal determinism is true or not (Fischer 2006, 6; 2012, 118).

Many compatibilists, such as Susan Wolf, Harry Frankfurt, Gary Watson, and Peter Strawson, argue that free will as the condition of acting for a reason should not be considered in the same way as free will as the condition of choosing *not* to act against good reason. According to Wolf, for example, the debate between compatibilism and incompatibilism that adopts a symmetrical account of freedom—that the conditions of freedom precede conditions of value and freedom has a similar role regardless of whether an agent performs a good or bad action—overemphasizes the concept of freedom as a condition of moral responsibility. Therefore, discussions seldom look beyond simple options. Wolf argues for an asymmetrical account of freedom that distinguishes between the conditions of being a free in sense of controlled actions (condition of freedom) and the conditions of being a moral agent in sense of responsibility (condition of value). According to her, the condition of freedom depends on the condition of value, not the other way around. An agent who is not psychologically determined is "so free as to be free from moral reasons," because abandoning absence of determinism implies that interests cannot determine actions, or external things (that are not in the mind of an agent) cannot determine interests. The absence of psychological determinism is thus not required for an agent to be morally responsible (Wolf 1986, 225–32). Wolf relativizes will by claiming that freedom of will and freedom to act are not entirely separated (since will is bound to the reason for action). By this she departs both from the traditional incompatibilism (that responsibility always requires freedom to do otherwise), and the standard compatibilism (that freedom to do otherwise is never required) and just claims that an agent can "act freely" (Wolf 1986, 1990). Her account serves as an example of the idea that a positive link can be seen between psychological—and perhaps also causal—determination and action for a moral reason. Even though her theory rests on an individualistic framework, it seems compatible with an enactivist account of mind and cognition.

John Martin Fischer is famous for his semicompatibilism, according to which, responsibility does not require the capacity to "make a difference" in the external world. He argues that instead of "control over" one's behavior, so called regulative control, it is enough for responsibility that an agent has moderate guidance control over behavior. Fisher (2012) agrees that defending responsibility requires that not all choices and behavior are consequences of the past and the laws of nature. The view focuses on different forms of freedom: while freedom to do otherwise might be incompatible with causal determinism, freedom required for moral responsibility is not. Decisive character of such modestly free actions providing responsibility is reason-responsiveness. Fischer's view allows one to think of responsibility as gradual, since all psychological mechanisms need not be reason-responsive in order to count an agent responsible.

Besides the nature of freedom, the notion of self, of who is the acting agent, also influences how the conditions of responsibility are considered. In the discussion on free will three main definitions of selfhood can be distinguished: self as a biological organism (an animal that may have mental processes or not), as a mental or psychological entity (an entity that has my mental processes, *is* me), and as something that *has* my mental processes (for instance, a soul). From the viewpoint of freedom, the psychological view can admit that actions are explainable by the processes of mind. However, as a popular interpretation of the psychological self is the one that reduces mental processes to the brain, a problem occurs regarding the source of freedom. What makes an agent's mental processes take part in generating and directing the actions in the sense that the actions are controlled? If the source of an act is in the mechanisms of brain and body, the act is not free in this sense. This conclusion supposes, however, quite a simplified concept of mind, and consequently, of agency, that reduces mental states to the determinants found in the brain and body, conceived as the brain and body of an individual human being. This reductive concept of mental states does not take into consideration the possibility of creative interactivity inside and outside the skin of an agent through which the mental states emerge and change. Even processes of biological interaction involve choices, not all of which are , according to biological understanding at least, predetermined. If this view is correct, the idea of psychological self famously defended also by Hume may imply that actions generated by mental states are not totally determined nor totally free, since neither are the mental states themselves.

Those who do not identify self as identical with mental states, but rather with something that *has* my mental states, struggle with the fact that neurological theories cannot locate such a command center in the brain. Their problem seems to emerge from the supposition that the requirement of responsibility is in the freedom that can be isolated in the mind internal to a particular homo sapiens. Some representatives of this view, however, have acknowledged the problem of reductionism and argue for a complex, systemic, and emergent notion of the self (e.g., Murphy and Brown 2007). A general feature of the discussion is that philosophers defending free will usually seek for a center of self-regulation supposing that responsibility needs to be a *centralized* system, while negating the type of agency included in other types of self-organizing systems.

My supposition is that from the point of view of what has been said about relational agency so far, both incompatibilism and the type of compatibilism that is grounded in an absolute categorical difference between causal and intentional activities are unconvincing. If we take causal and intentional elements in agency to be conceptually and categorically interlinked (if not belonging to the same category) rather than totally separated categories, relational agency refers to their mixed coexistence in the self-expression of agency. An agent can be self-organized even though intentionality as a concept (depicting the condition of responsibility) is not restricted to what is internal to the individual mind or brain. The difference between self-organizing systems and self-regulating systems is usually seen in that the self-organizing systems, such as the collectively acting shoal of fish, generate order as if they had a single mind without in fact having a central command above all its parts, while the self-regulating systems generate order from top to down. If the latter type of self-regulation is considered to be a condition of responsibility, autonomy is conceptually linked with the individualistic view of the mind. In contrast to this, an ecologically relational concept of agency allows for autonomy beyond an individualistic notion of the self.

In this sense, a relational approach adds a new perspective to the discussion of freedom and autonomy. Accordingly, a part of our very agency (the one that determines the action of self-expression, as well as that of "making a difference" in the world, if one believes it is possible) and external social, material, and cultural heritage are interwoven. On my view, the meaning and narratives an agent constructs interactively with others in participatory sensemaking and the ways she expresses herself as a self-organized system can in fact make a difference in the world—and in the character of her own agency. Some present determinants are thus consequences of the previous processes in which interactively provided meanings play a role. Widening the perspective, the determinants may be various for a relational understanding of moral agency. Despite limitations of freedom, the various determinants, such as body, identity, place, and past are, however, not just threats for responsibility but also possibilities for practicing autonomy. Absolute individual freedom is not necessary for moral responsibility. Yet, an important role that "freedom" plays in the context of relational agency has to do with *the ways an agent takes part* in interactions and participates in sensemaking, through which the character of an agent also changes. Character is not fixed. Interactive creativity as activity that provides for responsibility is extended in time and place.

Arguments for embodied and enactive cognition also offer support for this view. As the reader already knows, enactivism implies, according to Hanne de Jaegher, that the encounter based in caring and mattering between beings continuously changes the participants and deeply affects them to the extent that it can even retroactively modulate their intentions (De Jaegher 2021). Some others argue for a kind of chastened conception of freedom. Mark Johnson, for example, insists that ethics does not need the Kantian idea of radical freedom which supposes that "we are, or possess, a transcendent ego that is the locus of our capacity to negate any bodily, social, or cultural influence, habit, or tendency." The idea that we are "free to choose who and what we shall become" is too radical for an embodied and contextualized view of human agent. But like de Jaegher, Johnson also argues that humans have freedom to contribute to transformations of their own situation and, through that, to self-transformations (Johnson 2007, 280). A question then arises regarding how much "an individual" is responsible for cultural lifestyles or natural conditions that not just partly influence the actions of many, but also either enhance or degenerate one's own moral character which is embedded in those lifestyles and conditions. The relational notion of agency seems not to question the conceptual prerequisites of morality, though it calls for shifts in adopted concepts.

COLLECTIVE AGENCY AND THE
MEANING OF RELATIONSHIPS

Intentionality is normally connected with expressions of individual freedom. However, it is a widely held and justified view that in some cases operations of the mind, including reasoning and intentionality, can be considered as collective activities. Addressing rationality and intentionality in terms of collectives or group agents is important from the point of view of environmental responsibilities, and it opens new possibilities for normative discussion of environmental issues. But it also elucidates the ways in which social determinants and individual autonomy interact in both individual and collective responsibility. In this sense, discussion of collective agency is helpful for understanding the relational mechanisms of moral agency as providing nonindividualistic responsibilities.

An action can be called collective due to collectively directed intentions. Interpretations of collective responsibility vary in accordance with theories of collective intentionality. Collective agency can be based on (1) collective intentions that are non-summative actions of separate individuals (John Searle's definition; see Searle 1990), (2) collective intentions that are "shared intentions" of interrelated individuals (Michael Bratman's and David Copp's view; see Bratman 2007, 1993; Copp 2006, 2007), or even (3) special we-mode intentions, that exist when the collective nature of agential operations creates such features in the group that the group can be considered responsible as an agent (Raimo Tuomela's and Margaret Gilbert's position; see Gilbert 2001, 2014; Tuomela 2012, 2007; Tuomela and Mäkelä 2016). The crucial issue that divides different approaches concerns the role of an individual in the collective action. According to Gilbert's idea of strong collective agency, for instance, several individuals can form a plural subject that has collective intentions and intentional states, such as beliefs about moral aims and even collective reasoning, when the individuals form a joint commitment to act as a body (Gilbert 2015, 72). This means that a collection of individuals can act as a distinctive subject, and social rules can be seen as joint commitments of the society (Gilbert 2001; Gilbert 1989). Addressing moral agency to collectives raises questions about whether and how collectives can have reasons for action of their own, and whether and how motivation of an individual's action can be derived from a collective goal. Tuomela's theory of group reasons develops answers to these questions.

Tuomela distinguishes between two types of social reasons for action: "I-mode" reasons and "we-mode" reasons. For an "I-mode," group action holds that members of the group share each other's intentions as individuals, and reasons for intending a collective action are thus private "I-mode" reasons. But as a group the members can have a joint plan to be realized, and therefore, each member commits to the collective action (Tuomela 2013, 70–72; 2006, 35, 39–40). In contrast to that, a "we-mode" reason for collective action is a reason of the group agent. It is a reason "a group has for performing its action as a group. In turn, a group reason is a reason that a group gives to its members for their actions as individual group members," which means that the members "are assumed to function on the basis of their 'we-thinking' and 'we-acting' compatible with the group's ethos." A we-mode intention is then accepted by a group member qua group member. We-mode intention is one that satisfies three criteria: a group reason, a special collectivity condition derived from the members' being "in the same boat," and a collective commitment (Tuomela 2012, 404–5; 2013, 69). It should be noted, however, that Tuomela's social ontology is not an essentialist notion about collective agents, but a functional notion referring to group agency. Individuals can have intrinsic intentions, but when acting as group members "they only operate on the basis of their extrinsic mental states deriving from the group's 'mental' states" comparable with the actors' roles in a theater, although it is the members who have written the play and direct it (Tuomela 2016, 306–8; Tuomela and Mäkelä 2016, 300). Shared, as well as "I-mode" and "we-mode" collective intentions, highlight the role of participatory responsibilities for collective agency.

Tuomela's notion of group reason is especially interesting for two reasons. First, it emphasizes the creative role of interactivity. According to Tuomela, collective attitudes of members are products of complex interactions in the group. We-mode intentions and actions are thus irreducible to I-mode intentions and actions, though they emerge from them: interaction generates a collective reason which is more than the sum of individual reasons. The synergy effects from interaction cause the situation in which the group agent's actions and attitudes can emerge, and therefore, the group agent's reasons cannot be put in terms of private attitudes even when practiced by individuals (Tuomela 2006, 50–51; 2012, 406–7; 2013, 91–93). The function of the group agent depends on the member's functioning compatibly with the group ethos, but because of the synergy and interaction effects, the ethos of the group agent is not reducible to the individuals' attitudes. Therefore, changes in the group agent's attitudes take place through changes both in attitudes of the members and the *changed interaction*. This indicates that the nature of collective agency is relationality. Second, the interactive way of producing collective reasons implies that the motivation for an action is individual, but the motivation is not necessarily reducible to the individual attitudes or reasons, but rather, it can be addressed to the individual by the group reason, which is significantly influenced by the interactivity of the group in question. In other words, reasons providing individual motivation consist of two kinds of reasons: individual reasons and interactively produced group reasons. According to Tuomela, there are we-mode reasons "both for individual and joint action" (Tuomela 2012, 409–10).

The very agency in group reasoning is thus partly beyond the set of the individual members. I-mode reasoning of a group may motivate a different kind of behavior than we-mode collective reasoning in the same situation: reasons formulated interactively generate different actions than reasons formulated individualistically. This means that *interactivity* plays an important role in the *reasons for action* and in the motivation of both individual and group actions. According to Tuomela, human agents are generally disposed to engage in both we-mode and I-mode thinking and acting without supposing either perspective to be conceptually primary (Tuomela 2013, 93, 190–93). From the point of view of an individual, there then seem to be various levels of agency in which different rationalities take place. The relational composition of agency at the level of individual reasoning can be seen to have partly analogical features with we-mode collective agency. Those autopoietic cognitive partners (which can be any living organism, according to enactivism) that are constitutive for an individual's reasoning thus form a kind of joint agency or web of agency for that individual mind. For such an individual, agency is irreducible to the activity or influence of each partner or to the sum of them. If this analogy works as I suppose, individual agency is a collective of various sub-individual members that constitute the individual's identity, knowledge, and attitudes, besides being itself a part of other collective agencies. This interpretation of Tuomela's view implies that two issues should be recognized as decisive for the reason and motivation of an individual agent: the aggregation of the partners that each have an impact on individual agency—in both intersubjective and sub-subjective levels—and the interactivity between partners constructing the irreducible composition of the "individual" or "collective" agency.

Michael Bratman argues that agency should be approached from the perspective of action rather than that of psychological identity. He emphasizes interrelatedness and participatory intentions, which are related in a distinctive way: In a shared activity each participant intends that the subplans of each participant mesh when they follow participatory intentions. According to Bratman, collective intentionality can be based on the members' shared I-mode actions without a concept of group agency. Sharing generates a special bond that interlocks intentions (Bratman 1992, 331ff, 340; see also Tollefsen and Gallagher 2017, 98). The others' intentions thus have authority for the agent through a "bridge intention" to mesh individual plans with those of others: commitment to consistency and coherence as norms for an individual intention requires the participants to formulate their individual plans and intentions with an eye toward consistency and coherence with the other's plans and intentions (Bratman 2007, 26–32). This refers interestingly to a relational bond between the individual intentions as the subplans for actions. But it also means that the stability of shared agency is not bound to psychological continuity but to psychological connections. One way to overcome the weak stability of shared agency is to emphasize the role of we-narratives for the self (Tollefsen and Gallagher 2017, 99–104). Bratman also offers support to the argument for relational agency. On his interpretation, relational agency does not necessarily require a concept of collective group agent, but it denies that I-mode intentions embodied in individual actions are independent.

David Copp adds to Bratman's view that social rationality also has *normative force*: it is the glue that makes collective agency something more than the set of actions of member individuals. It is the normative force of social rationality. The requirement of meshing one's intentions with those of others is among the central norms for individuals. Social rationality functions as the glue between different participants, each of which may have a very different rationality. Therefore, responsibility and even a type of autonomy can be addressed to the collectives although they are not independent agents (Copp 2015, 3395–97; 2007a; 2006, 220–21). The we-mode intention and glue are not fixed entities, but rather impressionable webs of relationships. But once they emerge, they become constitutive for the collective agency and normative of all those taking part in the collective. This does not release the members from being accomplices. *Qua* members of the collective, they are partly responsible for the interactivity, which is the social "glue," and hence, for reliability of the reasons of the collective actions. An individual's intentional agency thus extends beyond the individual mind and body (Copp 2009b; 2015, 3392). It is also important to notice that the nature of intentional states of an individual does not essentially differ from that of collective ones, since both can be considered as relational states. Copp even suggests giving up talking in terms of agency individualism (Copp 2006, 207–10). The definition of the glue as interactivity implies that the collectives may include different types of participators; the decisive thing seems to be that the relationship between participants is interactive in the sense of mutual influence. Bratman's and Copp's views of agency can be defined as relational since it is the quality of relationships that makes a difference in their normative structure. They also open a way to consider individual agents as collectives of the interactive sub-processes. Both Tuomela's idea of we-mode intentions and the idea of social glue can thus be seen to conceptually exemplify *relational agency* irreducible to the activity of either each partner or the sum of them.

The issue of collective responsibilities is important in environmental social sciences, and it is of great value for societies aspiring to conduct sustainability transformation. But the worry about the clarity of designation of environmental responsibilities to various actors has raised questions about the grounds of collective responsibilities and the role of an individual in a group or a collective. Policy making that focuses on collective responsibilities is criticized especially for dismissing individuals who are the only agents that can "feel the pull of obligations," and therefore, such a policy makes only "minimal interference with individual liberty" (Cripps 2011). However, considering interrelatedness as constitutive for agency calls into question the traditional concepts of intentionality, freedom, and autonomy on which the debates that contradict individual and collective responsibilities also commonly rely (see Hourdequin 2012; van Grunsven 2018). Interrelatedness is not alien to the collective agency discussion, although theories of social cognition usually adopt a representational rather than enactive view of intersubjectivity (Fuchs and de Jaegher 2009). Let us briefly return to Tuomela. From the idea of "we-mode" intention it follows that the interaction produces collective reason and attitudes of the members. Because of the interaction effects, the ethos of the group agent is not reducible to the individuals' attitudes nor "(even) to we-mode attitudes" (Tuomela 2012, 407). This means that changes in the group agent's attitudes depend on both changes in attitudes of the members and changes in interaction. The idea of we-mode intention, thus, indicates a relational nature of collective agency, which means that in case of collective responsibility, moral criticism should be first and foremost targeted at the interactions responsible for the composition of the group. Interactively formulated reasons also generate different actions than "I-mode" reasons. For an individual, there are then different levels of agency in which different rationalities take place. Therefore, responsibilities also seem to cover a wide range of mental and physical processes and activities.

Complicity for collectively caused harms is easy to excuse when one's individual participation is marginal. Therefore, it is important, especially from an environmental point of view, to emphasize personal interactive responsibilities that the individuals have *qua* members of organized collectives and, especially, *qua* constituents of unorganized collectives through the idea of complicity as a form of liability (see Cripps 2011, 2013; Hormio

2017, 30–31, 145–54). Individuals can then be held blameworthy for collective harming as they participate to the constitution of the collective reasons for action and social norms as parts of various groups. So, responsibilities of individuals should be considered as responsibilities of the participators in the constitution of the collective, and such responsibilities can clearly be focused on with help of a relationally revised notion of agency instead of sticking to individualism. The advantage of relational agency here is that it points out how the private-level and the collective-level activities are intertwined.

The relational approach highlights the meta-level responsibilities of an individual for its own, collective-dependent reasons for action through cultivating the interactions by which they are constituted. According to classical virtue ethics, for instance, agents are responsible for the kind of agency they have. This means that they are responsible for the interactions that make their own—collective or individual—agency. The issues at stake for an individual regarding collective responsibility are, again, an aggregation of the partners and the interactivity itself. As a side effect, a relational approach turns the focus from the question of moral status of individual nonhuman beings based on their internal capacities (which has been central for extensional environmental ethics) and highlights the interactivity by which human and nonhuman entities together form the multispecies moral community. Regardless of the status as an individual, moral counting emerges from the fundamental interactivity of the collaborative partnership in sensemaking and agency. In summary, collective responsibilities are not sufficient without focusing on responsibilities for the mechanisms of how the collective agency is constituted and how they function. Respectively, responsibilities of a relationally considered individual agent are not sufficient without focusing on responsibilities for the mechanisms of how the individual agency is constituted and how it functions. I argue that considering agency as relational brings about meta-level responsibilities that are comparable with the responsibilities of individuals *qua* constituents of collectives.

AUTONOMY AS RELATIONAL

Processes crucial for moral agency conceived as relational deeply challenge the canonical version of autonomy: they question both individual autonomy and autonomy as a purely mental issue. But does this threaten responsibility? And especially: how does relational agency change the idea of responsibility for the environment? Autonomy is the crucial question for a relational account of moral agency. An interesting feature in the discussion is that enactivists and other interactionists who consider the problem of autonomy and responsibility of a relational agent mainly call upon the feminist notions of relational autonomy, in formation of which ecofeminists and other feminists interested in the biological and ecological agency have been active (see chapter 3). The environmental ethical tendencies I started with thus seem implicitly interwoven in the current discussions on enactivism, social ontology, and interactional agency.

A relational notion of autonomy is used especially by feminist ethics that criticizes the concept of autonomy that supposes a detached, isolated, incorporeal, rational, un-contextualized individual agent exemplified in independence, impartiality, and noncommitment. As described in chapter 3, the two main interpretations of relational agency in feminist ethics are the *procedurally relational autonomy* defended, for instance, by Marilyn Friedman (2000), and the *interactively relational autonomy* defended, for example, by Catriona Mackenzie (2000) and Diana Meyers (1989). While the procedural view conceives relationality mainly as a necessary means for making decisions as an autonomous person—which refers to the reflective self-understanding, internal coherence, and absence of manipulation—the interactive view considers relational interaction more radically as a constitutive element of autonomy, which refers to skills of active reflective engagement with, and actualization of, oneself in relation to others. According to both interpretations, autonomy is thus never entirely free from the essential particularities of an agent. Autonomy is a relational rather than an absolute thing, a dynamic process rather than a feature of an individual, and the same concerns moral rationality: they take place in engaged operations. According to Mackenzie, for instance, becoming critical in some relationship is possible only with the help of the rest of our social and cultural relationships (Mackenzie 2000, 144). But unlike the procedural approach, the interactive approach highlights the conceptual difference between the standard individualist humanist versus the relational notion of autonomy. Ecofeminists mainly prefer the interactive interpretation, and many evolutionary anthropologists, such as Michael Tomasello and Tim Ingold, also seem to conform to that (see Tomasello 2014, 2016; Ingold 2022). Ingold, for instance, considers an action of trust to mark the agent's relationally dependent autonomy. At this point, again, natural scientists and constructivist environmental philosophers who criticize the modernist idea of human agency as the core of the self-understanding of ethics approach each other.

A famous recent relational notion of agency is the one presented by Donna Haraway. She formulates an interactively relational idea of autonomy—intentionally or not—in terms that finds an echo in philosophers who try to articulate the ramifications of enactivism. This makes Haraway's approach especially interesting as it conceptually connects the discussions of feminist environmental philosophy and cognitive science, though she seems critical of the scientific approach. In contrast to the term *autopoiesis* used by enactivists to depict an embodied system, even a single cell, as something that produces itself and maintains itself as a self-organized system,[1] Haraway (2016, chapter 3) talks about *sympoiesis* to highlight that *nothing* makes itself in sense of pure autopoiesis or self-organization. Instead, every process of self-production and self-organization is a process of "making-with" other earthlings. Sympoiesis in a way "enfolds autopoiesis and generatively unfurls and extends it." On my view, Haraway's purpose is to emphasize the complexity, dynamicity, and large coverage of the constitutive interactivities of the self. The link between enactivism and the feminist notion of relationality and relational autonomy has also been present in enactivist discourse separately from the possible connection made by Haraway (Cash 2013, 66–69; see also Urban 2016, 2022).

The fact that enactivism questions the traditional way of separating free human actions and the act of nature entails revisions in the account of autonomy. Autonomy of the cognitive systems refers, first and foremost, to the self-organization of these systems under precarious circumstances as they take part in each other's sensemaking. Even simple organisms have some adaptive autonomy by virtue of their organization (De Jaegher 2018; de Jaegher and di Paolo 2007; Thompson 2007; Colombetti 2018). Although adaptive autonomy and more complex types of cognitive autonomy are not the same, neither of them is autonomous as a detached subject alone influencing their ("internal") cognitive actions. The practice of moral deliberation does not form an exception. Vulnerability of the living system makes it "continually seek interactions with its surroundings, to get the necessary energetic and material resources." According to Giovanna Colombetti, enactivism calls us to emphasize both biological adaptive autonomy and the autonomy emerging from lived experience, and to see "a mutual circulation between biological and phenomenological descriptions of the living organism." As "a network of interrelated processes" an organism "has to work continually in order to maintain itself, to counteract the unstable and decaying tendencies of its component processes" (Colombetti 2018, 574–75). To be an agent indicates that one cannot be indifferent to its environment. The concepts of intentionality, autonomy, and moral responsibility should thus be reconsidered accordingly.

The ethical implications of enactivism have recently been under increasing discussion. In their influential article, Colombetti and Steve Torrance (2009) criticize the traditional idea of individual responsibilities, in which agents can be held accountable in the world, and blamed or praised, only on the ground of their individual, intracranial, internal representational mental states—that is, causally efficacious beliefs and desires—and their following individual acts. According to their proposal, an inter-(en)active ethics, the focus for ethical appraisal should be interaction, and individual agents should be considered within the context of their processes of interaction. The meanings from which the ethical character of a situation partly, at least, arises emerge "out of the inter-relations between the participants in that situation." An interaction situation thus "has a 'life of its own,' and can be characterized as *interaction-autonomous*" (Colombetti and Torrance 2009, 517–20; Colombetti 2018, 572). This means that interactive processes themselves should be seen to have a relative autonomy, *interaction-autonomy*, in addition to the autonomies of the interactants. Cognitive systems that are not restricted to an individual mind but extended are essentially dynamical, interactively autonomous, and hence, self-organizing processes (Colombetti 2018, 578–79).

Colombetti and Torrance argue that interaction-autonomy takes place at the level of coordinated negotiation of physical movements between participants, but also in the level of coordinated social and ethical meanings: "significances are implicit in the situation of the encounter. . . . . There will also be myriad shared, complicit, disputed, resolved, dissolved, rebutted, etc., significances which emerge in a constantly shifting, more or less shadowy way, in any interactional situation." Such meaning-negotiation is a process that "modulates, and is in turn modulated by, the participant's own individually autonomous authorial perspectives on the situation" (Colombetti and Torrance 2009, 519–20; see also de Jaegher and di Paolo 2007, 490ff). The dynamics of meaning is thus not an individual issue. So, Colombetti's and Torrance's argument implies that the participants' agential autonomies are not detached from interaction-autonomy, and vice versa, which highlights that autonomy as a concept is in no case absolute but rather relational. Interaction-autonomy both enables and constrains individual agential autonomy, which is an achievement of relational processes. Agential autonomy partly relies on environmental factors that are beyond the control of agents, and individual responsibility is realized within particular situations.

This has an impact in the ethical appraisal: individuals do not necessarily have full responsibility in the traditional sense for certain situation. Therefore, Colombetti and Torrance claim that a shift in thinking about responsibilities is needed, and the focus should be turned especially to the quality of the interactions. Interactions have ethical qualities regarding their ability to enable or constrain participation or autonomy (Colombetti and Torrance 2009; see also de Jaegher 2018, 462). Interactive autonomy does not make us isolated or impartial, but, in a sense, maintaining autonomy is something that strengthens our moral commitment. As an enactive approach draws on empirical cognitive science, it can be seen to provide backing for the idea of relational autonomy formulated by (eco)feminist writers as well as for the ethical importance of interpersonal care and caring practices (see Urban 2015b).

The claims for an interactively revised conception of autonomy have also generated concerns. Similar to the criticism against the implications of collective agency for ethical appraisal, Janna van Grunsven (2018) argues in the context of inter-(en)active ethics, that a shift away from individual responsibility and an emphasis on interaction-autonomy makes an ethical appraisal normatively weak. She criticizes Colombetti's and Torrance's (2009) claim that to turn the focus "from making judgments of individual responsibility" to the interactions themselves is ethically "deeply problematic." According to van Grunsven, a relational turn toward a less individual-centric approach would mean that "we are never quite warranted to place blame on individual agents-in-interaction," which she considers as an "all-or-nothing stance." And if moral blame and praise could not be directed to individuals, "victims targeted in acts of violence or limited in their agency through oppressive social environments" would be characterized "as playing their equal part in their own degradation" (Van Grunsven 2018, 146–47; cf. Colombetti and Torrance 2009, 519–20). I do not quite subscribe to van Grunsven's criticism here, though the worry that victims cannot distance themselves from supporting oppressive structures is real. In feminist ethics of care, for instance, which she partly leans on in her own approach, oppressive structures are always social constructions that can be changed only though social emancipation. Although the victims cannot be blamed, the oppressed ones have their part to play in the process of emancipation. They are powerful because their interactive participation in the societal structures matters: through participating in interactions, they still have a little possibility to emancipate the dynamics of interactive structures. Not only are the enhancement and degeneration of their agential autonomy partly integrated in the social structures, those structures are also the platform for them to embody and enact their autonomy. Interaction-autonomy is not as absolute as is the autonomy of individuals. According to feminist notions of relational autonomy, autonomy can be relationally enhanced, and this can be seen to hold also for interaction-autonomy.

Van Grunsven seeks for an enactivist theory that would maintain the conceptually individualistic justification of personal responsibility. She proposes that the problems of inter-(en)active ethics could be avoided with the help of P. F. Strawson's conceptual framework, which allows a more nuanced understanding of the differences between agential, interactive, and situational conditions of actions. Instead of focusing on the agential excuses of autonomy that may "warrant a total repudiation of the reactive attitudes," we should focus on the situational or "injury" excuses that do not (van Grunsven 2018, 151–54; see Strawson 1962, 187–211). But this does not rule out the idea of interaction-autonomy. It seems that van Grunsven supposes that a relational notion of autonomy—or at least the ethical implications that Colombetti and Torrance derive from it—claims that attention should only be given to interactive autonomy, but it does not claim that it is the only perspective to which all instances of individual autonomy could be reduced. On my view, interaction-autonomy offers an important perspective to ethical appraisal, though it may only be partial.

The tension between interactional and individual autonomies and the worry for individual responsibility could be dispelled by more clearly characterizing the individual, that is, the human being, relationally anew and focusing also on the interactive constitution of what is "internal" or "individual" for the agent. An individualist conception of mind is not compatible with embodied or enactive cognition. But a nuanced understanding of various types of autonomy does not need an individualistic conceptual framework. The problem seems to be that the common ethical discussion is restricted to inter-*personal* relationships, that is, interaction between traditionally conceived individual beings whose agency is either their individual or, perhaps, socially distributed. The interpretation of relational moral agency I try to defend here is, however, different. If relationality of an agent is considered not only as social but also biological and ecological, the autonomous mechanisms at different (agential and social) levels of interaction and their mutually caused constraints would appear nuanced and richly complex.

I argue that relational autonomy does not have to be a weakness for an embodied, enactivist approach to ethics, but on the contrary, it can offer a revolutionary new way to justify normativity of social and environmental care. In this sense, it can enable a relational account of ethics to challenge the modernist humanist account without compromising "individual" responsibility and contribute in an interesting and fruitful way to environmental ethics. A relationally shifted notion of autonomy is exactly what can make relational ethics a serious moral theoretical alternative. If the practices of interaction are partly constitutive for conscious processes and perhaps even self-consciousness (Telakivi 2020), these interactions play a role in the agent's moral deliberation. However, this also shifts the status of these interactions from nonmoral to moral: relationships with the active partners of cognitive processes (whether they are human or nonhuman organisms) become highly morally relevant. Despite relevant criticisms, it seems that in the recent discussion on an enactive approach to ethics it is more common to recognize relational autonomy as offering more possibilities than threats (Cash 2013; Pescador Canales and Mojica 2022; de Jaegher 2021; Urban 2014, 2015a).

Hanne de Jaegher, for example, defends the interactive type of autonomy and argues along with Colombetti and Torrance that not just individual organisms are self-organized, but that interaction processes are too. They can be considered as instants that take "a life of their own" in the sense that the interaction dynamics may replace some cognitive functions in an intersubjective interaction (cf. "we-mode" collective agency by Tuomela).

The concept of participatory sensemaking used in context of intersubjective interaction may be elucidative in defining the relationship between individual and interactive responsibilities. According to de Jaegher, intersubjectivity requires, on the one hand, that "a co-regulated, mutual coupling" exists and leads to an operational closure and, on the other hand, that "the autonomy of the interactors is not destroyed in the process, though it can be decreased or increased" (De Jaegher 2021, 855, 866; see also de Jaegher and di Paolo 2007). Intersubjectivity is a matter of participating "in the creation and transformation of meaning together," between the interactants, each of which has its inherently meaningful although limited and constantly evolving perspective on the word, the other, and oneself "through acting and interacting." Participatory sensemaking should, therefore, do justice to both interaction processes and subjectivity "in its bodily, experiential, existential, and historico-sociocultural complexity." (De Jaegher 2018, 455, 462.) De Jaegher also calls attention to the fact that concrete, situated cognitive interaction already changes the future "objects" of knowledge, and thus, influences in what can be known. Such an interaction deeply affects both participants of the interaction. The influence of such interactivity in the intentions may be dramatic: the "existential dialectic of an encounter between beings (a relationship based in caring, in mattering), which unfolds over time and ongoingly changes the participants on both sides of it affects them deeply . . . and can even go so far as to retroactively modulate the knower's intentions" (de Jaegher 2021, 864).

Mason Cash was among the first to focus on how enactivism influences the concept of autonomy. He has formulated an idea of *distributed responsibility*, which makes use of the feminist notions of relational autonomy. According to Cash, distributed relational autonomy does not dismiss the individual aspects of responsibility; despite the constitutive role of the extracranial elements for cognitive systema, individual agents have relative "individual" autonomy enough for responsibility. But it is misleading to talk about the individual "ownership" of autonomy in a traditional sense. Responsibility does not require a "liberal" view of moral agent, a Cartesian internalist idea of mind, or an unencumbered individual who is independent from external influences. It allows for values and abilities to act morally to depend upon "the ways they are scaffolded and supported by" the social, cultural, and normative context and the various others we are engaged with. It is actually the normative nature of environmentally scaffolded constitution of agency that makes an individual responsible for her ideas and actions. However, our engagement with others and cognitive tools, practices, and institutions is still a critical engagement; the quality of bidirectionally influential interactions is not independent from the one who engages in them (Cash 2013, 66–67; for the critical engagement; see also Gallagher 2013).

In formulating the idea of distributive autonomy Cash draws especially on the interactionist type of the feminist account of relational autonomy (Cash 2010, 2013; cf. Meyers 1989, 2018; Mackentzie 2000). He thus considers an enactivist notion of autonomy to approach interactively relational autonomy and agrees with Colombetti and Torrance that the focus of the ethical concern should be shifted from the individual acts to the formulation and manipulation of the structures and contexts in which moral decisions take place. According to Cash, agency and responsibility are not primitive concepts. Instead, "the distinction between actions for which one should be held responsible and actions for which one should not be held (fully) responsible" is continually modified by the interactions and debates (Cash 2013, 68). He also argues that understanding autonomy as distributed can help address the "cognitive bloat" problem for externalism, because the limits of one's (relational) autonomy can be used to prescribe the limits of one's cognition. "A socially and physically distributed cognitive process counts as mine if it is appropriate to hold me responsible—to blame me or praise me, punish me or credit me—for the ideas or actions produced by this process." Although distributed responsibility is in a way "without borders," Cash highlights that there are still important reasons, for instance pragmatic, ethical, and political ones, to focus on the particular actions of "individuals" when the actions in question shape distributed practices (Cash 2013, 62, 67; see also Gallagher 2013; McCrew 2020, 369).

Philosopher and neuroscientist Xabier Barandiaran (2017) develops an enactivist notion of autonomy hand in hand with empirical neuroscience. He scrutinizes the tension displayed by the foundational enactivist proposal between autopoiesis that refers to sensorimotor adaptive autonomy and takes place even in simple living cells, and the operational closure that refers to the higher level of neurodynamic autonomy deployed as constitutive. Leaning on robotic simulation models, Barandiaran argues that despite the differences between these levels of autonomy they do not represent different realities: the crucial thing for both is how they are mutually interconnected. He focuses especially on reconsidering autonomy "at the level of sensorimotor neurodynamics" and argues that instead of focusing on the case of a single neurodynamic pattern we should move beyond that "to an *organization* of such patterns *in* interaction with the environment." As the robotic experiments show, the coherence of neurodynamic webs is essential for the sensorimotor functions, not only the other way around.

Barandiarian's theory of cognitive organization uses the concept of habit as "a *self-sustaining pattern of sensorimotor coordination* that is formed when the stability of a particular mode of sensorimotor engagement is dynamically coupled with the stability of the mechanisms generating it." Such habit adds the notion of plasticity to the neurodynamic pattern: "repeated enactments of a given sensorimotor correlation bear plastic reinforcing consequences on the mechanisms (e.g., synaptic branching) that support it." But a repeated habit "can take on a life of its own" and become "the cause and the consequence of its own enactment" at the same time. Individual agents, such as animals, can be seen as bundles of habits, and the notion of bundle or ecology of habits "both makes possible and depends on a sensorimotor environment, or *habitat*." An agent's effective environment is distinguished from the potential one "by habitually avoiding some correlations . . . selecting others, actively seeking some, sequentially switching from one to another, etc." (Barandarian 2017, 421–22; see also Buhrman, di Paolo, and Barandarian 2013). Sensorimotor autonomy emerges when the adaptive conservation of the bundles of habits "becomes the main principle of sensorimotor regulation; when sensorimotor compensations, accommodations, re-arrangements, etc. take place to maintain the capacity of the agent to keep behaving coherently." This generates a normative domain: the environment should not fail in collaborating in balancing between conflicting habits. One should "appropriately enact the right sensorimotor coordinations on which the tangle of habits depends for its systemic equilibrium." According to Barandiaran, the operational closure should not be considered "in terms of 'plain' neuronal activity" but "at the higher level of patterns of coordinated neuronal activity and sensorimotor coupling taken together" (Barandarian 2017, 412–13, 422–23).

This means that autonomy cannot be assimilated into autopoiesis—the basic autonomy in the biological realm—but neither can it be assimilated into purely neurological level operational closure. Instead, autonomy should be defined as the *coherent coupling* between the different levels. Autonomy depends on the topology of the webs that regulate neurodynamic changes: if that topology loses its shape, adaptivity of the system weakens, and it loses its ability to function. But what does this mean for the concept of moral autonomy or responsibility? It means that autonomy depends on the coherent interaction dynamics between the mutually dependent processes of basic biological and complex neural levels. And the processes in both levels are interactive in the sense that they involve environmental and extracranial partners. From this enactivist notion of *autonomy as coherence* Barandiaran derives a Kantian type of *imperative* that crystallizes a central ethical implication of the relational notion of agency: "behave so as to sustain your capacity to behave" (Barandiaran 2017, 424).

In case that human agency is embodied and relational, this also is remarkably an *environmental norm*. It justifies *responsibilities for the environment as responsibilities for one's own ability to act as a cognitive and moral agent.* I thus argue that instead of dispelling responsibility, enactivism defines environmental responsibility as a prerequisite of maintaining moral agency. Barandiarian's argument thus shows that an empirically sustained relational revision of the concept of agency can imply justification for the norm of extreme environmental carefulness even in the Kantian framework.

Giovanna Colombetti also highlights that autonomy in enactivism refers to both biological adaptive autonomy and lived experience, as well as to the need of "a mutual circulation between biological and phenomenological descriptions of the living organism" (Colombetti 2018, 573). The nature of enactive autonomy thus gives reason for a caring attitude towards the various components of the living system. The structure is reminiscent of that of virtue ethics. Although the focus of discussion on enactive autonomy has been in the intersubjectively shared or distributed autonomy among people, many of the given arguments hold for the interaction with other organisms too. As even simple organisms are cognitive agents, they participate in the construction of one's cognition and through that in one's relational autonomy. Regarding the worries about the possibility of blaming or praising individual agents, relational framework thus seems to give us *fewer* possibilities to excuse ourselves—as individuals as well as groups or organized collectives—from the constant vigilance in our relationships than the traditional individualistic one, and this also includes environmental relationships. Although responsibilities are in a way shared, they also extend in place and time. Responsibilities not only concern certain actions, but rather, they cover the entire course of being related and acting, by which the networks of agency transform through interaction.

There is then a *second-level category of responsibilities* concerning the practices of interaction, namely *responsibilities for relational moral agency, autonomy, and rationality*, on which the ability to be responsible rely. Relational responsibilities extend to the responsibilities for those whose cognitive processes, affections, and intentions we participate in and all that may influence these processes. Through changed circumstances, possibilities of autonomy also change. Hanne de Jaegher refers to a similar idea when she argues that sensemakers "are autonomous in the sense that they self-organize under precarious circumstances," which "makes a sense-maker sensitive to what is beneficial and what is pernicious for its self-maintenance, and capable of adapting to its circumstances in the service of self-organization" (De Jagher 2018, 457). Ability to practice moral agency in the future is influenced by whether the current interactions are beneficial or pernicious for the self-maintenance of the participating partners too. If so, Colombetti and Torrance (2009, 523) are right in claiming a shift in ethics to focus on the qualities of interaction. But the interactions we should care for involve participants in a multispecies community of organisms.

In environmental ethics, ecofeminists have been especially inclined to extend relational agency to the interaction with the material environment, and this continues in posthumanism and especially new materialism. Ecological cooperation is considered influential in both procedurally and interactionally relational notions of autonomy. A person becomes potent to act morally by not denying engagements but by making good use of them. Val Plumwood, for example, talks about cultural landscapes as products of mixed agency: land is a field of "multiple interacting and collaborating agencies, which can include humans but is never exhausted by them" (Plumwood 2006, 125). In turn, the landscape influences the agential abilities and the value construction of an individual. The interaction between those who participate in the modification of a particular landscape, such as the land use planners, residents, and the flora and fauna are partly responsible for the state of that landscape. And the outcome influences in turn, say, the intentions of land use planners. Relationally constituted eco-social features, such as gender, place, race, religion, social class, friends, landscapes, and opportunities shape one's way of being a self and modes of knowing (Warren 2000, 166). From the viewpoint of autonomy, environmentally and socially collaborative agency offers hope for possibility of genuinely new directions of agential development and creativity, which is usually seen as one of the main characters of free action. Therefore, extending agential abilities beyond the individual mind does not necessarily contradict the idea of freedom but relocates it to the bidirectional interaction instead of one-way causality. In creation of landscapes for other moral agents, for instance, one's part in the shared responsibility may appear to be more demanding than responsibility considered as an individual issue. Responsibility should, I think, be widened to concern the ecological and social structures that provide legitimate knowledge.

In mainstream contemporary philosophy, one distinctive way to conceptualize autonomy is the one put forward by Christine Korsgaard in the neo-Kantian spirit. According to her, autonomy has to do with the (relational) self-constitution of the agent. She explores the borderline between autonomous and determined actions by defining and defending animal agency (Korsgaard 2009b, 2011, 2012, 2018). Korsgaard aspires after a reconciliation between the evolutionary explanation of moral reasoning (naturally embedded) and moral autonomy (which requires normative self-governance). She accepts that "at least some of our mental attitudes are the products of the internalization: that our beliefs, desires, emotions, and so on, are the result of the new form of consciousness that emerged" through evolution. While this is usually seen to implicate non-convergence of moral judgments, and hence, relativism (at least if we do not accept ethical nonnaturalism), according to Korsgaard, it does not. The evolution of morality is not a story of specific contents of moral propositions but a story of normative commitment and the emergence of a normatively "self-governed animal" (Korsgaard 2010, 22–23).

The origin of moral autonomy or self-governance is not in awareness of our own mental attitudes, but *in the relationships* that we have with others:

only in relationships can we acknowledge the interconnectedness between our attitudes and the way the world is for us. We can thus distance our mental attitudes from the world. Mental attitude language can be used for distancing one's attitude from the world by recognizing that the way the world seems to oneself is not the same as the way it seems to others and that this is due to one's attitudinal contribution to the way the world is for oneself. According to Korsgaard, in natural history we began to assume that we have control over ourselves, and our responses, because we recognized the influence we had on the other's attitudes and, through that, to the way the world is for them. This resulted in an awareness of our own mental attitudes. Mental attitudes are thus first spotted in other people, and "we would never think of our own mind if we were never exposed to other people" (Korsgaard 2010, 21–22).

If we follow Korsgaard here, it means, first, that desires and attitudes should be seen as contributions to the way the world is for us, and second, that moral autonomy should be seen as a product of commitment, not an instantiation of unlimited individual freedom. But the content of commitment depends on the others to whom we are committed. So, self-governance has normative sources in others, and it binds us to those by whom we become aware of our own agency. The disputed issue about the relationship between justification (resulting from a cognitive state of mind) and motivation (resulting from an attitudinal state of mind) finds a new location through Korsgaard's analysis. In contrast to juxtaposing cognitive justification and conative motivation, they can be thought of as just different instantiations of how we use the attitude language about ourselves. Moral motivation does not just express its connectedness to our inner states but also to our interaction with external states of the world. But such interaction brings about both belief and commitment, not just commitment (Korsgaard 2008, 214, 227–29.)

Relational notions of autonomy also have metaethical implications. For example, taking autonomy as a relational concept seems to make the juxtaposition between semantic expressivism and semantic representationalism in moral language somewhat blurred because it connects the meaning of moral concepts to moral autonomy defined as an expression of the (real) ideal nexus of agency. Moral concepts should, perhaps, be seen to express the ideal constitution of the normative commitments that the speaker has due to the ideal interrelationships to which her body and mind take part. Therefore, actual moral judgments express a state of body and mind that is partly an outcome of its interactivity, namely the actual constitution of the agency. Such an outcome is not, however, purely subjective in the usual sense of expressivism because it results from the interaction between empirically real partners. The idea could, perhaps, be developed further. In the case of the ideal constitution of agency—which means that constitution of my agency commits me to all the niches in the nexus I live by (or partners with whom/which my agency actualizes itself), not limited to reasonable minds (social nexus)—the state to which my use of expressive concepts refers would be an outcome of something that is objective. Autonomous (moral) deliberation would then concur with the moral (at least in the sense of morally all-encompassing) reality.

Be this as it may, the relational understanding of agency has the potential to refresh both a Kantian and a virtue theory of ethics. The idea of relational moral autonomy indicates that questions of justification, good reasons to act, and good grounds for moral belief must be something to be approached by correct practicing of relationships with those partnering in the constitution of one's autonomy. What is left open in this interpretation, however, is the criterion for correct contribution to the way the world is in constructing one's agency. We shall return to that. According to Korsgaard, there is no conceptual difference between the relational constitution of human and animal agencies. The difference that makes moral criticism possible for humans but not for animals just emerges from the fact that when self-constitution takes place in human nature, principles according to which it is realized are selected by more complex processes (Korsgaard 2009b). She argues that self-determination can be used in two senses. In the first sense, to be autonomous or self-determined means "to be governed by the principles of your own causality, principles that are definitive of your will." In this sense every agent—animal or human—is autonomous. But in the second sense, to be autonomous means "to choose the principles that are definitive of your will," the instance that Kant calls "spontaneity." Korsgaard thinks that despite the animal nature of human agents, the quality of relationships by which a human can engage herself in external things exceeds the one by which other animals do. Responsibility can thus be seen to refer to the use of one's mental voluntary movements in actual relationships in enhancing rather than degenerating moral abilities (Korsgaard 2009b, 108–15). Such uses are, for instance, reasoning, collaboration, commitment, care, listening, deliberation, and love. Responsibility, then, does not require "spontaneity." If Korsgaard is right and I have interpreted her correctly, both natural and social engagements of agency, and the following modest notion of moral autonomy, are compatible with the (chastened, but basically) Kantian theory of ethics.

The modern concept of an autonomous human mind has been considered to guarantee the autonomy of ethics and its normative authority. Not too many ethicists have worried about the scientific credibility of the background presuppositions of this concept before, but the situation has changed. Since the definitions of agential autonomy rely on adopted understandings of human agency, changes in that understanding may have an impact that the traditional metaethical categories and battle lines between ethical theories also shift.

HUMANISM REVISED: QUESTIONS FOR ETHICS

This part has developed the concept of *ecologically relational moral agency* by exploring current understandings of human nature and the mental operations relevant for moral action. It brought together pieces of discussion on philosophical anthropology, philosophy of mind, epistemology, and philosophy of cognitive science complemented with supportive examples drawn from selected fields of empirical sciences to help in articulating the concept of relational human agency aspired for in environmental ethics. In the light of the given examples, the moral self, cognitive operations, knowledge, and even rationality and autonomy can be plausibly described as relational issues. It also became clear that all the relationships constitutive for one's mind and agency are not only relationships between similar types of agents, but also that the interactivity between various elements that form the "ecology" of the cognitive and conative processes are important. It is thus justified to argue that there is plenty of evidence in support of the relational conceptual shift of moral agency. Such a shift has both normative and metaethical implications. This means that various -isms in ethics—and especially humanism—that are based on the common interpretation of the modern concept of what a human is become substantially challenged.

Concerning the question of the source of moral obligations, for instance, it seems that ethicists defending relational agency cannot wholeheartedly follow either Kant or Hume. The key problem lies in how the central concepts of their ethical systems, "rationality" or "moral senses," are conceived. A relational shift implies that a theory of ethics should take into consideration the complexity of both rationality and moral senses. Two aspects in the relational concept of moral agency seem especially important for ethics. First, nondualism between the cognitive and intentional operations as elements of the complex processes to which moral rationality refers emphasizes the relevance of materiality and bodily life as determinants of reasoning, and second, collaborative interrelatedness (social and ecological) is at the core of the processes crucial for moral agency. Determined and voluntary actions are complexly intertwined in a way that makes it impossible to ignore the physical and social conditions of reasoning for the reasons of action.[2]

Responsibility should thus be seen to concern not just actions but also ways of reasoning, the quality of cognitive interactions, and the agent's ability to respond to those participating in her interactive agency. In a way, responsibility should be seen to concern the response-ability itself (see Haraway 2016). Through this, relational explanation of moral agency also offers certain *reasons for being moral* and contributes thus to a basic metaethical question about the normative force of moral reasons. Acting for moral reasons—to care, love, and be responsible—is motivated because they are also conditions for an "individual" to become a coherent being, to know, to act rationally, and to be response-able.

Reasoning considered as relational implies that actions are not just expressions of freedom made with the assistance of neutral knowledge. The quality of a relationship between "an agent" and "an object" dictates what one can extract from the object, whether it is knowledge or utility. Habits, performed actions, hopes, and memories direct and limit one's reasoning and decision-making. One needs to ask: How do my actions influence my understanding of humanity? Who should a human be? What drives me to my intentions and what role do I have through my everyday relationships in directing my rational processes? Because conditions of rationality partly depend on the material relationships and biospheric conditions of an agent, it is justified to consider "being moral" as including moral attitudes to the nonhuman world. The idea of responsibility does not only extend in the current webs of interactivity; it also extends in time. Agency is constantly re-constructed. For example, we owe a debt to our hunter-gatherer ancestors and their ecological environment in the savannah for many of our social instincts and moral sense. But can we praise or blame them for our current moral inclinations?

We saw that responsibility can be saved without an individualist or totally free notion of autonomy, but the focus of relational responsibility shifts through a relational turn in the account of autonomy. Responsibility concerns not just actions but also wider traits of behavior, such as cultural values, and even for some physical adaptations. Our autonomy may be limited due to our location in evolutionary time and ecological place, which include former cultural habits and social structures. But the elements of relative autonomy are involved in our active participation in the "narrative of agency" in our own place in the chain of generations from our own perspectives to the past (memories, history, evolutionary heritage), through response-able participatory sense-making and collaboration with the contemporary webs of social and ecological others, and through the imagination of the future. Hope for relatively autonomous choices is valid due to the operations of agency being constructed in relation to a wide enough and relatively harmonious, resilient entirety of nets of relevant interaction. Moral abilities, autonomy included, are constantly either cultivated or degenerated in actual interactions. Hence, we also play a part in the abilities of those to come. We carry inherited responsibility for the actions of past generations, participatory responsibility for the actions of our contemporaries, and influence responsibility for the actions of future generations. Broadly speaking, a relational shift in ethics approaches virtue tradition.

There are two discussions of metaethics to which the relational shift of agency especially seems to contribute: the relationship between *explanation and reason*, and the juxtaposition between *realism and relativism*. The hegemony of the common explanations of "action for moral reasons," namely Galilei's type of causal-mechanistic explanation, Aristotle's type of essentialist teleological explanation and the modern humanist freedom of will explanation, have been challenged by new types of explanation. The flaw of hardwired modernist positions can be located in their narrow conception of agency, which is partly based on a crude model of causation.[3] Relational explanation brings causal and intentional sides of action closer to each other by pointing out the non-radical nature of both causalities and intention, their complex mutual interrelatedness, and their copresence in cognitive processes in all levels. Explanations of being moral should not, however, be confused with the reasons for being moral, and explanations of moral commitments should be distinguished from morality as a conceptual system. Therefore, questions about the meaning of explanations should also be posed.

The claim that relational explanations are not irrelevant for ethics as a conceptual system calls for dissolving an extreme juxtaposition between explanation and reason. Arguments for morality that reduce moral motivation to some natural contingencies, for example desires, as they do, for instance, for Thomas Hobbes are thought to explain moral behavior rather than give moral reasons because the normative force is external to moral reason. In Hobbes's view, people want peace, security, and freedom as moral aims, but for egoistic rather than moral reasons. According to moral internalism, moral agency requires reason of its own type that has normative force by itself. Responses to such reasons are usually considered to be intentional, voluntary acts. However, a relational account of moral agency involves some explanatory features concerning motivation in the moral reasons so that they are partly mixed. Reasons and reasoning conditions should then not be seen totally separated, and neither should reason and motivation. For instance, enactivism seems to deny clear separation between reasoning and intention to act by denying the modal distinction between cognition and action (see Colombetti and Torrance 2009). This does not mean that people could not do anything they "know" as wrong, but such an inconsistency should perhaps be considered to emerge more from a narrow and inconsistent account of "knowing" rather than from an absolute isolation between reasoning and voluntary actions, as they are internally interrelated.

Unlike Hobbes, a defender of relational agency may hold that the whole structure of moral reasoning is tied to one's attitudes, or that the motivation considered as egoistic is tied to moral reasons. Motivation cannot be reduced to either natural desires or facts about relational human nature as they are intertwined. If a relational agent cannot act rationally or autonomously without taking into consideration the others on whom one relies, then the reason for a person to "voluntarily" take them morally into account is a kind of "mixed reason" including natural "ingredients." Relational reasoning refuses a strict division between "passive" objects of mental operations and "active" responses of the mind. Relational reasoning and participatory sensemaking as explanations of the agent's mental processes also play a role in the conceptualization of what is good and right without dictating their absolute contents (cf. Tomasello's independence hypothesis in 2016, 150–52).

The borderline between moral realism and antirealism can be defined in terms of the autonomy of ethics. Ethics may lose its autonomy in two ways: by reduction of moral beliefs either to objectively verifiable natural facts, or to subjective attitudes and voluntary preferences constructed by a freely floating individual mind or by a social group. While the former leads to extreme moral objectivism in the sense of determinism, meaning that moral beliefs are self-evident as they are, say, coded in the brain by the course of evolution, the latter leads to moral relativism. In their extreme forms both natural and cultural explanations of morality are reductionist: naive evolutionary naturalism reduces moral concepts to human psychological mechanisms explained by genes or evolutionary psychology, while hardwired constructivism reduces moral concepts to expressions of the free states of mind of individuals or groups. Since systemically complex agency cannot be explained reductively, it calls for a dissolving of extreme positions. In contrast to the reductionist positions on moral reasons, relationally modest forms of both naturalism and constructivism may represent non-reductionism. A relational shift concerning the concept of agency thus can have a potential for making a sound claim that contextual reasons do not threaten the autonomy of ethics. It seems that relational moral agency indicates a third route in between the objectivist (realist) and the subjectivist (constructivist) theories in ethics. The following parts will argue that autonomy and authority of ethics do not seem severely threatened by the relational shift, but the accounts of "objectivism" and "subjectivism" should be revised, as well as realism and antirealism, too.

Environmental ethicists usually seek an ethical theory that is scientifically sound, critically potent, and normatively committing. This leads them to a dilemma: on the one hand realism ensuring critical potentiality is preferred, while on the other it is the scientifically sound and committing constructivism that is preferred. The question is thus often raised whether moral realism is necessary for a plausible normative environmental ethic. I would rather ask what kind of realism would be both plausible and efficient for a normative environmental theory. The question thus is about *definitions of realism*. If we wish to defend moral realism, the truth-aptness of moral concepts and the measurements for the development of moral agency should also be defended. But how can better and worse relational reasoning be measured? What counts as progress or the cultivation of virtuous reasoning? Shadows of the metaethical debates of the last century still influence how moral realism is usually defined—against constructivism—as a view stating that the cognitive job of moral concepts is to offer representation of the moral reality which should be applied to action. The idea of relational agency challenges such concepts and calls for a redefinition of realism.

Many environmental philosophers are pleased to remark that interesting metaethical midway proposals have recently been defended. Dale Jamieson, for instance, recognizes "quasi-realism," "realist-expressivism," "internalist naturalistic moral realism," "sensible subjectivism," and "dispositionalism" as promising approaches. He claims that these "sensible center" positions share the suspicion towards both universalistic realism and modes of relativism (Jamieson 2008, 62–63, 68).[4] My supposition is that relational features in an ethical theory relate to metaethically hybrid shifts. Such midway initiatives attract environmental ethicists because of their potentiality to maintain both the critical force of ethics to compare and evaluate moral conducts (approaching moral objectivism) and the ultimate diversity and particularity of every actual moral perspective, even autonomy (approaching moral subjectivism). Since constitutive interactions involve not only an individual's cognitive and voluntary mental operations, but also external relationships, the conceptual clarity of starkly separating between belief and expression seems to vanish. Consequently, the philosophical juxtaposition between a factual and a constructed basis for moral conduct abates. If internal and external activities are constitutively interrelated, the borderline between moral subjectivism and objectivism will become blurred and, correspondingly, the juxtaposition between non-reductionist moral realism and cognitivist moral expressivism.

A preferable metaethical position for environmentalists seems to be the one that maintains both the normative authority and the autonomy of ethics. The problems for constructivism are how to save autonomy of ethics, avoid relativism, and achieve agreement. In the case of naturalism, the main problem is that the reduction of morality to the mechanisms of nature or psyche may offer objective grounds for conduct, but only in the sense of explanatory reasons. This kind of "moral science" lacks authority as a source of "ought." Problems with both hardwired positions thus largely originate in reductionism. Applying a non-reductionist relational notion of moral agency may thus *soften either view* in a way that reduces even the gap between the naturalist and constructivist positions in metaethics.

This part of the journey took us into the discussions on the relational conditions of being, knowing, and acting as a human moral agent. Although the examples of interdisciplinary support gathered here are in many ways fragmentary, they offer a convincing picture about the way modern ethics should revise its common presumptions about moral agency. Instead of a static, individualistic, and isolated core of humanity, human moral agency can be justifiably explained to be an interactive, nexus type of issue that extends far beyond the human sphere. Cognitive, affective, and voluntary processes of agency are embodied, embedded, enacted, and environmentally extended. Enactivism based on cognitive neuroscience and phenomenology appeared to offer fertile ground for continuing the discussion of relational agency started among environmental ethicists long ago.

NOTES

1. The term was launched by Humberto Maturana and Francisco Varela in *Autopoiesis and Cognition: The Realization of the Living* (Dordrecht, Boston, London: D. Reidel Publishing, 1972).

2. This links the issue with the discussion about moral reason, on the one hand, and the normative force of ethics on the other. For the discussion, see e.g., FitzPatrick 2005.

3. The implications of the flaw are, for instance, those connected with the moral role of ecosystems and nonhuman environment, collective responsibilities, and the timescale of rational choices. Although the crude model of causation was criticized already by Kant, the criticism has not profoundly influenced the concept of moral agency. See e.g., Kant, *Opus Postumum* (translated by E. Föster and M. Rosen, edited by E. Föster, *The Cambridge Edition of the Works of Immanuel Kant*, Cambridge: Cambridge University Press 1995), 22: 318, 421.

4. Jamieson acknowledges, especially, John McDowell, Christine Korsgaard, Simon Blackburn, David Copp, Michael Smith, and David Wiggins.

PART III

Shifts in Ethical Theories

Beyond Naturalism and Constructivism

In the previous part we traveled among the explanations of relational agency and found out that explanations of autonomy and rationality, especially, have further implications in ethics. As the journey goes on, we concentrate on the ethical and philosophical implications of adopting relational explanations. Through selected examples, we consider whether philosophical frameworks of ethics change due to a conceptual shift in the notion of agency in a way that offers more space for environmental ethics. Explanations are not traditionally seen as decisive in philosophy, because ethical concepts are seen as independent from contingent facts. However, if our self-understanding of ethics is that it should have practical relevance—even in this complex world we live in—it is not possible to dismiss the scientific plausibility of the conceptions of human mind and action adopted in an ethical theory. Can relational explanations of agency have real relevance for the foundations of normativity and develop criteria for the good and right? As we will see, relationally defined moral agency seems to offer at least valuable justificatory perspectives to normativity and a novel approach to the question of moral truth.

One of the key reasons why a relational explanation of agency has theoretical potential concerns its ability to avoid reductionisms without detaching moral reasons from the practically influential natural world. Various modes of ethical constructivism and naturalism are agent-dependent theories. But agent-dependency is often considered either as mind-dependency or as body-dependency, and these perspectives seldom properly meet. But relational agency reaches beyond this dichotomy and extends the common notion of "conscious mind." Does this extension add something, for instance, to discursive constructionist moral rationality that would make space for objectivism? A relational account of agency seems to imply that agent-dependent truth conditions and explanations of normativity blur the common borderlines between constructivism and naturalism. It thus abandons their extreme modes and moves them toward philosophically modest positions. An agent-based relational approach to ethics seems to allow consideration of moral beliefs as objectively evaluable, though not in a traditional sense. Relational objectivity refers to the optimal relational orientation or imagined hope for ideally inclusive relational reasoning as procedures for truth. Such proposals approach the idea that I shall call *relational realism*. On our way toward a relational view, we shall make use of some examples of modestly naturalist and chastened constructivist positions that in one way or another compromise with each other, or that already involve relational elements or support relationality, and apply a relational notion of agency to them. The exemplified outcomes include both hypothetical and realized positions.

Chapter 8

Shifted Naturalisms

WHAT IF EXPLANATIONS ARE RELATIONAL?

Evolutionary explanations have often been used reductively, and this has led either to extreme naturalist realism or to extreme reductionist antirealism. However, these extreme views usually adopt some simplistic evolutionary explanation of agency. Ethical arguments based on naive evolutionary psychology, for instance, either apply an idea of external authority to argue for the normativity of ethics or consider "ethics" as just another scientific description of human behavior. But the recent evolutionary and developmental explanations that focus on the relational factors of evolution—even morality as a system has been considered to play a cooperative role during evolution and the phenotype of the agent—undermine hardwired positions.

The metaethical worries connected to the evolutionary naturalist explanations of moral agency are that they may threaten moral reasoning as a means to achieve good and just reasons for action, the autonomy of action and, thus, moral responsibility by claiming determinism, and/or the objectivity of ethics by explaining moral beliefs, intuitions, and culturally reliable conducts as derived from contingencies. The first two worries concern the moral operations and capacity of agents, while the third concerns the general question of whether naturalist explanations undermine the autonomy of ethics and justify debunking nonsubjective arguments. The key tension between evolutionary explanations of moral agency and the possibility of ethics to guide actions concerns the tension between autonomous and natural moral agency. The authority of ethics is usually considered to require freedom at the level of the individual agent, but since scientific evolutionary explanations of agents often seem to contradict that, the easy options are to either derive moral guidance from nature (by deriving norms from what is), or to argue for debunking ethics. Both options are, however, reductionist.

Further options could be found by revising the notion of autonomous agency. Evolutionary debunking arguments, according to which scientific naturalism debunks the entire idea of ethics as if it is conceptually reducible to random empirical facts, are eager to use the genealogy of morality to undermine objective justifications of moral beliefs (see FitzPatrick 2015). The natural explanation of moral agency is seen to undermine moral realism and often also cognitivism. Belief in objective moral truth is an unnecessary addition if morality just refers to the origin of socialized behavior in evolved genetic inclinations (Joyce 2006, 179). But moral beliefs explained as adaptations can also be considered objective. According to such "moral science," morality is an output of psychological adaptations, evolved to solve the problems of social and environmental life in the societies of human ancestors (see Sober and Wilson 1998; D. S. Wilson 2002). Objectivity in this basically Humean mode of naturalism is based on the shared psychological structures and moral emotions of agents; moral propositions are true or untrue, but only in the context of how human brains have evolved to solve particular problems. According to such a straightforward derivation of ethics from evolutionary science, moral behavior is, in the end, the product of the human brain. Moral codes are better or worse in relation to the evolved mechanisms of the mind; therefore, they are not relativist. Objective conducts are found in evolved social structures (Wilson, D. S. 2002, 20–27). This kind of reductionist approach implies, however, a problematic computational view of the mind.

A typical philosopher's answer is to deny the role of scientific explanations by pointing to the naturalistic fallacy. But the question remains: "Despite the fact that ought never follows from an is, and despite the fact that the concept of the good cannot be identified with any empirical property, how should we understand the normative relevance of empirical facts in light of the empirical presuppositions of various normative commitments?" (Wilson, E. O. 1998, 278). The conceptual division between normative language and explanatory language is not, however, the only way to provide an answer. Relational empirical explanations of moral reasoning also invite us to reconsider naturalism in ethics. Many environmental ethicists are sympathetic to evolutionary ethics, but they are antipathetic to both robust reductionist naturalism and to ethical debunking arguments. More modest approaches are preferred.[1] Soft versions of antirealism, such as expressivism, Simon Blackburn's quasi-realism, and John Mackie's error theory have been among the most adopted positions by environmentalists who identify themselves as evolutionary ethicists. According to Michael Ruse, for example, Darwinism leads to moral antirealism, but not necessarily to noncognitivism (Ruse 1998). Error theory and quasi-realism can explain the cognitive nature of moral judgments without being entangled with realism. Mackie trusts that moral judgments are untrue (so called "atheistic skepticism"), while some others, for example evolutionary ethicist Richard Joyce, are skeptical about truth-aptness altogether (so called "agnostic skepticism"). According to Joyce, because of the agents' relational nature no one has the competence to evaluate the truth value of moral judgments. He claims that the denial of ontological moral realism is just what evolutionary psychology implies. Discovering relativism to be true is objectively good (sic!) because it lets people seek sustained rules on nonmoral grounds, leading to practically sustainable moral behavior (Joyce 2006, 222–23).

In contrast to this, Ruse follows more directly Mackie's skepticism and argues, in accordance with error theory, that belief in moral realism in fact gives the adaptational advantage to humans. Hence, belief in moral realism—whether it is true or not—is justified on an evolutionary basis. Ruse's interpretation admits the value of objectively moral reasons: He thinks that freedom and action for moral reasons has been profitable, or even necessary, for the evolution of the human mind and agency, but his meta-theory undermines trust in any moral reasons. Despite the fact that trust in truth-apt moral beliefs is preferable for human life and society, trust in truth-aptness and objectivity is *an illusion*; it is a lucky illusion, but an illusion in any case (Ruse 2004, 46–47; 1998, 101, 259; 1985, 198–201; 2010, 305–8; Ruse and Wilson 1986). The idea that the real reason to act in accordance with moral codes is beyond ethics—located in the "cheating mechanisms" of evolution that make us believe in reason—sounds fatalistic. The idea of freedom also is an instrumental one (Ruse 1998, 259). Would it not be the case that the recognition of illusion would turn the course of evolution and threaten the future of moral agency? If we recognize that belief in moral reasons is only a device for evolutionary progress, then morality loses all other truth value. Individuals would have little incentive to care about morality if it only has meaningful value on the macro scale of past human evolution and, hence, the evolutionary device loses its efficiency. Ruse's claim seems to be an argument from outside of the evolutionary history of human moral agents. Belief in moral reality has been fake and calling it a "lucky" fake does not imply anything ethically: ethics is only a part of the explanatory theory of who we are.

Metaethical positions connected with evolutionary explanations may be softened in two ways: either by not entirely reducing moral reasons to empirical explanations but to something less, or by avoiding reductionism by pointing out that evolutionary explanations of the world to which it is "reduced" are not facts that are entirely external but are also linked to intentionality and free agency. Relationality regarding human agency challenges reductionism especially in the latter sense: moral agency cannot be reduced to any ability to promote fitness. The complexity of the processes by which the facts about human nature (cognitive and motivational mechanisms) evolve and develop also preludes reduction of morality to either natural or social or cultural explanations. A relational account of agency also makes a difference in the implications of empirical explanations in ethics by involving the whole web of ecological others in the relational process of reasoning. At least when applied to an agent-focused approach to ethics, such reasoning can provide reasons for action. Contextuality of individual moral reasoning does not undermine modest moral realism. Interaction between various perspectives can be seen as a procedure for approaching what is right and good in a more objective sense, for instance, on the grounds of feminist and discursive ethics. But a relational notion of agency that fundamentally combines cognitive and noncognitive as well as internal and external elements of reasoning allows procedural ethics to be modestly naturalistic. According to a scientifically valid explanation, moral reasoning has emerged from natural sociality. But the fact that cognitive and noncognitive elements are dynamically intertwined in reasoning, which as such is extended beyond an individual mind and body, makes relational explanations of moral reasons non-reductionist.

According to Frans de Waal, for instance, moral emotions evolve in social interactions in a sense that both moral judgments (whether they are ontologically real or not) and moral motivation emerge from them (de Waal 2006, 16–20, 56–57; 1996, 17). Social interactions are thus not external to social emotions. This also explains collective agency: through the process of internalization, "the goals of others and the needs of our community" turn out to be my own. According to de Waal, this is the basis of moral reasoning, which thus cannot be reduced to emotions rather than to the social dynamics of relationships and communities to which the agent belongs. Because these relationships are complex and include a two-way impact, "reduction" is too strong a term to use here. The idea of naturally evolved moral capacity allows one to hold morality as uniquely human, in some sense, although "it never fully transcends primate social motives." Uniqueness relies on the nature of human natural good: it is interactive and dialogical to the extent that it has become unique on earth (De Waal 2006, 174–75). If operations of moral deliberation and behavior are relational, reductionism in the traditional sense is challenged. Naturalistic metaethics are also softened. Moral reason and experiences resulting from a complex nexus of mutual interactions are not external to the nature of the agent. But this does not involve a reduction to physical determinants in the exact sense.

The way that mainstream modern ethics protects ethical autonomy and prevents reductionism detaches moral agency from natural agency to an unnecessary extent. Nonnatural morality as external to human nature is connected to agential reality through some gateway capacities, such as abstract reasoning, impartiality, and free will. In the evolutionary discussion, the discontinuity thesis defended, for example, by Julian Huxley and Richard Dawkins, promotes this line of thought, too: if moral concepts are not reducible to (genetic) profitability, they must be based on external, nonnatural reality, such as God's will (see e.g., Dawkins 2016, 159, 180–81). Darwinian explanation offers, however, a slightly different starting point. Interactive explanations that question the reductive nature of evolution are compatible with the Darwinian continuity thesis: the idea of the naturalness of morality need not be denied. Such a relational evolutionary explanation a) criticizes the overplayed role of genes and highlights epigenetic processes as something taking place in both biological evolution and cultural development, b) considers evolutionary mechanisms as systemic level functions including both individual organisms and ecological environments, and c) conceives of interactions as taking primacy in development. In the dynamic process of development each interactant is both altered and altering (see e.g., Jablonka 2003; Griffiths and Tabery 2013; Oyama 1985; Lema 2014).

These systemic explanations of morality maintain, first, that there are complex evolved moral features (empathy, responsibility, intentionality, and reason) which are features of a nexus rather than of an individual, and second, that the existence and future of these features depends on the interactions between organisms and their environments, both altering along with that interaction. Therefore, reductionist explanations do not seem scientifically firm. Since relational agency challenges both reduction and detachment, it calls for a more nuanced approach to ethics. For environmental ethicists who prefer naturalism, evidence against reductionism may be welcomed: a non-reductionist nuanced approach may remain, however, naturalist. If evolution and the development of moral agency are mutually related, as systemic approaches claim, moral agency must not just be associated with an individual mind. In addition to that, factual processes, such as evolution and scientific practices, should be considered to partly result from the normative stance taken by the social community. This resembles the idea included in virtue ethics: in order to act virtuously, an agent needs to direct her attention to others with which/whom her ability to act morally develops.[2]

While a reductionist conception of agency applied to moral naturalism leads either to brute (determinist) objectivism or to relativism, applying a non-reductionist explanation makes room for *modestly naturalist realism*. A modest philosophical attitude to factual reality calls philosophical theorizing to be seen in continuity with natural sciences, though without fusing ethics to sciences as a "moral science" (see Kitcher 2007, 171–73; de Waal 1996; 2005). Identifying moral agency in the ecological nexus then requires revisions in the idea of moral naturalism; it draws naturalism to the metaethical borderline and to the edge of realism. At the same time, it draws constructionism to the same borderline from the other direction and to the edge of expressivism. For naturalism that acknowledges relational agency, moral knowledge does not result from an inquiry-type process, but from virtue-like activities that some philosophers call wisdom. This means that morality as an earthly phenomenon always remains unready and non-stable: even morality as a human phenomenon is an evolving issue. Therefore, adopting relational agency admits only a modest type of realism. A conceptually crucial question concerns the source of hope for the enhancement of morality through the self-transcendence of moral agency, and the possibility of (the teleological or causal) progress of ethics (Kitcher 2011, 209–52). For a relational type of non-reductionist naturalism enhancement of ethics relies on the commitment to and the role of the nonhuman and material others in the nexus of agency. Attitudes toward these various others and responses to their impulses are crucial for grasping moral insight and developing moral identity.

Relational processes of moral reasoning highlighted in many fields of science uncover weaknesses of the extreme metaethical positions. Not surprisingly, those who recognize the relationality of agential processes usually prefer midway metaethical solutions (see Jamieson 2008). These midway or "sensible center" theories are, however, often located closer to modest antirealism than realism, although I do not see any grounds to disdain modestly realist options. The empirical claims to define agency in radically relational terms seem, in fact, to advance the plausibility of modest realism. Fundamental relationality questions the way in which foundations of ethics have been located in moral realism *either* in nature *or* in reason. Environmental philosophers who wish for evolutionary theorizing to converge with normative reasons for actions have a notable interest in building a bridge between scientific naturalism and moral realism without falling into reductionism of any kind. Suggestions for starting points for them might then be approaches like a naturalist version of neo-sentimentalism (McShane 2011), Elliot Sober's "contrastive empiricism" (Sober 1994), and some neo-Aristotelian theories, such as Philippa Foot's (2001), Michael Thompson's (1995), and Martha Nussbaum's (2011, 2023) views.

However, talking about relational agency also undermines moral reasons as either objective or subjective. Whether a midway theory of ethics is convincing as a relational theory or not depends thus on whether the theory recognizes the conceptual relativity of both moral objectivity (that the moral concepts are external to the agent) and moral subjectivity (that the moral concepts are internal to the agent). The idea that the cognitive source of moral concepts is either "out there" *or* "in here" should be questioned. Modest realism can take either a noncognitivist (such as neo-sentimentalism) or a cognitivist form (such as natural teleology). But bringing relationality into the picture means that cognitive and noncognitive processes must be seen as inseparable, which also leads to a revised understanding of representationalism. Such a relational shift brings naturalism and constructivism to common ground. What most matters for morality is neither inner nor outer, nor noncognitive nor cognitive elements, but the change in moral agency itself, directed by the dynamics of the complex processes between these elements. Compromising with constructivism thus seems to increase the ability of naturalism to solve the metaethical dilemma of combining the cognitive content and normative force of moral concepts. Examples in what follows can be categorized in two ways: First, they adopt either a basically Humean sentimentalist theory or Aristotelian naturalism, and second, they end up with either modest metaethical realism or modest metaethical antirealism. The next sections are categorized according to the first category.

HUMEAN APPROACHES TO SOFT NATURALISM

Humean metaethics resonates with attempts to explain the dispositions of cooperation by an appeal to the empirical sciences. In the Humean framework, especially, moral sentimentalism is a favored starting point to combine an evolutionary or developmental explanation of morality and the normative force of moral codes. Moral senses also form a stage for the entrance of a relational conceptual shift (see e.g., Kitcher 2007, 2011). Neo-sentimentalism challenges traditional sentimentalism by highlighting the nature of senses as mixing biological and constructed aspects. Moral sentiments are not nonnatural, but they are not reducible to either biology or to sociology. According to Robert McShea, for instance, values are based on "human species-specific feelings," evolved in social and ecological contexts to promote appropriate relations between the members of an animal (or human) society and with other beings. Such feelings form a basis for moral judgments (albeit indirectly) as well as moral motivation. Neo-sentimentalism thus clearly disagrees with hardwired evolutionary psychology: moral sentiments cannot be understood without the biological and cultural conditions in which humans can flourish. As the genetic blueprint is altering all the time in response to evolution and human influence, the basis of value judgments also "moves on" (McShea 1990; see also de Waal 2006).

Neo-sentimentalism, such as McShea's "non-reductionist human nature theory of ethics," aspires metaethically to combine expressivism about moral language with a modestly realist theory of universal, but not static, moral facts. For McShea, feelings are experiences of altered bodily states. Success and failure, better and worse, are experiences in relation to these states and, therefore, they are not objective. But there is a universal ground for ethics included in the passions and their interrelationship with the intellectual operations with which they are involved (McShea 1990, 154–55, 181–87, 198–200, 266). Most neo-sentimentalists are non-reductionists and seek to somehow bridge error theory and moral realism without employing mind-independent moral facts. Consequently, they move toward the arena of metaethical mid-way positions, though constructive and innate elements are not easily combined on the theoretical level.

They often argue that realism is compatible with evolutionary explanations if only full-blown metaphysical moral realism is renounced (Allhoff 2009).[3] According to subjectivist realism, for instance, moral facts do not need to exist independently from the epistemic subjects. But subjectivity refers to an interactive collective rather than an individual or a divine entity, which means that the ability by which moral truth can be approached does not lie in any individual or shared feature or common agreement but in the processes of their interaction. Unlike error theory, subjectivist realism does not require separate metaphysical proof for the truth of moral claims, and therefore, there is no need to conclude that the seemingly realist form is a fake, as error theory claims. However, the alternatives to metaphysical moral realism usually connect the truth value of moral judgment with the subject's voluntary actions. Implicitly, this supposes that noncognitivism included in subjectivism would ensure metaphysical neutrality. Sticking to a contradiction between cognitivism and noncognitivism seems to inhibit neo-sentimentalists from reaching a sensible midway position (for a criticism, see Blackburn 1993). My supposition is that a simplistic identification of metaphysical neutrality with subjectivism could be rejected by focusing on the relational nature of agency: the co-development of cognitive and voluntary actions and the bidirectional interactions in the agent's ecological niche are facts about the natural world that may shift the viewpoint. Relationality of agency implicates that the idea of an agent-dependent truth condition exceeds traditional subjectivism but also mixes cognitive and affective operations in a way that questions traditional distinction between cognitivism and noncognitivism (see Colombetti 2018; Rowlands 2018). As this would shape a Humean sentimentalism that can approach naturalism, external theoretical help could be offered by neo-Aristotelians, such as Martha Nussbaum.

Linking moral reason with an evolutionary explanation is an ambitious project, but the idea could be developed by articulating a procedural value of the very processes of their relationship and by linking the nature of moral reasons with the systemic mechanisms of a consistent relational web of agency. The recent interpretations of evolutionary and cognitive science could be of help in that case. Compared to standard evolutionary psychology, Michael Tomasello's evolutionary explanation of morality, for example, is more complex and explains moral reasons for action by considering the moral subject as a cooperatively rational "we." Cognitive skills emerged from cooperative communication, for instance, do not directly provide morality, but "they structure the way that individuals understand their collaborative interactions and the participants in them." Cooperative rationality then explains the connection between motivation and moral reasons. The connection itself emerges from the process of conceptualization providing a sense of self-other equivalence (Tomasello 2016, 143–63).

A prominent contributor to this field, Philip Kitcher, develops his non-reductionist naturalism precisely on the idea of complex natural explanations. Kitcher's genealogy of morality interprets a Darwinian explanation of ethics in a non-reductionist way. Morality is clearly continuous to animal behavior, and it has developed and continuously develops under the same mechanisms as other complex behavior traits. Normative guidance has evolved naturally through hominid social life: We have an evolved "capacity for articulating rules . . . to shape our wishes, plans, and intentions, so that the frequency with which the altruistic tendencies that underlie cooperation are overridden is diminished" (Kitcher 2007, 172; 2011). Kitcher combines naturalism and non-reductionism by claiming that an inclination to articulate rules and to commit oneself to them is a feature that constitutes one's moral identity, but the articulated normative principles that generate moral identity are not themselves reducible to the natural well-being of those whose identity is in question. Motivation for commitment to the normative rules is naturally explainable, but the actual norms continue evolving through continued interaction (Kitcher 2011, 314). As an argument this represents ethical reductionism formally but not literally. In Kitcher's view, moral development is notably a progression issue: morality does not evolve in any direction whatsoever. Moral development takes place by continuously "extending . . . our psychological altruism . . . that made genuine human life (the social life that transcended the interactions of chimpanzees) possible." Progress is the creation of ever more effective moral codes to solve the underlying problems of social conflicts and to enhance social cohesion by mutual engagement, through which psychological altruistic dispositions are amplified and extended. The criterion for success of moral practices is that they improve social cohesion and the ability to promote such cohesion by the transmission of the normative system itself (Kitcher 2007, 175–78; 2011, 201–13, 223, 339–42; 2021). The possibility of moral progress in Kitcher's view is included in the interactive nature of the moral collective constituted of psychologically altruistic natural agents. Kitcher does not have to deny the Darwinian continuity thesis—although he seems to do so—since his notion of natural interactivity allows for claiming that relational moral agency emerges from a complex type of natural agency.[4]

In this sense, his approach seems to form an interesting naturalistic counterpart to Christine Korsgaard's constructivist argument. Both focus on the notion of agency and argue that moral actions do not directly grow from animal behavior, though they are not isolated either. For both Kitcher and Korsgaard, it is the notion of agency that denies any reductionist view.

Kitcher locates the element of novelty in the norms that are cognitive outcomes of this articulation of natural beings for social cohesion, while Korsgaard locates it in the "normative self-constitution" of the agency that articulates the principles (see Kitcher 2011, 2021; Korsgaard 2009b, 2010). Both approaches are interestingly relational, though in different ways. Kitcher talks about extension of collective psychological ability as a method toward something better in moral life. It refers to extension of our interactive agency in biological reality in order to enhance moral ability. For him ethics is a permanently unfinished phenomenon, which means that the normative outcomes of progressive morality never become ready or achieve the final "truth." To compare with Korsgaard, she considers extension of agency as extension of the reasoning agent's collective. While the relational extension of the agency in Kicher's view concerns the *noncognitive aspect* of agency, for Korsgaard it concerns the *cognitive aspect*. As I am trying to argue, however, cognitive and noncognitive aspects should not be separated. Therefore, I find these views to be counterpart approaches from opposing directions toward the same, meta-ethically novel perspective. We shall return to Korsgaard in chapter 9.

Because normative guidance is not cognitive, or at least not representational, for Kitcher, ethics should not be seen as objectivist. However, he argues for the idea of an objectively better and worse course of ethical development. The relation between progress and truth is thus complicated in his view. He dissolves the tension between truth and criteria of better and worse by talking in terms of a moral methodology. Unlike the "Discovery View," according to which progress relies on discovering more mind-independent moral truths, his method refers to the ways of approaching the ideal conversation, the one that would include the perspectives of all those who are affected by the problem in question. Kitcher's method for progress thus rests on mutual engagement, which makes it exemplify relationality in the sense constructed in the last part. Objectivity of the "progress" seems to concur with what I would call *procedurally relational idea of truth* (see chapter 10). On Kitcher's view, ethics is fundamentally something included in *engaging conversations*, and hence, the method for moral progress takes place, first and foremost, through emotional inclusiveness (Kitcher 2021, 13–40; see also 2011, 340–43).[5]

Kitcher's view of objectively better and worse is interesting for two reasons. First, it locates the "fixed point" in the correct *way of being related* with others in the shared social animality. Progress *via* the enhancement of mutual commitment echoes the relational idea of moral agency which partly aligns with feminist epistemology (see Kitcher 2002; cf. Longino 2002b). The included modest view of truth allows ethical naturalism to employ a plurality of practical truths. Both truth and the authority of ethics are social by nature: the content of moral reason is bound to the interactive "is," while moral authority is based on the joint capacity to reflect. Second, the "fixed point" is better defined as *the ability* rather than a property. The ability to remedy altruism failures works as the meta-criterion for objectivity providing progress. According to Kitcher, moral rationality does not require propositional definitions of the ideal conditions of reasoning. The truth is functional and constantly reconstructed in natural ways: "Some capacities for emotion and some emotional reactions are *apt*; others are not" (Kitcher 2011, 203–4, 210, 246; 2021). This embodies neither standard cognitivism nor standard noncognitivism, but Kitcher seems to make a link between moral precepts and natural facts by referring to social cohesion as central for human functioning in a way many cognitivist virtue ethicists also do (see Kitcher 2007; cf. Nussbaum 2011). The core of the evaluative criterion is, however, in the attitudinal positioning of oneself as part of a group (or web) called "social animals," although it does not have a permanent description. A surprising limitation of Kitcher's view is that it restricts social cohesion to human species. The examples he uses concern traditional human social issues: slavery, women's opportunities, and same-sex love (Kitcher 2011). Kitcher's meta-ethical position is not easy to locate, as he aspires beyond anti-realistic eliminativism (such as John Mackie's error theory) and reductionist realism, which both fail to take the human framework of ethics seriously. They both claim that in order to be real, moral facts must be objects of some scientific-like investigation, which is common for modernist metaethics. Kitcher's view is an example of how the turn of focus to the relationality of agency allows for renouncing outdated language about cognition when adopting a naturalist position. Such a shift also questions the necessity of the antirealist tone of the Humean positions.

NEO-ARISTOTELIAN APPROACHES TO SOFT NATURALISM AND RELATIONAL SHIFTS IN VIRTUE ETHICS

The neo-Aristotelian approach offers a strictly non-Humean alternative to those favoring a naturalist framework for earthly, agent-based ethics.[6] Especially theories grounded on the Aristotelian tradition but open to constructionist discourse often imply some type of a relational notion of agency, although they seldom clearly take into consideration material and ecological interactivity as essential for moral agency. Neo-Aristotelian virtue ethics, especially when it approaches constructivism, and constructionist ethics when it approaches virtue ethics, as well as care ethics, are open for relational definitions of agency. The recent discussion on the implications of enactivism for ethics has focused, especially, on the converging perspectives of enactivism and care ethics; both support the relational shift of moral rationality (Urban 2015a, 2015b, 2016; van Grunsven 2018). Enactivism interlinks the cognitive skills and functions of reasoning with the priority given to second-person engagement, and more widely, with the ability to care for one's interactions with the various others that take part in one's cognitive processes and functions of reasoning. The only reasonable attitude to the social and material environment, from the point of view of the functions of the mind, seems to be that of *care* (Varela and Thompson 2001; Colombetti and Torrance 2009; Rowlands 2009; Cash 2010; Urban 2014). Relational care ethics thus offers one of its natural counterparts in ethical discourse. I argue that interactive interpretation of human nature and natural human goods would also benefit virtue ethics by offering support to their included rationality of ethics. Explicit articulation of relational agency and its derived implications in ethics also could help environmental virtue and care ethics when they face criticism against their included naturalism and weak normativity.

According to a standard Aristotelian claim, virtues arise neither straight from nature nor without nature, but rather, nature offers the capacity to acquire virtues, and they are completed through habituation (Hursthouse 2012, 180). Criticism has been targeted both against its "earthliness" (human animality) and its pre-Darwinian, essentialist naturalism (earthliness considered as "improper"). Unlike classical Aristotelianism, non-reductionist neo-Aristotelian ethics derives moral concepts from the agent without reducing them to any essentialist nature of the subject agents. Despite building on human nature, the natural foundation of the virtues is thus notably non-reductionist, and a neo-Aristotelian agent-based virtue ethics is compatible with the Darwinian evolutionary notion of humanness. But at the same time, the foundation of natural goodness is vaguer than in traditional Aristotelian virtue ethics because prescriptive concepts referring to the nature of an organism, such as "natural good" or "function," do not refer to any fixed or sole definition of individual, genetic, or social success, either directly or indirectly. Morality belongs first and foremost to practical rationality. But rationality requires animality, and agency requires both corporeality and rationality: human nature and the contingent conditions of agency are thus integral for morally relevant notions of good.

Modern natural science undermines any large-scale teleology, usually adopted in virtue ethics, but it leaves open the idea of small-scale teleology in the sense of the functionality of an organism. Such a small-scale teleology is supposed by, for instance, Philippa Foot's natural teleology: the proper function of the heart is to pump blood, which again is explained by its function of distributing nutrients and removing waste. But is this enough for an ethical theory? Foot's natural teleology is often noted as an example of hard naturalism. It basically follows the Aristotelian idea that virtues and vices are character traits that either promote or impede the proper function of an organism, but two features deserve special attention. First, in Foot's theory, the function of an organism refers to an organism defined in terms of the modern biological idea of an organism rather than any essentialist conception. Second, the proper function of an organism, which represents the measure of the good direction in Foot's natural teleology, is a contextual concept and relies on the human organism. A function is evaluable only in relation to the context in which the human organism practices its virtues. The two usual candidates for function in natural teleology are "function" as an adaptation responsible for evolutionary profitability and "function" as a narrative concept, having a certain place in the life of certain individuals at certain time (Foot 2001, 5, 31–32; M. Thompson 1995). According to Foot, human function as a narrative concept is contextual regarding both internal purposes and external place. The question arises, then, of how a basically Aristotelian theory can renounce essentialism without losing the critical role of ethics while closely connecting "moral" with "prudential." What is the criterion to compare internally good narratives? This is an issue of continuous debate, to which, I think, discussion about relational moral agency can contribute.

Besides the question of the human function, the source of normativity is a common target of criticism against virtue naturalism. The relation between natural goodness (good for) and normative goodness (final good) is often too simple. However, according to Foot, virtues promote natural human flourishing, while vices impair it, but moral virtue that promotes final good is not reducible to human happiness (good for). Happiness cannot be identified with the life of virtue, since virtue (good-at) does not entail flourishing (good-for) but rather, a moral choice may include genuine tragedy. Happiness is "the enjoyment of good things" (Foot 2001, 97–98).[7] A modern critic may ask what then needs to be added to the concept of flourishing in order to determine the criterion for virtuousness. In Foot's view, human good is something that is conceptually natural but cannot be described by "success in the life cycle of development, self-maintenance, and reproduction" (Foot 2001, 51). Plants and animals have purposive actions which refer to their natural teleological purposes. In relation to these purposes, natural "good" and "bad" (good-for, bad-for) can be used to evaluate operations of nonhuman beings, perhaps even as natural "norms." For example, night vision for owls or cooperative hunting for wolves are examples of such natural norms, which are partly derived from general features (reproduction, nourishment), and partly from specific, less general ideas (eating, fruiting, fleeing). According to Foot, the logic of how normative virtues emerge from human natural good parallels how natural norms emerge from natural features of plants and animals: moral evaluation does not require any transcendental ability, and she considers the idea of human good in the sense of a "final good" as deeply problematic (Foot 2001, 33–36, 43).[8]

Natural teleology provides a case for naturalistic metaethics that follows Aristotelian teleology without adopting its metaphysical burden, *if only* its non-metaphysical "final" human good (the basis of telos) satisfies a proper explanation of function. The usual problem for virtue theories is that focusing on flourishing easily slides back either to essentialism or to a standard neo-Aristotelian idea of good narratives as the criterion for virtuousness.[9] Natural teleology seems to aspire beyond this division by at the same time highlighting the naturalness of the final good and insisting that it is non-reductive to any simple natural facts. The key may hide in the scientifically plausible, systemic, contextual, and interactive explanation of human function. The problem with Foot's view is, in my view, that it remains individualistic, and because of that, it is close to assimilating evaluative good (good-at) and natural final good (good-for). But as she does not actually make this assimilation, her Aristotelian view seems to be lacking something and she does not quite complete *what* should be added to the idea of natural flourishing in order to evaluate virtuousness. My supposition is that adoption of relational agency could facilitate the reconciliation of flourishing and virtuousness: A relational definition of "function" does not refer to subjects but to the processes involving multiplicity of interactive relationships by which agency is constituted.

There are at least three aspects of how neo-Aristotelian naturalism could be improved with help of the relational reading of humanity. First, turning the focus from the features of one (human) species to the organic development and structure of human functioning could offer a scientifically plausible way to redefine the relationship between human function and virtue. Second, highlighting the fact that human beings are social animals who are essentially bound to ecological conditions would uncover the non-individual nature of agency: mutual influence of intertwined partners and the support of a collective could even be seen as requirements for agency (see Hursthouse 2013a, 3575–77). Third, relationality of agency also implies that inquiry into human nature, which is used to evaluate human functioning, is an ongoing process; its success depends on practical virtuousness of the epistemic agents. According to an Aristotelian conception of practical science, action and understanding are mutually connected: the more aware of her own nature a human is, the more she can, again, practice virtues. To fully make use of these features, explicit articulation of the nonindividual, relational nature of the agent and her virtue would be helpful. It should be noticed that such a suggestion is not far from the aspiration of the neo-Aristotelian virtue approach. Unfortunately, philosophers often end the discussion before this point—or exclude the ecological side of relationality. But there are some encouraging exceptions to this trend.

One of them is Martha Nussbaum, who seems to aspire somewhat further. Her non-reductionist contribution to Aristotelianism and the capabilities approach form a promising ground for combining natural and constructed elements of moral concepts. However, the fact that Nussbaum's theory draws from contractarianism (especially Rawls's type) may impede withdrawing it from individualism and taking ecological aspects into account in the concept of a virtuous life.[10] Nussbaum links human good with the basic human capabilities to live a life that is worthy of the dignity of human beings, that is, "a life that has available in it 'truly human functioning.'" The list of basic capabilities that form a "threshold" theory of social justice includes, briefly put, the ten capabilities important for all: (1) life, (2) bodily health, (3) bodily integrity, (4) senses, imagination, and thought (which includes also reasoning and doing these things "in a 'truly human' way"), (5) emotions (which includes "being able to have attachments to things and people outside ourselves . . . to love, to grieve, to experience longing, gratitude, and justified anger"), (6) practical reason (which includes "being able to form a conception of the good and to engage in critical reflection about the planning of one's life"), (7) affiliation (which includes "being able to live with and toward others, to recognize and show concern for other human beings, to engage in various forms of social interaction; to be able to imagine the situation of another" and "having the social bases of self-respect and nonhumiliation"), (8) contact with other species (including "being able to live with concern for and in relation to animals, plants, and the world of nature"), (9) play, and (10) control over one's environment (which includes both political and material aspects) (Nussbaum 2003, 40–42; 2011, 33–34, 40–41). Compared to John Rawls's shorter list of "primary goods," Nussbaum's list is both complementary and corrective.

Three features of these capabilities are, I think, worth special attention. First, Nussbaum ties capabilities closely with experiences of a meaningful life. They do not describe factual situations, in which these experiences are realized, but the *experience* itself (e.g., Nussbaum 2013). These experiences are notably relational by nature. Second, capabilities are notably defined as the goods of an *active* agent, rather than just an existing subject. Action is thus essential for agents: they need to and wish to use their capacities for acting, which influences who they are going to be. This is compatible with the idea of "enacted" agency. Third, although capabilities belong to individuals, and "only derivatively to groups" (Nussbaum 2011, 35), they refer to the *relational features* of individuals. By not addressing capabilities to groups Nussbaum wishes to stress that no one may be used as a means for the capability of a group. This seems to make her theory confined to individualism.

However, Nussbaum adopts the social or cooperative constitution of human goods as capabilities of individuals, many of which are defined in terms of interaction that form good relationships. For example, bodily integrity, affiliation, contact with other species, and control over one's environment refer to good "positions" in the web of the world. Nussbaum also uses relational language, which emphasizes the role of sociality and relationality for the human good, in the sense of both "good for" and "good at." Skills and capacities, too, are something cultivated by the community together rather than internally by the individual. The descriptions include, for instance, being able "to have attachments to things and people outside ourselves," "to love, to grieve, to experience longing, gratitude, and justified anger," "to live with and toward others, to recognize and show concern for other human beings, to engage in various forms of social interaction; to be able to imagine the situation of another," "to engage in critical reflection about the planning of one's life," "to live with concern for and in relation to animals, plants, and the world of nature," and to have "the social bases of self-respect" (modified descriptions by Wells; see also Nussbaum 2011).

Although the listed capabilities tend to define political entitlements, they highlight that human good is highly relational by nature, and that freedom and autonomy important for good and virtuous lives are vulnerable issues. By claiming that the entitlements should not be seen as proportional to any "inner intelligence or skill" Nussbaum seems to refer to this relationality of freedom and autonomy; basic capabilities should not be bound to innate features. Social and material relationships and structures are capable of either harming or improving both the good of human beings and their autonomy. Everyone should be able to rise above "a certain threshold level of combined capabilities" in the sense that they *become free* "to choose and act," which politically is in line with standard feminist ethics that hold that "those who need more help to get above the threshold get more help" (Nussbaum 2011, 24). A meritocratic attitude to basic capabilities is not justified. This is mainly a political notion, but I am more interested in its side message: it refers to the fact that without favorable conditions and external aid, no one can cultivate her capacities for good or virtuousness. Virtues are thus, at least partly, relational, rather than individual.

Nussbaum's justification of the ten capabilities is neo-Aristotelian, and mainly naturalistic, but not reductionist. Human capabilities represent final goods, and they have a claim to also be realized in practice. But instead of defining them in terms of fixed properties, Nussbaum focuses on the structure of experiences that are described to a large extent in relational terms. Despite this, capabilities are claimed to be universal, as are virtues based on them even though experiences take various forms (Nussbaum 2013, 631–33). But although they take different representations in various times and cultures, they are natural enough to form a basis for claiming that capabilities based on them carry with them some normative claim. Common capabilities are, according to Nussbaum, empirically speaking, relatively stable: they have appeared in different societies throughout history. The list of capabilities must, however, remain abstract, because each society and cultural situation may have its own ways to define the concepts of good. The listed capabilities remain proposals (Nussbaum 1995b, 72–75; 2011, 36–40, 106–8). In order to justify the list, ongoing inquiry concerning the components and valuable human functioning for the good life is necessary. Such an inquiry does not merely provide justification for the list, it is also a guide in solving conflicts between the components. This kind of non-reductive naturalism has been widely acknowledged as the core of the attractiveness of Nussbaum's theory. The good life is not for her a "closed" case.

Nussbaum's non-reductionist theory mixes naturalism and constructivism. Features of the human good life in the sense of final good are only partly fixed. Justification of capabilities representing features of the good life is constructed, but nature sets constraints for constructivism. Most notably, human good is not reducible to the individual subject but spread into one's nexus of social and ecological relationships through which meaningful experiences can be realized. It seems, therefore, that one's experiences of the good may be unique, while the structure by which good experiences can emerge (for one's type of being) may be universal and objective. As experiences also may depend on the place of the experiencing agent, the definition of human good should be a pluralist concept in the limits of a certain type of universalism. To put it more exactly, Nussbaum revises Aristotelian naturalism by rejecting reductionism in regard to human nature and pointing to the cooperative structure and relational nature of valuable human agency. She thus rejects a reading of Aristotle that would contradict the (basically Humean) idea that morality is derived from attitudes rather than objective descriptions and points to a "non-internalist" definition of human good (Nussbaum 1995a, 102). Nussbaum's midway approach could be strengthened if definitions of final human goods were clearly articulated to correlate with the relational functions of agency, bound to collaborative features of human activity, and if the sphere of cooperation were not restricted to humans. In this sense, Nussbaum's extension of her focus to animal justice (Nussbaum 2023) is promising. Understanding the functions of human agency relationally would mean that they contain mutually transformative interactions between social and ecological constituents. Such processes constantly constitute their own function, which is the locus of the agent's experience and reasoning. In a naturalist ethics, the function of the agent defines both the "good for" the agent (natural good) and sets a reason for the agent to act ("final good"), from which virtue arises as the moral good, "good at." If the relational account of agency is adopted, however, the "fixed" point could be located in the activities constitutive of human functioning rather than in any fixed function as such.

The capabilities approach is among the potential tools that can aid in solving metaethical challenges faced by those—including many environmental ethicists—who aspire to combine and connect the following three avenues: non-reductionist natural explanations of good with modest moral realism; moral concepts (final goods) with natural concepts (goods for); and explanations of moral reasons as the cause of moral motivation of earthly beings with the critical force and autonomy of ethics. Nussbaum takes a position that is, in one sense, more Aristotelian and, in another sense, more constructivist than, for instance, Foot's position. The core value of the capabilities approach, metaethically speaking, is in its way to combine the ideas derived from naturalistic human goods (universal goods *for*) and constructed human goods (agent-based goods *for*) in the concept of moral goods (*final* goods). This can be called tentative realism (Hursthouse 2013b, 651). This tentativeness resonates with the idea of relational agents and the consideration that humans are embedded in an eco-social nexus of interactions. If Nussbaum would adopt the relational account of an agent, involving the material and nonhuman aspects of relationality, too, some normative implications would emerge. As the structures of experience and reasoning continuously alter through the practical interactions that take place in socioecological contexts, ensuring the capabilities requires two types of "metacapabilities." Breena Holland has argued that relatively stable environmental conditions form a metacapability for practical reasoning and all other capabilities (Holland 2012). But in addition to that, ensuring the "inner" conditions of reasoning and other capabilities of a relational agent requires another type of metacapability: a coherent mental structure and the capacity to interact in a way that enhances rather than degenerates the capabilities. The future of reasoning and enjoyable experiences needs to be preserved by cultivating and caring for the nexus of various others who participate in sensemaking with us.

The relational notion of agency challenges common naturalist explanations of moral reasons by pointing to the fact that capacities of agency emerge from and develop by the structures of interactive relationships which involve both natural and social/cultural aspects. Since such interactivity changes all participants, neither human nature nor the objects of her cognitive representations are fixed. Representations of the "good for" are thus never objective but contingent facts, plural and contextual by nature. But this does not have to rule out objectivity of better and worse. It only should be defined procedurally in terms of the methods of interaction, or intra-action, of relational agency, instead of as the fixed contents of good and bad. Although moral concepts in naturalism refer to natural issues, these issues do not have to be representational facts or entirely externally determined. In an actual situation, facts are always also constructed.

In summary, the implications of adopting an ecologically relational concept of agency in the case of naturalism turn the focus a) to human flourishing as flourishing of the interactive webs in which natural agents live in, b) from human nature to the conditions of human action and agency, c) to consider nature and its functions bound with constructed structures of agency, d) to consider virtue as an issue to guide the line of constant changes of agency, rather than as a stable character, e) from knowing moral fact to knowing how cognitive operations may enable ever better constructions of moral good, and f) from cognitive contents of moral judgments to the structures and epistemic mechanisms by which any content can be formulated. Metaethically speaking, the relational shift challenges the naturalist way of defining the source of normativity reductively. But what can make natural goodness a norm or final good if the agent is not defined as it traditionally is? Although the idea of natural good becomes both unsure and unstable, the idea of final good can still be anchored to the idea of flourishing: Normativity may arise from the dynamic nature of the capacity for reasoning, enjoyable experiences, and moral action—or capabilities, in Nussbaum's terms. Relational agency thus challenges the idea of robust naturalist moral realism and calls for a relational one instead.

NOTES

1. Environmental ethicist's sympathy for quasi-realism (Philip Kitcher), error theory (Michael Ruse), or neo-sentimentalism (for example, Katie McShane and Fritz Allhoff) arises especially from their worry about the scientifically plausible nature of moral agency.

2. Cor van der Weele, for example, calls an ethics based on DST "an ethics of attention" and compares it with the ideas of Iris Murdoch and Martha Nussbaum. See Van der Weele 2001.

3. For example, Michael Ruse and other sociobiologists are criticized for adopting a far too narrow view of moral realism.

4. Although Kitcher argues for entirely natural moral agency, he disputes Frans de Waal's critique of the discontinuity thesis that considers moral agency as a "thin veneer" over human animal nature. Discontinuity thesis separates human nature and moral agency and distinguishes humans from the other animals. On my view, this seems an unnecessary contradiction. See Kitcher 2007, 2011, 2013; cf. de Waal 2006, 7–12.

5. Kitcher's method of moral inquiry resembles John Dewey's method of scientific inquiry but in the context of morality.

6. Among the notable are Philippa Foot, Peter Geach, Rosalind Hursthouse, John McDowell, Alistair MacIntyre, Martha Nussbaum, and Michael Thompson, plus Elizabeth Anscombe because of her strong influence on the others. I shall focus here especially on Foot and Nussbaum.

7. Like John McDowell, Foot thinks that "there is indeed a kind of happiness that only goodness can achieve," but unlike McDowell she argues that in a moral choice "the genuine tragedy" may remain. See also McDowell 1998, chapter 8.

8. Like Rosalind Hursthouse, for example, Foot does not divide between "good persons" and "good human beings," which would lift moral agents above human social animality. See Foot 2001, 66; Hursthouse 2013a, 3575.

9. Evolutionary biology denies any definition of function by the overall flourishing or welfare of individuals, and hence, the concept of function used in natural teleology is questionable. Foot is aware of this and seeks to avoid it, but, according to Kitcher, without succeeding. See Kitcher 2011; Cf. FitzPatrick 2020.

10. While Nussbaum draws Aristotelian and contractarian philosophies closer to each other, Korsgaard, to whom I shall turn later, represents its neo-Kantian counterpart that complements a Aristotelian view with a neo-Kantian approach to value. Both are interesting from the relational point of view, but both also need some additional understanding or, at least, clarification about the role of nonhuman partners of human processes and derived notions of virtue or obligation.

Chapter 9

Constructivism Chastened by the Natural Relationships of Agency

ANCHORING CONSTRUCTIVISM TO NATURE

A familiar question that bothered Kant now bothers many environmental ethicists: How can moral rationality and autonomy of ethics be reconciled with the particular and contextual conditions of human reasoning and reflection? The usual way to avoid relativism is by settling the tension between pluralism and objectivity with the help of some procedural approach to the truth of moral concepts. We owe the procedural theories of moral rationality to the great variety of post-Kantian modern ethics. Most often procedural approaches reconcile contextual perspectives with the truth-aptness of moral reasons by appealing to the idea of shared moral rationality independent from particularities. The perspective of relational environmentalists has, however, a unique tone. While modern metaethics after Kant and Hume mainly focuses on moral rationality without questioning the idea of unique human reason as its basis, they question the humanist point of view, as well as the idea of non-embodied reason. Conceiving of the capacity of reasoning as inseparable from the practices of being related to others also challenges the conventional concept of moral rationality. This makes the Kantian question even more urgent, but it invites us to seek answers from a new direction.

Procedural methods that reconcile between the contingency of reasoning and noncontingent moral reasons make it possible for a constructionist theory to reject both relativism and agent-independent objectivist realism. Reliable examples of such methods are the overlapping consensus of rational deliberation (John Rawls), discourse (Jürgen Habermas), the structure of a functioning society (David Copp), and the self-constitution of an agent (Christine Korsgaard). Common to all procedural models, normative concepts are agent-derived. The proper use of an individual or social structure of agency thus functions as the measure for reliability. It is usually defined in terms of interactions—ethics is largely about appropriate ways of being related to different others (Korsgaard 2003, 105)—but the partners of interactive discourse are restricted to human individuals. As the conception of agency is central for both providing normativity and definitions of the procedures for moral truth, a relational account of agency results in different normative conclusions than the traditional, modernist one.

A relational approach to ethical theory parallels procedural ethics but the valid and reliable procedures are different. If the very functions of agency are embodied, embedded in, enacted with, and extended to material relationships, *so must be the procedure*. Procedures for moral conduct are valid only if they are grounded in the mechanisms of relationality rather than on the traditional humanist explanations of social interaction. The focus should be on the interactive mechanisms of being related as such (e.g., Colombetti and Torrance 2009). Relationality of agency entails that moral identities, knowledge, and actions are constrained by the structures and processes of external mind-independent reality. The idea that such constraining elements could have some positive impact is opposed to the traditional interpretation of constructivism, although the idea is present, for example, in feminist, posthumanist, and enactivist discourse (e.g., Warren 2000; Haraway 2016; de Jaegher 2021). For feminist constructionism especially, social structures are both the criteria of moral evaluation and an outcome of moral practices, which refers to the dynamicity of social interaction (Plumwood 1993, 55–59; Mellor 1997; Warren 2000, 90, 105; Hekman 1999, 110–13).

Applying relational agency to a constructivist theory implies that the practices of being related themselves add a *directive element* to social rationality. Therefore, truth-aptness should be seen to concern the *mechanisms of reasoning* more than the outcomes of reasoning, at least in the actual situations. Objectivity is not reachable by the practical reason of any individual or actual moral community alone, however inclusive the procedure is, since the ways in which individuals and communities practice reasoning changes the facts that are valid in actual situations (see e.g., Plumwood 2002; Haraway 1988). In this sense, relational agency draws the idea of moral *rationality* closer to the ideas of *care* and *virtue* than to a representative cognitive process. Common procedural theories thus seem to adopt simplified conceptions of rationality, autonomy, and the nature of moral knowledge in order to warrant the objectivity of outcomes, and consequently, they miss the systemic point of view that would involve other-than-human partners. From the relational point of view, Kantian rationalism, traditional procedural realism, and postmodern relativism share a similar kind of problem: reduction of moral reason to freedom considered as a simple concept referring to the internal capacity of human individual beings (Mann 2005, 58–60). However, if, in contrast, agency is conceived of in the interactive nexus of natural, social, and cultural relationships, rationality emerges from the proper ways of being related, internally and externally. Objective justification may thus be approached through the process of inclusive relational reasoning, but such reasoning requires benevolent recognition of all others. Therefore, *methods for procedurally realist ethics are commitment instead of impartiality, care instead of scrutiny, and love instead of investigation.*

According to the relational notion of autonomy and rationality, the ability to transcend one's own perspective is part of the creative force of relational interactions the results of which cannot be reduced to the creativity of the individual partners. As Mark Johnson and Christopher Preston argue, creative synergy, empowering recognition, and collaborative cocreation provide for transperspectivity (Preston 2003, 127; Johnson 2014). Whether a process of deliberation qualifies as rationality relies on whether the ways of interacting and being related function well and are inclusive enough. Objectivity would require perfect moral rationality, which means that it should take place in an ecologically and socially perfect, all-inclusive nexus of agency. Since this never takes place in the actual world, the focus of ethics, as well as epistemology, should be on the mechanisms of creating as perfect a situation as possible by advancing the quality of interactions and practices and inclusiveness.

The essential question then is, what makes mechanisms of interaction better or worse? For a constructivist normative theory, moral concepts refer to solutions of practical problems. These solutions result from actual embodiment of the process of agent formation, which is itself influenced by previous acts of reasoning. Apt reasoning is relative to that process. In each act, agency takes a new form and, therefore, a plurality of rational codes of action is inevitable. Although rational outcomes vary case by case, in each actual case one outcome may be the best. However, since the agent formation is complex, it is not possible in practice to know for sure whether the actualized case is the best or not. The perspective is always limited. But the mechanisms of reliable agent formation may be universal. In a relational type of constructivism, the agent-dependent idea of truth should thus be located in the processes of constructing moral propositions rather than in their contents. What counts as a reflected, justified proposition would then focus on the *advancement of the procedures* of moral rationality, instead of the results of the correct procedures. The relational perspective on the question of objective moral truths thus involves a temporal aspect: the question of realism turns into the question of whether changes in moral systems represent the progress of agency formation. In this sense, a constructivist normative theory adopting relational agency resembles non-reductive virtue theories.

Adopting relational agency seems to make a constructivist theory more abstract, on the one hand, and more naturalist, on the other. It seems to abandon practical knowledge considered in procedural terms, because there are no ready instructions which would allow the subject to accomplish a cognitive task (Rowlands 2009, 58). Relationality thus shifts the focus a step further from a theory of interaction to the metalevel conditions of reliable interactivity. But relational agent-dependency of moral reason also binds valid procedures to the agent-independent natural processes that provide for life and reasoning through external collaborators. These natural conditions of "good-for" should be seen as necessary for the final good, too. Morally relevant final goods are thus not entirely separated from nature. Constructionist truth value of moral concepts is usually connected with moral identity, which can be defined as social, communal, or collective identity (as in communitarian ethics), individual identity (as in discourse ethics), or relational identity (as in care ethics), but the concept of relational agency suggested in this book adds to them the embodied and ecological relationality that makes moral identity extend not only beyond one individual but also beyond one species. Compared to the more traditional notion of relational identity, it anchors moral identity to the conditions of nature in a wide sense. Relational proceduralism thus seems to be modestly naturalist in a sense that it resists relativism without denying that actual moral judgments are always constructed and partial.

TOWARD HYBRIDIZING METAETHICS: NATURALIST SHIFTS IN CONSTRUCTIVISM

Relational modes of feminist ethics and epistemology are enlightening when trying to sketch the implications of the relational notion of agency. Feminists often talk about a "human type of objectivity" that focuses on the process toward objectivity through optimally inclusive discourse, in which power relationships are taken into consideration. In feminist standpoint theory, for instance, methods to strengthen objectivity are inclusiveness and weighing of marginalized voices, as Sandra Harding (1991, 119–41, 160) argues (see also Haraway 1988, 586–99; Cf. Hekman 1995, 129–30,138–39). A few decades ago, feminists participated actively in the deconstruction of the modernist paradigm that divides narrative reality and the real world, but instead of straightforwardly supporting the narrative pole, many ecofeminists and feminists, especially those with a scientific background, constructed new alternatives to the conceptual polarization in order to also take materiality seriously. They argued that objectivity should always be seen as *embodied objectivity* (see Haraway 1988, 579–80). According to early ecofeminism, objects play active roles in knowledge construction, and therefore, accounts of the "real" world rely on socially, materially, and ecologically power-sensitive structures of "conversation" through which they are constructed. Objectivity is thus a constructive ethical *task* rather than an issue of pure representation. This idea is concurred upon by current philosophers leaning on embodied cognition extended mind thesis, and enactivism—who also often acknowledge what they owe to feminists (e.g., de Jaegher 2021; Johnson 1993, 2018; Rowlands 2005; cf. Haraway 1988, 589–90). Because rejection of a non-relational, non-embodied concept of agency in modern ethics was the main reason for many feminists to adopt postmodernism, material and ecological relational agency promotes their original aspiration to overcome the conceptual contradictions between nature and culture, or discourse and reality, without necessarily leading to relativism.[1]

Feminist modes of soft agential moral realism include textbook examples of the nuanced battle between realism and relativism. Despite the lack of success of some enterprises, the models developed at the edge of realism, for example, by Karen Barad, Donna Haraway, and Susan Hekman, should not be ignored when sketching the implications of an ecologically relational account of agency. In feminist ethics, better and worse usually refer to the emancipation of the society in which the moral codes are constructed. But it seldom claims that any actual political situation is, in terms of objective rationality, the best. Despite this, one situation may be *objectively better* than some others. This argument is not easy to defend, but a notable advantage brought about by this articulated concept of relational rationality is that it brings nonlinguistic and ecological communication between organisms into the discussion. This constrains, if not anchors, the idea of moral construction.

To take just one example of relational feminist approaches to embodied truth conditions, I want to introduce *agential realism*, a concept of Karen Barad, a physicist and feminist philosopher of science also known as one of the key figures of new materialism. It exemplifies the aspiration to overcome the discourse vs. reality dichotomy by focusing on the relationality of agency. As a scientist drawing especially on quantum physics, Barad highlights that according to an empirically accurate understanding, epistemological, ontological, and ethical considerations are fundamentally inseparable. Hence, Barad's agential realism is an "epistemological-ontological-ethical framework" concerning the role and meanings of "human *and* nonhuman, material *and* discursive, and natural *and* cultural factors in scientific and other social-material practices" (Barad 2007, 26). Her notion of material-mental "*intra-activity*" acknowledges the dynamic nature of reality and considers the relationship between cultural and natural elements as one of "exteriority within." According to the agential realist account, "matter is dynamic expression/articulation of the world in its *intra-active* becoming. All bodies, including but not limited to human bodies, come to matter through the world's iterative interactivity—its performativity. Boundaries, properties, and meanings are differentially enacted trough the intra-activity of mattering. The very nature of materiality is an entanglement" (Barad 2007, 93, 392–93).

Although this view is often called new materialism, the key issue is the relational activity that does not make a clear division between discourse and causality. Instead of making a choice between absolute types of exteriority and interiority, or between determinism and free will for a causal structure, Barad conceives agential intra-actions as causal enactments. If nature is "an antecedent entity" this means that "its very existence marks the inherent limit of constructivism" (Barad 2003, 824–25). Scientific practices do not reveal something that is already there but "what is 'disclosed' is the effect of the intra-active engagements of our participation with / in and as part of the world's differential becoming." Objectivity is a matter of "accountability for what materializes, for what comes to be. It matters which cuts are enacted: different cuts enact different materialized becomings." (Barad 2007, 361, 381). In agential realism, realism concerns phenomena that are ontologically inseparable components of agential intra-actions, instead of separate objects. This is a stronger claim than that of epistemological inseparability of observer and observed. Agential realism also draws the discussion beyond humanism to the sphere of posthumanism by claiming that nonhumans and material partners are important players in all kinds of natural-cultural practices.

Agential realism has both scientific and ethical implications. According to Barad, natural intra-actions always have a normative status. She talks about "ethics of mattering." Since observations and the agency of observation are "intra-actively" related, the construction of meaning is a material process, which implies that individuals are "responsible for the world of which we are a part, not because it is an arbitrary construction of our choosing but because reality is sedimented out of particular practices that we have a role in shaping and through which we are shaped" (Barad 2007, 390). Ethics does not just emerge from the relational structure of the world, but the ethical responses also are performative actions by which new matter is constructed: ethics is thus about "mattering and taking into account of the entangled materializations of which we are a part"; it is about "responsibility and accountability for the lively relationalities of becoming of which we are a part" (Barad 2007, 384, 393). Since moral agency exceeds the sphere of human beings, we should "meet the universe halfway to take responsibility for the role that we play in the world's differential becoming" (Barad 2007, 396). Agential realism blurs the distinction between given and constructed realities, and between determined and intentional actions. If each new materialization emerges as sedimented out of the previous states in which the given and the constructed are mixed, our self-construction as moral agents is intertwined in material reality, too. Moral realism that does not concern separate objects but ontologically inseparable phenomena as components of agential intra-actions combines elements of naturalism and constructivism that are traditionally considered metaethically contradicting. Naturalist concepts always refer to something constructed, and vice versa.

Concerning the legitimacy of moral notions, Barad's agential realism parallels the idea defended by Michael Tomasello from the viewpoint of evolutionary psychology and neuroscience. If normativity is explained by the hypersocial nature of human life, as Tomasello claims, moral conducts can have "a special power of legitimacy" in individual decision-making because of the "'we'>'me' psychological orientation," that makes "me" a part of "we" in a way that I am both judger and judged at the same time (Tomasello 2018, 668; 2016). Barad and Tomasello share the view that moral rationality is something bound to agency, however not any agency, but the agency in which material causalities and social constructions are inseparable. In such conditions, true moral concepts could, in theory, be rationally achievable. But because of relationality, actual procedures for rational justification are never inclusive and complex enough. The procedures for the best or the most truthful conduct are more like the procedures of agential virtuousness than the procedures of objective reason.

An important dividing element between postmodern feminism that celebrates the linguistic turn and ecofeminism arguing for modest realism concerns their views of agency. The systemic theories of nature in biology and physics encouraged early ecofeminists to develop the first steps toward relationally considered realism; despite criticizing robust realism, they wished to reject relativism. For those who wish to resist the linguistic turn and adopt a chastened version of social constructionism, the challenge for ethics is to balance between recognizing the power to construct and change the world and the limitations of that power. The truth "always escapes human efforts to know and control" (Peterson 2001, 211–12). Following this line of thought, responsibility concerns the mediation of truths by engaging in the self-construction of agency with these genuine others respectively, dialogically, and inclusively. Many feminist philosophers argue that ethics precedes knowledge as a condition for any objective epistemic proposition, partly following Emmanuel Levinas's way to give ethics the status of the first philosophy (Levinas 1969; cf. Warren 2000). Objectivity cannot be approached without commitment to transformative interactions, but the results of such interactions partly depend on the active recognized investment on the side of *all* relevant partners of the "participatory sensemaking," using the terms of enactivism. In theory, it is then possible to claim that such results are truth-apt in a modest sense of better and worse. Lacking objective moral senses and abstract rationality, the truth can only emerge from the irreducible nexus of interactions between the partners concerned. As Karen Warren, for example, argues, the "loving perception" for others is a precondition for both appropriate knowledge and action (Warren 2000, 65–66, 104–5). Interestingly, similar claims about the acknowledgment of cognitive partners have been recently put forward on the grounds of enactivism, perhaps most notably by Hanne de Jaegher (2021).

In relational ethics, instead of aiming for impartiality or the objective third person's perspective, care refers to the *reliability of a process for intellectual and moral advantage*. According to Warren, care is a condition for any appropriate method to approach truth, although care as such is not necessarily considered to be an instantiation of that truth (Warren 2000, 108–12). In this sense, Warren's view resembles neo-Aristotelian virtue epistemology defended by other ecofeminists, such as Lorraine Code and Linda Zagzebski. They argue that wisdom, *phronesis*, should be seen as the architectonic virtue: wisdom unites moral and intellectual virtues which are essentially unified in the constitution of agency (Code 2008, 189; Zagzebski 2003). However, taking ecological aspects of relationality into consideration, architectonic virtue should stress the relatedness of intellectual and moral abilities to the material and bodily conditions.

The naturalist twist in relationally revised constructivism has one especially interesting implication from the point of view of environmental ethics: the normative status of environmental responsibility lies in the complex interactive structure of moral reasoning and agency in which environmental others are engaged. *Responsibility for material things must precede any appropriate construction of moral (or epistemic) judgments.* Material structures and moral beliefs are reciprocally related and there is, in Christopher Preston's words, "a moral structure to material culture": environments are thick with constructed moral norms, and no moral culture can get rid of their influence. But the recognition of ecological others and material structures can make them more visible and thus sustain and reassert their role in the interaction, and this in turn enhances the moral culture of a place. But the risk of moral degeneration is always there: if material others are mainly generated or manipulated, the moral structure of material culture justifies beliefs that narrow or flatten the life of moral agents (Preston 2009, 175–82, 185–86; also Taylor, C. 1991, 6). Hope for moral progress lies in the fact that moral beliefs refer to material culture: the material things beyond construction, genuine otherness, wild things can contribute to the direction of construction, if only they are well recognized. According to Preston, this explains the normative status of claims against environmental manipulation. Relational agency blurs the dichotomy between considering moral concepts as either facts or constructions (or expressions). The content and construction of moral conduct cannot thus be conceptually separated in a traditional sense. Actual moral facts are necessarily plural, but it seems possible to claim that in the final sense of the moral facts, plurality converges if the perspectives become optimally intertwined through relational reconstructions of agency.

   I want to take two examples of hybridizing metaethics from a construction starting point that can be interpreted to refer to the relational nature of agency, though not explicitly argue for it. They are David Copp's realist-expressivism that considers moral agency emerging from social interactivity and Christine Korsgaard's constitutivism that refers to internal relationality of an agent. Analyzing these views as if they would include an articulated account of relational agency can, I think, enlighten the metaethical implications of the relational shift. Korsgaard and Copp defend soft moral realism without subscribing to the semantic thesis of robust realism. Both focus on "relationality" of moral agency as the ground to soften constructivism and justify normativity, which makes them fit for my experiment: Copp focuses on socially relational, collective agency and Korsgaard considers agency as reflectively structured. Despite admitting that moral reasoning is contextual, they argue that both normative authority and the autonomy of ethics can be defended. The difference between metaethical constructivism and realism concerns, according to Korsgaard, the use of normative concepts: while realists normally use them to describe normative facts (as independent from practical situations), constructivists use them as "schematic markers" for practical problems to be solved (Korsgaard 2013, 23; 2003, 115–19; 2015, 146; 2014, 419). Realism can thus be perfectly compatible with constructivism, although moral facts to which practical solutions refer are not evidently visible for those who do not face the problems (Korsgaard 2008, 325; 1996, 36, 113–14; 2003, 112–19).[2] My special focus here is, however, normativity.

   Copp's realist-expressivism is a hybrid theory that combines nonrepresentationalism concerning moral concepts with a pluralist-teleological explanation of normativity based on a collective idea of agency, while Korsgaard's neo-Kantian constitutivism explains normativity through the self-construction of agency on an individual level. Both thus offer a platform for a relational understanding of agency as the source of normativity. Both also admit that human morality is just a special type of animal morality, nothing exceptional, and share with non-reductionist naturalists the view that strict division between constructivism and naturalism results from an implausible notion of human morality (Copp 1995, 2007b, 2011; Korsgaard 2006, 2010). Korsgaard even argues that human and animal agencies can form a common collective (Korsgsaard 2013, 23–25). The concept of moral agency is the key that leads beyond the ordinary dividing lines between realism and expressivism in both theories (Copp 2001, 2008b; Korsgaard 2003, 2008, 2013). But Copp emphasizes the social structures of normativity based on collective moral autonomy (Copp 2007a, 2015), while Korsgaard, who highlights Kant's idea of communication as constitutive for reason, locates the source of normative self-reflection in agency that involves natural inter-personal relationships (Korsgaard 1996).

Copp's society-centered theory is a functionalistic type of constructivist naturalism that accepts the evolutionary adaptive link explanation of social structures. Moral reasons are constructed in the naturally evolved structures of collective agency, without being themselves reducible to natural facts: evolution provides a tendency to formulate moral beliefs in favor of social stability, peace, and cooperation (Copp 2007b, 13–26; 2008a, 198–201; 2009a; 2009b; 2011; 2013, 124–28). According to Copp, a moral proposition is true "if a corresponding moral standard is included in or implied by the moral code the currency of which in the relevant society would enable the society better to serve its basic needs than would the currency of other sets of norms and better than would be the case if no set of norms had currency in the society" (Copp 1995, 252–53; 2008a, 200). The truth conditions of moral propositions are described in terms of the status of corresponding standards: a proposition is true if the corresponding standard has relevant truth-grounding status, which is the status of being morally authoritative which, again, depends on the ability of the codes to serve the basic needs of a society. Normativity thus refers to society-like, nexus-type agency that authorizes the standards, rather than to a group of separate subjects. It emerges from the fact of pluralism which involves an aspect of teleology in a society-type entity. The truth value remains, however, approximate.

Copp's view can be seen as a generalization of John Mackie's idea of morality being a "'device' needed to solve 'the problem' faced by humans because of 'certain contingent features of the human condition.'" But contrary to Mackie's idea that "morality is normative only to the extent that it would be practically rational to adopt this device for a relevant purpose," Copp states that "the norms of practical reason themselves constitute a 'device' that is suited to ameliorating a 'problem of normative governance'" (Copp 2009b, 22; cf. Mackie 1977, 111, 121). This idea, which he calls the pluralist-teleological theory of normativity, underlines the mechanisms of collective agency as the source of normativity. While Mackie's view amounts to antirealist error theory, since he believes that moral judgments presuppose the existence of intrinsically prescriptive normative properties, which, he thinks, do not exist, Copp argues that such a presupposition is unnecessary, and the device theory is compatible with normative realism (Copp 2009b, 22–23; 2009a). So, normativity emerges from the practical rationality of a collective, or a society, as the collective requires a teleological aspect in which the plurality coheres. The expressive nature of actual moral judgments is bridged with realism about the teleological nature of normativity by autonomy: "the normative system with the function of dealing with the problem of autonomy is always relevant to evaluating deliberation." Whatever this system is, it "determines what we are rationally required to do" (Copp 2009b, 35–36). According to Copp, pluralist-teleological normativity can provide "a unified account of the truth conditions," since in all normative systems it is the problem of (collective) agency that determines the standards of practical rationality; autonomy is inseparable from the natural facts that make up its reflective form. The contents of the standard of autonomy represent truth, but autonomy also makes it possible for an agent to be directed by her own standards (Copp 2009b; 2015)

Environmental philosophers have recognized hybrid metaethics as promising midway approaches to combine the autonomy and authority of ethics with the normativity of actual environmental relationships (e.g., Jamieson 2008).[3] In my view, the most promising feature is included in the role some of them point to of collaboratively conceived agency for truth conditions and normativity. When appealing to the idea of collective autonomy, Copp's theory takes a relational tone: normativity is based on the constitution and functionality of the collective agencies. Objective and relative elements are hardly separable: "the moral truth is a function of the content of the moral code the currency of which in society would do most to ameliorate the problem of sociality" (Copp 2015, 3393). Such a code for sociality is ideal. Copp then stresses the division between realism and moral objectivism: actual normative systems need to be pluralist to ameliorate actual problems of society. Solutions should be "endemic to the human condition," but beyond them there is "a unified account of the truth conditions" (Copp 2009b, 36; see also 2006, 2007a). Using procedures as methods does not rule out that derivative principles can be true in a non-procedural sense: they provide moral principles the evaluative contents of which are not reducible to the procedure (Copp 2013, 125–28). I think it is worth making a distinction here between the evaluative and the descriptive content on the one hand, and between the actual and the final truth on the other (see Timmons 1999). While the descriptive content resulting from the evaluative content of the procedure refers to the actual truth, the ultimate evaluative content (the second level descriptive content)— the one that functions teleologically for ameliorating the constitution of the agency—refers to the final truth. One can well think that the descriptive content is (actually) true and that the evaluative force exists—because they are the outcome of the application of the procedure—without thinking that the evaluative content (or, final descriptive content) is an outcome of any actual application of the procedure.

From the viewpoint of relational agency, any individual actual agent cannot distinguish between the two meanings of content: one that represents the actual truth and another that represents the ultimate truth—or, in terms of naturalism, one that refers to what is *good for* the actual agency to enhance its constitution as agency, and another that refers to the ideal (teleological) state of agency in sense of the *(final) good*. A moral belief of any actual agent can only have descriptive contents in the first sense. But the awareness of the evaluative role of the latter may remain. Copp thus combines the plurality of normative reasons with the unified account of truth conditions through turning the focus from individual humans to the idea of collective moral agency, through which the pluralist notion of normativity becomes justified (Copp 2007a, 373, 386; 2006, 220–21). The theory exemplifies a simple type of relational moral rationality. Korsgaard's view is, however, perhaps even more inspiring.

NEW PROSPECTS FOR KANTIANISM THROUGH RELATIONAL CONSTITUTION OF AGENCY?

Christine Korsgaard makes an interesting shift in Kantian constructivism by focusing on the agent's constitution when grounding normativity in the self-governance of the agency. By this, she seems to open a track to detach a basically Kantian approach from modernist humanism in a way that invites us to pay attention to the relational constitution of moral agency. This section follows Korsgaard by interpreting her theory as if it adopts the relational notion of agency. I argue that considering the fundamental constitution of agency as a relational process changes the interpretation of Kantian ethics: the categorical imperative does not have to be the one between individuals sharing similar rationality, but it can concern the mechanisms of an interactive constitution of rationality in a multispecies web of agents.

Korsgaard criticizes the realist view of considering goodness as a fact of action since it would require another norm to dictate that one is obligated to perform that action, which exemplifies the normative gap. According to Korsgaard, normativity emerges at the level of the self-constitution of agency. The difference between metaethical constructivism and realism, which concerns the use of normative concepts, thus also refers to the difference in the concept of agency (Korsgaard 2013). Korsgaard argues that actions are morally good or bad by virtue of being good or bad as actions: their goodness is, thus, due to the function of action. This function is to constitute the agency, and by that, the identity of the agent. Conversely, the agent who acts "declares that what he does is good" (Korsgaard 2009b, 28–33; 2008, 228–29). By explaining the normative force in terms of practical problem solving, Korsgaard eliminates the additional normative question of why one should care. The source of obligations is a legislator, that is, the agent's own mind and will, which sets her theory to the side of voluntarism (Korsgaard 2013, 23; 2007a, 98). However, I argue that a relational definition of the agent as legislator makes a huge difference to what is commonly understood by a voluntaristic theory. I try to clarify this with the help of Korsgaard's view.

The key to Korsgaard's theory is, in my view, that moral agency (or the human mind, if the agent is defined as a human individual) has a reflective structure: moral authority is based on the *reflective structure* of self-consciousness, which is "the source of reason" and "the source of obligation" (Korsgaard 1996, 2007a, 2008, 2009a, 2014). There is no direct encounter with the *self* in human consciousness, but the reflective structure of the mind forces us to construct a "self-consciousness." The unity of agency is thus not given, entailing natural individuality. On the contrary, it is a normative *task*: "being the seat of a unified consciousness—sets you the task of constructing a unified mind, and a unified agency—in the normative sense." Korsgaard interprets Kant from this point of view: it is the structure of agency that establishes "a relation which we have to ourselves" which is a relation of authority—that is the source of obligation (Korsgaard 2007, 96–97; 2014, 209). Awareness of one's mental states, self-consciousness, "introduces a certain reflective distance between ourselves and our desires, so that we both can, and must, decide whether to act on them or not." To decide means to define what is good-for me in the final sense, that is, "to describe something's relation to my condition as having normative implications," which in turn is to sympathetically endorse my own condition (Korsgaard 2013, 23–24). The constitution of agency is thus the source of the reasons for action, and the authority of obligations.

My question is: can a relational notion of moral agency contribute to the discussion concerning moral reason? Carla Bagnoli formulates the criticists' question against the ability of a basically Kantian constructivism to combine normative and probative reason: "If the contents of reasons are decided, and if reasons are the products of the agent's deliberation how can they show anything about the world?" Even though the constructions of legislative reason have universal authority in a Kantian view, the worry remains concerning the possibility of moral knowledge. The criticism is justified: while reducing moral reasons to legislative decisions, constructivism is in danger of losing its capacity to account for the critical role of probative reason in making moral judgments (Bagnoli 2012, 149–50). A constructivist may be either realist or antirealist, although the borderline is not always clear. I argue that a decisive issue for the success of realism can be whether the concept of agency is defined in terms of modernist individualism or, as I suggest, of relational nexus. A relational notion bridges the agent's decisions with the world and the functions of the others, while an individualistic notion detaches normative and probative reasons of agency. It has been argued throughout this study that the activity of constructing agency takes place in the web of interactions that are perceptive, responsive, reflective, and dynamic. When Korsgaard claims that while making a choice you are at the same time constituting your identity, she is not far from accepting this relational account. By stating that choices do not take place between "you" and "the world" but are made "in the world" she denies detachment between the two (Korsgaard 2009a, 36–37; 1996, 18–26, 41–42, 100–2).

I do not see any reason to limit Korsgaard's idea of the self-constitutive construction of agency to under the skin of an individual human being. Unity of agency as a normative task remains the same even if the agency refers to the interactively constituted, embodied, and extended mind. If the relational account of mind is plausible, as I argue, cognitive processes include worldly constituents, and cannot be identified as detached from the world. Instead, external interactivity should be seen as constitutive for both reasoning and willing (e.g., Rowlands 2005, 25–26). These interactions are intertwined and unified in a knot of agency which is the actual agent. But each unification is a *task,* the performance of which determines who I am as an actual agent. To put it the other way around, responsibility for the relationships with social, environmental, and bodily partners constitutive for agency are responsibilities *for one's own moral agency.* According to Korsgaard, functions of agency are decisive for whether an action is governed by moral standards or not. Since decisive functions are interactive, autonomous agency is tied with the quality of interaction, as well as the function of the involved partners. The source of obligation can thus be seen in the self-constitutive construction of agency as relational.

If an embodied, ecologically relational notion of agency is correct, motivation and intention are compatible with non-subjectivism. Motivating reasons are actual moral reasons, and the source of these reasons is neither in the desires of individual subjects nor in the separate realm of facts, but in the interaction that constitutes agency. In Korsgaard's terms, the source of obligation is in conjunction with what we "do in (and to) the world." The contents of reason, while being "decided," are not detached from the world or from the quality of one's actions in relation to the world. According to Korsgaard, "the intimate connection between person and action does not rest in the fact that action is caused by the most essential part of the person, but rather in the fact that the most essential part of the person is *constituted* by her actions" (Korsgaard 2009b, 100). Although a fixed human identity is rejected, agency can function as the source of both obligation and moral reason (Korsgaard 2009a, 2009b, 2012). Adopting a relational view of agency does not prevent a theory from basing moral authority on it.

Autonomy is a crucial concept for Korsgaard, but autonomy required by reflectivity does not need to be defined in the traditional way. However, at this point it is relevant to talk about a special capacity of human beings that plays a role in moral agency: the knots of agency called human agents can, perhaps more than any other animal, be aware of the ways in which various relations operate on us and influence our action. This awareness gives each human being *an unusual obligation* for taking care of the optimal conditions and constitution of moral agency, that is, to ensure and develop moral capabilities. The fact that our choices "carry out the work of constructing a conception of the world and a self who is both a knower of that world and an agent within it" is the reason why "we human beings, unlike all the other animals, must justify our beliefs and actions" (Korsgaard 2009a, 39). The collaboration of the various physical and living partners taking part in the constitution of agency makes the agent conscious of itself as an agent, and thus, morally equipped. Whether the agent is morally equipped or not, thus, depends on whether the partners of this cognitive processes function well. Korsgaard's claim that normative self-constitution is an obligation can thus be seen to involve the conditions and capabilities of the entire web of relationships relevant for the constitution of our very agency. Relational moral agency in a way *justifies responsibilities for the body and the external environment already by definition*. Roughly put, if humans are not aware of themselves being obliged to enhance the conditions and capabilities of the nonhuman contributors in agency, the normative capacity to act for moral reasons becomes endangered.

Although a relational interpretation of the normative self-constitution of agency is an explanation of normativity, it is also organically linked with the idea of substantive normativity: one's obligation to justify one's actions arises from the possibility and need to reconceptualize the world and one's own agency. Together these tasks concerning the world and the agent constitute the activity of reason. "The principles of rationality . . . are principles of unification," which guide the activity of unifying both the experienced world and the self. Unifying oneself through interrelations with the environment is, according to Korsgaard, what practical reason aims at (Korsgaard 2009a, 33). She emphasizes the internal interaction of agency as the constitution of reason, which is the regulative principle for Kant. The idea of relational constitution of agency—which as such is a factual issue—makes a shift in the Kantian position. Commitment to the world through the constitution of agency involves some substantive conditions for agency: relationships need to be of a certain kind for them to bring about the unity of agency. This quality determines what is good, and at the same time, dictates the constitution of moral agency. There is thus *a normative quality to the commitment*. In this sense, Korsgaard's basically Kantian approach seems to share something important with virtue and care ethics. But since the quality of commitment is the method or procedure for unifying agency rather than the content of a normative concept, the content of moral concepts for an actual situation are not derivable directly from it.

Alongside its normative force, the autonomy of ethics that provides the non-relativist, critical point of view is an inalienable feature of moral realism that most environmental ethicists think is worth preserving. Korsgaard's transcendental argument of ethics is procedurally realist in a way that can explain its normative force without reducing the autonomy of ethics. A central element of her argument also is the action-based communicative structure of the agent's constitution, which is the source of obligation (e.g., Korsgaard 1996, 35–37, 112; 2009b). Although Korsgaard adopts the basically voluntarist claim about normativity—the source of obligations is a legislator, and we stand in that position to ourselves—it depends on the adopted concept of agency, whether the basically voluntarist argument for normativity distances or approaches moral realism. In Korsgaard's argument, it is the internal dynamics of agency that provide both reflectivity and normativity; the self-constitution of agency results conceptually from its relational structure (Korsgaard 2007, 2008, 2009b).

Although Korsgaard considers the relational structure of agency as internal to an individual agent, there seem to be no obstacles to make the argument for the case of the extended relational self-constitution of agency. If my analysis is correct, application of such an account implies a shift that can improve a basically Kantian ethics to meet the theoretical challenges of environmental ethics. It can also draw the theory interestingly toward metaethically midway positions. For Korsgaard, morality expresses the constitutive requirements of agency. The theory does not deny that moral concepts are real in the sense that actions are better or worse, but it denies the idea that moral truth would refer to propositional facts and relates it to the conditions of agency by which actions can be good or bad (Korsgaard 2009b; 2013, 22–25; 2015, 145–50). Korsgaard's way to combine elements from naturalist Aristotelian virtue ethics and Kantian constructivism makes it, in my view, especially insightful, and I argue that, combined with the idea of ecologically extended operations of agency, her theory can point to a track for a procedural and relationally realist notion of ethics. The basic argument for the source of normativity is much a Kantian one. In short, it says:

1. To rationally choose to do X, you must regard doing X as good.
2. You cannot regard doing X as good in itself, but can only regard doing X as good because it satisfies your needs, desires, inclinations, etc.
3. You cannot regard your desiring or needing to do X as making it good unless you regard yourself as valuable.
4. Therefore, you must regard yourself as valuable, if you are to make any rational choice. (Shortened formulations by Stern 2015, 2011.)

Thus far the argument only states that the reason to act is based on regarding things as valuable, not as whatever one desires or needs, but as what satisfies some of one's genuine needs or desires as a valuable agent. For example, it is impossible to make a rational choice whether to eat a piece of chocolate cake or not without valuing your genuine nature as the one who makes the choice for her genuine desire or need. But here we come to the definition of "yourself." To make rational choices, it is not enough to refer to the value of oneself (Korsgaard 1998, 54; 1996, 122, 249–50; Stern 2015; 2011, 89–90). According to Korsgaard, the problem vanishes by turning the focus on reflection. Reflection depicts reasoning and only its command can make an action obligatory. To reflect one defines "oneself" more generally, for example, in terms of humanity or personhood. An important conclusion then is that in order to act rationally, I should not value myself *qua* myself, but *qua* a rational agent (Korsgaard 1996, 101, 125, 164–65). But it should be noted that reflection is also an empirical fact about the cognitive processes, and the conclusion put in these words may thus still lead us in the wrong direction. To be precise, the idea that making a rational choice requires regarding oneself as valuable does not necessarily refer to any fixed human nature of the agent but that the agent is capable of making choices that are good for herself, meaning good for her genuine needs and desires. Korsgaard's argument can, in fact, be seen to refer to the nature of "agency" rather than to the nature of "humanity." This implies that it is the definition of *agency* rather than *humanity* to which moral concepts are connected. The crucial concept is practical identity that provides agency, which is the core of what must be valued instead of any substantial feature of human nature. If I am right, it is the *capacity of agency* defined through reflectivity that should be valued as the requirement for any rational choice for good. In this agency the double natures of identity—reasoning and legislating identity—coincide through communicative reflection (Korsgaard 1996, 165).[4]

In the argument based on the notion of practical identity, Korsgaard's definition of "yourself" no longer refers to the concept of humanity but rather to one's *identity* that has the general capacity of making it possible for an agent to live a life that contains reason, and to act in accordance with it. To make rational choices, choices that are good for you, you must value yourself *qua* rational agent. This points to the track for understanding the shift that a relational agency makes in Korsgaard's transcendental argument. Robert Stern formulates the transcendental argument as follows:

1. To rationally choose to do X, you must take it that doing X is the rational thing to do.

2. Since there is no reason in itself to do X, you can take it that X is the rational thing to do only if you regard your practical identity as making X the rational thing to do.

3. You cannot regard your practical identity as making doing X the rational thing to do unless you can see some value in that practical identity.

4. You cannot see any value in any particular practical identity as such but can regard it as valuable only because of the contribution it makes to giving you reasons and values by which to live.

5. You cannot see having a practical identity as valuable in this way unless you think that having a life containing reasons and values is important.

6. You cannot regard it as important that your life contain reasons and values unless you regard leading a rationally structured life as valuable.

7. You cannot regard leading a rationally structured life as valuable unless you value yourself *qua* rational agent.

8. Therefore, you must value yourself *qua* rational agent, if you are to make any rational choice. (Stern 2011, 90; Stern 2015)

Rational choice thus conceptually depends on valuing oneself as rational. But what does it require? It requires that I have a reason to act due to my practical identity (as a mother or as a teacher, for example), the reflectivity of which determines my actions. The acts are not independent from the actor in the sense that they have reasons in themselves; it is my practical identity as making X, which gives me reason to do X (step 2). But if the relational notion of moral agency is adopted, this does not only mean that "the acting self must in any case do what [the thinking self] says," but the reason dictating action is bound to "the fact that we are animals of a certain kind," namely "autonomous moral animals" (Korsgaard 1996, 165). This natural fact is *a contingent one*: it has not always been so, and it can change. Therefore, the influence between "the acting self" and "the thinking self" should be seen as *two-directional*. The meaning of practical identities for moral reason is that they contribute to giving us reasons and values by which we live. This is the way in which they get their value (step 4). Identity is an active part of agency, and therefore, it counts. Applying relational agency implies focusing on the activity which takes place in relationships by, for example, moving either toward or away, recognizing or ignoring, and joining with or distancing oneself from something. This something contains contingent natural issues by which the agent who has a particular practical identity lives. Going through to the seventh and eighth step we come back to the conception of "yourself." Rational choices require valuing of "yourself" (*qua* agent), but this refers to *things that make your agency capable*.

If rationality is considered relationally and practiced elementally in the socio-ecological nexus, then the argument would conclude that we must value our ecologically relational agency. Consider this: if we take reason and autonomy as collective issues, Korsgaard's conclusion turns out to claim that rational choices require us to value the collective and the conditions of collective reasoning. If the relational definition of human rationality and autonomy is correct, then the conclusion turns out to claim that making rational choices requires valuation of the balanced functioning of one's ecological, material, and social relationships, or valuation of the collective and each of its mutually related members. Five implications follow from adopting relational moral agency in Korsgaard's argument. First, since we are aware of the mechanisms realized in the constitution of our agency, which is the source of our obligations, we are *normatively bound* to taking care of relationships with social and material earthly others in a way that sustains our rational agency. The agency capable of constituting our rationality relies on the web of interactions between various earthly partners. Second, this means that there are some mechanisms to which moral concepts necessarily and objectively refer. Because moral concepts need to refer to the rational constitution of moral agency, which is the reason for action, in case of relational agency, moral concepts must refer to *the functions of the relational mechanisms* that constitute rational moral agency. These functions are not bound to any actual agent or situation. Instead, they are the fundamental conditions of moral agency.

Third, this implies that moral concepts are not expressions of some individual mind—even though they get their normative status by being such expressions: some mechanisms of interaction are *objectively better* than some others. Fourth, earthly others take part in the reflective processes that create the source of normativity, but the content of obligations reflects back to these partners in a way that also establishes how the contents of moral obligations play a role as conditions of rationality, although the actual contents are bound to actual situations. From the point of view of an agent, such obligations are—in a way—not just constructed. Fifth, moral responsibility is compatible with the limited freedom of will. If you are acting in the world, commitment to the mechanisms that constitute your rationality is a fact. In fact, you are committed to some relationships more than to others and focus on recognition of some more than others. Because of complexity of the world and the agent's cognitive operations, capacities at one moment, that is, for one particular actual "agent," are limited: you cannot focus on everything. Making choices is inevitable: you are always forced to choose between partners, and your interaction with them will contribute to constructing your practical identity. But these choices and interactions are not—at least not entirely—causally determined. Whether you recognize certain bodily messages or not influences the weight they have in your reasoning. This is the case with material, nonhuman, and social relationships that together form the ecological structure of your identity.

The idea of affordance used in an enactive approach to cognition could help in considering how the interactive nature of mind dissolves the subjective-objective dichotomy here. What you perceive are affordances of the world, which means that your ability to perceive is shaped in mutual interaction with the world (e.g., Gibson 2014). Your ability to encounter and recognize certain messages and the ways you can and will respond to them depends on your encountering them and on practices of recognition and response to such messages. "Freedom" of responding, focusing, or emphasizing relationships, and maintaining others by the interaction makes a difference in the constitution of your agency. These responses and participations implemented in the nexus of relationships make it justified to regard agents as *responsible for the direction in which their agency develops*.

AN ANIMAL TYPE OF AUTONOMY AND RESPONSIBILITY FOR AGENCY

For the Kantian notion of moral autonomy, normative self-governance guarantees that there is an ability to surpass determination. While normative constitution of agency is usually considered in terms of political philosophy, Korsgaard reconciles the idea of autonomy with natural (evolutionary) explanations of embedded moral reasoning: autonomy does not have to be something nonnatural or even unique for humans (Korsgaard 2011; cf. Copp 2008a, 198–201). According to Korsgaard, autonomy is not a uniquely human feature, but other animals can also have agency and act autonomously to a certain extent. The agencies of human and other animals share a lot, but humans are, however, the only animals *aware of* the constitution of agency and its mechanisms (Korsgaard 2012, 2018). Hence, they are *moral* animals: humans are conscious not only of their acts and intentions, but also of the reasons and principles that guide their actions and relationships (Korsgaard 2010, 21–23; 2009b, 104–8; 2011). Therefore, the ways they are related with other beings differs from the ways other animals are—in the sense that sets them *moral* obligations. Since the constitution of agency forms the source of obligations for the agent, humans are *normatively bound to care for* the constitution of their own agency. The difference between humans and other animals is, however, not of kind—as Kant claims—but of degree—as Darwin claims (Korsgaard 2006, 109).

Korsgaard argues that the mechanism of self-governance, and hence, normativity, has its origins in natural history: when members of a species became aware of the role of their own attitudes in how the world is for them, they began to assume control over themselves and their responses. You may distance your attitudes from your world when you recognize that the way the world seems to you is not the same as the way it seems to me, and that this is due to your attitudinal contribution to the way the world is for you. When acknowledging the interconnectedness between your attitudes and the way the world is for you, you may distance your mental attitudes from the world. In evolution, control over one's responses was first directed to ordinary activities, and this is common to autonomy of all species. But since an animal recognized that "conceptualizing, evaluating, and responding to the world are things that our minds do" she started to do them "self-consciously." According to Korsgaard, to be a normatively self-governed animal is to believe and act because of normatively committing thoughts (such as "'yes, this is what I believe' 'yes, this is the right thing to do'"), which starts carrying normative commitment and rising new questions about whether things we do are correct and what is a good reason to act or to believe (Korsgaard 2010, 21–23). Self-governance thus requires engagement in one's constitution, commitment to others, and interactive responses to the outside world. However, evolution is not a story about the origins of specific moral contents, but about how morality evolved through normative commitment and practical problem solving, from which the normatively "self-governed animal" emerged (Korsgaard 2011).

Korsgaard's view of autonomy thus has an important Darwinian tone: it is the precondition for taking reflective distance for beings whose evolved conscious abilities are complicated enough. Once this level is reached, a difference emerges between those who are responsible for their agency and those who are not. Continuity between the autonomy of human and other animals is unbroken but the ways to perform it differ. It is the actual constitution of identity that makes those who are aware of their attitudes and the potential influences of their attitudes morally responsible for the actions they are aware of (Korsgaard 2011, 102–3). If agency is considered relational, whether that constitution of identity succeeds or not relies on the ability of an agent to be responsive (response-ability) in the interactive relationships constitutive for her agency. According to Korsgaard, the mechanisms of moral agency are *laws for an agent aware of them.* Human agents constitute their agency by adopting laws to govern their actions, but these laws may "succeed or fail" in performing agency. Whether I succeed or fail in performing my own agency is due to my ability to follow the mechanisms that best constitute it; mental activity "consists in following rational norms" (Korsgaard 2014, 196–97, 203). Performing relational agency is not, however, an issue of an individual human being but takes place in the nexus of interaction with various others, which makes such self-governance possible.

The special feature that is recognized either as an advantage or a problem for Korsgaard's constitutivism is that it makes a connection between descriptive and normative elements of good *via* agency. As Korsgaard conceives of moral judgments as conclusions of practical reasoning rather than descriptions of facts or expressions of emotions, she avoids a contradiction between cognitivism and noncognitivism (Korsgaard 2003, 105). Contrary to both reductionist naturalism and nonnaturalism, normativity is based on the self-authenticating account of standards of practical reason. So "the reason for an action is not something outside of, or behind, or separate from, the action" (Korsgaard 2008, 214, 227–29).[5] However, one's awareness of her mental (and physical) states "introduces a certain reflective distance" between herself and her desires, and she "can, and must, decide whether to act on them or not" (Korsgaard 2013, 23). Normativity of the responses adds a special feature to the practical reason that makes the constitution of identity crucial for normative rationality. The practical constitution of moral identity, thus, plays a key role for what counts an obligation.[6]

But identity is not necessarily an individual thing or a stable state of affairs: self-constitution involves the adoption and maintenance of "practical identities" including "the roles and relationships in terms of which we value ourselves and find our lives worth living and our actions worth undertaking." Whatever promotes and constitutes practical identity is included in "the functional sense of good-for and therefore the final sense too" (Korsgaard 1996, 101; 2015, 149). If identity, rationality, and autonomy are to be defined relationally, the interactive mechanisms and function of the factual ecological nexus of life are—at least partly—decisive for the contents of normative concepts. Korsgaard could agree that normative self-governance is bound to the relationality of an agent, which would provide a normative link between an individual human and all by whom/which she becomes aware of her agency. The fact that she does not clearly articulate the meaning of ecological and material relations is, in my view, a weakness both normatively and metaethically.

In Korsgaard's view, an agent is at the same time a functional system having functional goods-for, and a conscious unit having efficacy to go for what is good from his point of view. He necessarily values his own efficacy, which means that he values his functional good "as an aspect of his final good." But Korsgaard rejects the naturalist idea that "the final good for people is survival and reproduction, or simple maintenance, or even to lead a healthy life of our kind . . . unless we take a capacious view of what is involved in self-maintenance, or in leading a healthy life of our kind" (Korsgaard 2015, 148–49). Despite being conceptually separated, both functional and final senses of good refer to "the same set of facts, but from two perspectives." Health, for instance, exemplifies good in a functional sense, but it is not valued as a means but as the excellence or goodness of the physical life. Virtues are not for something beyond them: "what the practice of moral virtue makes us capable of . . . is virtuous activity itself" (Korsgaard 2015, 143). Having final good is an essentially relational state; it "*just is* standing in relation to evaluative goodness that is made possible by consciousness" (Korsgaard 2013, 22). Leaning on Kant, Korsgaard argues for the idea of good (good *simpliciter*) "as a criterion for identifying, or better, for constructing, the good itself" or "looking for the ends that we can share." But a solution for the problem of shared ends, which is to be named "good," or "good-for all," requires—to put it in the terms used in this book—a relational understanding of identity. The reason to operate with moral concepts is that we are forced to face the task to construct conditions that are good for all. It requires an agency that is "capable of seeing the world through the eyes of others." Without cultivating proper relations, empathy, and commitment, it is not possible to meet the task to construct "a state of affairs that is, as far as possible, good-for us all" (Korsgaard 2013, 24–25). The moral obligation of promoting good-for all then calls for a good construction of moral identity and care for included interactivities.

Korsgaard's idea about the source of normativity in self-constitution seems compatible with the idea of relational agency—and in fact somewhat presumes it. Things that constitute and promote practical moral identities are good in some noninstrumental sense; "successful maintenance of our practical identities is the excellence of our lives." As has been argued above, on the grounds of given scientific evidence, it is justified to consider these processes as materially, ecologically, and socially relational. Subscribing to a relational view implies that unifying moral reason has to do with the mechanisms operating in relationships by which practical identities become maintained. It seems that adoption of an ecologically relational account of agency would not make dramatic changes in Korsgaard's theory as such. But it would make it possible to argue for the normative status of the nexus of our complex environmental relations and involved nonhuman and physical others. They are participants in our self-constitutive agency and their good-for is a prerequisite of our own functional and final good. The normative rationality and self-constitution should then be seen to include the balanced good-for of the wide nexus of various partners in which reasoning takes place.

Relational agency adopted to Korsgaard's theory thus has an important normative implication in environmental ethics. As part of one's self-constitution, and in order to maintain it, an agent is obligated to act in relation to the relationships that participate in forming her practical identity in a way that enables her own moral rationality and normative self-constitution. Taking the relational notion of agency as embodied and extended, as I have suggested, this is substantially an *environmental norm*. Responsibility for the good of the systemic webs of interaction in social and ecological environments becomes *normatively justified as responsibility for one's own agency*. Such a conclusion resembles what we saw to be an implication of enactivism for the concept of autonomy. Xabier Barandiaran even formulates it in a Kantian mode: "behave so as to sustain your capacity to behave" in relation to those collaborating with you in the participatory sensemaking or other extended, embodied, and enacted mental processes (Barandiaran 2017, 423–24; see also chapter 7). In my view, the fact that relationality involves the good of external material and nonhuman partners and their roles in enabling moral rationality strengthens Korsgaard's idea of metaethical convergence between constructivism and realism.

Korsgaard emphasizes the mutual relatedness of cognitive virtue, moral epistemology, and identity: "Importantly, because you are a functional system that works *by* tracking your own good through perception and thought, when you do get it wrong, you are malfunctioning. The very fact that you don't know what's good for you is, in a way, a large part of *what* is wrong" (Korsgaard 2015, 149). Tracking our good makes our functional system work, which in turn is made possible by us knowing what is good for us. Cognitive ability and functional efficiency are then inseparable in the concept of the good. According to critics, this forms a circular argument that may appear as a weakness of the constitutive theory (see Bagnoli 2011). However, an explicitly articulated notion of the ecologically relational functioning of mental operations—which can even be seen as implicitly present at some points of Korsgaard's texts—would benefit the theory. As a nonindividualist conception, a functional system refers to the complex, materially, and socially anchored web in which the actual good changes through each action, instead of through an isolated individual who both dictates and is dictated to. This could prevent circular arguments.

Adoption of relational concept of agency to a basically humanist type of constructivist ethics shifts the focus a) from discourse to discursive-material interactive processes, b) from social structures to ecological (including social) structures, c) from opposing reasoning and moral reason to the complex interconnections between the real and the constructed, d) from acceptance as justification to actual acceptance as natural-social reliability, e) from considering evolution as an ended process that produced conditions for autonomy and reasoning to considering it as a continuing process, the future influences of which partly depend on the current use of these capacities, and f) from considering the function of an actual individual agent as the measure for the proper constitution of agency and as the source of normativity to considering the mechanisms of the relational constitution of agency as methods for enhancing agency and as the source of normativity. If normativity is defined in terms of the self-constitution of agency, as for Korsgaard, but also in ecologically relational terms, the derived source of normativity is partly *external*, and hence, beyond the legislative freedom of an actual agent—and *real* in a certain sense. A relational notion of agency thus bridges the agent's legislative decisions with the *coherence of the interactive nexus of relations* in the external world. Cognitive and affective elements cannot be strictly separated as has been done in both traditional internalism and externalism. At least some aspects of the "external" world are "internalized" through mutual interaction. We could, perhaps, talk about "extended internalism" instead of opposing internalism with externalism. This would have further implications for the conception of moral motivation. Relational constitution of moral rationality also draws a theory toward a metaethically modest position, perhaps a hybrid one.

Constructivism in forms that Korsgaard and Copp understand it seeks to offer a metaethical option for defending moral objectivity without applying the ontological and epistemological load of nonnaturalist realism. However, its ability to offer distinctive moral semantics, its success at steering a middle way between metaethical realism and antirealism, and the tenability of its explanation of practical truths in terms of constitutive practical reasoning have been criticized (e.g., Bagnoli 2011; Bratman 2012). A relational perspective to moral activity can, however, make a conceptual shift that contributes to this discussion: constructivism could survive better as a metaethical framework for environmental ethics striving for scientifically plausible and slightly realist ethical theory if the construction of moral reasons were located in relational reasoning involving material, ecological and social interactions.

SOME CONCLUSIVE REMARKS

What has been said so far proves that a relational account of moral reasoning and autonomy can have theoretical and normative implications in addition to explanatory clarification. Applying relational moral agency to either naturalist or constructivist ethics can support their modestly realist forms. This became especially clear in that relationally shifted forms of both carefully deny every type of drastic reductionism. Reductionist explanations of moral concepts and actions for moral reason become undermined through denying that any one definable reality (whether physical, psychological, evolutive or social) survives alone as an explanatory reality.[7] But at the same time, explicating moral agency as relational ensures that moral concepts cannot be detached from external reality. Some of the differentiating issues between moral realism and antirealism, such as the gap between constructed and factual realities, therefore become unclear.

To summarize the features of the relational shift that have philosophical implications in both ethical naturalism and constructivism, four issues are worth emphasizing. First, relationality calls for a critical stance against nativist naturalism because relationships between the brain and consciousness, or physical objects and mental operations, are seen as mutually interactive and collaborative, instead of purely causal. The traditional views of causality and natural determinism of the nonhuman world become questioned, and freedom and intentionality revised. Second, relationality of the mind means that it involves external bodily, environmental, and social interactants. Therefore, natural relationships constitutive for agency are not reducible to physical causalities. Mental operations resulting either in descriptions or prescriptions cannot be defined in terms of internalized minds. Third, relationality supports a basically Darwinian interpretation of human naturalness in the sense that human mental capacities used in moral reasoning differ from the capacities of nonhuman animals in degree, but not in kind. Fourth, each entity taking part in the interaction share vulnerability and dependency on each other: the autonomy of each partner is essentially dependent on others and the actions of each can fundamentally harm the autonomy of the others (Pescador Canales and Mojica 2022). In this sense, interactive agency makes the fates of different entities mutually intertwined.

This part of the journey led us to touch on some metaethical and normative implications of relational agency. There are two general conclusions. First, a relational approach shares much with the ethics of care and virtue ethics. Adoption of relational agency into naturalist approaches highlighted the possibility of a relational account of agency to enhance virtue ethics in solving problems concerning the relationship between natural good and final good, which may mean a substantial contribution to the virtue discussion. Second, relational agency is adoptable even to a basically humanist Kantian ethics. As our experiment to adopt a relational account of agency to Christine Korsgaard's argument for normativity showed, such a combination results in the normative justification of responsibility for material and nonhuman companions of reasoning (as well as for social ones) as necessary for the responsibility for one's own moral agency. If the source of normativity is in the self-constitution of agency, as Korsgaard argues, agency considered as relational—meaning that construction of agency partly relies on these external environmental partners—involves these partners and the interactivity binding them together as partly constitutive for the self-constitution of agency. Hence, it is not indifferent from the viewpoint of the moral agent's ability of self-regulation whether she cares for the good of these others or not.

NOTES

1. Attempts toward such a shift are, for instance, Sandra Harding's constructivist materialism, Lynn Hankinson Nelson's empiricism as community-based knowledge, Lorraine Code's regulative realism, Bruno Latour's agency of nonhuman entities, Andrew Pickering's world filled with agency and the embodied intellect, and Karen Barad's agential realism. See Hekman 2008, 89–94,103–4, 109, 110–12. Susan Hekman, who prefers to define agency as *discursive* rather than as *relational*, ends up denying objectivism and realism. See Hekman 1995, 72–76, 110–12, 138–39, 160.

2. For criticism of Korsgaard's notion of realism, see e.g., Crisp 2006 and FitzPatrick 2005.

3. According to Sinnott-Armstrong, Copp's theory is the only successfully hybridist one that falls into realism. See Sinnott-Armstrong 2009 and 2007.

4 Elements by which reasoning and legislating identities coincide refer to Korsgaard's neo-Kantian interpretation of unified reasons (Kant's theoretical and practical reason) through communicative or relational practices. See also O'Neill 1989.

5. The disputed issue about the relationship between justification (resulting from a cognitive state of mind) and motivation (resulting from an attitudinal state of mind) can be relocated through the analysis Korsgaard gives. Instead of locating justification in the objective world (reached by cognition) and motivation in the subjective world (reached by conation), they are different instantiations of how we use attitude language about ourselves.

6. When Kantian philosophers say "the agent must think of herself as a citizen of the Kingdom of Ends," meaning that practical reason is linked with one's practical identity, they argue that the coverage of the moral law derives from how the agent identifies herself. Korsgaard 2007, 96, 106.

7. Since no single faculty can explain moral agency, even though each individual feature of moral agency would be relativized, this does not necessarily entail that moral agency as a whole could. See Light 2000, 63; Rowlands 2005; Preston 2001.

PART IV

Ethics for Relational Agents

The journey has brought us to the point where we need to ask where the relational conceptual shift of moral agency will take us. What is beyond humanism as we knew it? Is it a new type of humanism, posthumanism, or something entirely new? And what does it offer to environmental ethics? Ethics is usually divided into three distinctive fields: descriptive, normative, and metaethics. Descriptive ethics as a field of empirical morality and metaethics as a field of conceptual analysis are separated from normative theories that are concerned with "oughts." While normative ethics asks, what should I do, and why should I do it, metaethics asks, why should I care what I should do. The contextual limits of deliberation and action are normally recognized in terms of descriptive ethics: they concern the explanations of morality as a phenomenon, and it cannot justify any prescriptive principles and rules; the moral reasons for action are autonomous from nonmoral, explanatory reasons. However, if moral agency is considered as relationally constructed, claims for such isolation seem both mistaken and morally narrowing. Relational explanations of "knowing" and "expressing" or of the fundamental dynamicity of the relationship between the world of "objects" and the world of "agency" make changes in these common categories and question the common way of distinguishing between (descriptive) explanations and (prescriptive) ethics without supposing reduction between them.

Is the agent-based relational conceptual shift then relevant for normative ethics and/or metaethics, or does it just offer alternative explanation of the contingent facts that play a role as means in moral deliberation? And how does relationality contribute to ethical debates about the problems faced by the modernist presumptions in environmental ethics? In the previous part I argued that when explanations concern the core elements of moral agency, such as autonomy and reasoning, they also have philosophical, metaethical,

217

and normative implications. Implications of the relational explanations were briefly exemplified by adopting such a view to some of the known ethical theories. It also became clear that the relational shift persuades constructivism and naturalism, as well as the empiricist and the rationalist theories, to approach each other. Now it is time to find out what a relational approach to ethics could offer us on its own.

In this part I shall initially sketch a relational approach to ethics. My special interest is still in environmental ethics, especially in how a relational approach would answer basic questions concerning normativity and truth-aptness of moral concepts: Why should I care for the environment? And is it possible to make a difference between better and worse? Environmentalists would widely welcome a route that rejects both reductionism and nonnaturalism of moral agency but can save the normative authority and the evaluative autonomy of ethics. In my view, a relational approach can offer a novel option. At the first stop of this last part of our journey we shall discuss relational ethics as a metaethical position and my initial notion of relational realism as a midway model. At the second stop we shall articulate the main normative implication of relational agency in environmental ethics and open the discussion on the practical implications in environmental ethics and policy making. Reconceptualizing moral agency relationally relocates the basic aspiration of environmental ethics and turns the focus to the fact that interactions constitutive for the agency are, on the one hand, internal to extended human rationality and intentional operations in a way that they can be called *intra-actions,* and on the other hand, they take place between the knots of the interactive nexus, that is, between individual members of the multispecies community (see chapter 9). Cultural values, personal habits, and scientific and political practices should be assessed from the perspective of sensitivity and care they can provide for the relationships constitutive of moral agency. Normative relational ethics seems best to be articulated in terms of virtue ethics, though in nontraditional ways.

Chapter 10

Relational Foundations for Environmental Ethics

THE DILEMMA STARTS TO DISSOLVE

Actual moral cultures can be seen to develop in the sense of advancement through the development of agency in practices of ecologically inclusive care. But the claim that one direction of development is better than some other supposes moral realism. I argue that although a relational approach challenges common interpretations of realism, it refers to the metaethical position I would call *relational realism* (Nurmi 2020). My aim in this chapter is to open the discussion concerning relational realism and an agential relational approach to ethics rather than to complete a definite view. The most critical questions about the possibility of a relational agent-based ethics to survive as realist concern the compatibility of normative authority of moral propositions (implemented in motivation), and the autonomy of moral concepts (implemented in their truth value) with an ethical theory that conceives moral rationality as relational. Relational ethics should offer proper solutions to avoid both threatening ends for any modest theory: reductionism lurking inside of naturalism, and relativism lurking inside of constructionism.

A robust form of moral realism is committed to three theses. According to the semantic thesis, moral predicates refer to moral properties in a way that moral statements represent moral facts, and propositions of the statements are (at least approximately) true or false. According to the thesis concerning truth, some moral properties are true. And according to the metaphysical thesis, the truth value of moral propositions relies on the metaphysical status of moral facts and properties to not be relevantly different from the status of nonmoral facts and properties. While the most usual modes of minimal realism exclude the metaphysical thesis and defend (nonnaturalist) moral universalism, constructivists usually contradict the semantic thesis: moral properties refer semantically to the internal activity of the agent(s), and the source of obligation is in the subjects and their mutual communication. While this is often seen to correlate with antirealism, a relational constitution of identity, knowledge, and action denies simplified division between (determined) external facts and (free) internal activity. In accordance, antirealism becomes softened. Concerning the semantic thesis of realism, a relational shift implies that the clarity of the division between semantic categories, on which the representational suppositions rely, vanishes. Since body-based intersubjectivity is constitutive for moral agency, even constructed propositions are closely tied with external natural facts, whatever they are, which softens the conceptual division between expressivism and cognitivism.

Concerning the thesis on truth value, a relational shift increases uncertainty and highlights the direction of the processes: constructed propositions always remain partial and none of the actual propositions can fulfill the conditions of truth alone. But some actual conducts approach the truth better than some others due to the inclusive procedures of interactivity, and thus reflect the correct direction. Concerning the metaphysical thesis, relationally constructed agency can admit without contradiction that moral facts and properties have a certain natural connection. However, both natural and moral facts should be defined non-reductively. This may refer to a slightly naturalist type of realism, but not in a robust mode. Moral facts can neither be reduced to nonmoral facts nor to free choices. Relational agency relocates the discussion by distinguishing truth about the reliable and justified moral conducts of an actual situation from the procedural truth about the constitution of agency, which also has semantic implications for the concept of truth itself. Truth (in a final sense) concerns ideal agency formation, the process of which embodies itself better or worse in each construction of actual conducts. Despite being constructed, actual truths rely on reality; cultural narratives by which moral concepts acquire their meanings, are not independent from the objective elements they involve. At the metaethical level, conceptual relationality questions both robust realism and standard expressivism, but modest forms of both relationally procedural realism and expressivism seem defendable in the sense that do not require stability of actual truths. Relationality softens the differences of constrained constructivism and agent-focused non-reductionist naturalism into nuances.

Tension between freedom and nature counts among the fundamental problems for those who wish to argue for authority and autonomy of ethics and, at the same time, take seriously the empirically plausible notions of human naturality. A weakness of traditional rationalism in ethics is that it assumes exceptional human uniqueness and freedom. Empiricism does not need such an assumption, but its weakness is in its capacity of defending the autonomy of ethics. These problems reflect the most crucial theoretical dilemma for environmental ethics. Aspirations to overcome the tension by unifying natural and moral agencies by an appeal to ontological holism or Romanticism are common in environmental ethics, but they easily lead to a blind alley. Environmentalists should not just conflate human moral community with natural ecological relationships or derive guidance directly from natural sentiments. However, the previous chapters have posed the question of whether these metaethical poles are properly located if they are described in the humanist way. Can "the human moral community" as the source of rationality be confronted with "the natural environment" as an empirical object? How are they intertwined?

According to Kant's third antinomy, antinomy of freedom and nature, *causality* is a category for the experiences and understanding of natural reality as it appears to us, while *reason* is a category that pushes toward universal principles. While aiming toward autonomous moral principles, reason is faced with the dilemma of two metaphysical dogmas about causality: the empiricist dogma about unbroken chains of causalities and the rationalist dogma about the first cause(s) that begins new chain(s) of causal connections. Kant's famous solution is to reject both as transcendental illusions and to argue that as the thesis and the antithesis of an antinomy they are both legitimate perspectives that do not offer as such access to the transcendent world. There seems to be an irreducible ambiguity at the core of moral experience. But Kant's separation between the standpoints of "the two worlds" of nature and freedom sets significant limitations for environmental ethics. As Robert Kirkman asks (2009, 219), what can be the grounds for "a moral vision of harmony in the relationship between humans and our environment when that relationship is always dual"? The relational approach denies that the options are restricted to separation and unification. If there is something basically natural that enables certain acts to be called autonomous ("free") through relationally constituted agency, a third option is defensible.

Although each individual feature and each actual stage of moral agency can be relativized, good moral agency as whole cannot, because it is not reducible to any single faculty or stage of actual agency. The mechanisms and structures of relatedness are decisive for the quality of agency in the sense that concepts like good and right can be subjected to them. Actual moral reasons are influenced by the contextualities of reasoning, but also vice versa: actual moral conducts influence the reasoning processes through the consequences of actions that make differences in the constituents and, hence, self-constitution of agency. Embodied agency, whether it is natural (animal type) or moral (human type), makes changes in the world in which the agency itself is collaboratively constituted. Therefore, all such acts count normatively. Relational reasoning pays attention to the nondescriptive implications of factual states of affairs and conditions of life and thus questions the idea of normative ethics as restricted to the guidance of narrowly defined moral (deliberated, individual) actions (also Preston 2003, 2009). The sphere of actions that fall under moral evaluation thus extend beyond the traditional definition of moral actions since factual premises concerning agency are involved in normative rationality. There are moral actions in which the actual individual agent is not autonomous in the traditional sense when implementing an act. Therefore, the idea of moral responsibility also becomes extended in time and spread among individuals. Besides actual responsibilities, there are responsibilities for the conditions of agency, including for future generations. There are also responsibilities that one must carry without being blamed as an individual for the action itself, for instance, because of the acts of previous generations (as climate ethics well exemplifies) or because of being a powerless member of a collective or society active in question.

But all this is not just a descriptive fact about the contingent contextuality of ethics. A relationally shifted ethical theory also seems to support a metaethically demanding, realist claim: the constitution and active use of agency can make the world better or worse, at least in some semi-objective sense derived from the functions of agency. The shift of empirical stance in contemporary science toward describing moral operations relationally has implications for both moral reasoning and moral rationality. Relational agency mixes factual causalities and intentional operations in a complex way that makes clear division between determined operations and free actions impossible. This, again, implies that the categories of constructed and non-constructed realities, to which different premises of a moral argument separately refer, become vague. As was described, in the case of naturalist ethical theories relationality implies that the possibility of sound moral deliberation must be grounded in the proper use of natural relationships that are dynamic and dialogical, and that moral rationality must also concern the relationships to and conditions of interactants in the "external" environment. This makes strict difference between anthropocentrism and ecocentrism in environmental ethics irrational. In the case of constructivist ethics, it implies that intentional elements providing autonomy are not necessarily free in the traditional sense, but that the course of action can change indirectly through the process of the constitution of agency, and that successful moral construction requires cultivating the conditions of autonomy and rationality, meaning that external conditions and partners need to be cared for. As naturalism and constructivism that adopt relational agency no longer fit into hardwired metaethical positions to which they have been usually classified, ramifications of the relational turn contribute to the metaethical debates of normativity and truth-aptness of moral propositions.

The concept of moral realism, as well as expressivism or antirealism, seems to need redefinition. In the previous part I used two heuristic means to explain how metaethically opposing perspectives can be mediated into hybridity or compatibility: by making a conceptual distinction between actual and final moral reasons, and by locating the non-conditional truth of moral concepts in the methodological issues by which ecologically relational agency is constituted. These methods are also important when trying to sketch an alternative midway proposal based on the relational conceptual shift. To argue that the fundamental relationality of moral agency does not rule out realism means that there is at least some ground to argue that moral concepts have noncontingent linkage, some autonomy as a regulative conceptual system is not reducible to the explanations of moral life, and some normative authority over moral agents in the sense that it can somehow guide and move them. The authority of ethics is linked with nondetermined explanations of the source of moral obligations. Admitting the constitutive role for the contingent relationships of practical identity in moral rationality seems, at first glance, to undermine its authority. However, as was seen in the case of Korsgaard's theory, there are strong arguments for locating the source of normativity in the mechanisms of the self-constitution of agency. Instead of considering normativity emerging from either inside or outside the subject, from either individual (or social) legislative mind or reason, (which options presuppose such divisions to be strict), the source of normativity can be located to the processes of interaction taking place in the extended agency. The legislative activity is a mixture. In the self-constitution as a subject of embodied, extended, and enactive agency, natural causalities are involved in the constitutive rationality of the agent.

Claiming the noncontingency of normatively committing obligations requires explanation of non-conditional normativity. Enlightenment philosophers such as Kant and Hume solved the problem of authority for nonrelative ethics by basing the notion of authority either on shared moral rationality (Kant's idea of the fact of reason as reflective) or shared moral psychology (Hume's idea of common moral senses)—both referring to fixed humanity itself in one way or another. Beyond the contingencies that govern the actual reasons for action, a fixed point for the moral system lies, in their views, in the fact that all human beings belong to the unique party of humankind, which forms the moral community. This explains universal moral rationality and the grounds of evaluation in modern post-Enlightenment ethics. If moral rightness and wrongness are internal to the world of human beings, features of humanity form the measure for the currency of judgments. One's identity is one's relation to humanity itself (Korsaard 2007a, 101). However, "humanity itself" requires definition, and definitions given by Enlightenment philosophers do not convince. The current vivid discussions at the interface of natural sciences and philosophical anthropology should not be disregarded. Discussions introduced in part 2, for instance, take critical positions against the concept of agency adopted in humanism. Since the relational shift in the concept of agency denies a simplistic idea of humanity, it becomes useless as the source of shared normativity. As cognitive and conative operations also are intertwined in each mental process of agency, the distinction between the Kantian and Humean traditions also needs to be rethought.

Some theories that basically echo Enlightenment humanism could also apply to ecologically relational agency and benefit from it. A justified way to argue for the authority of relationally constructed moral obligations can, for instance, be based on Korsgaard's constructivism, as it argues that unconditional obligations can be accounted for in terms of practical identity. Considering practical identity in terms of ecological relationality is then compatible with Korsgaard's argument in favor of normativity without sub-scribing to the Kantian grounds for ethics in unique human reason: moral rationality emerges from the extended notion of reason. This also holds true for the self-constitution of agency as the source of obligation: environmental constituents take part in it. For relational ethics, elements providing actual "oughts" cannot be stable elements of human nature, but they refer to coop-erative mechanisms of the constitution of agency. The conceptual division between positions that argue for external "oughts" (provided by "them" as the external facts) and positions that argue for internal "oughts" (provided by "me," the agent's will, or reason) are thus not totally separable. Normativity that is considered to rely on the "the laws of reason" can then extend beyond the individual mind and embody environmental elements.[1] The critique of reason led Kant to base ethics on the purified core of moral agency, namely the autonomous self. But the relationality of the self makes the picture of a fixed core unclear: The self is not isolated from its contingent contextualities. If I am right in claiming that the traditional concept of agency can be replaced by a relational one in a Kantian argument, the conclusion follows that agency, which is the primary source of normativity, involves external collaborators and ingredients in terms of the extended subject of self-governance. As moral agency which represents dignity for Kant should be preserved and cultivated, so should environmental others that participate in one's self-governance.

If correct, this is an influential normative claim that makes *the environ-ment fundamentally relevant for ethics*—not only for environmental ethics but ethics *in general*. The role of the environment in ethics fundamentally changes: moral obligations should always include the concern for interac-tions with various others relevant to influencing and participating in the construction of agency. The obligation to care for rationality and moral abil-ity implies maintaining and advancing sensibility, commitment, and respect for material and biological others. By modifying environments—landscapes, organisms, cultures, and ecosystems—practical "nonmoral" actions also have moral status. The very conditions of moral rationality are connected to factual relationships within material and mental ecosystems. The relational constitution of agency as normative self-construction thus implies a *second-level normativity*: the way one's own agency functions determines what counts as the source of its actual obligations. According to a relational approach, the focus of ethics should be turned to this meta-normative level of obligations.

Agency formation being a relational process thus means that the reasons that count as my own reasons and the meanings that count as meanings for me are constructed in a systemically functioning nexus of interactions. In this sense, meta-level normativity is also illustrative of how naturalism enters constructivism. Natural processes are conditions of my normative self-constitution, and the constitution of agency emerges through commitments. The reflective structure of agency relies on the previous states of agency and the quality of the relationships by which it is constituted, and the actual process of self-construction of agency influences, again, the external others that will take part in the further constitution of agency. Meta-normative obligations ensure continuity and enhancement of reflection and reasoning. The meta-normative level obligations emerge from the conditions and mechanisms of the self-constitution of agency: if there are conducts that are necessary for the self-constitution of relational agency, they have the status of *universal normativity*. A Kantian idea that moral reasons should be understood as reasons for all seems thus justified at this level. A relational explanation then implies that in an actual situation everyone has a reason to promote her own ability to reason through cultivating her *agential partners'* good.

Responsibility for those partners and for further interactions seems evident. Korsgaard, for instance, subscribes to the meta-normative level of "transforming oneself" into the cause of moral activity: "To act is not just to cause an end, but to make yourself into the cause of the end, and so to *make yourself into* the kind of thing that achieves that end. To be an agent is to transform yourself into a certain kind of cause. The activity we exhibit in action is a kind of *self-determined* efficacy" (Korsgaard 2014, 197). At the meta-level of normativity we can talk about the "joint progress" or "joint corruption" of the partners involved in the construction of moral agency. There are thus some universal conditions for the better and worse constitution of moral agency that concern the quality of interactions and the inclusiveness of cognitive processes. Interactive actions themselves are means for practicing the virtue of moral agency. I find this interpretation of the normative constitution of agency helpful for understanding the procedure by which moral conducts regarding environmental relationships can be approached.

As we saw, naturalist virtue ethics and constructivism are close to converging with each other in relational ethics: moral abilities, such as empathy and solidarity, can be seen partly "given by nature," but nature itself is partly "constructed," or influenced (to use a more causal terminology), by the actions of actual performances of agency. The constituents of agency are, however, mutually inseparable in agency because of the systemic nature of their interconnectedness. Moral concepts are thus not reducible to any actual natural features. Instead, they refer to the process of completing the constitution and actualization of moral agency by ever better honing the relational mechanisms. In a sense, the final goods for an agent do not precede the agent. Compared to traditional virtue ethics, a theory of human virtues should then be replaced by a theory of the virtuous constructions of relational agency. Neo-Kantian constructivism and neo-Aristotelian virtue ethics approach each other's positions through the revised notion of agency. In the constructivist view, natural facts need to be seen to be involved in the source of normativity through relational agency—without lapsing into naturalistic fallacy. Seen from another perspective, natural facts as relationally active are, in fact, such that it is relevant to talk about them as constructions—but this does not involve relativizing what is good for the agents. It thus seems possible to argue that moral abilities enhance or degenerate through evolutive types of mechanisms, and that they are influenced continuously by everyday practices that reflect the actual moral landscape and the capacities of agency. If I am right, perspectives emerging from ecologically relational agency encourage ethical theories representing (realist or modestly antirealist) constructivism and (modestly realist) naturalism to take steps toward each other in a way that appreciates the diverse processes behind both "representation" and "expression."

TOWARD RELATIONAL REALISM

To argue that moral rationality is something bound to relational agency implies that the autonomy of ethics cannot be understood in an absolute way. According to the common definitions of moral realism (by, for instance, G. E. Moore, John McDowell, and Hilary Putnam), defending moral realism implies that moral concepts refer to descriptive facts (natural or supernatural), the cognitive content of which is evaluative measurement, that moral concepts are truth-apt and sensitive to the conditions of morality, and that a morally qualified agent can evaluate the truth value of moral propositions. A relational ethical theory can adopt, and even persuades us to adopt, a form of modest moral realism, but the definition needs to be reconsidered. Initially put, relational realism calls for three correctives: First, moral concepts refer to natural or supernatural facts, which may have some cognitive meaning but are not necessarily describable in a non-conditional way. Second, moral judgments are truth-apt, but this does not rule out plurality of *actual* truths which may converge in the *ultimate* truth *via* their nonpropositional features. And third, there are moral abilities by which an ideally qualified agent could evaluate the *actual* truth value of moral propositions, but these abilities are never fully realized in an individual or a group at any moment of time. The ultimate truth thus escapes any actualized abilities, although the development of these abilities may approach it.

Moral rationality in an actual state of agency is bound to its constitutive relationships, which means that normative concepts in any actual state refer to truths that are somehow contingent. But interactive relationships are not determined by the individual interactants. Agency continuously alters itself through mutually changing interactions/intra-actions, and the direction of this altering is what matters (also Barad 2007; de Jaegher 2021). The idea of limited autonomy of any actual, embodied agent includes, in fact, the possibility that the complex as a whole can develop. The construction of one's practical identity takes place by ways of responding to the other's communicative initiatives, by recognizing or ignoring the affordances, and by focusing on some interactions while bypassing others. Noncontingency in the development of agency is thus located in the *best possible ways to respond* to all the relevant relationships in reflective mutuality, in so called response-ability (see Haraway 2016).

The relational theory of moral concepts has two special features: First, since practical identities are various and change in time, partly through practical actions, *actual* goods and rights must be distinguished from goods or rights in some absolute or *final* sense. And second, since practical identities can better solve practical problems when developing the function of agency, that is, when the complex relationships that are constitutive for it function better, moral concepts refer to *processes* rather than facts. The actual meanings of good and right can be addressed to the function of the webs, referring to the involved partners and the ways of their mutual interaction. As the functional structure of agency includes various (including both linguist and material) relationships, ethics (values or conducts)—even as a "human issue"—can never be detached from the contingent, natural world. Final meanings of moral concepts differ from actual ones in that they refer to some teleological aim for the continuous construction of agency. In each actual stage, moral rationality concerns the quality of actual interaction and the direction of changes. Rationality is thus tied with cognitive states internally bound to the outside word. This kind of "active externalism" of the vehicles of knowledge highlights the nature of rationality as a process of interactivity (Rowlands 2003, 2005; Noë 2004; Clark and Chalmers 1998).[2] Relational realism does not require the actual privilege of any perspective or value absolutism. On the contrary, partiality of the truth value of actual conducts is among the elements that make universal truth approachable by partial agents This is in alignment with feminist epistemologies.

The main difference between procedurally realist constructivism and substantive realism is how the problem of practical reason is identified, and what the role of the procedure is: a procedural approach offers a logic for solving moral questions, while the substantive approach applies moral facts to them. Relational realism is comparable with procedural realism, but the logic differs from modern procedural theories. The function of moral concepts also distinguishes constructivism from both substantial realism and antirealism. Truth-apt normative concepts, according to constructivists, have a practical function: they refer to whatever solves the problem. So, they name solutions to practical problems rather than represent mind-independent reality (Korsgaard 1996; 2003, 116; 2008, 302; O'Neill 1988; 1989, 206; Bagnoli 2011, 20) Someone who defends a relationally realist approach does not need to object. However, the relational approach emphasizes that this is the *actual* sense of truth-aptness, and the focus needs to be on the level of *virtuous mechanisms* for balanced relationships in a moral ecosystem (of different kinds of ingredients), instead of on political mechanisms, such as reflective equilibrium, or other quasi-impartial contents. The idea of moral truth must be scrutinized, because not only does the meaning of moral terms vary from context to context, so too do the representations of the truth-making object. What is "real" in relationally considered moral concepts must refer beyond all such particularities (whether they are psychological, cultural, or material). As relational realism may somewhat look like Hilary Putnam's internal realism, it is worth noticing their significant difference. According to Putnam, the truth conditions are internal to the cultural context and cannot exceed it, while for relational realism, truth conditions that are located in *interactivity* hold regardless of the variety of epistemic contents. The mechanisms of relationality in every context share features that may refer to truth: some features can be advantageous for relational agency objectively. In this sense, relational realism is more closely connected to truth-making objects.[3]

As actual moral claims are constructed in relation to the real world, according to a relational theory of ethics, moral concepts that refer to the agent, such as virtue and vice, refer to the *quality of these real relations*, not to essential humanness, cultural commonality, or shared awareness. Interrelatedness between "internal" and "external" reasoning makes a theory hybrid in the sense that expressive and non-expressive elements are inseparable in moral reasons. *Hope for the (moral) truth lies in the very web of interactivity.*[4] While metaethical midway paths usually locate the source of moral reasons in either cognitive or noncognitive operations, a relational approach locates it in the interactivity between the "constructed" and "constructing" elements;

reduction to either expression or fact does not make sense. If both expressions and beliefs are outcomes of the complex processes involving cognitive and noncognitive elements, moral goodness should refer to something that is neither clearly "real" nor "constructed." Instead of referring to either (cognitive) content or (conative) expression, moral concepts refer to the logic of interaction between them. Addressing moral concepts just to one or another would imply that they escape from earthly moral agents who cannot divide them. Both modest realism and soft expressivism could be compatible with a relational approach, but it seems more plausible to pursue a relationally minimal realism: proper mechanisms of agency are related to the world through, for example, the agent's natural needs, cognitive processes, cultural practices, personal experiences, landscapes, and religious beliefs.

Even though dichotomizing objectivism and relativism has been criticized for decades, a relational approach differs from other alternatives by focusing on the *organic nature of moral agency*. Considering ecosystems of intimate relationships as central for the agential definitions of moral concepts (either as solutions for practical problems or as facts about the final good of the agent) opens a new route for discussion. On this route, contingent conditions of moral reason do not rule out the critical authority or autonomy of ethics, nor some objectivity, since moral rationality "for all" rests on the shared measures for the mechanisms of good interaction. The conditions of reasoning located in (real) systemic structures support an argument for a basically constructivist modest realism.[5] Relational "procedures" focus on *virtuous relatedness*, in which also nonhuman and material others are acknowledged to contribute to the very process of construction. Moral languages or narratives to which a constructivist theory may refer are not isolated but heavily interwoven. However, the idea of truth refers, first and foremost, to the method of achieving ever more encompassing results, instead of the results themselves. Therefore, truth-aptness is not "internal" to a moral landscape but can cross traditions through encompassing mechanisms (cf. Putnam 1988, 1990). Beyond the justifications of each narrative there is a *metanarrative about the relatedness of viewpoints*: as parts of the nexus of narratives, partial justifications are connected by the mechanisms of the functioning nexus of narratives. Relational moral rationality thus may help in overcoming the contradiction between foundationalism and coherentism.[6]

From the perspective of naturalistic realism, reductionism remains an issue worthy of critical discussion. One way to elucidate the implications of a relational shift to naturalism is to see how it influences the evolutionary debunking arguments of ethics. They are problematic because they rely on a fundamental disconnection made between different types of evolutionary forces and the supposition that non-reductionist capacities cannot, therefore, be natural, naturally evolved and trainable (FitzPatrick 2017, 6–7; 2018, 551).

Since the debunking arguments are reductionist and grounded in simplistic explanations of moral agency, they seem to dissolve through the relational shift. According to relational ethics, it is the function of relational agency in connection to the natural conditions of vital interactivity that enables moral capacity. This function is shared, and it marks the continuity between human and nonhuman agencies, echoing the Darwinian continuity thesis. Responsibility for nonhuman entities do not need other "similarity arguments" than the shared relational structure of the basic functions of agency: through fundamental relationality, we can harm and benefit each other and each other's vulnerable, gradual autonomy in a way that binds us normatively (Pescador Canales and Mojica 2022). The important job for philosophers who wish to debunk the debunking argument is to properly articulate a concept of moral agency that does not suppose nonnatural features to be requirements for moral reasoning. A relational notion of agency shows such an appeal unnecessary.

Even minimalist realism indicates cognitivism of some sort. At the same time, a relational understanding of agency casts suspicion over the traditional division between cognitivism and noncognitivism. Resistance to the contradiction between cognitivism and noncognitivism can be defended from both naturalist and constructivist origins, as various hybrid metaethical theories show (e.g., Korsgaard 2003; Copp 2009b; Kitcher 2013; Sinnott-Armstrong 2007, 2009). Modestly realist constructivism and naturalism often differ from classical realism regarding the view of normative concepts. Historically speaking, moral realism was given a new, narrow meaning in the twentieth century when it was closely connected with reductionism of moral concepts. As moral language was closely connected with the verificationist theory of meaning, moral philosophers came to doubt whether moral concepts can have cognitive content at all, and as the line of debate was then cemented between the realists and the rest, a wide range of "noncognitivist" proposals were developed (Korsgaard 2003, 104). In contrast to such a narrow interpretation, a relational naturalist would argue that moral concepts refer to natural states of affairs, but they do not represent certain states of affairs. Concerning moral knowledge, such a view is skeptical toward representationalism (e.g., Foot 2001, 2002; Nussbaum 1998, 2006, 2011). Cognitivism does not require that the contents of moral concepts are empirically verifiable, even though they would be natural. A relational approach to ethics holds that actual normative concepts refer to the *principles of the relational logic of practical reasoning*. Although the contents of actual moral concepts are plural, they are thus not mere expressions.

If it is plausible to talk about the relational theory of ethics, as I argue, it seems possible to defend it as a realist approach which includes an account of moral concepts that refer to the facts about (the function of) agency, but these facts combine constructed as well as non-constructed elements. Normative concepts thus do not *represent* stable features of reality, but they name the mechanisms required for achieving solutions to practical problems, such as eco-social harmony. These mechanisms can refer to reason in the case of a relational approach to relational reason. And reason as relational implies that environmental conditions partly determine our problems. Because the construction of agency is conceptually prior to human reason, according to relational realism, moral judgments that are true in an actual sense can be seen as developing along with the agency. There are some features that resemble, on the one hand, what a Kantian constructivist, Onora O'Neill (1992), argues to be features of modestly realist constructivism, and on the other hand, what an evolutionary ethicist Philip Kitcher (2011) argues to be features of modestly realist naturalism. But from the relational perspective, development of actual meanings of moral concepts results neither from natural factors nor rational revisions of self-scrutinizing reason alone but from the ongoing practicing of relational virtues that combine them. The virtues of relatedness and collaborative togetherness include, for instance, recognition, listening and respect for others, together with whom/which reasoning must be practiced. In consequence, agency develops, and capacities of reasoning expand. This whole process of the development of agency and reasoning is connected to the real, physically and ecologically structured world, in which normative concepts can approach truth over time.

On the grounds of what has been said, Martha Nussbaum's capabilities theory appears one option for developing normative relational ethics. It accounts for metaethically mixed position and exemplifies a non-essentialist virtue ethics, in which the genuine possibility of practicing human capabilities works as the actual measurement for evaluating virtue. Capabilities are not absolute but may, to some extent, vary due to circumstances (Nussbaum 2011). Objective human morality refers in Aristotelian virtue ethics to the "appropriate functioning in each human sphere," but this does not imply relativism. According to Nussbaum's interpretation, only actual goodness can serve as a measure for agents, and each actual good is relative to the constituents of a certain human sphere. But although the grounding of good is in actual human experiences, the critical point remains: it arises from a "more inclusive account of the circumstances of human life and of the needs for human functioning that these circumstances call forth." A good rule is, in a way, "a good summary of wise particular choices." Nussbaum thus claims that Aristotelian virtues can balance between general rules and awareness of particulars. Good and virtuous decisions being context-sensitive does not imply them being "right only *relative to*, or *inside*, a limited context." On the contrary, she argues, "[i]t is right absolutely, objectively, anywhere in the human world, to attend to the particular features of one's context; and the person who so attends and who chooses accordingly is making, according to Aristotle, the humanly correct decision, period." (Nussbaum 2013; see also chapter 11) Critics are not, however, convinced, and some argue that Nussbaum's concessions to relativism take her approach too far from realism.

Conceiving moral agency as relational in the sense it has been described in this book involving systemic, organic, and material relationships could add the missing piece that would strengthen Nussbaum's modestly realist meta-ethics. Goods and, hence, capabilities of a relational agent rely on the actual constitution of human agency, rather than a specified definition of universal humanity. Goods and capabilities may change by (virtuous or vile) practicing of agency, that is, by cooperating (virtuously or viciously) with others in agential ecology. It is then the proper *mechanisms of constituting a function of agency* that form the reference for what counts as good. But such mechanisms are not "relative to, or inside, a limited context" rather than *objective*. Relational interpretation of Nussbaum's theory represents a nontraditional account of moral realism that draws on Aristotle's remark about the sketch for the good, to which Nussbaum refers: "It looks as if we have to draw an outline first, and fill it in later. It would seem to be open to anyone to take things further and to articulate the good parts of the sketch" (Nussbaum 2013, referring to Aristotle, *Nicomachean Ethics* 1098a20-26). According to a relational approach, the source of obligation cannot be reduced either to nature (empirical facts as determining what is good) or to construction (human freedom as the legislative law) alone, since normative legislation entails a creative interactivity between them. Therefore, the actual state of moral truth can be imagined as separated from the ideal state: although actual truth always remains a partial construction, through the ideal mechanisms of relationality developing the functions of agency, constructed concepts can have truth-aptness even in the ideal sense of truth. In this work I have defended relational ethics as a form of realism, albeit a modest relational one.

RELATIONAL TRACKS TO MORAL TRUTH

A relational account of agency refers to an agent-based theory of ethics in which the dynamic process of moral development is realized through continuously reshaped agency. The cognitive contents of moral propositions cannot then be truth-apt in the sense of traditional representationalism, which is impossible for embodied relational cognition. The idea of representational truth value does not even serve objectivity as it stabilizes partial descriptions of moral concepts.

Practiced patterns of body-environment coupling influence conscious acts of meaning-making and knowledge formation by determining fundamental human experiences of the environment and, hence, cognition (Johnson 2007, 20, 50–57). Processes from which the meanings of moral concepts emerge are thus neither merely emotional nor cognitive but fundamentally relational. Body-based intersubjectivity cannot be ignored in the notion of truth-aptness of moral concepts. Relationally constructed moral concepts can, however, be considered as "relationally objective," which is, I argue, enough to form a reliable ground for transforming further constructions better. Although moral philosophy remains uncertain about moral truths, it can offer objectivity concerning better and worse, and hence, grounds for hope. The constraints provided by bodily and environmental experiences limit alternatives in a way that may significantly assist in achieving reliable directions for continuous constructions. An absolute universal governance theory remains, however, an illusion. In Mark Johnson's words, ethics "will help us struggle to discern better from worse possibilities within a given situation" (Johnson 1998, 65–67).

The relational concept of agency *relocates truth conditions* from the ability of an actual proposition to represent (moral) facts to the interaction in which propositions (at each actual moment of time) about those facts are constructed. Conditions of moral truth neither represent preexisting facts nor attitudes in any straightforward sense. This kind of non-representational position is a realist one but not in a robust sense. The basic difference between relationally constructivist and robustly realist positions, from a cognitivist perspective, concerns verification of truth and certainty. The idea of truth in uncertainty, and the agnostic attitude about the possibility of achieving absolute truth is common for many constructivists, feminists, and pragmatists, as well as early environmentalists like Ralph Waldo Emerson and Henry David Thoreau (see Thoreau 2016; Emerson 2019, *Essays: Second Series,* chapter 2; *Representative Men,* chapter 4). But their idea of truth hidden in skepticism should be distinguished from both Cartesian methodological doubt and the skepticism claimed by Hume. For Thoreau, for instance, skepticism does not mark a failure of cognitive effort, but recognition that the primary relation to the world is not cognitive but ethical in nature (Pihlström 2005, 74–80). The moral value of cognitive uncertainty is that it underlines the ability to seek—and to some extent even act in accordance with—the truth instead of owning it as a static belief. Cognitive uncertainty forces agents to constantly reshape moral judgments, beliefs, and practices by humbly asking whether all relevant partners have been recognized in the production of agency. Without such recognition, agency cannot implement moral truth in the best way. The central feature of ethics is the move toward the better. Supplementing a basically cognitivist view with radical uncertainty underlines the meaning of noncognitive moral conditions of sensitizing oneself in approaching knowledge. It seems that current cognitive science can better support the basic aspiration of the early environmentalists than did the scientific understanding of mind in their time: If the affective and attitudinal elements play a role, by definition, already in cognition, it is not necessary to formulate arguments for external non-cognitive conditions of knowledge.

Relationality calls for dynamic self-understanding of ethics: ethics is something that compels agents to ever better self-constructions to achieve ever better understanding of the goods. Although the good retains uncertainty in actual situations, any realist approach to ethics should define the truth condition, however minimal it may be. While according to representational-ism, there must be a way to judge which of the conflicting propositions is true or closer to the truth, an agent-derived truth condition has to do with the method of evaluating *what kind of agency* would end up with the best state-ments, rather than the statement itself. Practical moral ability changes with time: moral agency evolves (in terms of naturalism) or develops (in terms of constructivism) due to the collaborative process by which the agency of a particular being is constituted. The chain of constitutions of agency may take different directions, and in the direction of both individual and collective agencies the individual choices in interactions play a role. In actual situations, neither absolute true moral statements nor actualized perfect moral agency is required in order for the practical moral judgment to face some truth condi-tion. Practical moral judgments can have truth-aptness as judgments concern-ing the means of moral flourishing of ecologically relational agency. But how can the *better and worse direction* of development be measured? What enhances moral flourishing of agency? Whether one direction of development is better than another in some objective sense is a question that relational real-ism also needs to answer.

In the case of actual judgments, truth value refers to what is appropriate for an actual system of well-functioning relationships rather than any fixed propositional truth. The measure for better and worse is *a process*: whether it enhances or degenerates the ability of agency. Although constructed, such a process is objective in an actual situation. One option to connect the actual truths with more general good simpliciter can be enlightened by Korsgaard's comments on what it needs to constitute oneself as a moral agent: we need to commit ourselves to constructing "a state of affairs that is, as far as pos-sible, *good-for us all*," because otherwise we cannot constitute ourselves as moral agents (Korsgaard 2013, 24–25, italics added). Without caring for the others of "us all" and improving their good-for, the agency that we construct together cannot function in the best possible way. In any actual situation the fixed feature of the "better" is then based on the natural structure of the world—in the fact that acquiring the best possible situation from the point of view of good-for all is necessary for constituting oneself as moral agent—although the natural world itself is not fixed. The nexus of environmental relationships is constitutive for the agency we regard as our own agency. This is a sufficient reason to talk about "good *simpliciter*, and not just of good-for this or that person or animal" (Korsgaard 2013, 43).

Although this is a constructivist claim, conceiving of the self-constitution of agency relationally in terms of ecological relationality—which is located in evolutionary and social history, in place, and in the ecological conditions and structure of earthly life—anchors it to the real, though evolving, world in the sense that makes it slightly naturalistic. What is left as the unconditional good concerns interrelatedness between beings and things in space and time. Although the structures and conditions of agency change, evolve, and develop, in each actual situation the capabilities of moral agency require relationships and interactivity that at each moment is as inclusive and as loving, attentive, and respectful as possible. Commitment to even an unknown good simpliciter is needed for the ability of agency to construct objectively better judgments, although "the best" always escapes even the best possible knowledge. The best as a kind of teleological final good can then work as the content of hope for the agents to make progress and take steps that can approach the truth.

Relational ethics thus emphasizes virtuous dynamics and directedness instead of epistemic certainty or representational truths. Truth-aptness of moral propositions should concern the meta-normative level of obligations. Even actual propositions can, however, be "truth-apt" in an indirect sense as they are connected to the teleological second-level truth-apt propositions through procedural mechanisms. But a distinction must be made between the actual truth referring to actual moral facts connected with the construction of practical identities for solutions in the actual conditions of reality, and the final truth referring to the transcendent moral facts about the ideal direction of the relational processes. Truth in the actual sense requires that certain relationships hold between mutually coherent "states of mind," which refers, internally, to the commitment and best function of all relevant partners in agency, and externally, to the proper expression of provided knowledge (see also Hyman 2015, 164). Final truth is the aim that remains transcendent without ruling out the possibility of improving moral and epistemic abilities to approach it gradually. Moral knowledge understood as an ability connects the concept of truth with the processual nature of relational agency. At each moment, particular truths can participate in approaching more general truth, and through collaborative participation enhance the advance toward the better, that is, reach closer to the best or the good. Hence, truth can be many, on the one hand, and singular on the other. In the ideal case, mechanisms of interactivity generate moral agency to function optimally in an actual eco-social situation: inclusive, active, and reflective interactions emerge in which each participant can optimally play its role in reasoning. The hint of objective truth is embedded in the attitudes provided by such ideally functioning agency. In this sense, moral truth is expressive by nature.[7] The normative focus is thus on the quality and conditions of interaction in the actual eco-social environments to endow us with moral competence.

While John Mackie's error theory or Michael Ruse's fake realism claim that there are practical or evolutionary reasons to *believe* that actual moral claims can be true, though they *are not*, from the relational point of view there are moral reasons to be *skeptical* about any *claimed* moral truth (especially put forward in propositional language), though the truth *exists*. This skepticism means that instead of sticking to any proposition, one should commit oneself to the interactions through which, *via* the development of agency, actual truths can approach the final truth, though it will always remain transcendent. Actual agents do not have access to it, but actual conduct can be evaluated in light of their ability to reflect appropriate procedures. The truth *persuades*, in a way, as process philosopher A. N. Whitehead would say: correctly practiced sensitivity in the interactions maintains and advances practical moral identity, and hence, the ability to solve practical problems, which attracts us and calls us to follow its course (Whitehead 1978). Marks of an appropriate procedure may be, for example, increasing harmony, systemic vitality, and flourishing of the agential knots. Perhaps the best candidate, rich enough to define such a procedure, could be *love*.

One can still wonder whether relational realism is just a form of coherentism. I do not think it is. The criterion for measuring better or worse must be in line with the procedures for approaching coherence of all the mutually intertwined functions of agency at a certain moment of evolutionary history, *and* with the procedures of preserving and advancing the ability of all to commit to them. An awareness of the environmental relationships on which our deliberation and intentions rely is thus not only central for moral ability but also for the actual measures of good. The outcome we get from a collaborative process of agency, such as moral deliberation, depends on who we recognize, pay attention to, listen to, give space, and trust. The objects of epistemic processes emerge for the reasoning agent through them being related with each other and through efficiently participating in agency.[8] According to a relational view, beliefs as acts and representations as states of affairs are constitutively related. Commitment to the appropriateness of the relations constituting moral agency is a moral virtue, just as commitment to the world is an epistemic virtue. Such virtues are, in turn, related to the correct contents of beliefs or judgments.

Relational agency that refers to "extended internalism" (instead of either externalism or internalism) has both epistemic and motivational implications. As it covers "inherently normative and motivational entities" that exist in the form of "people, and the other animals," these others can, roughly put, both "tell us what to do" and "make us do it" (Korsgaard 1996, 166, 210–18). To put it in terms of the relational approach, realism is right in that there are extant entities that meet the dual criteria of providing both direction and motive: They can be addressed to ideally functioning structures of ecologically relational moral agencies. The actual evaluative standard can simply refer to the method of constructing the ideal constitution of the nexus of recognition, care, and attention: It is objectively the best way to approach the truth, however transcendent it is. This method can be described in terms of virtuous relations and collaboration.

As mentioned, separation of actual/contextual and final/noncontextual truth refers to a teleological nature of ethics: the continuous moral constitutions of agency aim at truth as their *telos*. But unlike the usual notions of teleology, the aim in a relational approach is derivable neither from the essential nature of the agent (in the Aristotelian way) nor teleological unification (in the Hegelian way), but from the ideal way of constituting agency in relation to everything else. Qualified interactivity, by which all partners of knowledge formation are respected, wondered about, trusted, and taken responsibility for, is a means for objectivity: although objective truth escapes, hints are located in collaboration aimed at advanced mutuality.[9] A regulative power for developing agency is generated in real relationships, which means that "external" reality is involved in the relational autonomy that directs the reflective ability and constitution of agents. Not even actual moral judgments can be justified without involving complex earthly interactants in the (self-) reflection. Inner diversity is needed for the structure of agency to function as the basis for reflection.[10] The moral aim for an individual is thus to develop her agency to be inclusive, loving, and persuading in order to approach objectivity and the ability to act accordingly (good at). The ideal case would ensure the final good.

A relational account of moral truth could be roughly summarized in a sentence: the truth can be approached on the grounds of the ideal constitution of relational agency, but any actual approach to moral truth at any moment is necessarily partial. Therefore, the focus of ethics should primarily be on the method of approaching truth rather than its content. The truth escapes all grasps not only because it transcends all partial perspectives, but also because the totality of the contingent facts of the real world continuously changes due to actions taken, and how they are enacted. The only way to evaluate the truth value of actual moral judgments concerns the changes they entail in the relational constitution of moral agency, and their ability to solve for better or worse the practical problems of relationships by which they are constituted. Modestly thinking truth-aptness of a moral concepts does not require that any of its actual definitions represent absolute truth. Moral concepts refer to the *method of constructing better normative systems* through the development of agency. The currency of a moral code can emerge from the ideal method of constituting agency reflected by the relational interaction. The ideal constitutions are plural and can vary from context to context, despite the uniting method. The point of evaluation possible in any actual situation can at best concern the quality of the interactivity constitutive for the agencies.

NOTES

1. For instance, Korsgaard's formulation of the source of normativity differs from the basic Kantian view regarding the idea of moral autonomy. Instead of individual self-governance, her view can be seen to refer to a modest, relational type of autonomy that can be appointed to an embodied agent that extends—through embodiment—to eco-social environments. Consider, e.g., this: "I *must* interact with the conscious inhabitants of my body, because I must act with my body. But I *may* also interact with other people, and when I do, then their reasons, as well as my own, become as it were incentives in the deliberative process that we undertake together, resources for the construction of our shared reasons." Korsgaard 2009b, 200. Emphasis original.

2. The idea of "active externalism" of the vehicles of the content of experience owes a debt to Ludwig Wittgenstein's solution to the skeptical paradox, according to which, meaning and understanding can only be achieved in the world in practice (1958) and Daniel Dennett's (1991) distinction between content and vehicle externalisms. According to Dennett, it is not possible to read off the properties of vehicles of cognitive operation from the resulting cognitive content. Clark and Chalmers (1998) add that the vehicles loop out of the head and brain into the world.

3. Although judgments can be evaluated and corrected by judgments about their truth "in an idealized epistemic condition," according to internal realism, we cannot know that we are in an idealized epistemic condition, which easily leads to an infinite regress argument. See Putnam 1981, 55–56. Hiroshi Ohtani tries to solve this by adopting a Kantian notion of a regulative ideal, which would mean adopting the idea of "the ideal of human moral flourishing." This could draw internal and relational positions closer to each other. See Ohtani, 2011, 190.

4. The Cartesian skeptic question could ask: if I am what my webs make me to be, how can I trust anything? But instead of making the Cartesian division between the *inner* awareness as the source of certainty and the *external* world of uncertain (moral) objects, trust—if not certainty—emerges from their connectedness in agency.

5. This can be compared with circumstantial relativism, which is, unlike ethical relativism, a realist position: moral rightness of action being relative to the facts about the agent is compatible with the existence of truth, although contextual justifications of beliefs are not founded in that truth. The regress of justification does not end in firm foundations, but neither is it endless. See Timmons 1996, 296–97.

6. Susan Haack formulates an idea of foundherentism that defends a somewhat similar idea. According to her, both foundationalism and coherentism rest on an unconvincing view of human rationality, and she argues for overriding the dichotomy

between them by turning the focus to how contextual narratives are mutually inter-related. According to foundherentism the justification of beliefs is then not unidirectional. Haack 1993, 73–94.

7. This may resemble an ideal observer argument, but it is not. The main differences concern the content and timing of the moral truth. From an ideal observer's viewpoint, the cognitive contents of propositions are truth-apt regardless of the context or time, while in a relational theory the truth-aptness concerns the process of relatedness directed toward the higher levels of moral capabilities.

8. The contribution of any object in a cognitive relationship amounting to representation is partly up to the subject's actions. See Code 2006a; Rowlands 2005; Preston 2009. An agent's contribution concerns the very way another exists as "an object of knowledge," besides its meaning to the epistemic agent. E.g., Clark and Chalmers 1998.

9. Kant argues that the truth of a proposition lies in the ways it is reached, that is, how agency is constituted, realized, and practiced. Relational agency can be applied to the neo-Kantian notion of a regulative ideal: moral judgments need to be continuously corrected through an ever-enhanced constitution of agency. Unlike Kant, however, a relational view underlines that moral flourishing relates to the earthly world. The "external" reality is involved in the relational autonomy that directs the constitution of agents.

10. Relational realism resembles here the feminist standpoint epistemology and the idea of "strong objectivity." See e.g., Harding 1991, 142–49.

Chapter 11

Responsibilities for Relational Agency

RESPONSIBILITY RELOCATED

If there is objectivity for moral goodness, it cannot be derived either from external facts or expressions of legislative reason: instead, moral concepts refer to the mechanisms of the interactive processes by which moral agency is continuously constituted. But these processes intimately involve nonhuman and material relationships, too: human agents belong to nature and are parts of complex natural webs of interaction as "moral" agents as much as "natural" agents. Human types of cognitive, affective, and intentional processes are embodied and embedded in the dynamic interactivity of the systemic multispecies collective. And to this interactivity, we owe both rationality and affectivity, as well as moral autonomy. In terms of environmental ethics, reconceptualizing moral agency relationally relocates its basic normative aspiration by highlighting interactive agency in which human mental operations coincide with the processes of a multispecies community and interaction between its members and their environments in a way that revises the entire meaning of moral rationality. Actions, cultural values, personal habits, and scientific practices should all be assessed from the perspective of this ecological interactivity. Sensitivity and care for the dynamic interactivity constitutive for agency are decisive for its function. Relational ethics thus seems best articulated in terms of some type of *virtue ethics.* As such, it emphasizes *responsibility for moral agency* as a central virtue that is exemplified in loving and caring relationships and interaction (e.g., Barandiaran 2017).

A relational shift in ethics opens an entirely new perspective to environmental ethics. Regarding responsibility, relational agency as a premise has twofold implications for environmental ethics. First, it widens the concept of

241

responsibility for moral agency to include responsibilities for the multispecies, ecological, and social interactivity that constitute agency. The cooperative partners of agency should be treated so that their transactional impacts
enhance rather than degenerate agential (collective and personal) functions.
Second, it widens the perspective of responsibilities for nonhuman beings and
external environments. The ethical focus cannot only be on individual entities
or even populations or species. It should also be on the systemic mechanisms
that enhance the function of mutually beneficial interactivity. The practices
influencing the mechanisms of interrelatedness in the structures of the material environment, as well as the quality of interaction between various others also have implications in the core processes of (human) moral agency.
Environmental relations and ecological issues thus rise from the margin of
applied ethics to the center of any ethical theory. The entire role of the nonhuman world in ethics must be reconsidered since moral reasons are achievable
only through cultivating the complex type of agency.

Colombetti's and Torrance's argument for inter-(en)active ethics calls for
a shift in thinking about responsibilities and encourages us "to focus on the
ethical qualities of the interaction itself" instead of individual acts, since "the
ethical content or valuation of a given situation" emerges "as much from the
interaction of the participants as from the autonomous decision-making or
original authorship of the participants themselves" (Colombetti and Torrance
2009, 523). Interactions have ethical qualities also with regard to their ability
to enable or constrain participation and autonomy. According to Colombetti
and Torrance, this is likely to make a transformative impact in "how we ethically evaluate our own and others' roles in situations. For if action takes shape
more in the melting pot of collective extemporisation than as an aggregation
of individual moves in an interactional chess game, then it appears that we
have to be more humble in our ethical appraisals." There are at least two reasons for this humbleness: first, we need to accept that we share co-ownership
of "the less attractive features of how others act in a given situation," and
second, we need to concede to others "a liberal share of co-ownership of
those aspects of our own acts that seemed to put us in a personally flattering
light." Another shift that an inter-(en)active ethics calls for concerns the way
of conceiving of social interaction. It may be that "the negotiative dance of
participatory sense-making is inevitably ethical in nature: that what we participate in is, to its very bones, an ethical communal sense-making or value-
making" (ibid.; see also de Jaegher 2018, 462).

Responsibilities are not only individual and direct, but we share the
co-ownership of both blame and praise with other interactants. This means,
of course, that the indirect responsibilities to take care of the conditions and
capacity of all interactants to support good decisions are heavy. And especially
important for environmental ethics is that interaction whatsoever can be seen

as an inevitably ethical "dance of participatory sense-making." Everyday life practices and so called nonmoral decisions thus have ethical status as good or bad actions. Responsibilities concern the entire course of being of relating and acting by which the networks of agency transform through interaction, not just certain actions. As argued earlier, there is thus *a secondary level category of environmental responsibilities*, namely responsibilities for relational moral agency, autonomy, and rationality, on which the ability to be responsible rely. Relational responsibilities should then be extended to all those who participate in our cognitive processes, affections, and intentions.

Consequences of actions that change the environment to which we "adapt" through cultural practices and institutions may be far reaching both in time and place because changes in circumstances also change possibilities of reflection and rationality. Responsibilities for agency are heavily environmental by nature since interactions between an organic self and its environments are constitutive for the relational subjectivity of a sensemaker. Although all sensemakers are autonomous "in the sense that they self-organize under precarious circumstances" due to their relational self-organization, every sensemaker needs to be "sensitive to what is beneficial and what is pernicious for its self-maintenance, and capable of adapting to its circumstances in the service of self-organization" (de Jaegher 2018, 457). Whether an event of interaction is beneficial or pernicious for the self-maintenance of participating partners influences the further realizations of agency. Colombetti and Torrance are right, I think, when they claim a shift in ethics to focus on the qualities of interaction, but it is necessary to acknowledge that the interaction we should care for takes place not only among individuals of one species. It takes place in the webs of different living and material partners, and transforms the cognitive, ecological, social, or cultural systems to which they are connected. If it is justified to consider moral agency as relational in a way that, for instance, enactivism suggests, it is justified to claim that there are *responsibilities for* the environmental others *for the sake* of relational moral agency—besides other reasons.

The idea of responsibility for agency refers to the *metaphilosophical attitude* that has been emphasized especially in feminist care ethics. Not surprisingly, those who have explored the ethical implications of enactivism after Colombetti and Torrance most often find support and merging perspectives from care ethics and the feminist notion of relational autonomy (Urban 2015b, 2016; Cash 2013; van Grunsven 2018). According to both ecofeminists and care ethicists, there are moral reasons that should be given priority in, for instance, epistemology: knowing requires a "loving perception" of others in order for them to become available (e.g., Warren 2000, 104–5). Care is an appropriate method to distinguish between reliable and unreliable knowledge, as well as to evaluate moral principles. We are responsible for mediating moral truths by acting dialogically and caringly with earthly others and the world to which our moral agency extends (e.g., Peterson 2001, 211–12). A plausible account of knowledge should acknowledge that knowledge and action are intertwined and refuse a traditional description of knowledge as a true, justified belief.

If environmental others are not only objects of knowledge or actions but collaborative partners, they take part to the cognitive and intentional processes that make us believe something or act in a certain way. Responsibility for moral agency entails then both epistemic responsibility and exercise of caution in practical, everyday choices toward the environment. Knowledge can be seen a virtuous ability to approach truth, where the truth-aptness of moral concepts refers to the correct care for the conditions of moral agency (*perhaps besides other issues*).[1] Plurality of actual truths does not rule out a justified hope for approaching convergent objective truth, though it is not realized in any belief-like statements. While non-conditional truths cannot be acquired as states of mind, they can be approached through the search for ideal recognition and respect for everyone and all that counts. The nature of knowledge as ability or skill also implies a norm to take care of the conditions of virtuous agency and to virtuously practice relational reasoning. Epistemic ability is something we are responsible for (Code 2006a).

A few philosophers have recently critically questioned the epistemological myths based on the modern but currently scientifically implausible conception of human agency. Relationalist, as well as reliabilist, virtue epistemologist, and neo-Aristotelian approaches to moral knowledge question or revise one or more of the central aspects of traditional moral epistemology, which are cognitivism, epistemic necessity of justified true belief, epistemic internalism, and priority of epistemic structure. They also share an effort to naturalize moral epistemology without reducing the justification of a moral belief to any description about either physical or social reality. According to virtue epistemologist Margaret Olivia Little, for example, knowledge is linked with the way the object of knowledge is recognized and "listened to" (Little 1997), and John Hyman argues for knowledge as ability (Hyman 2015). In the light of relational moral agency, such epistemologies imply that the truth-aptness of moral concepts should be seen to refer to—in addition to some other things, perhaps—the practical care for the relational interactivity of agency itself. Sensitivity to the conditions of morality and the virtuous practicing of relational reasoning thus have a normative status that includes nonhuman entities and the material world through their role as collaborators in the nexus of agency. Proponents of relational ethics are neither cognitivists nor noncognitivists because the cognitive and noncognitive elements of reason are mixed (cf. Haack 1993).

Throughout modern ethics it has been commonly thought that any ethical theory that does not accept nonnaturalism with *a priori* access to moral facts should rely either on a posteriori moral knowledge based on evidenced natural facts (such as human flourishing), or on desire-based constructions. Conceiving epistemic agency as relational dissolves such contradiction by mixing cognitive and conative operations. In this sense it also questions the common understanding of the distinction between natural and moral epistemologies: perception and reasoning may have similar mechanisms that should be cared for to successfully perceive or reason. In modern theories, Kantian and utilitarian alike, distinction between epistemic and moral spheres has strengthened the dualist account of humanity, and the division between actor and spectator. Consequently, empirical and moral facts have been distanced. But agency considered as generating normative authority through natural interactivity questions the detachment between free and determined instances of moral reasoning. Following virtue epistemology, knowledge requires objects of knowledge to be involved in the epistemic process by adopting a virtuous attitude toward them: the relevant "informants" need to be acknowledged, paid attention to, and trusted (e.g., Code 2006a). The way the objects are approached, perceived, or treated influences their contribution to the epistemic process (Noë 2004).

Virtue epistemology, as well as Hyman's idea about knowledge as ability, fit with the relational theory of ethics. If knowledge is a skill or ability, the *task of moral epistemology* is not to describe moral facts but to reveal actions that make us able to be guided by good and right. It means, first, that the way to gain knowledge is through situated actions in which the agent is *aware* and *responds* to the reality embodied in the situation. Moral knowledge is nothing to be stated, but instead something received by doing good things and offering in turn the ability to be guided by right things. Second, it means that moral knowledge is bound to the nature of agency: actions by which we respond and are aware of take place in the constitution of agency. Third, the truth can be expressed only through action: having moral knowledge causes actions to be guided by the right, which includes a hint of truth. Correct action is then an expression of the ideally practiced ability to be guided by what is right—which refers to the correct constitution of agency. Fourth, knowledge is gradual because it is a learning process linked to action: it can be weaker or stronger relative to epistemic ability. The truth by which we seek to be guided does not change, though the expressions vary (see Hyman 2015, 209–10). Each expression of morally correct action in a particular situation enhances the ability of moral knowledge and realizes a trace of truth. An enactive approach to knowledge supports the implications of relational agency in epistemology. As de Jaegher (2021) claims, human knowledge at its best is *love*.

If knowledge is an ability to produce correct or reliable outcomes by practicing virtuous activities, such activities are essential for moral reasoning. To be fully rational, one needs to be responsible for and response-able to whoever (or whatever) might carry valuable perspective to a practical problem as a partner of the epistemic process. The better the interaction, the more reliable the outcome. Virtue, thus, takes part in arranging favorable conditions for agency. To put it in Nussbaum's terms, interactive virtues promote the capabilities of a relational agent.

The normative status of taking care of environmental relationships makes them responsibilities. But to argue that the relational account of agency has such normative implications requires a justified account of normativity. Discussion of the source of normativity in relational or enactivist ethics is only beginning. I have referred to three approaches to the normativity of interactions, which partly overlap each other, that are worth bringing together. Two of them are deontological types of arguments for normativity, and they combine the interactive account of autonomy with the notion of autonomy as normatively committing. The third is the virtue ethic argument that refers to the interactive nature of human function. We shall return to that in the following sections.

A relationally modified version of a constitutivist argument of the source of obligations argues that normativity emerges from the *relational self-constitution of agency* (cf. Korsgaard 2019). Agency considered in terms of relationality entails that autonomy, as well as knowing, reasoning, and acting, are constituted in the interactive web of relationships. Hence, interactions—which also have autonomy of their own—take part in the directive function of agency. The source of obligation is thus included in the self-constitutive construction of agency, which involves external partners. If reflective self-consciousness is the source of obligation, as Korsgaard argues, normativity of the obligations for enhancing interactivity emerges from the normative self-constitution of agency as all normativity does in a neo-Kantian ethics. As interactivity internal to autonomous agency influences norms, practicing and cultivating of relational autonomy has normative nature (Korsgaard 1996, 2007, 2009, 2014). The unity of agency as a task remains the same even if the agency refers to extended, interactive agency. Normativity can thus be agent-based without reduction: The source of reasons is not in desires or in external facts but in the interaction that constitutes the agency. Such normativity is in conjunction with what we "do in (and to) the world" (Rowlands 2005, 2006; Korsgaard 2009, 2014). Responsibilities for the body and the external environment can be justified by the nature of moral agency, the normative self-constitution of which is linked with the conditions and capabilities of a wider web of interactions. This theory for normative authority can be seen to inform and support relational virtue ethics.

Another argument for normativity is based on the *shared vulnerability of autonomy*. As an argument that relies more clearly on an enactive account of autonomy and applies a deontologist justification of normativity, it highlights that mutual interactivity in agency can either harm or enhance the autonomy of interactants. The possibility of the participants of interaction substantially changing one another's autonomy leads to a moral type of responsibility for each to care for one's own autonomy as well as the others'. According to Cassandra Pescador Canales and Laura Mojica (2022), agents have a "possibility of irrevocably . . . harming or expanding each other's autonomy," and moral normativity "regulates and, in some cases, constitutes this very possibility." Therefore, agents are "morally responsible for caring about their own and others' autonomies in interaction." As an embodied, situated, and affective issue moral normativity "is constituted in social practices and maintained in interaction."

As normativity here is grounded in reciprocity, Pescador Canales and Mojica restrict the argument to interpersonal relationships and, perhaps, relationships between participants considered "similar" enough to have reciprocal duties. According to them, necessary conditions for normativity to arise are the embodied constitution of agents and the sociolinguistic nature of the human type of deliberation by which human agents can make normative distinctions between actions (Pescador Canales and Mojica 2022). On my view, however, a relational concept of agency allows for wider interpretation. Since enactivism is right in that even simple organisms can have adaptive autonomy (in the sense of autopoiesis), which gradually increases in accordance with the complexity of the organic system, the possibility to harm and to be harmed can also concern nonhuman interactants that do not share the sociolinguistic nature of deliberation. Responsibility (and thus, application of normativity) also increases gradually. Normativity can be seen to hold for humans even though the influence of the other parties of interaction in their autonomy results only from their adaptive autonomy. Hence, if the relational, nonhumanist nature of human agency is taken seriously, the argument need not be restricted to human interpersonal relationships: justification based on shared vulnerability and possibility to harm one another's autonomy can also apply to asymmetrical interspecies relationships.

Both arguments for interaction normativity highlight the connection between responsibility for one's own agential ability and responsibility for the various others one interacts with. Care for the interactivity in environmental relationships then gets its normative status from the interactants being influential in one another's agency—regardless of whether their agencies are just partly dependent on the mutually influential interactive processes or also partly constituted by them (see chapter 5 for modest and radical enactivism).

Self-constitution of agency being relational means that the quality of various interactions influences autonomous actions as an internal part of the source of normativity; the interaction is, in a way, "inner" to one's self-constitution (see chapter 9). Supposing that the relational account of the agency is plausible, care for environmental relationships (as well as social ones) is a condition for a moral agent's cognitive processes to function well and to be deeply influential in, if not constitutive for, her self-consciousness. Responsibilities for the quality of interaction are thus metalevel responsibilities implicitly present wherever deliberation for action takes place.

An embodied, relational account of moral agency thus alters the very place of environmental relationships in ethics, which entails changes in normative environmental ethics. The relevance of the question of moral status of nonhuman entities by which we started this book, for example, becomes secondary, if not entirely trivial. The very aspect in which humans are "unique"— though, in degree rather than in kind—as beings having conceptualized morality and ability to take responsibility, seems included in the naturally developed capacities of response-ability, care, and love. A loving attitude and care for the ways of being related with human, nonhuman, and even material others, and for the possibilities of each partner to contribute to the interaction, increase by practicing them which, again, widens the cognitive perspective. Agential moral capabilities thus can either increase or decrease due to affective relationality and interaction autonomy. Caring for the quality of interactivity and those taking part in the interactive nexus is also all about caring for one's own moral ability.

One can still wonder, whom does the normativity concern? How can relational responsibilities as responsibilities addressed to a relational agent commit an individual? The question of moral autonomy is the most criticized point in the interactive, relational, and enactive approaches to ethics, as well as in the more traditional care ethics, to which the given arguments for normativity, at least partly, answer. The notion of relational autonomy introduced in this work (see chapters 3 and 7) refers, on the one hand, to mutually dependent, relationally constrained autonomies of "individual" agents and, on the other hand, to interaction-autonomy of the interactive processes, not entirely reducible to individual autonomies. Interactive processes that have relative interaction-autonomy of their own both enable and constrain individual agential autonomy, which is an achievement of relational processes. Agential autonomy thus partly relies on environmental factors that are beyond the control of agents (Colombetti and Torrance 2009, 517–18). According to critics, the emphasis on interaction-autonomy evaporates responsibility, which is thought to require unconstrained individual autonomy that would be compromised by the relative autonomy of interactions (e.g., van Grunsven 2018). But saving responsibility does not require conceptual individualism or a traditional humanist framework. Relationality does not mean *reducing* individual autonomies to the interactive one or vice versa. Instead, one is a constituent of the other. Autonomy is not an either-or issue, but a gradually emerging aspect of life—from the simplest biological organism on. Discussions about freedom and determinism and about their mutual compatibility offer different approaches to the idea of constraint freedom. Freedom can also be seen as asymmetrical in the sense that conditions of free, uncontrolled actions depend on the conditions of responsibility but not the other way round (e.g., Wolf 1986, 1990; see chapter 7). Autonomy that is enough for responsibility does not require absolute freedom.

But the idea of responsible agents also becomes more diverse with the relational shift. Identifying procedural types of interaction responsibilities, besides individual and collective ones, can also make the systems of cooperation directing ways of thinking and doing things together subjects of shared responsibility. If collective responsibilities are characterized as institutional responsibilities, interactive responsibilities could be characterized as *cultural* ones. Cultural mechanisms of interaction are continuously changing but at any actual moment they cannot be entirely changed even if all the interactants would wish that: the autonomy of each interactant partly remains under the influence of the mechanisms of interaction inherited from the past. Yet, interactants do not need to passively pass these mechanisms further. They can use their relative autonomy to fulfill their responsibility for the ways of interactive. As Diana Meyers and Mason Cash argue, being autonomous differs from failing to be autonomous in that one is not passive but reflectively engages with the determinants that partly shape her life (Meyers 1989, 53, 59, 82–84; Cash 2010, 2013). Being responsible for one's autonomy means that one cannot avoid being partially responsible for the interactive mechanisms that influence in her. If relational autonomy is accepted, it can thus introduce a novel type of responsibilities concerning participation to the interactive processes and the personal attitude toward the other, and through that, an entirely a new perspective to environmental ethics.

The moral role of environmental others shifts from being objects of individual actions into partners of agency in those actions, especially if they are living others, ecological systems or, for instance, cultural normative institutions, which all have clear influence in the circumstances of our sense-making. Relational ethics I have defended here has shifted the focus of ethical concern from individual acts to the formulation and manipulation of the interaction and structural contexts in which the constitution of moral agency and decision making takes place and to one's ways of contributing to them. Environmental ethics is thus encouraged to focus on the structural and functional backgrounds of environmental problems. Moral autonomy being relative to inter- or intra-activity that includes nonhuman partners,

and responsibility considered to require response-ability practiced and cultivated in the multispecies communities, fundamentally alters the meaning of
"humanist" ethics. There is no ethics distinct from environmental or ecological ethics.

ARISTOTLE MEETS ENACTIVISM: VIRTUES
AS ECOLOGICAL DISPOSITIONS

According to what has been said about the implications of an ecologically
relational account of agency for the foundations of normative environmental
ethics, care ethics, on the one hand, and virtue ethics, on the other, are perhaps
the best collaborative theoretical frameworks for a relational environmental ethics. I focus here on the virtue tradition, which can, in my view, take
advantage of the relational shift. At the level of normative ethics, relationally
shifted parallel agendas of naturalist and constructivist environmental ethics share the key idea that the ability of moral agency should be cultivated
to handle environmental problems. Both lines of thought have thus stepped
into the sphere of virtue ethics and ask what it means to be responsible for
the future of the conditions of morality. However, the traditional answers of
virtue ethics do not satisfy them. What, then, would be required for an appropriate account of virtue in relationally shifted environmental virtue ethics?
Relationality is not unfamiliar for virtue ethics, but it is framed in terms of
upbringing, role models, and social impact, as well as practicing the virtues in
everyday life, all of which play a central role in developing and maintaining
virtuous life. Many virtues also are relational by nature: among Aristotelian
virtues, for instance, justice, liberality, wittiness, modesty, righteous indigna-
tion, and magnanimity are fundamentally relational virtues. Even the basic
virtue ethical concept "phronesis" referring to wisdom or intelligence as such
refers to practical virtue that has "perceptual sensitivity" to the requirements
of a factual situation and context (McDowell 1979). However, relationality
is usually not considered to concern moral agency other than in the instrumental sense, namely in that a human person needs to be raised and trained
to become virtuous.

Relational agency differs from Aristotelian and other common virtue
theories concerns, especially, in the criterion for moral enhancement toward
virtuousness. Since this is among the weakest points of non-essentialist virtue
theories, according to critics, rethinking the nature of agency as relational
may be of help. Instead of connecting the virtue-guiding final good to the
human function based on essentialist human nature, as Aristotle does, the
virtue-guiding element can be based on of the relational nature of agency. It
then refers to the methods of constructing the nexus of relationships for the

agency. Taking this line of thought, which is, I think, justifiable, would then philosophically locate the idea of relational ethics among the neo-Aristotelian agent-based alternative types of virtue ethics (see Slote 2011, 2013).[2] This would also have metaethical implications. According to the common interpretation, moral realism in virtue ethics is based on the fact that the concept of final good relies on the essentialism of human function and flourishing. However, if it is possible for an Aristotelian ethics to accept that function and flourishing are relational by nature and that cognition and other mental operations are environmentally extended, this would not be the case. Flourishing capable of providing a noncontingent action-guiding element can also refer to the relational *harmony of an ideally collaborative nexus*, to the agency of which each individual agent participates, manifestations of which, however, always remain contingent

Virtue as a disposition also can be located in different ways. First, it can be seen as an internal feature of an agent connected to the agent's good that is understood, in an Aristotelian way, as harmonious life from the point of view of her life as a whole. In this interpretation, virtue benefits (real) human flourishing, or the flourishing of a wider collective, exemplified in the harmonious function of the society or environment. It is then the individual flourishing of the agent that drives people to virtuous environmental acts and virtuous acts toward the nonhuman and environmental others. This interpretation represents metaethically traditional realism. Second, virtue can be considered as a collective feature, referring to the good or the flourishing of a society or other collective. Metaethically speaking then, the grounds of virtuousness are related to the (relative) notions of cultural or societal harmony or, perhaps, with the (strictly naturalistic) notion of ecological harmony. The relational notion of agency offers a third interpretation: Virtue as a disposition refers to the *mechanisms of the flourishing of relational agency* that combines perspectives of both other interpretations. But against the first one, virtue character cannot be considered as a permanent disposition but rather as something that should change along with a changing context since the nature of the agent is not permanent. While standard virtue ethics justifies virtuous action by referring to how a virtuous person would act in a certain situation, which implies a permanent virtuous character, relational virtue ethics refers to the processes of virtuously engaging oneself in a situation and in virtuous interactivity. *Relationally virtuous practices* amount to a virtue.

If a virtuous agent is conceived as ecologically relational rather than an individual in the traditional sense, virtuousness refers to how the agency consists of systemically intertwined ecological, material, and social niches. There is then a certain *way of relatedness* that can best provide the best possible flourishing for each actual constitution of agency in each actual situation. Virtuousness thus implements the *virtuous mechanisms of relatedness* at the level of the constitution of agency, rather than a fixed or experienced final good that could be expressed by propositions concerning the state of the agent. These mechanisms take place in the complex embodied cooperation that provides agency and they can be implemented better or worse from the point of view or the function of relational agency. Virtue as an ecological disposition also contains external elements, not just what is traditionally considered to belong to one's character. Therefore, evaluation of a person's disposition should be refocused to cover contextual, collaborative features, and external others in companion with whom any character is generated. Instead of being either a permanent trait of an individual or a feature of occurrence (see Hurka 2006, 69–74), moral character is at each moment bound to take shape in *practical situations* through the actual beliefs, wishes, imagination, physical and biological abilities, and ecological awareness of both the individual and his close community. But as practicing virtue is traditionally conceived to do, practicing relational, ecological virtues also do: they *cultivate the agent* and make her ever more virtuous. The difference between the virtuous and the non-virtuous agent thus emerges from the processes of their constitution as agents. Different agents—virtuous and less virtuous—also are mutually related, but their mutual connection is not just in the dialogue in which the less virtuous only should ask the virtuous one for advice. Instead, the dialogue, or "multilogue," takes place inside the complex cooperation that provides benevolent agency. The function of such "multilogue" persuades participants to listen to each other, to understand, and to love. For a systemic agency, such a harmony also advances the possibility of critical assessment.

The main problem of a non-essentialist virtue theory as a normative theory is usually seen to concern the action-guiding element, namely normativity. In a virtue approach, the action-guiding element should emerge from the specification of a virtuous agent, which can be specified *via* the specification of virtues. According to the standard neo-Aristotelian theory, "virtue is a character trait a human being needs for *eudaimonia*, to flourish or live well," but this specification can be criticized to fail in being action-guiding (Hursthouse 2013b, 647). Virtue should *motivate*, although virtuousness does not always result in the good life. How can an agent be motivated to become and be virtuous even though the tragedy of life is a fact? One way that a relational notion of agency may contribute to this challenge is through pointing out that *eudaimonia* is not a state of individual life—neither at any actual moment nor from the perspective of the whole process of life. Virtues that refer to the mechanisms of relatedness are linked with the final good that is realized in the harmony of the entire collaborative nexus of agency—from the viewpoint of *its* total "life." A virtuous individual that suffers can thus be motivated by the results of her virtuousness although her personal life seems to be only suffering. As a part of her relational agency, her virtuousness significantly contributes to the direction of the nexus which, again, can offer better conditions of life for each of its participants at each moment, herself included.

Virtuous features can then be based—in addition to some "internal" traits, perhaps—on the mutually responsive relationships between the living participants of agency and between them and the material, physical, and cultural world in which they are embedded. Virtue can thus be satisfactorily justified neither by permanent character traits nor by the agent's total life as a life of an individual, but as relationality always tethered to the world and the communicative relationships constituting agency. For a relational agency, environmental actors are not determinants but internal partners of agency, and thus, partners in virtue, as well. It depends on the environmental situation and the external partners of mental operations whether moral insight can or cannot take real advantage of the collaboration with them. It is thus part of virtuousness to take care of the ability of environmental partners (or "ingredients") to enhance moral ability. Moral responsibility for one's virtuousness includes responsibility for all those that influence one's character traits. Attention should be paid to the traits or dispositions that have the virtue of enhancing environmental conditions for virtuousness, and not just to the character traits that enhance individual virtuousness. A relational approach to virtue ethics thus also makes virtue theory cross the classical metaethical categories. But not only do constructivism and naturalism metaethically approach each other when the notion of relational agency is adopted, as was shown, but so do normative virtue ethics and Kantian deontology. The break between them dissolves into mere difference in details.

Environmental virtue ethics has mainly utilized the traditional conceptions of virtue and the virtuous agent. The notion of ecological virtue can, however, contribute to the discussion in a way that makes it relevant for practical political debates. Ronald Sandler, who was among the first to develop environmental virtue ethics, defends a theory of virtue that is appropriately informed by environmental values. He denies, however, that the virtue-oriented approach could properly count as an environmental ethic, because the virtue approach "does not suppose that interactions and relationships with the environment constitute a discrete ethical sphere, or that environmental problems and issues require a distinctive form of practical reasoning, moral epistemology, method of ethics, set of evaluative resources, or metaethical framework" (Sandler 2007, 142). Sandler's view depicts a wider trend of how a great deal of the philosophically oriented environmental ethics locates itself. Virtue ethicists as defenders of an agent-focused ethical theory are, of course, among the first to acknowledge that the global environmental crises force us to critically reflect on our philosophical tradition. However, not even Sandler defines how environmental virtue ethics provides the dynamic alternative to Western theoretical ethics. My endeavor has been to draw the discussion a step further by introducing the idea of ecologically relational moral agency. The account uncritically adopted from modernist discussions requires conceptual revision.

Definition of virtue as a disposition of an ecologically structured nexus of agency amounts to an environmental demand. The development of virtue, like the formation of knowledge, requires that the relationships between participants function together in a way that generates the best possible conditions to practice and train virtues—including both moral and epistemic virtues, which are interconnected *via* agency (see e.g., Little 1997; Hyman 2015. Also chapter 3). Because of the biological and material relationality of agency, there is a close and complex connection between virtue and knowledge, and both are to be practiced in relation to material environments, like landscapes. But how does relationality modify virtue ethics to bring about practical implications for environmental ethics? It clarifies at least four issues. First, both *inclusiveness* and good—including loving, caring and response-able—*interactivity* play a central role in the virtuousness of an agent's life. They form the core of *relational virtue* that should be the criteria for other virtues. In this sense, relational virtue should be considered to have a somewhat similar role to that which moderation has among Aristotelian virtues. Second, not even a virtue perspective can be restricted to a human perspective, even if it is considered more widely as a human "eco-social" perspective. Construction of values and valid virtues requires that an individual actor continuously *questions her own perspective* as a member of the dominant species. Third, implementation of relational virtues is bound to *ecological contexts and situations*. For example, relational virtues implemented in regard to dietary habits may vary from arctic indigenous people to city people to tropical rain forest people since the relationships that should be taken into account, for instance, between a hunter and a deer, are complex and do not hold only between two individuals. Fourth, actual virtues should also be distinguished from the optimal ones toward which cultivation of virtues aims, and the focus should be on the cultivation. The cultivation of virtues takes place through how they are implemented in practical situations. This requires that each actual virtuous habit (such as dietary habits) must be under continuous critical evaluation from the viewpoint of the harmonious interactivity of the entire nexus of agency. One difficulty that may remain concerns the reliable principles in each actual moral context when balancing between cultivating the relational capacity of moral agency and cultivating ecological flourishing of the ecosystems in which it is embedded. This is especially true when the latter endangers good of some human individuals in an actual situation (as far as it is possible to identify such good distinct from the flourishing of ecosystems). Since the members of the human species are the only currently known actors who can exhibit highly developed moral capacities, total extinction of our species would probably not (as far as a human from her perspective can estimate) enhance the cultivation of relational moral capacity in the world. Extremely self-destructive environmental conducts and values thus seem not to represent the right direction.

Although it is not possible in the limits of this book, I think that it would be worth considering how the lists of virtues—or capabilities—may shift if the virtue of relationality is used as the leading virtue which is traditionally held to be moderation or reasonableness. I argue that such a shift would open entirely novel possibilities to also approach practical environmental questions and challenges.

RELATIONAL VIRTUES, CAPABILITIES, AND THE FINAL GOOD

Let us return to the question of normativity and specification of virtue in a bit more detail. In virtue ethics categorized as neo-Aristotelian naturalism, theories of normativity spring from the relation between the natural good ("good for") and final good which refers to virtue ("good at"). Leaning on Aristotle, moral life and reasoning generate and develop virtuous character, and the authority of morality rests on the fact that virtues are linked with what is good for the agent. The problem, however, is the definition of human nature, on which criteria for virtues are based. The challenge is this: If the fixed points, such as essential humanness, are ruled out, what can serve as the naturalist criterion for evaluation? How can the final good be defined? What can be the grounds for judging whether the changes in character instantiate progress or degeneration? According to a relational approach, definitions of universal moral ability or final good based on universally shared supreme human nature or supernatural features of human beings is neither plausible nor necessary. However, some grounds for the evaluation of character is required for us to determine the difference between virtues and vices.

According to Martha Nussbaum, this ground is partly found in factual human nature, but it can also partly be bound to the societal expressions of the good in different contexts. Nussbaum defends the Aristotelian idea that human capabilities represent the final good in the sense that they have a claim to be realized (Nussbaum 1995b, 2011; for more, see chapter 8). But instead of essentialism and metaphysical realism, she argues that the existence of capabilities is an empirical matter: a somewhat similar set of human capabilities have marked the good life in all types of human societies throughout history (see Nussbaum 2011, 33–34). But different actual communities—which can, I suppose, be considered as multispecies communities—can and will to some extent construct the list differently, and therefore, she argues, the list of capabilities should be tentative and open-ended (Nussbaum 1995b, 72–75;

2011). The interpretive function of the cognitive faculties of living beings should be appreciated. Due to the varying practices of a community, there can be more than one actual truth about the conception of virtues. Some may think Nussbaum has given up too much to be a realist. The criticism can be targeted, especially, against the weakness of moral authority: if the authority of morality relies partly on objective human nature, and partly on relative desires or deliberations, something should be added in order for a theory to plausibly represent realism. I think that Nussbaum's view is compatible with realism, but it unnecessarily divides between two types of grounds for defining capabilities, namely objective (naturalistic human nature) and relative (particular social context) grounds. This is the point where relational realism differs from more traditional realism. While Nussbaum argues that a good rule is "a good summary of wise particular choices," a relational approach would turn the focus to the mechanisms that *connect* the particular and objective human nature, each of which Nussbaum argues to be a *partial* ground for virtues, instead of just summarizing them. I agree with her that good and virtuous decisions being context-sensitive does not imply them being "right only *relative to*, or *inside*, a limited context" (Nussbaum 2013). But I argue that conceiving of moral agency as relational could add the missing piece that would appreciate Nussbaum's modestly realist metaethics.

Capabilities have inspired environmental philosophers, especially those who discuss environmental justice and climate ethics. The question of normative authority has also been discussed. Regarding Nussbaum's list of capabilities, Breena Holland proposes adding an extra capability to the list: a relatively sustainable environment should be seen as a *meta-capability* beyond all the ten others, she argues. "Because a stable climate system provides the necessary ecological context for engaging in personal, social, material, and political relationships that Nussbaum defines as basic to any minimally decent notion of human flourishing, . . . such a system should be understood as part of a broader 'environmental meta-capability' that enables all the capabilities worthy of protection as constitutional entitlements" (Holland 2012, 147; see also 2008). Meaningful human life requires a relatively safe environment. Environmental sustainability as meta-capability involves "being able to live one's life in the context of ecological conditions that can provide environmental resources and services that enable the current generation's range of capabilities; to have these conditions now and in the future" (Holland 2008, 324). Another climate ethicist, Elizabeth Cripps, criticizes Holland's view by questioning whether environmental risks and damage in the future will necessarily harm individual flourishing now. She asks why such damage should matter, "except insofar as it threatens my life, health, or affiliation, or insofar as engagement with the natural world is central to my plan or life or conception of the good?" (Cripps 2013, 40).[3] It is a justified question to ask whether the fact that human good is always engaged with the natural world entails that a stable environment should be seen as a meta-capability for meaningful human life in the normative sense. According to Cripps, such a connection could only be made by an agent's act of valuation. However, if the scientific grounds of the relational human action, knowledge, and will are correct, and I have interpreted them plausibly, such a connection *could* be seen as an empirical fact. Namely, Holland does not explicitly suppose that "meaningfulness" is bound to a certain ecological state of affairs, but rather that capabilities that are bound to one's life embedded in an ecological context. Such an understanding of capabilities sounds interesting, and the normative argument could, I suppose, be strengthened if the relational account of agency were applied.

Three points need elaboration from the point of view of a relational approach. First, capabilities reflect the good for agents whose agency is constructed in cooperation with other living and nonliving partners in her surroundings. This means that the environment does not only provide external conditions for the agent but that the interactions in that environment substantially change her agency. In this sense the environment can be considered as a meta-capability that has a normative role. Second, all capabilities should be seen to refer to good interactivity. Therefore, the possibility to practice good co-operating skills, which is implicit in most of the capabilities of Nussbaum's list, should be emphasized. And third, capabilities do not only concern the individual but also those taking part in the interactive processes by which her agency is constituted. Capabilities becoming real also depends to some extent on the interactive "capabilities" of the nonhuman others participating in the interactive construction of agency. Promoting someone's capabilities is thus not separable from promoting the capabilities of others in the multispecies, biophysical community. Normativity of the responsibilities to those others emerges, however, from the relational, interactive structure of agency as such. Environmental responsibilities then arise even if only strictly humanist reasons for action are accepted: if we are to respect the capabilities of human life, responsibility for the life-enhancing capacities of all the relevant interactive others—and for our ability to respectfully communicate with them on personal and political levels—is involved. As conscious persons humans are responsible for the existence of moral agency, as well as for the ability to construct proper epistemic and moral judgments. Epistemic responsibility concerns not just the processes of knowledge formation, but also the formation of the conditions of knowledge formation (see e.g., Hyman 2015). This means that even *epistemic responsibility*, for instance in science, *implies environmental responsibility*. In order to get proper information or construct proper measurements for moral evaluation, we need to love those we rely on.

The missing part of Nussbaum's conception of capabilities could then be characterized as objectively virtuous ways of continuously constituting moral agency; this consists of engaging oneself in the webs of interactivity in which mutually influential interactions with various others must be loving and caring for systemic reasons since this is what complex abilities of moral agency rely on. Virtuous agencies are not reducible to any single concept, definition, or appearance (of an absolutely virtuous agent), but nonetheless, virtuousness expresses what "is right absolutely, objectively, anywhere in the human world" in attending "to the particular features of one's context" in sense that "who chooses accordingly is making . . . the humanly correct decision, period," as Nussbaum defines her vision (Nussbaum 2013; see 5.1.2). Objectivity does not originate in distance. Narratives interwoven with the organic physical aspects of the constitution of agency question the opposing natures of naturalism and constructivism. The preservation and enhancement of moral rationality and autonomy requires preservation and enhancement of the mechanisms of reflective cooperation, wherever it takes place. They include issues like care, love, trust, commitment, and wonder. Everyday life actions also have moral implications when they change environmental conditions even though they are not categorized as "moral actions" in the traditional sense. All decisions concerning the environment involve us in constituting the prerequisites of moral agency; through this we modify the moral future. A serious question for the actual moral life then is, do our *morally approved*, or perhaps even praised, lifestyles and moral codes degenerate the future conditions of moral agency by degenerating the capacity of the natural and cultural environments to provide conditions for moral reasoning and deliberation, and hence, our most important capabilities that are conditions of flourishing human life?

Though compatible with the relational view, Nussbaum's theory does not oppose standard notions of individualism and humanism. David Wong, who himself argues for a relational type of Confucian virtue ethics, criticizes the capabilities approach regarding the separateness of individuals and argues that the unnecessary supposition of separateness should be replaced by cultural pluralism resulting from the engagements of human life (Wong 2006; cf. Nussbaum 1995b, 79–80, 85). However, the relational account of agency leads us further than just cultural relationality. It calls for focusing on the mechanisms of connectedness as the common ground of ethics, though even the list of the best actual mechanisms should be left open as the mechanisms themselves continuously develop, too. The mechanisms of connectedness make the variety of engagements with others (cultural pluralism) commensurate. I suppose that Nussbaum's theory can offer fruitful ground for a normative ethical theory based on relational agency. It denies essentialist humanity and defines the actual measurement of virtuousness by referring to the genuine possibility of practicing empirically explicable human capabilities. The latter is especially important: virtues do not have to be relative although each of their embodiments would be.

Philippa Foot as an Aristotelian virtue ethicist, too, seems to acknowledge that mechanisms of connectedness can make the particularities commensurate. She also defends strong naturalism regarding the definitions of the good life. As I argued earlier, the challenge for Foot's natural teleology concerns its non-metaphysical basis of teleological virtue in human "function" (see chapter 8). She emphasizes that objectivity lies in an understanding of human nature and its function: particular social standards and individual flourishing are not detachable from human "function." But all moral disagreements are not rationally resolvable. Human function refers to certain lives, biological conditions, place, and time, besides referring to the final good (Foot 2001, 32 fn.). Foot avoids the problem of a simplified identification between virtue (good-at) and a human nature-based view of flourishing (good-for) but does not quite complete *what* then should be added to the idea of natural flourishing in order to evaluate virtuousness (Foot 2001). The missing part here, too, could be found in the relational definition of "function," which does not refer to subjects but to the processes involving multiplicity of interactive relationships by which agency is constituted. Flourishing identified by the *function of relational agency* could connect the actual contingencies of certain agents with the objective aspects of the final good as the telos. These aspects appear in how human "function" is related with the function of the systemic webs of interaction providing social and ecological sustainability, enhancement, and harmony.

Virtues cannot be derived from nature or the environment if we reject metaphysical essentialism. But I argue that the functioning of systemic interactivity *can* offer guidance for the agent who is forced to somehow contribute to it by her inputs. There seems to be an imbalance in terms between virtue and flourishing if relational extension concerns only the concept of good-for but not of virtue. While virtue as a term refers to the input of certain instances of moral agency (individual agents) to contextual reality, flourishing as a term refers to the state of affairs amounting from a certain ecological system of natural things. Flourishing of a human, for example, is linked with certain functioning of ecosystem services, structures of the biosphere, and genetic diversity, etc. The environment enters an agent's happiness. What then is the relationship between virtues and nature? If we consider human "function" as based on ecological (including social) relations which are constitutive of agency, the evaluative criterion of virtue can be seen to have its natural reference in mechanisms for balanced, benevolent, and inclusive environmental interactivity, though the final good remains indefinable. Human function cannot then be understood as a stable state. Actual human function is also necessarily a plural concept because of the varieties in particular places, evolutionary time, and the players of an ecosystem. Consequently, my virtuous actions may differ from virtues of those living in different environments. Particular value systems do not survive as the final good. The only points of evaluation that may be worthy of replacing Aristotelian essentialist human nature or neo-Aristotelian narrative type flourishing must persist despite contextual changes, running time, and continuing evolution. Such "fixed" points can include the quality of interaction, ways of "communicating" with different others for enhancing the functioning of agency by creating sustainable and creative webs and, most importantly, moral agents. Yet, however imprecise such a measurement would be, it is conceptually potent to challenge the idea of stable fixed points.

A problem in using the concept of good *simpliciter* is that *the* good can never in reality replace the particular goods that are necessary for actual lives in particular cases which are best for maintaining and enhancing moral agency. Good is, in this way, connected to "real life," as Aristotle claims. But a relational account emphasizes that the "procedures" for establishing appropriate criteria for approaching the concept of the final good are restricted neither to a natural (evolutive) nor social (discursive) structure, but to them both. Related to this, Korsgaard criticizes Foot's original project, arguing that it should be complemented with a neo-Kantian idea that all our values are relative to "our valuing capacities: the capacity to find something pleasant, interesting, enchanting, satisfying, or stimulating—and of course to experience the opposite responses as well" (Korsgaard 2012, 10). I agree that valuing capacities play a role in the idea of human good, in the sense of both natural flourishing and virtuousness. They also express something of the "final good." However, the neo-Kantian description of valuing capacities is too narrow, and thus incomplete, because such capacities are not individual. Moral and rational flourishing and value capacities are issues that emerge from the ideally interactive constitution of agency. The practice of ideally balanced interactivity in relationships with both material and intellectual others can represent the good and virtuous life.

The point in which relationally constructivist and relationally naturalist positions seem to coincide, and in which the final good may acquire its evaluative standard, is derivable from the idea of the relational moral flourishing of agency, including the capacity of valuing. If this train of thought is plausible, we should accept that any description of actual human good is partial because it is part of some particular ecological good. Moral concepts can only concern the direction toward the final good, but never reach that end. Although the aim of virtuousness (the final good) cannot be descriptively articulated, some hints about the right direction can be reasoned from the systemic, ecological structure of agency. The idea of the *relational virtue* of agency plays a role as the primary good—like *care* in care ethics.

To sum up, being a virtuous agent at any actual time and place is a pluralist characterization as the embodiments of virtuous agency are bound to the conditions of nature. But, according to relational ethics, moral concepts can be modestly truth-apt, meaning that they may approach truth, although it is in fact impossible for any actual judgment ever to reach it. In this sense, relational ethics is *teleological* by nature. All actual moral judgments, however ideal the situation would be, are incomplete. Not even total agreement between *all* agents could guarantee the truth concerning a moral judgment: any *actual view of the final good*—even if it is shared by all the reasonable agents or held from a third person's perspective—cannot survive as *the good* for a conceptual reason. The "solution for the problem of shared ends," to put it in Korsgaard's terms, is not fixed to the *content* but to the *way* in which the ends are constructed and shared. Therefore, it is crucial for an ethical "procedure" to seek for the ideal way for members of a relational agency to communicate, and for the sympathy they cultivate for each other. Rather than talking about procedures for moral truth as emerging from discourse, we should talk about procedures for approaching truth or the best as emerging from organic dialogues. An ethical theory that adopts ecological relationality of moral cares about the ecological virtuousness of the moral agent.

TOWARD TACKLING SYSTEMIC PROBLEMS

What difference then does relational moral agency make in the practical discussion on environmental ethics? I have argued in this book that one of the main reasons why modern ethics has become paralyzed in front of the complex issues that extend beyond the moral community of individual human agents—like the most urgent problems today do—originate from its account of moral agency. My view is that the ecologically relational concept of moral agency will significantly help ethics to overcome this paralysis and to deal with questions of the multispecies community and environmental conditions of life. According to a relational approach, the good for an agent or moral community cannot be separated from good interactivity between intracranial, bodily, and external biological, material, and sociocultural elements and environmental others, which is constitutive for agential processes. The practical discussion to which this will lead would be a subject of another book, but a couple of starting points are worth initially sketching here.

In the age of climate and biosphere crises, we are in the situation that species and ecosystems, and perhaps the whole mode of human life as we know it, are widely threatened by human influence. For example, the number of animals in the wild species populations of terrestrial, freshwater, and marine vertebrate animals has declined 69 percent from 1970 to 2018 despite thirty years of work to stop biodiversity loss (WWF 2022, 32). The situation we live in is a consequence of political and moral actions that were pretended to promote human good. The most environmentally disastrous issues do not result from crimes but from widely accepted and appreciated lifestyles. We have not been rational, even in terms of self-interest. Economic and institutional decisions still take place daily that weaken our possibilities to promote human good. The problem partly lies in a *flawed notion of rationality* and *implausible facts about human and nonhuman agency*. In the age of the Anthropocene, we start seeing ourselves, our own image, reflected in the external world that was supposed to offer us the diversity in relation to which we should develop our agency. Consequently, focus slides more and more toward social and cultural interactivity while the role of other relationships diminishes. This implies a real danger of degeneration of rational and moral capabilities by narrowing our inter-agential and intra-agential diversity.

The biosphere is approaching a tipping point because of the total amount of the manipulated and destroyed ecosystems that are due to, on one hand, direct human activity, such as deforestation, monocultural agriculture, overfishing, construction, and pollution. On the other hand, they are due to the degenerative impacts of indirect activity, most notably climate change and the poorly managed overpopulation of the planet by people and domesticated animals which has led to the massive overconsumption of natural resources. Human generated planetary-scale critical transition caused by so-called threshold effects is very likely to take place in the near future. The drastic change becomes visible in light of what is currently known about the global mass extinctions in natural history. Drastic planetary scale stage shifts that have led to mass extinctions share a notable statistical similarity with today's reality: when the earth's terrestrial ecosystems are critically transited—for whatever reasons—to the extent that their percentage approaches 50 percent, they lead to "state shifts, which abruptly override trends and produce unanticipated biotic effects." This can be called a tipping point, because "once a sufficient proportion of Earth's ecosystems have undergone transformation, the remainder can change rapidly": the planetary web of systems shifts into a new state, and it is nearly impossible for the previous state of ecosystems to return. Dominant species diminish or go extinct and new or formerly rare organisms replace them, food webs change, and new types of biological communities and direction of evolution gradually takes place. Such a state shift makes the conditions of earth unsuitable or unviable for most of the previous species—even for the most intellectual one. The data published already in 2011 gives a picture of the scale of human impact: During the last three years, which means, after Kant's birth, human impact on 1–2 percent of the ecosystems has grown into the critical level. Human created ecosystems (croplands, pasturelands, timber plantations or land modified by logging or human caused erosion and sedimentation, etc.) showing state shifts covered approximately 47 percent of all ice-free land, in addition to approximately 7 percent of built areas. According to widely accepted studies, without quick and drastic changes in global politics, due to the threshold-crossing effects, a likely irreversible shift of the biosphere will take place before the middle of this century (Barnosky et al. 2012, 54–56).

This kind of scenario is not easy to split into questions about individual duties, face-to-face relationships, or debates between various human interests. Solutions to the type of complex problems we face today are not achievable by the individualistic moral theories resulting from the traditional humanistic logic of ethics. One challenge for practically efficient environmental ethics is, of course, to use correctly identified metrics for the adaptive capacity of ecosystems and conditions for sustainability in global changes. Wide scientific assistance is necessary, but philosophers need to do the conceptual job, which is also required. The modern humanist background presuppositions of the most used normative theories concerning both nature and human being are not convincing under scientific scrutiny. Both the nature of the moral problems we in fact face and the presuppositions of the moral theories offered to solve these problems need to be critically scrutinized in the light of the best scientific and philosophical understanding. The fact that modern humanist moral theories are successfully utilized in conceptualizing social political issues does not reveal anything about their efficiency in enhancing sustainability. Political conduct requires change in order to be able to guide the tackling of environmental problems, and achieving proper changes requires philosophical help. Politically oriented environmental ethics plays a practical central role in mediating between ethics and politics to confront the urgent crisis. The conceptual framework applied in that discussion influences the efficiency of environmental politics. Therefore, conceptual philosophical work should not be dismissed in political environmental ethics.

Conceptual tools we use also change the focus and topics of ethical discourse. For example, due to the dominance of humanistic individualism in ethical frameworks, the criteria for the moral status of nonhuman entities long dominated theoretical discussions of environmental ethics. But that discussion has little to offer for guidance in systemic environmental problems, though the question of moral status remains relevant for animal ethics aiming at changing political and social conduct regarding, especially, domesticated animals. The most urgent environmental problems, however, do not concern mistreatment of individuals but the balance of various entities on earth. The relational shift liberates environmental ethics from the shackles of an individualistic approach to focus on the structures and functions of vital systemic webs of interaction as a central measure of good and right in environmental politics and action. The claim that the relational nature of human agency calls for turning the focus of ethics to interactivity as, for instance, Colombetti and Torrance (2009) argue, highlights the moral responsibility for the systemic good. Systemic good of the interactive wholes turns, again, the focus to the conditions of ecological and social systemic resilience, and to the existence and development of functioning systems. The interactive nature of the knots of agency and systems on the largest scale refers to the resilience of these knots and systems, and hence, it emphasizes the moral relevance of the balance between the flourishing of individuals and the vitality of the wholes.

The relational concept of agency thus implies a shift of values and conduct that should focus on the functions of systemic webs. Such a shift does not, however, require adoption of any metaphysical or ontological system to make values concern systemic wholes. And unlike environmental ethical theories that lean on metaphysically loaded notions of moral holism, the relational approach does not undermine plurality. On the contrary, the relational approach appreciates variety, and value of, and responsibilities for, the plurality of embodiments of agency, such as human and animal individuals. This makes systemic issues like biodiversity, ecosystemic resilience, climatic balance, and sustainability of marine systems natural targets of ethical preservation. The value of such systemic processes and "wholes" then rests neither on the valuation of external human valuers nor on the objective value of some natural systems but on the interactive relationality that highlights both their interactive autonomy and the autonomy of each of their participants. Systemic relationality makes them conceptually subjects of value. Diversity of interactants is also an example of a crucial condition for resilient natural and social systems. Such systems may refer, for example, to the diversity of genetic material, species, ecosystems, populations, numbers of living organisms, or biotopes, and to cultural diversity, which is important for human societal resilience.

Let us take biodiversity as an example to briefly consider normative ramifications of the relational shift. Biodiversity maintains biological resilience, and cultural diversity, especially flourishing of various indigenous cultures, maintain resilience of the humankind. Cultural evolution and social resilience also are inseparable from biological change. Sustainability and resilience of ecosystems, which is strengthened by biodiversity, is required for the emergence of good social normative order and cultural flourishing. Biodiversity is widely valued as an important aspect of the good life and functioning systems by human agents, but axiologically such values become easily trivialized in the mainstream context of discussion, especially when confronted with the value of individual *human* lives. Human lives should—from the point of view of relational agency, too—be prioritized in the context of inter*personal* interactivity; as Kant claims, the consequences of violence against one's fellow creatures are disastrous for agency. *But* relational agency shows that juxtaposition between interpersonal and relational perspectives is a delusion: *all interactions extend beyond individual persons* because of the systemic nature of human life. A resilient biosphere and human life are intimately connected normatively, not just as facts. Relationality thus makes axiological and justificatory deliberation more nuanced but also harder because it does not allow easy solutions to complex issues. But the fact that it forces us to consider the complexity of systemic problems with a more nuanced toolbox is something that is highly needed to improve the practical relevance of environmental ethics. Therefore, it is not possible, for instance, to choose between prioritizing protection of one or another animal species simply due to their quantity or the strength of population. For example, in the case that an individual couple of some endangered species would die if a population of a more common species were not destroyed, moral deliberation needs to focus on, at least, four types of consideration. Besides the quantity and quality of suffering, one needs to consider, first, the vitality of biodiversity, as well as of the populations, from the viewpoint of evolutionary resilience. Second, one needs to consider the influences of different options in the quality of systemic interactivity of the ecological nexus combining bio-eco-socio-cultural interactants in the area and beyond it. Third, critical consideration should be focused on the political and personal reasons for action from the viewpoint of the relationality of agency and, hence, the quality of interaction should reflect the attitudinal and relational justification of intervention. One must always consider the responsibility of human species, the actual community that makes the decisions, as well as oneself as a relational, influential participant of them, to the balance between the good of the whole and the good of the individual species and individual members of the systemic nexus. Fourth, the focus should also be on the quality of personal attitudes and actions when encountering others in the multispecies community. For example, there are famous narratives among indigenous peoples about the mutual respect and understanding between the hunter and the hunted animal and about care for the vitality of its own social and ecological community. A large part of indigenous religious rituals originates from the aspiration to ensure the balance of nature and to enhance the loving and respecting interaction between the human community and its nonhuman companions—from the perspective of individuals and populations, as well as from, for instance, a forest or a mountain as a whole (see e.g., Pentikäinen 1996). Cultures that practice such rituals and tell these narratives are empirically proven to be ecologically more sustainable than those that do not. This exemplifies, that the moral acceptability of, for instance, hunting cannot be separated from the way it is done and the systemic context. In terms of relational ethics, these habits are constructed to preserve and enhance "response-ability," borrowing Donna Haraway's concept. The results of these types of deliberations are not easily simplified into standardized political rules.

Since human life and genuine human abilities, such as moral deliberation and consciousness, as well as the entire direction of the evolutionary future, are intimately interwoven into the functioning of the interactive processes of the biosphere, the normative status they have is justified regardless of human social recognition of such status. These processes are influential in way or another in the conceptual starting point of every moral deliberation. Enabling reliable cognitive processes, warranted affective responses, and responsibility requires practicing sensitive perception of the variety of living organisms and other planetary companions, respecting the affordance they express in these relationships, and responding to them with love and care. A relational account of agency thus gives new types of reasons to protect biodiversity, in addition to the usually given (and mutually somewhat opposing) reasons: an axiological reason derived either from the intrinsic value of the good of the biosphere or from the human voluntary act that addresses value to the vitality of the biosphere, and an ontological reason derived from the metaphysical status of diversity as such. To preserve epistemic and moral abilities entails preserving the dynamic flourishing of the environmental structures that influence cognitive processes, values, affections, and a sense of responsibility. Caring for variety and balanced interactivity between various partners is a condition of moral rationality and autonomy.

From the viewpoint of relational agency, any actual type of biodiversity that consists of certain species cannot, in theory, be self-evidently better than some other. From the interactive perspective, the species may change without decreased value, *if* balanced interactivity and creative potentiality for interactive agency to flourish and provide autonomy for the interactants will be equally well maintained. In principle, any biodiversity that maintains global and local resilience is good and should be protected. However, since biological evolution is a slow process, the consequences of extinctions always involve unknown side effects, and extinct species will not be automatically replaced, human-caused loss of any species should be prevented. In the lifetime of current and becoming human generations, the question of the composition of biodiversity also is irrelevant since the protection of diversity requires protection of vitality of every species left on earth. Although the composition of species may vary between equally good states of biodiversity, conceiving of agency as a nexus of interactivity that is a skill to be protected and enhanced means that complex organisms and systemic structures deserve special protection. Although the idea of humanity requires revision and harmful human influence on earth must be radically cut, extinction of the human species would also certainly be a great loss of value from the viewpoint of interactive agency.

Biodiversity has yet another value from the viewpoint of the dynamics of cognitive architecture. Cognition enacted interactively in relation to the environment highlights the importance of the everyday life environments in which identities, values, and affective and epistemic abilities are shaped. The mental architecture of human persons and the cultural architecture of society are place-based. Therefore, cultural habits and everyday environments are highly important for the possibility of respectful, reflective, and morally valid environmental politics. As highlighted in (human) developmental psychology, childhood experiences of environments and interactivity in multispecies communities highly influence a person's worldview and moral attitudes, especially regarding environmental issues (see e.g., Pike 2017). Encounters with diverse types of life, and especially engagement in close interaction with them, also make the individual and social human cognitive processes better able to adapt to changes in natural and social ecosystems, and to act in accordance with local and actual needs. While the relational approach to ethics emphasizes the second person's perspective in ethics—which can be criticized for dismissing the more objective third person's perspective (see van Grunsven 2018)—since it claims that no perspective can ever be impartial enough to be called a third person's perspective, the more diverse the encounters are the wider perspectives they offer, though without absolute objectivity. From the biological perspective, it is widely known that monoculture destroys flexibility and adaptability of plants and areas and makes them fragile in multiple ways (genetic degeneration, vulnerability against diseases and pests, etc.). In the case of an individual cognitive agent, the lack of diversity of perceptual interaction and participatory sense-making, which could be described as cognitive monoculture, degenerates cultural adaptability and resilience, but also impoverishes an individual's emotional abilities and epistemic and rational skills which, again, influence her political activity and decision making.

Since experiences of multispecies interactivity influence one's response-ability as a human agent, possibilities to encounter different others, to practice sensibility and care, and to commit oneself to different others should be present for all in everyday life circumstances. This means that in practical political actions, such as urban and land use planning, societies should consider that there are good routine ways for people to develop their relational sensibility. The immediate environments should offer individuals diverse possibilities to experience the shared vulnerability and precariousness of life with nonhuman others and the material conditions of sustainability, and to practice multispecies care and love. Places to encounter wild living others and perceive their ways of life indicate not only ecologically more sustainable cities but also develop cultural and moral capacities of human citizens to live in the multispecies community. A relational approach to agency may thus also offer a new and innovative method for urban and land use planning. Experiences in which the meaning of life, well-being, and happiness are seen as bound to respectful encounters with different others can enhance cultural conditions of the sustainability transition. For the purposes of both implementing sustainability and supporting sustainable well-being of individual citizens, it is also important to understand the connection between human moral development and the quality of the ecological environment where individuals grow up and cognitively adapt. Urban biodiversity, nearby natural areas, green spots, roofs, and walls should not be seen as nice additions to wealthy neighborhoods but as essential starting points in the land use planning of any neighborhood. Understanding the role of relational interactivity for human mental processes could also help societies to improve psychological, eco-social, and moral well-being. Diversity is important not just for ecological but also for cultural and moral sustainability.

The examples and notions given here do not, of course, take us far into the practical questions of environmental ethics. Such issues form the subject of another book. The fact also may be that the ecologically relational idea of moral agency provides sightly various practical outcomes when applied to different theoretical contexts. However, I argue that the relational conceptual shift based on the relational account of agency and, as I suggest, holding the virtue of relationality as the leading virtue, will open significantly novel perspectives for normative environmental ethics, too.

SOME CONCLUDING REMARKS

The last part of the journey we have made led us to the relational conceptual landscape of ethical discourse. We touched just a few of the perspectives that seem to follow from the relational, interactive agent-based focus in ethics, and it also appeared that the definition of relational agency still needs further examination and clarification. However, I argued that this initiative to articulate normative ethics suitable for relational moral agents shows, at least, that the presumptions of agency play a powerful role for the outcomes of environmental ethics. Because of the credibility and practical efficiency of ethics, any ethical theory should accurately scrutinize its conceptual basis concerning the idea of a human, and the role it plays in the theory and its outcomes. This is especially important for environmental ethics. I claim that philosophical groundwork is an important and inseparable part of an effective environmental ethics. This philosophical work should not be detached from interdisciplinary scientific work, and philosophers are required to formulate valid ethical arguments on the grounds of empirical explanations. But in contrast to those who claim that environmental ethics should identify itself only as a part of applied environmental sciences, since the philosophical work is, according to them, inefficient, I argue that environmental philosophy has a mission in ethics that exceeds its own discussions: it should open the track beyond the ingrained narrowly humanist presumptions of ethics. This mission is an important part of the cultural sustainability transformation.

The relational revision in ethics that I have called for means shifting the perspective from individualist and traditionally humanist background presumptions to conceptualizing the cognitive, epistemic, and normative processes of agency as inter- and intra-active mechanisms that systemically rely on the quality of the nexus of past and present interactivities. This has both theoretical and practical implications, as well as metaethical ones. The conceptual shift changes ethical discourse by highlighting that the constitutive elements of agency are relationally constructed. If operations transformative to the construction of agency cannot be clearly located in either natural causalities or in absolute freedom, but in the processes of relational cooperation that mix elements in a complex way, the central concepts for moral agency, such as autonomy, rationality, and acting for moral reason, should be considered from the meta-perspective as issues resulting from actual agency construction. This I argued not to compromise the philosophical method, nor to require applying certain metaphysical doctrines about relational nature from which normative obligations should be derived. I described here relationality as a fact, the awareness of which is important because actual moral rationality possible for human animals is always constructed in the context in which they live. This does not overrule the modest idea of moral realism: the mechanisms of relatedness may be objectively better or worse.

In case of environmental ethics this means that the dilemma that has bothered environmental ethics dissolves away. Aspirations to defend autonomy and the authority of ethics—that is, moral realism and a valid concept of normativity—and at the same time, defend a scientifically plausible idea of natural moral agency, are compatable through a relationally revised notion of moral agency and, consequently, ethics. Normatively speaking, the mechanisms of interactivity and the systemic processes they create—which precisely have been problematic for modern moral theories to deal with—rise to the center of assessment in relational ethics. If processes of agency engage active elements of surrounding environments, as I argued, the environments in which moral agency is continuously constructed significantly contribute to the outcomes of moral reasoning. This shifts the place and role of contingent environmental facts *even in the most humanist moral arguments*: assessment of environmental interactivity is present *wherever* moral deliberation takes place.

As the reader has noticed, relationality can be seen as an umbrella term for slightly different approaches. However, my purpose has been to clarify the specific nature of relationality as an *agential* approach to ethics. Agential relationality also makes the ramifications of interactivity in ethics more understandable, and perhaps even more acceptable than would, for instance, a metaphysical approach. Agential relationality emphasizes that regarding the faults of the concepts underlying modern humanist ethics, the tip of criticism is in their presumptions concerning the concept of moral agency. I have defended the relational concept as a plausible, philosophically and scientifically valid way to call into question the humanism of modern ethics in the mode we are used to understanding it and to reach beyond it.

The journey beyond humanism has not stopped. My personal journey with relational moral agency has already taken more than twenty years, but after lonely wandering through the landscapes, I am now grateful to notice that the arguments I have made in this book participate in the vivid discussion to which many great philosophers now take part. I have here referred to some of them, but as the discussion seems to evolve, I am eager to hear multiple voices join. Around the world, environmental scientists, enactivists, and various others who are critical of the modern type of humanism are continuously working on issues relative to what I have here articulated as relational agency and its ethical implications. My argument is that this discussion has significant implications for the self-understanding of modern ethics. It is especially significant for environmental ethics.

NOTES

1. I agree with Colombetti and Torrance in that ethical meanings in a situation emerge, at least partly, from the interactive processes to which various interactantas take part. See Colombetti and Torrance 2009, 520; Colombetti 2018, 572.

2. Michael Slote argues for the relational dimension of not just virtues but also goods and calls for further work with "the idea of dependent values," which means that "our profiling of the virtues ought to have a relational dimension in addition to the more familiar internal one. . . . such profiling should be applied to goods and not just virtues." Slote 2011, 126–27.

3. As a consequentialist, Cripps herself argues for weakly collective moral duties on the grounds of collective self-interest. Cripps 2013, 48.

Bibliography

Alaimo, Stacy, and Susan Hekman, eds. 2008. *Material Feminisms.* Bloomington: Indiana University Press.

Alanen, Lilli. 2003. *Descartes's Concept of Mind.* Cambridge, MA: Harvard University Press.

Allhoff, Fritz. 2009. "The Evolution of the Moral Sentiments and the Metaphysics of Morals." *Ethical Theory and Moral Practice* 12: 97–114.

Attfield, Robin. 1987. *A Theory of Value and Obligation.* London: Croom Helm.

Ayala, Francisco J. 2010. "What the Biological Sciences Can and Cannot Contribute to Ethics." In *Contemporary Debates in Philosophy of Biology*, edited by Francisco J. Ayala and Robert Arp, 316–36. Oxford: Wiley-Blackwell.

Bagnoli, Carla. 2011. "Constructivism in Metaethics." In *Stanford Encyclopedia of Philosophy*, edited by Edward N. Zalta. http://plato.stanford.edu/entries/constructivism-metaethics/.

Bagnoli, Carla. 2012. "Reason in Ethics." In *Reason and Reasons*, edited by C. Amoretti and N. Vassallo, 139–56. Frankfurt: Ontos-Verlag.

Barad, Karen. 2007. *Meeting the Universe Halfway: Quantum Physics and the Entanglement of Matter and Meaning.* Durham, NC: Duke University Press.

Barad, Karen. 2003. "Posthumanist Performativity. Toward an Understanding of How Matter Comes to Matter." *Signs: Journal of Women in Culture and Society* 28 (3): 801–31.

Barandiaran, Xabier. 2017. "Autonomy and Enactivism: Towards a Theory of Sensorimotor Autonomous Agency." *Topoi* 36: 409–30.

Barkow, Jerome H., Leda Cosmides, and John Tooby, eds. 1992. *The Adapted Mind: Evolutionary Psychology and the Generation of Culture.* New York: Oxford University Press.

Barnosky, Anthony, E. Hadly, J. Bascompte, E. Berlow, J. Brown, M. Fortelius, W. Getz, J. Harte, A. Hastings, P. Marquet, N. Martinez, J., A. Mooers, P. Roopnarine, G. Vermeij, J. Williams, R. Gillespie, J. Kizes, C. Marshall, N. Matzke, D. Mindell, E. Revilla, A. Smith. 2012. "Approaching a State Shift in Earth's Biosphere." *Nature* 486: 52–58. DOI: 10.1038/nature11018.

Beauvoir, Simone de. 2011. *The Second Sex.* New York: Vintage Books.

Berger, Peter, and T. Luckmann. 1966. *The Social Construction of Reality: A Treatise in the Sociology of Knowledge*. Garden City, NY: Doubleday.

Bernstein, J. M. 1995. *Recovering Ethical Life: Jürgen Habermas and the Future of Critical Theory*. London: Routledge.

Blackburn, Simon. 1993. *Essays in Quasi-Realism*. Oxford: Oxford University Press.

Braidotti, Rosi. 2019. *Posthuman Knowledge*. Cambridge: Polity Press.

Braidotti, Rosi. 2018. "Afterword: The Proper Study of the Humanities Is No Longer 'Man.'" In *Italy and the Environmental Humanities: Landscapes, Natures, Ecologies*, edited by S. Iovino, E. Cesaretti and E. Past, 242–45. Charlottesville: University of Virginia Press.

Bratman, Michael E. 2007. *Structures of Agency: Essays*. Oxford: Oxford University Press.

Bratman, Michael E. 1992. "Shared Cooperative Activity." *The Philosophical Review* 101: 327–41.

Bratman, Michael E. 1993. "Shared Intention." *Ethics* 104: 97–113.

Bratman, Michael E. 2012. "Constructivism, Agency, and the Problem of Alignment." In *Constructivism in Practical Philosophy*, edited by J. Lenman and Y. Shemmer, 81–98. Oxford: Oxford University Press.

Brennan, Andrew. 1988. *Thinking about Nature: An Investigation of Nature, Value and Ecology*. London: Routledge.

Brink, David O. 1989. *Moral Realism and the Foundations of Ethics*. Cambridge: Cambridge University Press.

Buber, Martin. 1970. *I and Thou*. Translated by W. Kaufmann. New York: Scribner's.

Buhrman, Thomas, Ezequiel Di Paolo, and Xabier Barandarian. 2013. "A Dynamical Systems Account of Sensorimotor Contingencies," *Frontiers of Cognitive Science* 4, no. 285.

Callanan, John J. 2013. *Kant's Groundwork of the Metaphysics of Morals*. Edinburgh: Edinburgh University Press.

Callicott, J. Baird. 1999. *Beyond the Land Ethic: More Essays in Environmental Philosophy*. Albany: State University of New York Press.

Callicott, J. Baird. 1980. "Animal Liberation: A Triangular Affair." *Environmental Ethics* 2, no. 4: 311–38.

Callicott, J. Baird. 2002. "The Pragmatic Power and Promise of Theoretical Environmental Ethic: Forging a New Discourse." *Environmental Values* 11: 3–25.

Callicott, J. Baird. 2008. "The New New (Buddhist?) Ecology." *Journal for the Study of Religion, Nature, and Culture* 2: 166–82.

Cash, Mason. 2010. "Extended Cognition, Personal Responsibility, and Relational Autonomy." *Phenomenology and the Cognitive Sciences* 9: 645–71.

Cash, Mason. 2013. "Cognition without Borders: 'Third Wave' Socially Distributed Cognition and Relational Autonomy." *Cognitive Systems Research* 25–26: 61–71.

Cela-Conde, Camilo J., and Francisco J. Ayala. 2007. *Human Evolution: Trails from the Past*. Oxford: Oxford University Press.

Chalmers, David. 2018. "Extended Cognition and Extended Consciousness." In *Andy Clark and His Critics*, edited by M. Colombo, E. Irvine and M. Stapleton, 9–20. New York: Oxford University Press.

Cheney, Jim. 1989. "Postmodern Environmental Ethics: Ethics as Bioregional Narrative." *Environmental Ethics* 11: 117–34.

Cheney, Jim. 2005. "Truth, Knowledge and the Wild World." *Ethics and the Environment* 10: 101–35.

Cheney, Jim and Anthony Weston. 1999. "Environmental Ethics as Environmental Etiquette: Toward an Ethics-Based Epistemology." *Environmental Ethics* 21: 115–34.

Clark, Andy. 1998. *Being There: Putting Brain, and World Together Again.* Cambridge: MIT Press.

Clark, Andy. 2007. "Curing Cognitive Hiccups: A Defense of the Extended Mind." *The Journal of Philosophy* 104, no. 4: 163–92.

Clark, Andy and David Chalmers. 1998. "The Extended Mind." *Analysis* 58: 10–23.

Clayton, Philip. 2004. "Biology and Purpose: Altruism, Morality, and Human Nature in Evolutionary Perspective." In *Evolution and Ethics: Human Morality in Biological and Religious Perspective*, edited by P. Clayton and J. Schloss, 318–36. Grand Rapids, MI: William B. Eerdmans Publishing Company.

Cobb, John Jr. 1972. *Is It Too Late? A Theology of Ecology.* Bruce and Glencoe.

Code, Lorraine. 1987. *Epistemic Responsibility.* Providence, RI: Brown University Press.

Code, Lorraine. 2006a. *Ecological Thinking: The Politics of Epistemic Location.* Oxford and New York: Oxford University Press.

Code, Lorraine. 2005. "Ecological Naturalism: Epistemic Responsibility and the Politics of Knowledge." *Dialogue and Universalism* 15, no. 5/6: 87–101.

Code, Lorraine. 2006b. "Skepticism and the Lure of Ambiguity." *Hypatia* 21: 222–28.

Code, Lorraine. 2008. "Thinking about Ecological Thinking." *Hypatia* 23: 187–203.

Code, Lorraine. 2013. "Reason and Woman." In *Reason and Rationality,* edited by M. C. Amoretti and N. Vassallo, 71–91. Berlin: De Gruyter.

Coeckelbergh, Mark. 2012. *Growing Moral Relations: Critique of Moral Status Ascription.* Houndmills: Palgrave Macmillan.

Colombetti, Giovanna. 2018. "Enacting Affectivity." In *The Oxford Handbook of 4E Cognition,* edited by A. Newen, L. de Bruin, and S. Gallagher, 571–88. Oxford: Oxford University Press.

Colombetti, Giovanna, and Steve Torrance. 2009. "Emotion and Ethics. An Inter-(en)ctive Approach." *Phenomenology and the Cognitive Sciences* 8, no. 4: 505–26.

Copp, David. 1995. *Morality, Normativity, and Society.* Oxford: Oxford University Press.

Copp, David. 2007b. *Morality in a Natural World: Selected Essays in Metaethics.* Cambridge: Cambridge University Press.

Copp, David. 2001. "Realist-Expressivism: A Neglected Option for Moral Realism." *Social Philosophy and Policy* 18: 1–43.

Copp, David. 2006. "On the Agency of Certain Collective Entities: An Argument from 'Normative Autonomy.'" *Midwest Studies in Philosophy 30, no. 1*: 194–221.

Copp, David. 2007a. "The Collective Moral Autonomy Thesis." *Journal of Social Philosophy* 38: 369–88.

Copp, David. 2008. "Darwinian Skepticism about Moral Realism." *Philosophical Issues* 18: 186–205.

Copp, David. 2009a. "Is Society-Centered Moral Theory a Contemporary Version of Natural Law Theory?" *Dialogue* 48, no. 1: 19–36.

Copp, David. 2009b "Toward a Pluralist and Teleological Theory of Normativity." *Philosophical Issues* 19: 21–37.

Copp, David. 2011. "Jesse Prinz, *The Emotional Construction of Morals* (Oxford: Oxford University Press, 2007): Prinz's Subjectivist Moral Realism." *Noûs* 45, no. 3: 577–94.

Copp, David. 2013. "Is Constructivism an Alternative to Moral Realism?" In *Constructivism in Ethics*, edited by Carla Bagnoli, 108–32. Oxford: Oxford University Press.

Copp, David. 2015. "Social Glue and Norms of Sociality." *Philosophical Studies* 172, no. 12: 3387–97.

Cornejo, Carlos. 2014. "On Trust and Distrust in the Lifeworld." In *Dialogical Approaches to Trust in Communication*. Ed by I. Marková and P. Linell, 237–53. Charlotte, NC: Information Age Publishing.

Cosmides, Leda, and John Tooby. 2013. "Evolutionary Psychology: New Perspectives on Cognition and Motivation." *Annual Review of Psychology* 64: 201–29.

Cripps, Elizabeth. 2011. "Climate Change, Collective Harm and Legitimate Coercion." *Critical Review of International Social and Political Philosophy* 14, no. 2: 171–93.

Cripps, Elizabeth. 2013. *Climate Change and the Moral Agent: Individual Duties in an Interdependent World*. Oxford: Oxford University Press.

Crisp, Roger. 2006. *Reasons and the Good*. New York: Oxford University Press.

Crisp, Roger. 1999. "Teachers in an Age of Transition: Peter Singer and J. S. Mill." *Singer and His Critics*, edited by Dale Jamieson, 85–102. Oxford, Malden: Blackwell Publishers.

Cuomo, Chris. 1998. *Feminism and Ecological Communities: An Ethic of Flourishing.* London: Routledge.

Curry, Patrick. 2008. "Nature Post-Nature." *New Formations* 26: 51–64.

Darwin, Charles. 2001. *The Descent of Man, and Selection in Relation to Sex.* 2nd ed., with an essay by T. H. Huxley (1877), *The Works of Charles Darwin.* Electronic edition. Part 1. Charlottesville: InteLex Corporation.

Davion, Victoria. 1994. "Is Ecofeminism Feminist?" In *Ecological Feminism,* edited by Karen Warren, 8–28. New York: Routledge.

Dawkins, Richard. 2016. *The Selfish Gene.* 40th Anniversary Edition. Oxford: Oxford University Press.

De Jaegher, Hanne. 2018."The Intersubjective Turn." In *Oxford Handbook of 4E Cognition*, edited by A. Newen, L. De Bruin and S. Gallagher, 454–68. Oxford: Oxford University Press.

De Jaegher, Hanne. 2021. "Loving and Knowing: Reflections for an Engaged Epistemology." *Phenomenology and the Cognitive Sciences* 20: 847–70.

De Jaegher, Hanne, and Ezequiel Di Paolo. 2007. "Participatory sensemaking. An enactive approach to social cognition." *Phenomenology and the Cognitive Science* 6: 485–507.

De Jaegher, Hanne, Ezequiel Di Paolo, and Ralph Adolphs. 2016. "What Does the Interactive Brain Hypothesis Mean for Social Neuroscience? A Dialogue." *Philosophical Transactions of the Royal Society B* 371: 20150379. http://dx.doi.org /10.1098/rstb.2015.0379.

De Waal, Frans. 1996. *Good Natured: The Origins of Right and Wrong in Humans and Other Animals.* Cambridge, MA: Harvard University Press.

De Waal, Frans. 2005. *Our Inner Ape.* New York: Riverhead Books.

De Waal, Frans. 2006. *Primates and Philosophers*, edited by Stephen Macedo and Josiah Ober. Princeton: Princeton University Press.

Deane-Drummond, Celia. 2004. *The Ethics of Nature.* Malden: Blackwell Publishing.

Deane-Drummond, Celia. 2014. *The Wisdom of the Liminal: Evolution and Other Animals in Human Becoming.* Grand Rapids, MI: Eerdmans Publishing.

Deane-Drummond, Celia. 2015. "The Uses and Abuses of Science in Religious Environmentalism." *Journal for the Study of Religion, Nature and Culture* 9: 169–75.

Dennett, Daniel. 1984. *Elbow Room.* Cambridge: MIT Press.

Dennett, Daniel. 1991. *Consciousness Explained.* Boston: Little, Brown and Co.

Desmond, Adrian. 1994. *Huxley: From Devil's Disciple to Evolution's High Priest.* New York: Perseus.

Devall, Bill. 1990. "Ecocentric Sangha." *Dharma Gaia*, edited by A.H. Bandiner, 155–64. Berkeley: Parallax Press.

Di Paolo, Ezequiel. 2009. "Extended life." *Topoi* 28, 9–21.

Di Paolo, Ezequiel, and Hanne De Jaegher. 2012. "The Interactive Brain Hypothesis." *Frontiers in Human Neuroscience* 6: 1–16.

Dryzek, John S. 1987. *Rational Ecology: Environmental and Political Economy.* Oxford: Basil Blackwell.

Dryzek, John S. 1990. "Green Reason: Communicative Ethics for the Biosphere." *Environmental Ethics* 12: 195–210.

Emerson, Ralph Waldo. 2019. *Essays: Second Series*, and *Representative Men* in Works of Ralph Waldo Emerson, Project Gutenberg. https://www.gutenberg.org/ files/58994.

Farber, Paul L. 1994. *The Temptations of Evolutionary Ethics.* Berkeley: University of California Press.

Ferré, Frederick. 2001. *Living and Value: Toward a Constructive Postmodern Ethics.* Albany: State University of New York Press.

Fischer, John Martin. 2006. *My Way: Essays on Moral Responsibility.* Oxford: Oxford University Press.

Fischer, John Martin. 2012. "Semicompatabilism and Its Rivals." *Journal of Ethics* 16: 117–43.

FitzPatrick, William. 2005. "The Practical Turn in Ethical Theory: Korsgaard's Constructivism, Realism, and the Nature of Normativity." *Ethics* 115, no. 4: 651–91.

FitzPatrick, William. 2015. "Debunking Evolutionary Debunking of Ethical Realism." *Philosophical Studies* 172: 883–904.

FitzPatrick, William. 2017. "Human Altruism, Evolution and Moral Philosophy." *Royal Society Open Science* 4: 170441. DOI: http://dx.doi.org/10.1098/rsos .170441.

FitzPatrick, William. 2020. "Evolutionary Biology and Appeals to Natural Teleology in Ethics." *Stanford Encyclopedia of Philosophy*, edited by Edward N. Zalta. http:// plato.stanford.edu/entries/morality-biology/natural-teleology-ethics.html.

Foot, Philippa. 2001. *Natural Goodness*. Oxford: Oxford University Press.

Foot, Philippa. 2002. *Moral Dilemmas and Other Topics in Moral Philosophy*. Oxford: Clarendon Press.

Fox, Warwick. 2003. "Deep Ecology: A New Philosophy of our Time?" In *Environmental Ethics: An Anthology*, edited by A. Light and H. Rolston, 252–61. Malden: Blackwell Publishing.

Friedman, Marilyn. 2000. "Autonomy, Social Disruption, and Women." *Relational Autonomy: Feminist Perspectives on Autonomy, Agency, and the Social Self*, edited by C. Mackenzie and N. Stoljar, 35–51. Oxford: Oxford University Press.

Froese, T., and Di Paolo, E. A. 2011. "The Enactive Approach. Theoretical Sketches from Cell to Society." *Pragmatics and Cognition* 19, 1–36.

Frye, Marilyn. 1983. *The Politics of Reality: Essays in Feminist Theory*. Trumansburg, NY: Crossing Press.

Fuchs, Thomas, and Hanne De Jaegher. 2009. "Enactive Intersubjectivity: Participatory Sense-Making and Mutual Incorporation." *Phenomenology and the Cognitive Sciences* 8: 465–86.

Gallagher, Shaun. 2005. *How the Body Shapes the Mind*. Oxford: Oxford University Press.

Gardiner, Stephen M. 2011. *A Perfect Moral Storm: The Ethical Tragedy of Climate Change*. Oxford: Oxford University Press.

Geertz, Clifford. 1973. *The Interpretations of Cultures*. New York: Basic Books.

Gibson, James J. 2014. "The Theory of Affordances." In *The People, Place and Space Reader,* edited by J. J. Gieseking and W. Mangold. New York: Routledge.

Gilbert, Margaret. 1989. *On Social Facts*. New York: Routledge.

Gilbert, Margaret. 2014. *Joint Commitment: How We Make the Social World.* Oxford: Oxford University Press.

Gilbert, Margaret. 2001. "Social Rules as Plural Subject Phenomena." In *On the Nature of Social and Institutional Reality*, edited by Lagerspetz et al. Jyväskylä: SoPhi.

Gilligan, Carol. 1982. *In a Different Voice: Psychological Theory and Women's Development.* Cambridge, MA: Harvard University Press.

Goodpaster, Kenneth E. 1978. "On Being Morally Considerable." *Journal of Philosophy* 75: 308–25.

Griffiths, Paul E., and Richard D. Gray. 2001. "Darwinism and Developmental Systems." In *Cycles of Contingency: Developmental Systems and Evolution*, edited by S. Oyama, P. E. Griffiths and R. D. Gray, 195–218. Cambridge, MA: MIT Press.

Griffiths, Paul E., and James Tabery. 2013. "Developmental Systems Theory: What Does It Explain, and How Does It Explain It?" *Advances in Child Development and Behaviour* 44: 65–94.

Grosz, Elizabeth. 2008. "Darwin and Feminism: Preliminary Investigations for a Possible Alliance." In *Material Feminisms*, edited by S. Alaimo and S. Hekman. Bloomington: Indiana University Press.

Gruen, Lori. 2009. "Attending to Nature: Empathetic Engagement with the More than Human World." *Ethics and the Environment* 14, no. 2: 23–38.

Haack, Susan. 1993. *Evidence and Inquiry: Towards Reconstruction in Epistemology.* Oxford: Blackwell Publishers.

Haidt, Jonathan. 2001. "The Emotional Dog and Its Rational Tail: A Social Intuitionist Approach to Moral Judgment." *Psychological Review* 108, no. 4: 814–34.

Haraway, Donna. 1991. *Simians, Cyborgs, and Women: The Reinvention of Nature.* New York: Routledge.

Haraway, Donna. 2007. *When Species Meet.* Posthumanities, Vol. 3. Minneapolis: Minnesota University Press.

Haraway, Donna. 2016. *Staying with the Trouble: Making Kin in the Chthulucene.* Durham, NC: Duke University Press.

Haraway, Donna. 1988. "Situated Knowledges: The Science Question in Feminism and the Privilege of Partial Perspectives." *Feminist Studies* 14, no. 3: 575–99.

Haraway, Donna. 2019. "It Matters What Stories Tell Stories; It Matters Whose Stories Tell Stories" *a/b: Auto/Biography Studies* 34, no. 3: 565–75.

Harding, Sandra. 1991. *Whose Science? Whose Knowledge? Thinking from Women's Lives.* Milton Keynes: Open University Press.

Harding, Sandra. 1998. *Is Science Multi-Cultural? Postcolonialisms, Feminisms, and Epistemologies.* Bloomington: Indiana University Press.

Harding, Sandra. 2004. "Rethinking Standpoint Epistemology: 'What Is Strong Objectivity?'" In *The Feminist Standpoint Theory Reader: Intellectual and Political Controversies,* edited by S. Harding, 127–40. New York: Routledge.

Hartsock, Nancy. 1998. *The Feminist Standpoint Revised: Other Essays.* Colorado: Westview Press.

Hayles, Katherine. 1991. "Constrained Constructivism: Locating Scientific Inquiry in the Theater of Representation." *New Orleans Review* 18, no.1: 76–85.

Hayles, Katherine. 1995. "Searching for Common Ground." *Reinventing Nature? Responses to Postmodern Deconstruction*, edited by M. Soulé and G. Lease, 47–64. Washington, DC: Island Press.

Hekman, Susan. 1995. *Moral Voices, Moral Selves: Carol Gilligan and Feminist Moral Theory.* Cambridge: Polity Press.

Hekman, Susan. 1999. *The Future of Differences: Truth and Method in Feminist Theory.* Cambridge: Polity Press.

Hekman, Susan. 2004. "Truth and Method: Feminist Standpoint Theory Revised." In *The Feminist Standpoint Theory Reader: Intellectual and Political Controversies,* edited by S. Harding. New York: Routledge.

Hekman, Susan. 2008. "Constructing the Ballast: An Ontology for Feminism." In *Material Feminisms,* edited by S. Alaimo and S. Hekman, 85–120. Bloomington: Indiana University Press.

Hoagland, Sarah. 1999. "Engaged Moral Agency." *Ethics and the Environment* 4: 91–99.

Hoffmann, Tobias. "Duns Scotus and William of Ockham." In *The Cambridge History of Moral Philosophy,* edited by Sacha Golob and Jens Timmermann, 181–91. Cambridge: Cambridge University Press, 2017.

Holland, Breena. 2008. "Justice and the Environment in Nussbaum's Capabilities Approach: Why Sustainable Ecological Capacity Is a Meta-Capability." *Political Research Quarterly* 61, no. 2: 319–32.

Holland, Breena. 2012. "Environment as Meta-capability: Why a Dignified Human Life Requires a Stable Climate System." In *Ethical Adaptation to Climate Change: Human Virtues of the Future,* edited by J. Bendik-Keymer and A. Thompson, 145–64. Cambridge, MA: MIT Press.

Hooker, Richard. 1996. "Pico Della Mirandola: Early Modern Italian Renaissance." Washington State University, http://www.wsu.edu/~dee/REN/PICO.

Hormio, Säde. 2017. "Marginal Participation, Complicity, and Agnotology: What Climate Change Can Teach Us about Individual and Collective Responsibility." Diss. Faculty of Social Sciences, University of Helsinki.

Hourdequin, Marion. 2012. "Empathy, Shared Intentionality, and Motivation by Moral Reasons." *Ethical Theory and Moral Practices* 15: 403–19.

Hourdequin, Marion, and David B. Wong. 2005. "A Relational Approach to Environmental Ethics." *Journal of Chinese Philosophy* 32, no. 1: 19–33.

Hurka, Thomas. 1993. *Perfectionism.* New York: Oxford University Press.

Hurka, Thomas. 2006. "Value Theory." In *Oxford Handbook in Ethical Theory,* edited by D. Copp, 357–79. Oxford: Oxford University Press.

Hursthouse, Rosalind. 2012. "Human Nature and Aristotelian Virtue Ethics." *Royal Institute of Philosophy Supplement* 70: 169–88.

Hursthouse, Rosalind. 2013a. "Neo-Aristotelian Ethical Naturalism." In *The International Encyclopedia of Ethics,* edited by H. LaFollette, 3571–80. Blackwell Publishing Ltd.

Hursthouse, Rosalind. 2013b. "Normative Virtue Ethics." In *Ethical Theory: An Anthology.* 2.ed, edited by R. Shafer-Landau, 645–52. Chichester: Wiley-Blackwell.

Hutto, Daniel, and Erik Myin. 2013. *Radicalizing Enactivism.* Cambridge, MA: MIT Press.

Huxley, Julian. 1941. *The Uniqueness of Man.* London: Chatto and Windus.

Huxley, Thomas Henry. 2009. *Evolution and Ethics,* edited by Michael Ruse. Originally published 1894. Princeton: Princeton University Press.

Hyman, John. 2015. *Action, Knowledge, and Will.* Oxford: Oxford University Press.

Ingold, Tim. 2022. *The Perception of the Environment: Essays on Livelihood, Dwelling and Skill.* London: Routledge.

International Commission on Stratigraphy. 2019. "Working Group on the 'Anthropocene': Results of Binding Vote by AWG. Released 21st May 2019." *The Subcommission on Quaternary Stratigraphy.* http://quaternary.stratigraphy.org/working-groups/anthropocene/.

Jablonka, Eva. 2003. "The Systems of Inheritance." *Cycles of Contingency: Developmental Systems and Evolution,* edited by S. Oyama, P. E. Griffiths, and R. D. Gray, 99–116. Cambridge, MA: MIT Press.

Jamieson, Dale. 2008. *Ethics and the Environment: An Introduction.* Cambridge: Cambridge University Press.

Johnson, Mark. 1987. *The Body in the Mind.* Chicago: University of Chicago Press.

Johnson, Mark. 1993. *Moral Imagination: Implications of Cognitive Science for Ethics.* Chicago: University of Chicago Press.

Johnson, Mark. 2007. *The Meaning of the Body: Aesthetics of Human Understanding.* Chicago: University of Chicago Press.

Johnson, Mark. 2014. *Morality for Humans: Ethical Understanding from the Perspective of Cognitive Science.* Chicago: University of Chicago Press.

Johnson, Mark. 1998. "How Moral Psychology Changes Moral Theory?" In *Minds and Morals: Essays on Cognitive Science and Ethics,* edited by L. May, M. Friedman, and A. Clark, 45–68. Cambridge, MA: MIT Press.

Johnson, Mark. 2008. "What Makes a Body?" *Journal of Speculative Philosophy* 22, no. 3: 159–69.

Joyce, Richard. 2006. *The Evolution of Morality.* Cambridge, MA: MIT Press.

Kagan, Sally. 1989. *The Limits of Morality.* Oxford: Clarendon Press.

Kant, Immanuel. 1987. *Critique of Judgment,* edited by Mary Gregor. Translated by Werner S. Pluhar. Indianapolis: Hackett Publishing.

Kant, Immanuel. 1990. *Foundations of the Metaphysics of Morals.* Translated by Lewis W. Beck. New York: Macmillan Publishing, 2nd ed.

Kant, Immanuel. 1996. *Metaphysics of Morals.* Translated and edited by Mary Gregor. Cambridge: Cambridge University Press.

Kant, Immanuel. 1997. *Lectures on Ethics.* In *Moral Philosophy: Collins's Lecture Notes. The Cambridge Edition of the Works of Immanuel Kant,* 37–222, edited by P. Heath and J. Schneewind. Translated by Peter Heath. Cambridge: Cambridge University Press. doi:10.1017/CBO9781107049512.004

Keller, Evelyn Fox. 1985. *Reflections on Gender and Science.* New Haven: Yale University Press.

Keller, Evelyn Fox. 1992. *Secrets of Life, Secrets of Death.* London: Routledge.

Keller, Evelyn Fox. 2001. "Secrets of God, Nature, and Life." In *The Gender and Science Reader,* edited by M. Lederman and I. Bartsch, 98–110. London: Routledge.

Kendal, Jeremy, Jamishid J. Tehrani, and F. John Odling-Smee. 2011. "Human Niche Construction in Interdisciplinary Focus." *Philosophical Transactions of the Royal Society B* 366: 785–92.

Kirkman, Robert J. 2009. "Darwinian Humanism and the End of Nature." *Environmental Values* 18: 217–36.

Kitcher, Philip. 2021. *Moral Progress,* edited by Jan-Christoph Heilinger. New York: Oxford University Press.

Kitcher, Philip. 2011. *The Ethical Project.* Cambridge, MA: Harvard University Press.

Kitcher, Philip. 2002. "Reply to Helen Longino." *Philosophy of Science* 69, no. 4: 569–72.

Kitcher, Philip. 2007. "Biology and Ethics." *The Oxford Handbook of Ethical Theory,* edited by D. Copp, 163–85. Oxford: Oxford University Press.

Kitcher, Philip. 2013. "Pragmatic Naturalism." In *Philip Kitcher—Pragmatic Naturalism*, edited by Marie Keiser and Ansgar Seide. Frankfurt: Ontos Verlag.

Kittay, Eva. 1999. *Love's Labour: Essays on Women, Equality, and Dependency*. New York: Routledge.

Kittay, Eva. 2011. "The Ethics of Care, Dependence and Disability." *Ratio Juris: An International Jounal of Jurisprudence and Philosophy of Law* 24, no. 2: 49–58.

Kivinen, Osmo, and Tero Piiroinen. 2013. "Human Transaction Mechanisms in Evolutionary Niches—a Methodological Relationalist Standpoint." In *Applying Relational Sociology: Relations, Networks, and Society,* edited by François Dépelteau and Christopher Powell, 83–100. New York: Palgrave Macmillan.

Klein, Jürgen. 2016. "Francis Bacon." *The Stanford Encyclopedia of Philosophy* (Winter 2016 Edition), edited by Edward N. Zalta. https://plato.stanford.edu/archives/win2016/entries/francis-bacon/.

Korsgaard, Christine M. 1996. *The Sources of Normativity*. Cambridge: Cambridge University Press.

Korsgaard, Christine M. 2008. *The Constitution of Agency: Essays on Practical Reason and Moral Psychology.* Oxford: Oxford University Press.

Korsgaard, Christine M. 2009b. *Self-Constitution: Agency, Identity and Integrity*. Oxford: Oxford University Press.

Korsgaard, Christine M. 2010. *Reflections on the Evolution of Morality*. Amherst Lecture in Philosophy. The Department of Philosophy at Amherst College

Korsgaard, Christine M. 2018. *Fellow Creatures: Our Obligations to the Other Animals.* Oxford: Oxford University Press.

Korsgaard, Christine M. 2003. "Realism and Constructivism in Twentieth-century Moral Philosophy." *The Journal of Philosophical Research,* APA Centennial Supplement, Philosophy in America at the Turn of the Century: 99–122.

Korsgaard, Christine M. "Morality and the Distinctiveness of Human Action." In Frans de Waal, *Primates and Philosophers*, edited by Stephen Macedo and Josiah Ober, 98–119. Princeton: Princeton University Press, 2006.

Korsgaard, Christine M. 2007. "The Authority of Reflection." In *Foundations of Ethics: An Anthology*, edited by R. Shafer-Landau and T. Cuneo, 93–106. Blackwell Publishing.

Korsgaard, Christine M. 2009a. "The Activity of Reason." *Proceedings and Addresses of the American Philosophical Association* 83, no. 2: 23–43.

Korsgaard, Christine M. 2011. "Interacting with Animals: A Kantian Account." In *The Oxford Handbook of Animal Ethics,* edited by T. Beauchamp and R. G. Frey, 91–118. Oxford: Oxford University Press. Oxford Handbooks Online.

Korsgaard, Christine M. 2012. "Moral Animals, Lecture One: The Origin of the Good and Our Animal Nature." Harvard University. http://www.people.fas.harvard.edu/~korsgaar/CMK.MA1.pdf.

Korsgaard, Christine M. 2013. "The Relational Nature of the Good." *Oxford Studies in Metaethics,* Volume 8, edited by R. Shafer-Landau, 1 – 26. Oxford: Oxford University Press.

Korsgaard, Christine M. 2014. "The Normative Constitution of Agency." *Rational and Social Agency: Essays on the Philosophy of Michael Bratman,* edited by Manuel Vargas and Gideon Yaffe, 190–214. Oxford: Oxford University Press.

Korsgaard, Christine M. 2015. "On Having Good." In *Philosophers of Our Times,* edited by Ted Honderich, 135–54. Oxford: Oxford University Press.

Korsgaard, Christine M. 2019. "Constitutivism and the Virtues." *Philosophical Explorations* 22, no. 2: 98–116.

Krebs, Angelika. 1999. *Ethics of Nature: A Map.* Perspectives in Analytical Philosophy 22. Berlin: Walter de Gruyter.

Lakoff, George, and Mark Johnson. 1999. *Philosophy in the Flesh. The Embodied Mind and Its Challenge to Western Thought.* New York: Basic Books.

Laland, Kevin, Blake Matthews, and Marcus W. Feldman. 2016. "An Introduction to Niche Construction Theory." *Evolutionary Ecology* 30: 191–202.

Latour, Bruno. 1991. *We Have Never Been Modern.* Transl. by Catherine Porter. Cambridge, MA: Harvard University Press.

Latour, Bruno, and Steve Woolgar. 1979. *Laboratory Life: The Social Construction of Scientific Facts.* London: Sage.

Lema, Sean C. 2014. "The Ethical Implications of Organism-Environment Interdependency." *Environmental Ethics* 36: 151–69.

Leopold, Aldo. 1949. *A Sand County Almanac.* New York: Oxford University Press.

Levinas, Emmanuel. 1969. *Totality and Infinity: An Essay on Exteriority.* Transl. by Alphonso Lingis. Pittsburgh: Duquesne University Press.

Lewontin, Richard. 1991. *Biology as Ideology: The Doctrine of DNA.* New York: Anansi Press Limited.

Light, Andrew. 1996. "Environmental Pragmatism as Philosophy or Metaphilosophy? On the Weston-Katz Debate." In *Environmental Pragmatism,* edited by A. Light and E. Katz, 325–38. London: Routledge.

Light, Andrew. 2000. "What Is an Ecological Identity?" *Environmental Politics* 9, no. 4: 59–81.

Light, Andrew. 2012. "Finding a Future for Environmental Ethics." *Les Ateliers de l'Éthique* 7, no. 3: 71–80.

Little, Margaret Olivia. 1997. "Virtue as Knowledge: Objections from the Philosophy of Mind." *Nous* 31, no. 1: 59–79.

Little, Margaret Olivia. 1995. "Seeing and Caring. The Role of Affect in Feminist Moral Epistemology." *Hypatia* 10, no. 3: 117–37.

Longino, Helen. 2002a. *The Fate of Knowledge.* Princeton: Princeton University Press.

Longino, Helen. 2002b. "Science and the Common Good: Thoughts on Philip Kitcher's *Science, Truth, and Democracy.*" *Philosophy of Science* 69: 560–68.

Longino, Helen. 2002c. "Reply to Kitcher." *Philosophy of Science* 69: 573–77.

Lovelock, James. 1979. *Gaia: A New Look at Life on Earth.* New York: Oxford University Press.

Mackenzie, Catriona. 2000. "Imagining Oneself Otherwise." In *Relational Autonomy: Feminist Perspectives on Autonomy, Agency, and the Social Self,* edited by Catriona Mackenzie and Natalie Stoljar, 124–50. New York: Oxford University Press.

Mackenzie, Catriona, and Natalie Stoljar, eds. 2000. *Relational Autonomy. Feminist Perspectives on Autonomy, Agency, and the Social Self.* New York: Oxford University Press.

Mackie, John L. 1977. *Morality: Inventing Right and Wrong.* Harmondsworth: Penguin.

Mann, Bonnie. 2005. "World Alienation in Feminist Thought: The Sublime Epistemology of Emphatic Anti-Essentialism." *Ethics and the Environment* 10: 45–74.

Marková, Ivana. 2016. *The Dialogical Mind: Common Sense and Ethics.* Cambridge: Cambridge University Press.

Marková, Ivana, and Per Linell. 2014a. "Trust and Distrust in Interaction: Some Theoretical and Methodological Points." In *Dialogical Approaches to Trust in Communication*, edited by P. Linell and I. Marková,: 213–35. Charlotte, NC: Information Age Publishing.

Marková, Ivana, and Per Linell. 2014b. "Epilogue: Trust Seen as Embodiment, Culture, Language and Morality." In *Dialogical Approaches to Trust in Communication*, edited by P. Linell and I. Marková, 255–57. Charlotte, NC: Information Age Publishing.

McDowell, John. 1998. *Mind, Value, and Reality.* Cambridge, MA: Harvard University Press.

McDowell, John. 1979. "Virtue and Reason." *The Monist* 62, no. 3: 331–50

McCraw, Benjamin. 2020. "Thinking with Others. A Radically Externalist Internalism." *Acta Analytica* 35: 351–71.

McFague, Sally. 1997. *Super, Natural Christians: How We Should Love Nature.* London: SCM Press Ltd.

McShane, Katie. 2011. "Neosentimentalism and Environmental Ethics." *Environmental Ethics* 33: 5–23.

McShea, Robert. 1990. *Morality and Human Nature: A New Route to Ethical Theory.* Philadelphia: Temple University Press.

Mellor, Mary. 1997. *Feminism and Ecology.* Cambridge: Polity Press.

Mellor, Mary. 2000. "Feminism and Environmental Ethics: A Materialist Perspective." *Ethics and the Environment* 5: 107–23.

Merchant, Carolyn. 1993. *The Death of Nature: Women, Ecology and the Scientific Revolution.* San Francisco: Harper & Row.

Meyers, Diana. 1989. *Self, Society, and Personal Choice.* New York: Columbia University Press.

Meyers, Diana. 2000. "Intersectional Identity and the Authentic Self? Opposites Attract." In *Relational Autonomy: Feminist Perspectives on Autonomy, Agency, and the Social Self,* edited by C. Mackenzie and N. Stoljar, 151–80. Oxford: Oxford University Press.

Meyers, Diana. 2018. "Emotion and Heterodox Moral Perception: An Essay in Social Moral Psychology." In *Feminists Rethink the Self,* edited by Diana Mayers, 197–218. New York: Routledge.

Meyers, Diana. 1978. *Beast and Man: The Roots of Human Nature.* London: Methuen.

Meyers, Diana. 1984. *Wickedness: A Philosophical Essay.* London, Boston, Melbourne, Henley: Routledge and Kegan Paul.

Meyers, Diana. 1985. *Evolution as a Religion.* London: Routledge.

Meyers, Diana. 1994. *The Ethical Primate: Humans, Freedom and Morality.* London: Routledge.

Meyers, Diana. 1998. *Animals and Why They Matter.* Athens: University of Georgia Press.

Meyers, Diana. 2004. *The Myths We Live By.* London: Routledge.

Meyers, Diana. 1979. "Gene-juggling." *Philosophy* 54: 439–58.

Meyers, Diana. 1995. "Duties Concerning Islands." In *Environmental Ethics,* edited by R. Elliot, 89–103. Oxford: Oxford University Press.

Midgley, Mary. 2000. "Consciousness, Fatalism and Science." In *The Human Person in Science and Theology,* edited by N. H. Gregersen, W. Drees, and U. Görman, 21–40. Grand Rapids, MI: Eerdmans.

Mies, Maria, and Vandana Shiva. 1993. *Ecofeminism.* London: Zed Books.

Muraca, Barbara. 2010. *Denken in Grenzgebiet: prozessphilosophische Grundlagen einer Theorie starker Nachhaltigkeit.* Freiburg, München: Karl Alber Verlag.

Murphy, Nancey, and Warren Brown. 2007. *Did My Neuros Make Me Do It? Philosophical and Neurobiological Perspectives on Moral Responsibility and Free Will.* New York: Oxford University Press.

Næss, Arne. 1973. "The Shallow and the Deep, Long-range Ecology Movement: A Summary." *Inquiry: An Interdisciplinary Journal of Philosophy* 16: 95–100.

Næss, Arne. 1988. "Self-Realization: An Ecological Approach to Being in the World." In *Thinking Like a Mountain: Towards a Council of All Beings,* edited by Seed et al., 19–30. Philadelphia: New Society Publishers.

Næss, Arne. 1998. "The Deep Ecological Movement: Some Philosophical Aspects." In *Environmental Philosophy: From Animal Rights to Radical Ecology,* 2nd ed, edited by M. Zimmerman, J. B. Callicott, G. Sessions, K. Warren, and J. Clark, 193–212. Upper Saddle River, NJ: Prentice Hall.

Narayan, Uma, and Sandra Harding, eds. 2000. *Decentering the Center.* Bloomington: Indiana University Press.

Newen, Albert, Leon De Bruin, and Shaun Gallagher, eds. 2018. *The Oxford Handbook of 4E Cognition.* Oxford: Oxford University Press. Oxford Handbooks Online.

Nielsen, Kai. 1972. "Why Should I Be Moral?" In *Problems of Moral Philosophy,* edited by Paul W. Taylor, 539–58. Encino: Dickerson Publishing Company.

Noddings, Nel. 1984. *Caring: A Relational Approach to Ethics and Moral Education.* Berkeley: University of California Press.

Noë, Alva. *Action in Perception.* 2004. Cambridge, MA: MIT Press.

Norton, Bryan G. 1987. *Why Preserve Natural Variety?* Princeton: Princeton University Press.

Nurmi, Suvielise. 2011. "Relational Agency: Beyond Constructivism and Naturalism." In *Ecological Awareness: Exploring Religion, Ethics and Aesthetics,* edited by S. Bergman and H. Eaton, 221–42. Berlin: LIT Verlag.

Nurmi, Suvielise. 2020. "Ecologically Relational Moral Agency: Conceptual Shifts in Environmental Ethics and Their Philosophical Implications." Dissertation. Faculty of Theology. University of Helsinki. http://urn.fi/URN:ISBN:978-951-51-5815-4.

Nussbaum, Martha. 2006. *Frontiers of Justice: Disability, Nationality, Species Membership*. Cambridge, MA: Harvard University Press.

Nussbaum, Martha. 2011. *Creating Capabilities: The Human Development Approach*. Cambridge, MA: Harvard University Press.

Nussbaum, Martha. 2023. *Justice for Animals. Our Collective Responsibility*. Simon & Schuster.

Nussbaum, Martha. 1995a. "Aristotle on Human Nature and the Foundations of Ethics." In *World, Mind and Ethics*, edited by J. E. J. Altham and R. Harrison, 86–131. Cambridge: Cambridge University Press.

Nussbaum, Martha. 1995b. "Human Capabilities, Female Human Beings." *Women, Culture, and Development: A Study of Human Capabilities*, edited by Martha C. Nussbaum and Jonathan Glover, 61–104. Oxford: Oxford University Press.

Nussbaum, Martha. 1998. "Aristotelian Social Democracy." *Necessary Goods: Our Responsibilities to Meet Others' Needs*, edited by Gillian Brock. Lanham, MD: Rowman & Littlefield Publishers.

Nussbaum, Martha. 2003. "Capabilities as Fundamental Entitlements: Sen and Social Justice." *Feminist Economics* 9: 33–59.

Nussbaum, Martha. 2013. "Non-Relative Virtues: An Aristotelian Approach." *Ethical Theory: An Anthology* (2nd edition), edited by Russ Shafer-Landau, 630–44. Malden: Wiley-Blackwell.

Nussbaum, Martha. 2016. "Introduction: Aspiration and the Capabilities List." *Journal of Human Development and Capabilities* 17, no. 3: 301–8.

Ohtani, Hiroshi. 2011. "Putnam's Moral Realism," *Bulletin of Death and Life Studies* 7: 176–96.

O'Neill, Onora. 1988. "Constructivisms in Ethics: Presidential Address." In *Proceedings of the Aristotelian Society* 89: 1–17.

O'Neill, Onora. 1989. *Constructions of Reason*. Cambridge: Cambridge University Press.

O'Neill, Onora. 1992. "Vindicating Reason." *The Cambridge Companion to Kant*, edited by P. Guyer. Cambridge: Cambridge University Press.

Oshana, Marina. 2013. "Self-identity and Moral Agency." *Autonomy and the Self*, edited by M. Kühler and N. Jelinek. Philosophical Studies Series 118. Dordrecht, Heidelberg, New York, London: Springer, 231–52.

Oyama, Susan. 1985. *The Ontogeny of Information: Developmental Systems and Evolution.* 2nd ed. Cambridge: Cambridge University Press.

Oyama, Susan, Paul E. Griffiths, and Russel D. Gray. 2001a. "Introduction." *Cycles of Contingency: Developmental Systems and Evolution*, edited by S. Oyama, P. E. Griffiths, and R.D. Gray, 1–12. Cambridge, MA: MIT Press.

Oyama, Susan, Paul E. Griffiths, and Russel D. Gray, eds. 2001b. *Cycles of Contingency: Developmental Systems and Evolution.* Cambridge, MA: MIT Press.

Pentikäinen, Juha, ed. 1996. *Shamanism and Northern Ecology*. Religion and Society Book 36. Berlin: De Gruyter.

Pescador Canales, Cassandra, and Laura Mojica. 2022. "Making us Autonomous: The Enactive Normativity of Morality." *Topoi* 41 (2): 257–74.

Peterson, Anna L. 2001. *Being Human: Ethics, Environment, and Our Place in the World.* Berkeley: University of California Press.

Peterson, Anna L. 2006. "Toward a Materialist Environmental Ethic." *Environmental Ethics* 28: 375–93.

Pettigrove, Glen. 2018. "Alternatives to Neo-Aristotelian Virtue Ethics." In *Oxford Handbook on Virtue*, edited by Nancy E. Snow, 359–76. New York: Oxford University Press. Oxford Handbooks Online.

Pickering, Andrew. 1995. *The Mangle of Practice: Time, Agency, and Science.* Chicago: University of Chicago Press.

Pihlström, Sami. 2005. *Pragmatic Moral Realism: A Transcendental Defense.* Amsterdam: Rodopi.

Pike, Sarah. 2017. *For the Wild: Ritual and Commitment in Radical Eco-Activism.* Berkeley: University of California Press.

Plumwood, Val. 1993. *Feminism and the Mastery of Nature,* London: Routledge.

Plumwood, Val. 2002. *Environmental Culture: The Ecological Crisis of Reason.* London: Routledge.

Plumwood, Val. 1994. "Nature, Self and Gender: Feminism, Environmental Philosophy, and the Critique of Rationalism." In *Reflecting on Nature: Readings in Environmental Philosophy*, edited by L. Gruen and D. Jamieson, 142–59. New York: Oxford University Press.

Plumwood, Val. 1996. "Anthrocentrism and Androcentrism: Parallels and Politics." *Ethics and the Environment* 1, no. 2: 119–52.

Plumwood, Val. 1999. "Ecological Ethics from Rights to Recognition: Multiple Spheres of Justice for Humans, Animals, and Nature." In *Global Ethics and Environment*, edited by Nicolas Low, 188–212. New York: Routledge.

Plumwood, Val. 2006. "The Concept of a Cultural Landscape: Nature, Culture and Agency in the Land." *Ethics and the Environment* 11: 115–50.

Preston, Christopher. 2003. *Grounding Knowledge: Environmental Philosophy, Epistemology, and Place.* Athens: The University of Georgia Press.

Preston, Christopher. 2000. "Conversing with Nature in a Postmodern Epistemological Framework." *Environmental Ethics* 22: 227–40.

Preston, Christopher. 2001. "Intrinsic Value and Care: Making Connections through Ecological Narratives." *Environmental Values* 10: 243–63.

Preston, Christopher. 2002. "Animality and Morality: Human Reason as an Animal Activity." *Environmental Values* 11: 427–42.

Preston, Christopher. 2005. "Epistemology and Environmental Philosophy: The Epistemic Significance of Place." *Ethics and the Environment* 10: 1–4.

Preston, Christopher. 2009. "Moral Knowledge: Real and Grounded in Place." *Ethics, Place, and Environment* 12, no. 2: 175–86.

Preston, Christopher. 2010. "Materializing Ethics: Shaping the Environment that Shape Us." *Minding Nature* 3, no. 1: 6–11.

Putnam, Hilary. 1981. *Reason, Truth and History.* Cambridge: Cambridge University Press.

Putnam, Hilary. 1988. *Representation and Reality*. Cambridge: The MIT Press.

Putnam, Hilary. 1990. *Realism with a Human Face*, edited by J. Conant. Cambridge, MA: Harvard University Press.

Rawls, John. 2003. *A Theory of Justice*. Revised edition. Cambridge, MA: Harvard University Press.

Raz, Joseph, and R. Jay Wallace. 2003. *The Practice of Value*. Oxford: Oxford University Press.

Regan, Tom. 1983. *The Case for Animal Rights*. Berkeley: University of California Press.

Rolston, Holmes, III. 1999. *Genes, Genesis, and God: Values and Their Origins in Natural and Human History*. Cambridge: Cambridge University Press.

Rowlands, Mark. 1999. *The Body in Mind: Understanding Cognitive Processes*. Cambridge: Cambridge University Press.

Rowlands, Mark. 2001. *The Nature of Consciousness*. Cambridge: Cambridge University Press.

Rowlands, Mark. 2002. *Animals Like Us*. New York: Verso.

Rowlands, Mark. 2003. *Externalism: Putting Mind and World Back Together Again*. Chesham: Acumen.

Rowlands, Mark. 2006. *Body Language: Representing in Action*. Cambridge, MA: MIT Press.

Rowlands, Mark. 2012. *Can Animals Be Moral?* Oxford: Oxford University Press.

Rowlands, Mark. 2005. "Environmental Epistemology." *Ethics and the Environment* 10, no. 2: 5–27.

Rowlands, Mark. 2009. "Enactivism and the Extended Mind." *Topoi* 28: 53–62.

Rowlands, Mark. 2010. *The New Science of the Mind: From Extended Mind to Embodied Phenomenology*. Cambridge, MA: MIT Press.

Rowlands, Mark. 2018. "Disclosing the World: Intentionality and 4E Cognition." In *Oxford Handbook of 4E Cognition*, edited by Albert Newen, Leon De Bruin and Shaun Gallagher. Oxford: Oxford University Press.

Ruddick, Sarah. 1989. *Maternal Thinking: Toward a Politics of Peace*. Boston: Beacon Press.

Ruse, Michael. 1985. *Sociobiology: Sense or Nonsense?* 2nd ed. Dordrechtr: D. Reidel Publishing Company.

Ruse, Michael. 1995. *Evolutionary Naturalism: Selected Essays*. London: Routledge.

Ruse, Michael. 1998. *Taking Darwin Seriously: A Naturalistic Approach to Philosophy*. Amherst, NY: Prometheus Books.

Ruse, Michael. 1999. *Mystery of Mysteries: Is Evolution a Social Construction?* Cambridge, MA: Harvard University Press.

Ruse, Michael. 2001. *Can a Darwinian Be a Christian? The Relationship between Science and Religion*. Cambridge: Cambridge University Press.

Ruse, Michael. 2004. "Evolutionary Ethics Past and Present." In *Evolution and Ethics: Human Morality in Biological and Religious Perspective*, edited by P. Clayton and J. Schloss, 27–49. Grand Rapids, MI: William B. Eerdmans Publishing Company.

Ruse, Michael. 2010. "Biological Sciences Can Act as a Ground for Ethics." In *Contemporary Debates in Philosophy of Biology*, edited by Francisco J. Ayala and Robert Arp, 297–315. Malden: Wiley-Blackwell.

Ruse, Michael, and Wilson, Edward O. 1986. "Moral Philosophy as Applied Science." *Philosophy* 61: 173–92.

Ruse, Michael. 1989. "The Evolution of Ethics." In *Philosophy of Biology*, edited by M. Ruse. New York: Macmillan.

Salleh, Ariel. 1997. *Ecofeminism as Politics: Nature, Marx and the Postmodern*. London: Zed Books.

Sandler, Ronald. 2007. *Character and Environment. A Virtue-Oriented Approach to Environmental Ethics*. New York: Columbia University Press.

Schloss, Jeffery. 2004. "Introduction." In *Evolution and Ethics: Human Morality in Biological and Religious Perspective*, edited by P. Clayton and J. Schloss, 1–26. Grand Rapids, MI: William B. Eerdmans Publishing Company

Searle, John. 2004 *Mind: A Brief Introduction*. Oxford: Oxford University Press.

Sideris, Lisa H. 2003. *Environmental Ethics, Ecological Theology, and Natural Selection*. New York: Columbia University Press.

Sideris, Lisa H. 2017. *Consecrating Science: Wonder, Knowledge, and the Natural World*. Berkeley: University of California Press.

Sideris, Lisa H. 2007. "Evolving Environmentalism: The Role of Ecotheology in Creation/Evolution Controversies." *Worldviews* 11: 59–82.

Sideris, Lisa H. 2015. "Science as Sacred Myth? Ecospirituality in the Anthropocene Age." *Journal for the Study of Religion, Nature and Culture* 9, no. 2: 136–53.

Singer, Peter. 1991. *Animal Liberation*, 2nd ed., London: Thorsons.

Singer, Peter. 1993. *Practical Ethics*, 2nd ed. Cambridge: Cambridge University Press.

Singer, Peter. 1995. *Rethinking Life and Death: The Collapse of Our Traditional Ethics*. New York: St. Martin's Press.

Singer, Peter. 1976. "All Animals Are Equal." In *Animal Rights and Human Obligations*, edited by T. Regan and P. Singer. Englewood Cliffs, NJ: Prentice Hall.

Singer, Peter. 1999. "Ethics Across the Species Boundaries." In *Global Ethic and Environment*, edited by N. Low, 146–57. London: Routledge.

Singer, Peter. 2006. "Morality, Reason and the Rights of Animals." In F. de Waal, *Primates and Philosophers*, edited by Stephen Macedo and Josiah Ober, 140–58. Princeton: Princeton University Press.

Sinnott-Armstrong, Walter. 2007. "Expressivism and Embedding." In *Foundations of Ethics: An Anthology*, edited by R. Shafer-Landau and T. Cuneo, 485–94. Malden: Blackwell Publishing.

Sinnott-Armstrong, Walter. 2009. "Mixed-Up Meta-Ethics." *Noûs* 43: 235–56.

Slote, Michael. 2011. *Impossibility of Perfection: Aristotle, Feminism, and the Complexities of Ethics*. Oxford University Press.

Slote, Michael. 2013. "Agent-Based Virtue Ethics." In *Ethical Theory: An Anthology*. 2.ed, edited by R. Shafer-Landau, 653–63. Chichester: Wiley-Blackwell.

Smith, Mick. 2001. *An Ethics of Place: Radical Ecology, Postmodernity, and Social Theory*. Albany: State University of New York Press.

Sober, Elliot. 1994. *From a Biological Point of View: Essays in Evolutionary Philosophy*. Cambridge: Cambridge University Press.

Sober, Elliot, and David Sloan Wilson. 1998. *Unto Others: The Evolution and Psychology of Unselfish Behavior*. Cambridge, MA: Harvard University Press.

Solomon, Robert. 2003. *Not Passion's Slave: Emotions and Choice*. Oxford: Oxford University Press.

Spencer, Herbert. 1851. *Social Statics, Or the Conditions Essential to Human Happiness Specified and the First of Them Developed*. London: J. Chapman.

Stenmark, Mikael. 2001. *Scientism: Science, Ethics and Religion*. Abingdon: Routledge, 2001.

Stenmark, Mikael. 2012. "Theories of Human Nature: Key Issues." *Philosophy Compass* 7/8: 543–58.

Sterelny, Kim. 2001. "Niche Construction, Developmental Systems, and the Extended Replicator." In *Cycles of Contingency: Developmental Systems and Evolution*, edited by S. Oyama, P. E. Griffiths, and R. D. Gray, 333–49. Cambridge, MA: MIT Press.

Stern, Robert. 2011. "The Value of Humanity. Reflections on Korsgaard's Transcendental Argument." In *Transcendental Philosophy and Naturalism*, edited by J. Smith and P. Sullivan, 74–95. Oxford: Oxford University Press.

Stern, Robert. 2015. "Transcendental Arguments." In *The Stanford Encyclopedia of Philosophy* (Summer 2015 Edition), edited by Edward N. Zalta. https://plato.stanford.edu/archives/sum2015/entries/transcendental-arguments/.

Strawson, P. F. 1962. "Freedom and Resentment." *Proceedings of the British Academy* 48: 187–211.

Stump, Eleonore. 2003. *Aquinas*. London: Routledge.

Swimme, Brian, and Thomas Berry. 1992. *The Universe Story from the Primordial Flaring Forth to the Ecozoic Era: A Celebration of the Unfolding of the Cosmos*. New York: Harper Collins.

Tao, Julia. 2004. "Confucian Environmental Ethics: Relational Resonance with Nature." *Social Alternatives* 23, no. 4: 5–9.

Taylor, Charles. 1991 *The Ethics of Authenticity*. Cambridge, MA: Harvard University Press.

Taylor, Paul. 1989. *Respect for Nature. A Theory of Environmental Ethics*. Princeton: Princeton University Press.

Telakivi, P. 2020. *Extending the Extended Mind. From Cognition to Consciousness. Dissertation*. University of Helsinki: Faculty of Arts, Department of Philosophy, History and Art Studies. http://urn.fi/URN:ISBN:978-951-51-6437-7

Thompson, Evan. 2007. *Mind in Life: Biology, Phenomenology, and the Sciences of Mind*. Cambridge, MA: Harvard University Press.

Thompson, Michael. 1995. "The Representation of Life." In *Virtues and Reasons*, edited by R. Hursthouse, G. Lawrence, and W. Quinn. Oxford: Clarendon Press.

Thoreau, Henry David. 2016 (1849). *Walden, and On The Duty Of Civil Disobedience*. CreateSpace Independent Publishing Platform.

Timmons, Mark. 1996. "Outline of a Contextualist Moral Epistemology." In *Moral Knowledge? New Readings in Moral Epistemology*, edited by W. Sinnott-Armstrong and M. Timmons, 293–325. New York: Oxford University Press.

Timmons, Mark. 1999. *Morality without Foundations. A Defense of Ethical Contextualism*. Oxford: Oxford University Press.

Tollefsen, Deborah, and Shaun Gallagher. 2017. "We-Narratives and the Stability and Depth of Shared Agency." *Philosophy of the Social Sciences* 47, no. 2: 95–110.

Tomasello, Michael. 2009. *Why We Cooperate?* With Carol Dweck, Joan Silk, Brian Skyrms, and Elisabeth Spelke. Cambridge: MIT Press.

Tomasello, Michael. 2016. *A Natural History of Human Morality*. Cambridge, MA: Harvard University Press.

Tomasello, Michael. 2014. "The Ultra-Social Animal." *European Journal of Social Psychology* 44: 187–94.

Tomasello, Michael. 2018. "Précis of a Natural History of Human Morality." *Philosophical Psychology* 31, no. 5: 661–68.

Torrance, Steve, and Tom Froese. 2011. "An Inter-Enactive Approach to Agency: Participatory Sense-Making, Dynamics, and Sociality." *Humana Mente* 15: 21–53.

Tucker, Mary Evelyn. 2001. "Confucianism and Ecology: Potential and limits." *Chinese American Forum* XVI/3: 18–20.

Tuomela, Raimo. 2007. *The Philosophy of Sociality: The Shared Point of View*. Oxford: Oxford University Press.

Tuomela, Raimo. 2013. *Social Ontology: Collective Intentionality and Group Agents*. Oxford: Oxford University Press.

Tuomela, Raimo. 2006. "Joint Intention, We-Mode and I-Mode." *Midwest Studies in Philosophy* 30: 35–58.

Tuomela, Raimo. 2012. "Group Reason." *Philosophical Issues* 22: 402–18.

Tuomela, Raimo, and Mäkelä, Pekka. 2016. "Group Agents and Their Responsibility." *Ethics* 20: 299–316.

Työrinoja, Reijo. 1995. "Regularity of Will and the Problem of Egoism." In *Moral and Political Philosophies in the Middle Ages* vol. 2., edited by C. Bazán, E. Andújar, L. G. Sbrocchi, 949–63. New York: Legas.

Urban, Petr. 2014. "Toward an Expansion of an Enactive Ethics with the Help of Care Ethics." *Frontiers in Psychology* 5 (November): 1354. DOI: 10.3389/fpsyg.2014.01354.

Urban, Petr. 2015a. "Enacting Care." *Ethics and Social Welfare* 9, no. 2: 216–22.

Urban, Petr. 2015b. "Enactivism and Care Ethics: Merging Perspectives." *Filozofia* 70, no. 2: 119–29.

Urban, Petr. 2016. "Foregrounding the Relational Domain: Phenomenology, Enactivism and Care Ethics." *Horizon* 5, no. 1: 171–82.

Van der Weele, Cor. 2001. "Developmental Systems Theory and Ethics: Different Ways to Be Normative with Regard to Science." In *Cycles of Contingency: Developmental Systems and Evolution*, edited by S. Oyama, P. E. Griffiths, and R. D. Gray, 351–362. Cambridge, MA: MIT Press.

Van Grunsven, Janna. 2018. "Enactivism, Second-Person Engagement and Personal Responsibility." *Phenomenology and the Cognitive Science* 17: 131–56.

Varela, Francisco. 1999. *Ethical Know-how: Action, Wisdom, and Cognition.* Redwood City, CA: Stanford University Press.

Varela, Francisco, and Evan Thompson. 2001. "Radical Embodiment: Neural Dynamics and Consciousness." *Trends in Cognitive Science* 5, no. 10: 418–25.

Varela, Francisco, Eleanor Rosch, Evan Thompson. 1991. *The Embodied Mind: Cognitive Science and Human Experience.* Cambridge, MA: MIT Press.

Waller, Bruce. 2003. "Empirical Free Will and the Ethics of Moral Responsibility." *The Journal of Value Inquiry* 37: 533–42.

Warren, Karen. 1996. *Ecological Feminist Philosophies.* Bloomington: Indiana University Press.

Warren, Karen. 2000. *Ecofeminist Philosophy: A Western Perspective on What It Is and Why It Matters.* Lanham, MD: Rowman & Littlefield Publishers.

Warren, Karen. 1990. "The Power and the Promise of Ecological Feminism." *Environmental Ethics* 12: 125–46.

Warren, Karen, and Jim Cheney. 1991. "Ecological Feminism and Ecosystem Ecology." *Hypatia* 6: 179–97.

Wells, Thomas R. 2012. "Sen's Capability Approach." In *Internet Encyclopedia of Philosophy*, edited by J. Feiser and B. Dowden.

Werner, Konrad, and Magdalena Kiełkowicz-Werner. 2021. "From Shared Enaction to Intrinsic Value. How Enactivism Contributes to Environmental Ethics." *Topoi* 41 (2): 409–23.

Weston, Anthony. 2009. *The Incompleat Eco-Philosopher: Essays from the Edges of Environmental Ethics*. Albany: State University of New York Press.

Weston, Anthony. 2004. "Multicentrism: A Manifesto." *Environmental Ethics* 26: 25–40.

Westermark, Edvard. 1917. *The Origin and Development of the Moral Ideas*, vol. 2., 2nd ed. London: Macmillan.

Whitehead, Alfred North. 1956. *Modes of Thought.* Capricon Books edition. New York: Putnam's Sons.

Whitehead, Alfred North. 1978 (1929). *Process and Reality. An Essay in Cosmology.* Corrected ed., edited by D. R. Griffin and D. Sherbune. New York: The Free Press.

Whitehead, Alfred North. 1951. "Immortality." In *Philosophy of Alfred North Whitehead,* edited by P. Schlipp. New York: Tudor Publishing Company.

Wilson, David Sloan. 2002. *Darwin's Cathedral: Evolution, Religion, and the Nature of Society.* Chicago: University of Chicago Press.

Wilson, Edward O. 1975. *Sociobiology: The New Synthesis*. Cambridge, MA: Harvard University Press.

Wilson, Edward O. *On Human Nature*. Cambridge, MA: Harvard University Press.

Wilson, Edward O. 1998. *Consilience: The Unity of Knowledge.* New York: Vintage Books.

Wittgenstein, Ludwig. 1958. *The Blue and Brown Books: Preliminary Studies for the 'Philosophical Investigations.'* Oxford: Basil Blackwell.

Wolf, Susan. 1990. *Freedom within Reason*. Oxford: Oxford University Press.

Wolf, Susan. 1986. "Asymmetrical Freedom." In *Moral Responsibility*, edited by J. M. Fischer, 225–40. Ithaca: Cornell University Press.

Wong, David B. 2006. *Natural Moralities: A Defense of Pluralistic Relativism.* Oxford: Oxford University Press.

Wong, David B. 2004. "Relational and Autonomous Selves." *Journal of Chinese Philosophy* 31, no. 4: 419–32.

Wright, Robert. 1994. *The Moral Animal: Why We Are the Way We Are: The New Science of Evolutionary Psychology.* New York: Pantheon.

WWF, World Wildlife Fund. 2022. *Living Planet Report 2022—Building a Nature-positive Society*, edited by R. E. A. Almond, M. Grooten, D. Juffe Bignoli, and T. Petersen. Gland, Switzerland: WWF.

Zagzebski, Linda. 2003. "Intellectual Motivation and the Good of Truth." In *Intellectual Virtue: Perspectives from Ethics and Epistemology*, edited by M. DePaul and L. Zagzebski, 135–54. Oxford: Clarendon Press.

Index

4E cognition, 105, 107–11, 120. *See also* enactivism

affection, 86, 107–9, 157, 165, 241, 243, 247–8, 266–7; and cognition, 107–9, 135, 176, 213, 233. *See also* enactivism; 4E cognition

agency: blank paper vs. full paper theory of, 38, 68, 83; dichotomized, xii, xiii, 12, 14–15, 49, 84; embodied, xiii, 28, 90, 92, 95–7, 111, 122, 135, 146, 165, 190, 192, 202, 211, 221, 227, 238, 247–8, 252; environmentally scaffolded constitution of, 154; exceptional, xiv, 15, 19–20, 24, 27, 30, 34, 39–40, 42, 87; of humus, 111; interactive, 85, 161, 178, 185, 224, 214, 241–2, 246, 257, 266; modern conception of, xiii, xiv, 19, 92, 132, 160; moral vs. natural, 15, 32, 48, 57, 172, 177; nexus of, 86, 111, 159, 165, 172–4, 185–6, 191, 195, 198, 201, 206, 208–11, 213, 218, 225, 144, 148, 250–4, 266; non-individual, 75, 85–7, 143, 182, 212; reflective structure of, 74–5, 102, 149, 197, 199, 201, 225, 227, 235, 237, 246, 249, 258; relational nature of, 171, 176, 182, 185, 197, 250, 264, 269; unity of, 90, 201–3, 246; virtuous, 224, 244, 251–3, 258, 261; in web, 111, 115,128, 1145–6, 155–6, 162, 172, 176, 201, 203, 211–2, 246–7, 259, 260. *See also* animal agency; autonomy; collective agency; epistemic agency; human; normativity, in self-constitution of agency; subjectivity; relational autonomy; relational autonomy; virtues

agential realism. *See* Barad, Karen; realism

altruism, 40–1, 43–4, 52–6, 97, 177, 179

analogy argument. *See* environmental ethics

animal agency, 48, 84, 88, 102, 158, 160, 208, 230, 262; moral, 104, 197

Anthropocene, 28–30, 66, 262

anthropocentrism. *See* environmental ethics

antirealism, 119, 164, 169–70, 174–5, 213, 220, 223, 228. *See also* realism; relational realism

Aristotelian: naturalism, 56, 175, 180–7, 255; virtue ethics, 180, 204, 231, 259. *See also* naturalism, neo-Aristotelian; virtue ethics

Aristotle, 185, 231–2, 250, 255, 260

About the Author

Suvielise Nurmi is a Postdoc Researcher in Ethics and Environmental Philosophy at the University of Helsinki. She has worked as a University Lecturer of Ethics in the Faculty of Theology for five years and taught ethics, philosophy, and sustainability science another ten years at the University of Helsinki, where she has also actively promoted the establishment of the Helsinki Institute of Sustainability Science. Dr. Nurmi is also engaged in public philosophy, and she gives further education in ethics and sustainability issues to professionals in the Church of Finland, the public sector, and at NGOs. In addition to several articles, she has published four textbooks on ethics, environmental philosophy, and multicultural education. Her research interests include environmental ethics and philosophy, ethical theory, philosophical anthropology, philosophy of mind and cognitive science, social ontology and epistemology, environmental humanities, science and philosophy interaction, sustainability science, philosophy of religion, and metaphysics. Her focus is currently on the relational understanding of mind and cognition and its implications for the humanist framework of ethics and moral theories, especially concerning the role of nonhuman beings and material culture in ethics. Her present project concentrates on the ramifications of enactivism for the idea of responsibility and on a theory of relational ethics.

Ingram Content Group UK Ltd.
Milton Keynes UK
UKHW010617010523
421006UK00003B/47